MENTAL RETARDATION
The Developmental-Difference Controversy

MENTAL RETARDATION
The Developmental-Difference Controversy

Edited by

EDWARD ZIGLER
DAVID BALLA
Yale University

LAWRENCE ERLBAUM ASSOCIATES, PUBLISHERS
1982   Hillsdale, New Jersey   London

Copyright © 1982 by Lawrence Erlbaum Associates, Inc.
All rights reserved. No part of this book may be reproduced in
any form, by photostat, microform, retrieval system, or any other
means, without the prior written permission of the publisher.

Lawrence Erlbaum Associates, Inc., Publishers
365 Broadway
Hillsdale, New Jersey 07642

Library of Congress Cataloging in Publication Data
Main entry under title:

Mental retardation, the developmental-difference controversy.
   Includes bibliographical references and indexes.
   1. Mental deficiency.   I. Zigler, Edward Frank,
1930–   . II. Balla, David A. [DNLM: 1. Mental retardation. 2. Mental retardation, Psychosocial. WM 300
M55424]
RC570.M42   1982   616.85'88   82-8798
ISBN 0-89859-170-8   AACR2

Printed in the United States of America
10 9 8 7 6 5 4 3 2 1

Contents

PART I: THE DEVELOPMENTAL APPROACH

1. **Introduction: The Developmental Approach to Mental Retardation** 3
   Edward Zigler and David Balla

   The Developmental Position *4*
   The Difference Positions *6*
   The Developmental-Difference Controversy *7*

2. **Motivational and Personality Factors in the Performance of the Retarded** 9
   Edward Zigler and David Balla

   Factors Influencing Motivation in Retarded
     Persons *11*
   Conclusions *22*
   References *22*

3. **Learned Helplessness and the Retarded Child** 27
   John R. Weisz

   Research on Learned Helplessness in
     Retarded Populations *29*
   Some Thoughts on Future Directions for Research
     on Helplessness in Retarded Children *36*
   References *38*

4. **Impact of Institutional Experience on the Behavior and Development of Retarded Persons** 41
   David Balla and Edward Zigler

   Conclusions 55
   References 56

   PART II: THE DIFFERENCE POSITIONS

5. **Rigidity—A Resilient Concept** 61
   Edward Zigler and David Balla

   The Lewin-Kounin Formulation 62
   The Criticisms of Goldstein and Werner 66
   Empirical Tests of the Lewin-Kounin
     Formulation 70
   The Motivational Alternative to the
     Rigidity Formulation 74
   Contemporary Variants of the Rigidity
     Position 78
   References 80

6. **Psychological Studies of Mental Deficiency in the Soviet Union** 83
   A. R. Luria

   References 98

7. **The Developmental-Difference Controversy in Verbal Mediation of Behavior** 99
   Rosa Cascione

   References 119

8. **Research Perspectives in Mental Retardation** 121
   Norman R. Ellis and Albert R. Cavalier

   References 149

   PART III: THE DEVELOPMENTAL-DIFFERENCE CONTROVERSY

9. **The Rationale and Irrational in Zigler's Motivational Approach to Mental Retardation** 155
   Norman A. Milgram

   References 161

10. **Developmental Versus Difference Theories of Mental Retardation and the Problem of Motivation** 163
 Edward Zigler

 Developmental Theory and a Model of
  Cognitive Development *165*
 Cognitive Level and the Role of the MA *169*
 Representative Difference or Defect Positions *177*
 Relevance of the Two-Group Approach *181*
 References *186*

11. **A Behavioral Research Strategy in Mental Retardation: Defense and Critique** 189
 Norman R. Ellis

 References *202*

12. **Mental Retardation** 203
 Morton Weir
 References *205*

13. **MA, IQ, and the Developmental Difference Controversy** 207
 Edward Zigler
 References *210*

14. **Piagetian Evidence and the Developmental-Difference Controversy** 213
 John R. Weisz, Keith O. Yeates, and Edward Zigler

 The Developmental-Difference Controversy:
  Two Attendant Hypotheses *214*
 Evidence on the Similar-Sequence Hypothesis *218*
 Status of Evidence on the Similar-Sequence
  Hypothesis *239*
 Critique of the Evidence *240*
 Toward Improved Research *241*
 Evidence on the Similar-Structure Hypothesis *242*
 Methodological Issues Involved in
  Structuring a Fair Test *242*
 Surveying the Studies *245*
 Status of Evidence on the Similar-Structure
  Hypothesis *261*
 Overview and Concluding Comments *269*
 References *269*

15. **Possible Contributions of the Study of Organically Retarded Persons to Developmental Theory**   277
Dante Cicchetti and Petra Pogge-Hesse

Introduction   277
Processes Involved in Skill Acquisition   280
Ways in Which the Investigation of Abnormal Development Contributes to the Formulation of Theories of Normal Development   282
The Organismic/Developmental ("Liberal") Position   284
Zigler's Developmental ("Conservative") Position   289
Expansion of Zigler's Position in Terms of the Liberal Developmental Model   290
An Organizational View of Development: Illustration from the Study of Down Syndrome Infants and Toddlers   292
Future Perspective   308
References   313

Author Index   319
Subject Index   327

This book is dedicated to Julius Richmond and George Tarjan, whose indefatigable efforts and greatness of vision have touched the lives of so many.

Acknowledgments

The editors would like to acknowledge their special indebtedness to Winne Berman for her work on this book. Thanks are also extended for the important work of Margaret Houghton, Melissa Maier, Sally Styfco and Peppie Weiss.

MENTAL RETARDATION
The Developmental-Difference Controversy

THE DEVELOPMENTAL APPROACH

1 Introduction: The Developmental Approach to Mental Retardation

Edward Zigler
David Balla
Yale University

There is a central issue and unifying theme of this book: the developmental-difference controversy in the area of mental retardation. Stated most simply, this controversy centers around the question of whether the behavior of those retarded persons with no evidence of central nervous system dysfunction is best understood by those principles in developmental psychology that have been found to be generally applicable in explaining the behavior and development of nonretarded persons, or whether it is necessary to invoke specific differences over and above a generally lower rate and asymptote of cognitive development. This controversy is of importance because at least 75% of all those identified as retarded have no evidence of organic brain dysfunction.

Retarded persons with no evidence of organic brain dysfunction are referred to by the American Association on Mental Deficiency as suffering from "retardation due to psychosocial disadvantage." The older and more widely used term is "cultural-familial retardation." We use this latter term throughout the book. We prefer this term in that this form of retardation is best understood as involving a combination of environmental (cultural) and genetic (familial) causes. Thus, the term *cultural-familial* seems to us to be a more precise diagnosis than "retardation due to psychosocial disadvantage." According to the developmental theorist, the familially retarded person is viewed as a normal individual in the sense that he falls within the normal distribution of intelligence dictated by the gene pool. He or she is normal in exactly the same sense that a person who is in the lower third percentile of height is considered to be normal. This person will be called "short" but will not be seen as being abnormal. As a consequence of the developmental theorists' view of a familially retarded person as a normal individual, these theorists predict that the performance of this retarded person and a nonretarded person of equivalent developmental level (most typically defined by mental age [MA] on an IQ test) on a cognitive task should be exactly the same. The difference theorist would maintain that retarded and nonretarded persons even of equivalent developmental levels should differ in cognitive performance because of intrinsic differences over and above intellectual slowness.

This book is divided into three major sections. Firstly, the developmental position is presented. Then, several of the major difference positions are discussed. Finally, a series of chapters on the developmental-difference controversy are presented.

THE DEVELOPMENTAL POSITION

In order to understand the developmental position, it is necessary to discuss several issues in the area of mental retardation: the developmentalist's view of "intelligent" behavior, motivational determinants of retarded behavior, the effects of institutions on retarded persons, and the effects of etiology of retardation on performance. We present a brief overview of each of the issues.

Many would agree with the proposition that ultimately the crucial defining feature of mental retardation is low intelligence in comparison with some general reference group. Although such a statement may seem self-evident, difficulties arise when we attempt to define intelligence and to measure it. Of course, intelligence is most often measured with an IQ test and the resulting score is used as an index of intellectual level. The IQ score is not a pure measure of formal cognition. By "intelligence" or formal cognition, we mean such processes as ability in short-term memory, abstracting ability, reasoning, speed of visual information processing, as well as other variables that have been of interest to cognitive psychologists. Many of these cognitive variables have been investigated at great length by the difference theorists represented in this book.

Formal cognition, although of great importance, is only one of the factors that influence performance on an intelligence test or, for that matter, almost any behavior. Performance is also affected by achievement factors. Two individuals with identical cognitive capacities may have had very different experiences in the learning of such items as "What is a slipper?" or "Who wrote *Faust?*". We must draw a clear distinction between formal cognition and achievement. If we ask a person "Who wrote *Faust*" and he/she replies that he/she does not know, we might assume that there is something inadequate about his/her memory or retrieval system, which are aspects of the formal cognitive system. On the other hand, if in the person's experience he/she has never encountered the work *Faust,* he/she will fail the item even though his/her memory and retrieval systems are perfectly adequate. This cognition–achievement distinction is quite similar to the familiar process–content distinction in developmental psychology.

Finally, intelligence test performance is influenced by a variety of motivational and personality variables that have little to do with either formal cognition or achievement. A person can achieve a low score on an IQ or achievement test even when formal cognitive factors and general achievement are adequate. Such a person's motivational stance may preclude optimal or adequate behavior in a test-like situation. One example of such a motivational variable is fear or wariness in a test situation. These motivational personality variables have a major role in the developmental approach to mental retardation. Whenever differences in performance are found between retarded and nonretarded groups of individuals matched on MA, the developmental theorist typically looks for differences in motivation between the two groups.

Much of the work of the developmental thinkers in the area of mental retardation has focused on motivational differences between retarded and nonretarded persons. Retarded persons have been found to be more responsive to social reinforcement from a supportive adult than nonretarded persons of equivalent developmental level. This heightened responsiveness to social reinforcement stems from a history of social deprivation. Often, retarded persons are more interested in interacting with a kindly adult in a testing situation than they are in solving the problem at hand. Paradoxically, retarded persons have also been found to be more wary of strange adults than nonretarded persons. We refer to the heightened responsiveness to social reinforcement and increased wariness as positive and negative reaction tendencies, respectively. The retarded are also less likely to trust their own cognitive resources in problem-solving attempts and rather to rely on possible solutions provided by others. This increased imitativeness is often detrimental to problem solution. We refer to the imitative problem-solving style as outerdirectedness. Frequent failure is also observed in many retarded persons. Because of this high preponderance of failure experiences, the retarded often have a low expectancy of success in problem solving. In addition, their behavior can often be seen as aimed at avoiding failure rather than achieving success. The expectancy of success variable is extensively discussed in a chapter to follow. Different classes of reinforcers have been found to be differentially effective with retarded and nonretarded persons. The retarded are typically more responsive to concrete reinforcement than to intangible reinforcement. "Learned helplessness" has also been seen to characterize the performance of retarded individuals, a phenomenon that is discussed in Chapter 3.

In any consideration of the developmental position it is necessary to discuss the effects of institutional experience on the behavior of retarded persons. In many studies where nonretarded and retarded groups have been compared, the comparison has involved institutionalized retarded individuals with nonretarded individuals living at home. Thus, it is impossible to determine whether any results obtained reflect cognitive differences between retarded and nonretarded groups or the effects of institutionalization. Paradoxically, though researchers have all too often ignored the institutionalization variable, it is generally assumed that institutions have uniformly catastrophic effects on development. We have found that the effects of institutionalization are by no means uniformly negative. Any comprehensive understanding of the effects of institutionalization requires a consideration of the characteristics of the retarded person, his/her preinstitutional life experience, the nature of the institution, and the assessment of a variety of outcome variables on the part of the resident.

As noted previously, the developmental position is limited to those individuals with no evidence of organic brain damage. Seventy-five percent of all retarded individuals have no evidence of central nervous system dysfunction. Those persons with known central nervous system dysfunction, either due to genetic or environmental causes, indeed, can be seen as possessing a "defect." However, all too often in research in mental retardation, the question of etiology has been ignored, and groups of retarded individuals comprised of persons with both cultural-familial and organic diagnoses have been compared with groups of nonretarded individuals. In such studies involving retarded groups with heterogeneous diagnoses, it is difficult to determine if any results obtained reflect intellectual slowness per se or the effects of organic brain damage that might be found at any level of intelligence. Any true experimental confrontation between developmental and difference positions must be limited to the cultural-familial retarded. As is discussed in Chapter 14, the difference position has often been supported if etiology is not taken into consideration in the research, whereas the developmental position has most often been supported if etiology is considered.

THE DIFFERENCE POSITIONS

The second major section of this book is devoted to a presentation of some of the major difference positions in mental retardation. These difference positions have their roots in the area of cognitive psychology, and consequently relatively little attention has been given to the motivational variables that have been of great concern to developmental theorists. Another characteristic of most difference theories is their focus on relatively small subsets of the possible number of cognitive processes; for example, short-term memory.

Historically, the oldest and most influential of the difference positions is the work of Lewin and Kounin on rigidity in the retarded. While this position is far too complex to summarize here, the general view that the retarded are inherently more rigid in their behavior than are nonretarded persons of the same MA has been extremely influential in the area of education and training of retarded persons. Although this position has been regarded by some as little more than an historical relic, variations of the rigidity theme continue to be propounded to the present day.

The retarded have also been characterized as suffering from a deficit in verbal mediation ability. This position is most closely identified with the work of the late Russian psychologist, Alexander Luria. Luria maintained that retarded individuals do not use verbal mediators to guide their behavior as effectively as do nonretarded persons. This verbal mediation deficiency has been said to involve an underdevelopment or general inertness of the verbal system and a dissociation of this system from the motor or action system. A review of this position is presented in Chapter 7.

Another deficit said to characterize the retarded involves relative inadequacy in short-term memory. The work in this area is most closely associated with Norman Ellis. Again, the original work in this area relied heavily on what at that time appeared to be a quasiphysiological construct, stimulus trace. More recently, the work has moved more toward the mainstream of cognitive psychology, with emphasis on flow charts; constructs such as primary, secondary, and tertiary memory, and the study of encoding, rehearsal, and retrieval strategies. However, stimulus-trace theory has by no means been abandoned, and recent evidence in support of this is discussed in Chapter 8.

THE DEVELOPMENTAL-DIFFERENCE CONTROVERSY

The third major section in this book is devoted to the controversy that has arisen around developmental and difference approaches in the area of mental retardation. The major criticisms of the developmental position are presented in chapters by Norman Milgram and Morton Weir. Milgram has characterized the developmental approach as constituting a motivational theory of mental retardation and as giving insufficient attention to cognitive approaches to the problem. He also maintained that the developmentalist's insistence on comparing nonretarded and retarded groups of equivalent mental age in experimental tests of the developmental-difference controversy was "untenable," in that identical MA scores may be arrived at in numerous ways, reflecting myriad patterns of strengths and weaknesses. Weir asserted that if IQ is a measure of the rate of cognitive development, a low IQ score should index a slower rate of learning on any task, including the measures typically used in laboratory research. Thus, according to Weir, retarded individuals should do more poorly than nonretarded individuals of the same mental age on any cognitive task. In Chapter 13, Weir's criticism is responded to from the developmental perspective.

The Piagetian approach to mental retardation is also discussed in this section. This approach, adopted by the Geneva group, especially Inhelder, has been interpreted as consistent with both the developmental and difference positions. In a comprehensive review of empirical research inspired by the Geneva group, written by John Weisz and presented in Chapter 14, it is concluded that the developmental position was strongly supported.

In summary, a comprehensive discussion of a major controversy in the area of mental retardation, that between developmental and difference theorists, is presented in this book. The developmental and major difference positions are presented. In the course of these presentations, several key issues in the area of mental retardation and general developmental psychology are discussed: the most appropriate research methodology for the study of the phenomenon of retardation, the relative importance of cognitive, achievement, and motivational factors in human development, and the relative importance of various cognitive subsystems (ie., short-term memory, attention) in the understanding of retarded behavior.

2
Motivational and Personality Factors in the Performance of the Retarded*

Edward Zigler
David Balla
Yale University

In much of the thinking concerning mentally retarded persons, it appears to be assumed that retarded behavior is simply a consequence of low intelligence or inadequate cognitive functioning. This assumption is made despite the commonplace view in psychology that any behavior cannot simply be a function of formal cognitive functioning. In addition to cognitive determinants of behavior, achievements and motivational factors also play a crucial role (Seitz, Abelson, Levine, & Zigler, 1975; Zigler & Butterfield, 1968). These authors have argued that performance on an IQ test or any "cognitive task" reflects a combination of three factors: (1) formal cognitive processes such as memory, reasoning, and abstracting ability; (2) achievement factors involving specific knowledge of the problem to be solved; and (3) a wide range of personality and motivational factors. In this chapter we discuss personality determinants of retarded behavior. The demonstration of the importance of personality and motivational factors in retarded behavior has been the focus of much of our work. The fact that our work is focused on such factors does not mean that we believe that the cause of retardation lies in motivational or personality differences: The cognitive functioning of retarded individuals has a profound and pervasive influence on their behavior. The crucial questions are: Just how great is this influence, and how does it vary across tasks with which retarded persons are confronted?

---

*Portions of this article appeared in "Personality factors in the performance of the retarded: Implications for clinical assessment". *Journal of the American Academy of Child Psychiatry*, Winter, 1977, *16*(1), 19-37.

For many years, many investigators have noted that personality factors are as important in the adjustment of at least mildly retarded persons as are cognitive factors (Penrose, 1963; Sarason, 1953; Tizard, 1953; Windle, 1962; Zigler, 1971). Even some of the early workers in this country, such as Fernald, who have been predominantly identified with a genetic view of the etiology of retardation, felt that the difference between social adequacy and inadequacy in that large group of borderline retarded individuals was a matter of personality rather than intelligence. This view has been confirmed in a number of studies (see McCarver & Craig, 1974, and Windle, 1962, for previous reviews of the importance of personality factors in the adjustment of retarded persons). Perhaps the most notable of these studies was conducted by T. Weaver (1946) of the adjustment of 8000 retarded persons inducted into the United States Army, most of whom had IQs below 75. Of the total group, 54% of the males and 62% of the females made a satisfactory adjustment to military life. The median IQs of the successful and unsuccessful groups were 72 and 68, respectively. Weaver (1946) concluded that: "personality factors far overshadowed the factor of intelligence [p. 243]" in the adjustment of the retarded to military service.

The tendency to overemphasize the importance of the intellect in adjustment has been documented by Windle (1962), who found that most institutional personnel presume that intelligence is the critical factor in adjustment after release. However, as both Windle and McCarver and Craig pointed out, the majority of studies have reported no meaningful relation between intellectual level and adjustment after release from institutions. Rather, in this literature, factors suggested as associated with poor social adjustment include anxiety, jealousy, overdependency, poor self-evaluation, hostility, hyperactivity, and failure to follow orders, even when requests were well within the range of intellectual competence.

It is hardly surprising that many retarded individuals evidence such difficulties in light of their often atypical social histories, whose specific features and the degree to which they are atypical may vary widely. At one extreme, a familial retarded child may ultimately be placed out of the home, not because of lack of intelligence, but because his own home represents an especially debilitating environment. At the other extreme, a familial retarded set of parents may provide their children with a relatively good home environment, even though it might differ in values, goals, and attitudes from the typical home in which the parents are of average or superior intelligence. In these two hypothetical cases, the children may not only experience quite different socialization histories while living with their parents but also differ to the extent that out of home placement affects their behavior and development. To add even more complexity, the socialization histories of the familial retarded differ markedly from those of retarded individuals with documented central nervous system dysfunction who do not differ from the general population in the frequency of good versus poor home environments.

In the face of such complexity, we need not assert that each retarded child is so unique that it is impossible for us to isolate those factors that may influence the retarded child's level of functioning. If we conceptualize the retarded person as occupying a position on a continuum of normalcy, we can allow our knowledge of normal development to give direction to our efforts. This does not mean that we can ignore the imporatnce of lower intelligence per se, because personality traits and behavior patterns do not develop in a vacuum. In some instances, personality characteristics will reflect environmental factors that have little or nothing to do with intellectual endowment. For example, many of the effects of institutionalization may be constant regardless of the person's intellectual level. In other instances, we must think in terms of an interaction; that is, given a lower intellectual ability, a person may well have certain experiences and develop certain behavior patterns differing from those of a person with higher intelligence. An obvious example is the greater amount of failure that the retarded child typically faces. Even here, the behavior pattern developed may not differ in ontogenesis from that of an individual of average intelligence, who, by some environmental circumstance, also experiences an inordinate amount of failure. By the same token, if the retarded person could be guaranteed a more typical history of success, we would expect his behavior to resemble more nearly that of the intellectually average individual, independent of intellectual level. Within this framework, we discuss the personality factors that have been found to influence the performance of the retarded.

In interpreting the research findings presented in the following sections, it should be noted that improved performance following a manipulation of the child's motivation should not be interpreted as evidence that basic cognitive capacity has been changed. Rather, these studies may suggest ways in which the cognitive functioning of retarded persons may be maximized.

FACTORS INFLUENCING MOTIVATION IN RETARDED PERSONS

Social Deprivation

It has become increasingly clear that the behavior of institutionalized retarded individuals is related to preinstitutional social deprivation (Clarke & Clarke, 1954; Kaplun, 1935; Zigler, 1961). Our definition of social deprivation includes a lack of continuity of care by parents or other caretakers, an excessive desire by the parents to institutionalize their child, impoverished economic circumstances, and a family history of marital discord, mental illness, abuse and/or neglect. Each of these factors has been found to affect a wide variety of behaviors. For example, social deprivation has been found to be associated with behavioral variability, and highly deprived retarded individuals have also been found to be more verbally dependent and more wary than less-deprived children (Balla, Butterfield, & Zigler, 1974; Butterfield & McIntyre, 1969). Perhaps the largest and most important body of research has shown that social deprivation can result in a heightened motivation to interact with a supportive adult—an increased responsiveness to social reinforcement (Balla & Zigler, 1975; Balla et al., 1974; Zigler, 1961; Zigler & Balla, 1972; Zigler, Balla, & Butterfield, 1968). In these studies we have typically used the marble-in-the-hole game to assess responsiveness to social reinforcement. The person is instructed to drop marbles of one color into one hole of a large box and marbles of a second color into a second hole. He or she is allowed to persist at the task until satiated. The correct holes for the colored marbles are then reversed, and the subject again drops marbles until satiated. The measure of responsiveness to social reinforcement is the total time that the person persists on both parts of the task. The person is periodically reinforced by the adult experimenter with one of four randomly ordered comments: "that's fine," "very good," "you really know how to play this game," "you really know how to play marble-in-the-hole." According to our rationale, the socially deprived person will be more responsive to the attention and support of the adult than a nondeprived person and, consequently, will persist at the task longer. Early support for this formulation was obtained by Zigler (1961), who used a clinical estimate of the extent of preinstitutional social deprivation with a group of institutionalized retarded persons and found that highly deprived individuals persisted at the task significantly longer than less-deprived individuals. This finding has since been replicated with groups of institutionalized retarded individuals in four additional institutional settings, using the more objective measure of social deprivation described earlier (Zigler, Butterfield, & Goff, 1966). This heightened motivation to interact with a supportive adult stemming from a history of social deprivation certainly seems congruent with the sort of behavior often seen in retarded individuals—actively seeking attention and affection.

However, in certain circumstances, increased social deprivation may lead to an attenuation of social reinforcer effectiveness (Balla, Kossan, & Zigler, 1980; Irons & Zigler, 1969). Whether or not social deprivation results in an increased or decreased responsiveness to social reinforcement may well depend upon differences in psychological defenses employed by particular groups of subjects. For example, in the Irons and Zigler study, the subjects were acting-out children whose response to social deprivation might well have been hostility or negativism, which could result in social reinforcers becoming less effective.

It should be noted that heightened motivation for social reinforcement has been used as an indicator of an important phenomenon discussed in the general child-development literature, namely, dependency. Thus, with an almost imperceptibly slight shift in terminology, we might conclude that a general consequence of social deprivation is overdependency. We cannot place enough emphasis on the role of such overdependency in the behavior of retarded persons. Given some minimal intellectual level, the shift from dependence to independence is perhaps the single most important factor that enables retarded persons to become self-sustaining members of society (Zigler & Harter, 1969).

Some indication of the pervasiveness of the atypical dependency of institutionalized retarded persons may be found in a study by Zigler and Balla (1972). Intellectually average and retarded children of three MA levels, approximately 7, 9, and 12, were compared in terms of their responsiveness to social reinforcement, as measured by the marble-in-the-hole task. In keeping with the general developmental progression from helplessness and dependence to autonomy and independence, both retarded and intellectually average children of higher MAs were found to be less motivated for social reinforcement than children of lower MAs. However, at each MA level, the retarded children were more dependent than the intellectually average children. This disparity in dependent behavior was just as marked at the highest as at the lowest MA level. Indeed, the oldest retarded group persisted at the marble-in-the-hole task almost twice as long as the youngest intellectually average group.

The relationship between preinstitutional social deprivation and social reinforcement was strongest for the youngest retarded group, suggesting that the younger the child, the more his behavior depends on life experiences within the family context. Perhaps as the child grows older and interacts with a broader spectrum of socializing agents, his or her motivation for social reinforcement will become less determined by the quality of social interaction he or she has experienced within the confines of the family life. Such a view is certainly consistent with the observation that, as a child grows older, his personality structure is more influenced by peers, teachers, and other nonfamily socializing agents.

In the Zigler and Balla (1972) study we also found evidence that retarded children who maintained contact with their parents or parent surrogates were less dependent than children with more limited contact. Thus, it seems possible to modify excessively dependent behavior by having increased contact with important other people.

Positive- and Negative-Reaction Tendencies

A phenomenon that appears to be at considerable variance with the retarded individual's increased desire for social reinforcement has been noted: namely, the retarded child's reluctance and wariness to interact with adults. This apparent inconsistency has been a part of a controversy over whether social deprivation leads to an increase in the desire for interaction or to apathy and withdrawal (Cox, 1953; Freud & Burlingham, 1944; Goldfarb, 1953; Irvine, 1952; Spitz &

Wolf, 1946; Wittenborn & Myers, 1957). Experimental work to date has suggested that social deprivation results both in a heightened motivation to interact with supportive adults (positive-reaction tendency) and in a reluctance and wariness to do so (negative-reaction tendency).

The negative-reaction tendency construct has been employed to explain some of the performance differences between retarded and nonretarded individuals originally reported by Kounin (1941). The original interpretation of these studies is presented in Chapter 5. Kounin employed a simple two-part task highly similar to the marble-in-the-hole task discussed earlier. A recurring finding in studies utilizing such two-part tasks (Kounin, 1941; Zigler, 1958, 1961) has been that retarded individuals have a much greater tendency than intellectually average individuals to spend more time on task two than on task one. Zigler (1958) suggested that this difference was due to a greater negative-reaction tendency of institutionalized retarded individuals, a consequence of the more frequent negative encounters that they have experienced at the hands of adults.

In our own work we have measured the negative-reaction tendency in two ways. In several studies we have obtained the measure on the marble-in-the-hole task in conjunction with the measure of responsiveness to social reinforcement. In explaining the puzzling finding that some retarded people actually persisted at the second part of the test longer than they did at the first part of the test, it was hypothesized the retarded children are both excessively desirous of reinforcement from supportive adults and wary of them. The wary child would utilize the first part of the task to insure that the adult would not punish him. Once this determination is made, he is able to be responsive to social reinforcement and may actually persist at the second part of the task longer than the first. On the marble-in-the-hole task, therefore, negative-reaction tendencies have been measured by a cosatiation score (time part I − time part II/time part I + time part II).

In an early experimental study (Shallenberger & Zigler, 1961), both intellectually average and institutionalized retarded individuals experienced either a positive or negative interaction with an adult prior to the administration of the marble-in-the-hole measure. In the positive interaction condition, all the subject's responses met with success and were praised. In the negative condition, all the subject's responses met with failure, and disapproval was indicated. For both the retarded and nonretarded individuals, greater wariness was demonstrated following the negative than following the positive condition. In addition, the retarded children were more strongly affected by the negative interaction than were the nonretarded children.

In other studies, a more direct measure of the negative-reaction tendency has been utilized—how far a person situated himself from a stationary adult and how this position changed over a series of trials (S. J. Weaver, 1966; S. J. Weaver, Balla, & Zigler, 1971). Both positive and negative preconditions were also used in these studies. S. J. Weaver (1966), utilizing noninstitutionalized retarded children, found that children who had experienced a negative interaction prior to the criterion task were more wary than those who experienced a positive interaction. S. J. Weaver et al. (1971) investigated institutionalized and noninstitutionalized retarded children as well as intellectually average children. In this study, the institutionalized children were found to become more wary following the negative condition and less wary following the positive interaction.

In several studies of the negative-reaction tendency, experimental preconditions were not employed. Harter and Zigler (1968) found that institutionalized retarded people seemed to have a generalized wariness of strangers, whether they were adults or peers. Balla et al. (1980) found that after approximately 8 years of institutional experience retarded individuals with a history of high preinstitutional social deprivation were more wary than less-deprived individuals. Thus, there is some evidence that socially depriving experiences can cause a wariness of adults that is quite longstanding. Balla, McCarthy, and Zigler (1971), utilizing a group of institutionalized retarded individuals, found that those institutionalized at a younger age were less wary than those institutionalized when older. Apparently, the institution used in that study structured its program for the residents in such a way as to make them less wary of strange adults over the course of institutionalization. Excessive wariness is not an inexorable consequence of institutionalization.

Failure and the Performance of the Retarded

Another factor frequently mentioned as a determinant in the performance of retarded persons is their high expectancy of failure. This expectancy has been viewed as a consequence of a history of frequent confrontations with tasks with which retarded persons are ill equipped to deal. The experimental work employing the success–failure dimension has proceeded in two directions. The first has been an attempt to document the pervasiveness of feelings of failure in the retarded. The work of Cromwell (1963) and his colleagues has lent support to the general proposition that retarded individuals have a higher expectancy of failure than those of average intellect. In a further series of studies (MacMillan, 1969; MacMillan & Keogh, 1971; MacMillan & Knopf, 1971), the experimenter prevented children from finishing several tasks and subsequently asked why the tasks were not completed. In all these studies, the retarded children consistently blamed themselves for the tasks not being completed, whereas nonretarded children did not place blame on themselves.

The second line of research has focused upon the effects of success and failure expectancies on problem-solving behavior. The task typically employed in these studies is a three-choice discrimination problem in which one stimulus is partially reinforced and the other two stimuli are never reinforced. Children with low expectancies of success, as gauged by aspiration level or need–achievement measures, were more likely to display a maximizing strategy (persistent choice of the partially reinforced stimulus) on this task than children with high expectancies of success (Gruen, Ottinger, & Zigler, 1970; Kier & Zigler, 1975; Ollendick & Gruen, 1971).

Such findings are consistent with Goodnow's (1955) analysis of the determinants of choice behavior. Goodnow suggested that greater maximizing behavior would be found when a subject accepted less than 100% success as an acceptable outcome, whereas less maximizing behavior would be found when a subject expected 100% success, or a level of success greater than that allowed in the situation. Thus, on the three-choice probability task, children with higher expectancies of success would be expected to engage in strategies other than maximizing, in the hope of achieving 100% reinforcement.

Consistent with the expectancy of success formulation, retarded children have been found to exhibit more maximizing behavior (selecting the reinforced stimulus) than children of average intelligence (Gruen & Zigler, 1968; Stevenson & Zigler, 1958). However, the tendency of retarded individuals to employ a maximizing strategy could also be interpreted in terms of the cognitive rigidity position of Lewin and Kounin (see Chapter 5). That is to say, the inherent rigidity of retarded persons might have led them to perseverate on the choice of one of the three stimuli and not to abandon the choice, even when it proved maladaptive. In an attempt to resolve this issue, Ollendick, Balla, and Zigler (1971) employed relatively long-term success and failure conditions and observed the subsequent task behavior. They found that failure experiences resulted in a low expectancy of success, whereas success experiences resulted in a higher expectancy of success. From these data it seemed plausible to assume that the greater maximizing behavior observed in retarded individuals is motivationally based, rather than being indicative of cognitive rigidity. Gruen, Ottinger, and Ollendick (1974) attempted to determine whether the success–failure findings could be replicated in a more life-like school setting. As predicted, retarded children in regular classes (presumably being exposed to repeated failure) were found to have higher expectancies of failure than retarded children in special classes (being exposed to relatively higher levels of success). However, Caparulo (1979), who investigated mildly retarded boys who were either partially or totally mainstreamed, did not find the expectancy of success or failure to be systematically affected by the intensity of the mainstreaming experience.

The Reinforcer Hierarchy

Due to experiential factors, the retarded individual's motivation for incentives may differ from that of intellectually average individuals of the same MA. Stated somewhat differently, the position of various reinforcers in the reinforcer hierarchies may differ in retarded and nonretarded children. Much of the experimental work on the reinforcer hierarchy has focused on tangible and intangible reinforcement (Havighurst, 1970). It has been argued that certain factors in the histories of retarded children cause them to be less responsive to intangible reinforcement than are nonretarded children of equivalent MA (Zigler, 1962; Zigler & deLabry, 1962, Zigler & Unell, 1962). This work is of special importance, because intangible reinforcement (information that a response is correct) is the most immediate and frequently dispensed reinforcement in real-life tasks. When such a reinforcer is employed in experimental studies comparing retarded and nonretarded individuals, any group difference found might be attributable not to differences in intellectual capacity but rather to the different values that such reinforcement may have for the two types of individuals. The importance of the specific reinforcer dispensed in studies with the retarded was highlighted by both Plenderleith (1956) and Stevenson and Zigler (1957), who found that when the tangible reinforcers were given, institutionalized familial retarded individuals were no more rigid than nonretarded subjects of the same MA on a discrimination reversal-learning task.

Clearest support for the view that the retarded child is much less motivated to be correct for the sake of correctness than is the middle-socioeconomic-status (SES) child (so typically employed in comparisons with the retarded) is contained in a study by Zigler and deLabry (1962). They tested MA-matched middle-SES, lower-SES, and retarded children on a concept-switching task (Kounin, 1941) under two conditions of reinforcement: (1) the information that the child was correct; and (2) the child was rewarded with a toy of his choice if he switched from one concept to another. In the "correct" condition, both the retarded and lower-SES groups were poorer in their concept-switching than the middle-SES children. However, no differences were found among the three groups who received tangible reinforcers. Furthermore, no differences in the ability to switch concepts were found among the three groups receiving what was assumed to be their optimal reinforcer (retarded, tangible; lower-SES, tangible; and middle-SES, intangible). Interestingly, both retarded and upper-SES children were found to switch concepts more readily in a tangible than in an intangible reinforcement condition (Zigler & Unell, 1962).

These studies highlight an assumption that has been noted as erroneous by many educators; namely, that the lower-SES child and the retarded child are responsive to the same types of reinforcers as the typical middle-SES child. However, although retarded children as a group may value being correct less than do middle-SES children as a group, this may not hold true for any particular child; the crucial factor is not membership in a particular social class or being retarded per se, but rather the particular social learning experience.

This point is aptly underlined in a study by Byck (1968), who examined the performance of groups of institutionalized Down syndrome and familial retarded subjects (matched on MA, CA, IQ, and length of institutionalization) who received either tangible or intangible reinforcement for their performance on a concept-switching task. Superior concept-switching for the Down syndrome children was found in the intangible as compared to the tangible condition, whereas the reverse pattern was found for the familial groups. This finding is consistent with the social-class and reinforcer-effectiveness literature noted earlier, if one remembers that the institutionalized familial retarded almost invariably come from a lower-SES background, whereas children with Down syndrome are more likely to come from middle-SES homes. It would appear that the social learning experiences acquired fairly early in the child's life and prior to institutionalization are particularly influential in determining the potency of various reinforcers.

In more recent work, attention has shifted to the more general phenomenon of the intrinsic reinforcement that inheres in being correct, regardless or whether or not an external agent dispenses a reinforcer for such correctness. This shift in orientation owes much to White's (1959) formulation concerning the pervasive influence of the effectance or mastery motive. There can be little question that White's effectance concept provides a rubric for a variety of behaviors that appear very central in the individual's behavioral repertoire (e.g., the desire for optimal levels of sensory stimulation, manipulation, exploration, and curiosity). A series of studies (Shultz & Zigler, 1970; Zigler, 1966a, b; Zigler, Levine, & Gould, 1967) has given some support to this view that using one's own cognitive resources to their fullest is intrinsically gratifying and thus motivating.

As with the case of intangible reinforcers, the strength of the effectance motive may be different for retarded and nonretarded individuals. Evidence on this point has been provided by Harter and Zigler (1974), who constructed several measures of effectance motivation, including variation seeking, curiosity, mastery for the sake of competence, and preference of challenging tasks. On these measures, intellectually average children demonstrated more effectance motivation than retarded children. Institutionalized retarded children also displayed less curiosity than did noninstitutionalized retarded children. In summary, retarded children seem to be both less responsive to intangible reinforcers and less motivated by intrinsic effectance motives than the child of average intellect.

Outerdirectedness

Findings (Green & Zigler, 1962; Zigler, Hodgden, & Stevenson, 1958) that retarded children are more sensitive to cues provided by an adult than intellectually average children of the same MA have led us and our coworkers to the study of a general style of problem solving referred to as outerdirectedness (Achenbach & Weisz, 1975; Achenbach & Zigler, 1968; Balla, Styfco, & Zigler,

1971; Sanders, Zigler, & Butterfield, 1968; Turnure & Zigler, 1964; Yando & Zigler, 1971; Zigler & Abelson, 1975). This style has been defined as the degree to which the individual uses external cues to solve problems rather than relying on his own cognitive resources.

In the latest revision of the outerdirectedness formulation (Balla et al., 1980; Zigler & Abelson, 1975), three factors have been advanced as important in determining the child's degree of outerdirectedness—the general level of cognitive development, the relative incidence of success the individual has experienced when employing his cognitive resources in problem-solving situations, and the extent of the individual's attachment to adults. Either too little or too much imitation of adults is viewed as a negative psychological indicator. Some intermediate level of imitation is viewed as a positive developmental phenonenon reflecting the individual's healthy attachment to adults and responsivity to cues that adults emit, which can be utilized in the child's problem-solving efforts.

In general, the developmental aspect of the outerdirectedness formulation has received experimental support. With nonretarded children, outerdirectedness has been found to decrease with increasing MA (MacMillan & Wright, 1974; Ruble & Nakamura, 1973; Yando & Zigler, 1971; Zigler & Yando, 1972). This developmental shift has also been found in institutionalized retarded persons (Turnure, 1970a, b). In groups of noninstitutionalized mildly retarded people, decreasing outerdirectedness with increasing MA has been found by Balla, Styfco, & Zigler (1971) and Gordon and MacLean (1977).

The success/failure aspect of the outerdirectedness formulation has generated the prediction that retarded persons, because of their histories of failure, are more outerdirected in their problem-solving behavior than nonretarded persons of the same MA. This prediction has been confirmed in several of the studies cited previously. Both nonretarded and retarded children have been found to become more outerdirected following failure than success experiences.

To this point, outerdirectedness or imitativeness has been discussed as if it were a unitary psychological dimension. Actually, in different studies, at least two somewhat conceptually different measures have been employed. These measures each bear somewhat differently on the success/failure aspect of the outerdirectedness formulation. In some studies, a learning measure has been utilized where a cue extrinsic to the task could either help or hinder performance. There was clearly a right or wrong answer. It seems reasonable to expect that children living in an environment adjusted to their developmental level would be less imitative in this task than children living in an environment where they are confronted with their intellectual shortcomings and experience considerable failure. Indeed, Achenbach and Zigler (1968) found that noninstitutionalized retarded children were more reliant on external cues on this task than were institutionalized retarded children. A second measure of imitation that has been utilized has been a sticker game, where an adult first makes a design and then asks the child to make a design of his own choosing. The child's designs are subsequently scored for extent of imitation of the model. This is not a learning task, and there are no right or wrong answers. This task may well tap extent of conformity or compliance with adults. It seems reasonable to expect that in environments where a high degree of compliance has adaptive value, such as in total institutions, greater imitation would be found. In two studies (Lustman, Zigler, & Balla, 1979; Yando & Zigler, 1971), institutionalized retarded persons have been found to be more imitative on this task than noninstitutionalized retarded persons.

In regard to the attachment-to-adults aspect of the outerdirectedness formulation, there is some evidence that individuals who have not formed healthy attachment to adult caretakers will have an atypically low level of outerdirectedness (Balla et al., 1980). In this study we found that institutionalized retarded individuals whose caretakers had negative attitudes concerning them were less outerdirected than those whose caretakers had positive attitudes concerning them. Thus, individuals who are responded to in a negative manner may learn to ignore cues provided by adults and thus become less imitative.

Self-Concept

The self-concept construct has had a central role in general personality theory but, surprisingly, has received relatively little attention in the mental retardation literature (Balla & Zigler, 1979). Traditionally, a person's self-concept has been seen exclusively as a function of his life experience. An alternative view has been proposed by Zigler and his colleagues (Achenbach & Zigler, 1963; Katz & Zigler, 1967), who have advanced a developmental view of the self-image construct. In this work, three aspects of the self-concept have been measured: the real self-image—the person's current self-concept; the ideal self-image—the way the person would ideally like to be; and self-image disparity—the difference between real and ideal self. It has been argued that the growth and development of an individual must invariably be accompanied by an increasing disparity between assessment of the real self and the ideal self. From the developmental point of view, the magnitude of self-image disparity is considered an index of the level of maturity attained.

This thesis is based on the assumption that two of the determinants of the scores on typical self-image disparity measures are developmental in nature. The first such determinant is an individual's capacity to experience guilt, a capacity that increases over the course of development with a growing ability for incorporating social demands, mores, and values (Phillips & Rabinovitch, 1958; Phillips & Zigler, 1961; Zigler & Child, 1969). Secondly, an even more general determinant involves the phenomenon of increasing cognitive differentiation with development (Light, Zax, & Gardener, 1965; Werner, 1948; Witkin, Dyk, Faterson, Goodenough, & Karp, 1962). In any cognitive act, a person at a higher developmental level would be expected to make finer distinctions within each category than an individual at a lower developmental level. The use of a larger number of categories should increase the probability of greater disparity between any two complex judgments, including those regarding real and ideal self-images. The developmental approach to self-concept has received empirical support in studies of psychiatrically disturbed and nondisturbed adults (Achenbach & Zigler, 1963; McCormick & Balla, 1973), as well as with groups of normal and emotionally disturbed children and adolescents (Katz & Zigler, 1967; Katz, Zigler, & Zalk, 1975; Phillips & Zigler, 1980).

Although there has been a relative emphasis on the developmental aspects of the self-concept in the preceding studies, we have also recognized that there is certainly an experiential component in the development of the self-image, and that any comprehensive understanding of the issue requires a synthesis of both developmental and experiential postions. In one study concerned with the self-concept of retarded persons (Zigler, Balla, & Watson, 1972), institutionalized and noninstitutionalized retarded and nonretarded children were administered a self-concept inventory tapping real-image, ideal-image, and self-image disparity. Groups of nonretarded children were matched on both CA and MA with the retarded children. Consistent with the developmental approach to self-concept, the older nonretarded children had lower real self-images, higher ideal self-images, and greater self image disparity than the younger nonretarded children. Consistent with the experiential position, the retarded individuals had lower ideal self-images than did the nonretarded children. In another study where the self-concepts of retarded children were compared with those of both MA- and CA-matched nonretarded children (Leahy, Balla, & Zigler, in press), lower real and ideal self-images were also found in the retarded children. These findings concerning the ideal self-image among the retarded seemed to indicate that one consequence of being identified as retarded is a lowering of goals and aspirations; an interpretation certainly consistent with the expectancy of success literature cited earlier. In the Zigler et al. (1972) study, the institutionalized individuals in general were found to have lower real and ideal self-images as well as greater self-image disparities than the noninstitutionalized children. Thus, institutionalized individuals seemed to have low senses of self-esteem as well as setting low standards for themselves. In summary, both developmental and experiential interpretations of the development of the self-concept in retarded persons have received empirical support in our work.

CONCLUSIONS

In conclusion, we might ask the question: What is the burden of the total body of evidence concerning personality and the retarded person? We think that many of the reported differences between retarded and intellectually average children of the same MA are a result of motivational and emotional differences that reflect variations in experiential histories. This is not to say that we believe that the cause of mental retardation can be explained in terms of personality differences. The cognitive functioning of the retarded unquestionably has a profound effect on their behavior. As mentioned previously, crucial questions are, just how great is this influence, and how does it differ across tasks with which the retarded are confronted. We would like to think that if it were possible to change the personality structures of many retarded persons they might be more likely to become self-sustaining members of society.

REFERENCES

Achenbach, R., & Zigler, E. Social competence and self-image disparity in psychiatric and nonpsychiatric patients. *Journal of Abnormal and Social Psychology,* 1963, *67,* 197-205.

Achenbach, T., & Weisz, J. R. A longitudinal study of relations between outerdirectedness and IQ changes in preschoolers. *Child Development,* 1975, *46,* 650-657.

Achenbach, T., & Zigler, E. Cue-learning and problem-learning strategies in normal and retarded children. *Child Development,* 1968, *3,* 827-848.

Balla, D., Butterfield, E. C., & Zigler, E. Effects of institutionalization on retarded children: A longitudinal cross-institutional investigation. *American Journal of Mental Deficiency,* 1974, *78,* 530-549.

Balla, D., Kossan, N., & Zigler, E. *Effects of preinstitutional history and institutionalization on the behavior of the retarded.* Unpublished manuscript, Yale University, 1980.

Balla, D., McCarthy, E., & Zigler, E. Some correlates of negative reaction tendencies in institutionalized retarded children. *The Journal of Psychology,* 1971, *79,* 77-84.

Balla, D., Styfco, S. J., & Zigler, E. Use of the opposition concept and outerdirectedness in intellectually average, familial retarded, and organically retarded children. *American Journal of Mental Deficiency,* 1971, *75,* 663-680.

Balla, D., & Zigler, E. Personality development in retarded persons. In N. R. Ellis (Ed.), *Handbook of mental deficiency* (2nd ed.). Hillsdale, N.J.: Lawrence Erlbaum Associates, 1979.

Butterfield, E. C., & MacIntyre, A. Cognitive and motivational factors in concept switching among the retarded. *American Journal of Mental Deficiency,* 1969, *74,* 235-241.

Byck, M. Cognitive differences among diagnostic groups of retardates. *American Journal of Mental Deficiency,* 1968, *73,* 97-101.

Caparulo, B. K. *Mainstreaming and teachers' attitudes toward mainstreaming: Their influence on the behavior of mildly retarded children.* Unpublished manuscript, Yale University, 1979.

Clarke, A. D. B., & Clarke, A. M. Cognitive changes in the feebleminded. *British Journal of Psychology,* 1954, *45,* 173-179.

Cox, F. The origins of the dependency drive. *Australian Journal of Psychology,* 1953, *5,* 64-73.

Cromwell, R. L. A social learning approach to mental retardation. In N. R. Ellis (Ed.), *Handbook of mental deficiency.* New York: Mc Graw-Hill, 1963.

Freud, A., & Burlingham, D. *Infants without families.* New York: International Universities Press, 1944.

Goldfarb, W. The effects of early institutional care on adolescent personality. *Journal of Experimental Education,* 1953, *12,* 106-129.

Goodnow, J. J. Determinants of choice distribution in two-choice situations. *American Journal of Psychology*, 1955, *68*, 106-116.

Gordon, D. A., & MacLean, W. E. Developmental analysis of outerdirectedness in noninstitutionalized EMR children. *American Journal of Mental Deficiency*, 1977, *81*, 508-511.

Green, C., & Zigler, E. Social deprivation and the performance of retarded and normal children on a satiation-type task. *Child Development*, 1962, *33*, 499-508.

Gruen, G., Ottinger, E., & Ollendick, T. Probability learning in retarded children with differing histories of success and failure in school. *American Journal of Mental Deficiency*, 1974, *79*, 417-423.

Gruen, G., Ottinger, D., & Zigler, E. Level of aspiration and the probability learning of middle- and lower-class children. *Developmental Psychology*, 1971, *3*, 133-142.

Gruen, G., & Zigler, E. Expectancy of success and the probability learning of middle-class, lower-class, and retarded children. *Journal of Abnormal Psychology*, 1968, *73*, 343-352.

Harter, S., & Zigler, E. Effectiveness of adult and peer reinforcement on the performance of institutionalized and noninstitutionalized retardates. *Journal of Abnormal Psychology*, 1968, *73*, 144-149.

Harter, S., & Zigler, E. The assessment of effectance motivation in normal and retarded children. *Developmental Psychology*, 1974, *10*, 169-180.

Havighurst, F. J. Minority subcultures and the law of effect. *American Psychologist*, 1970, *25*, 313-322.

Irons, N. M., & Zigler, E. Children's responsiveness to social reinforcement as a function of short-term preliminary social interactions and long-term social deprivation. *Developmental Psychology*, 1969, *1*, 402-409.

Irvine, E. Observations on the aims and methods of child rearing in communal settlements in Israel. *Human Relations*, 1952, *5*, 247-275.

Kaplun, D. The high-grade moron. *Proceedings of the American Association on Mental Deficiency*, 1935, *40*, 68-89.

Katz, P., & Zigler, E. Self-image disparity: A developmental approach. *Journal of Personality and Social Psychology*, 1967, *5*, 186-195.

Katz, P., Zigler, E., & Zalk, S. Children's self-image disparity: The effects of age, maladustment, and action-thought orientation. *Developmental Psychology*, 1975, *11*, 546-550.

Kier, R. J., & Zigler, E. *Success expectancies and the probability learning of children of low and middle socioeconomic status.* Unpublished manuscript, Yale University, 1975.

Kounin, J. Experimental studies of rigidity: I. The measurement of rigidity in normal and feebleminded persons. *Character and Personality*, 1941, *9*, 251-272.

Leahy, R., Balla, D., & Zigler, E. Role taking, self-image, and imitation in retarded and nonretarded individuals. *American Journal of Mental Deficiency*, in press.

Light, C. S., Zax, M., & Gardener, D. H. Relationship of age, sex, and intelligence level to extreme response style. *Journal of Personality and Social Psychology*, 1965, *2*, 907-909.

Lustman, N. M., Zigler, E., & Balla, D. *Imitation in institutionalized and noninstitutionalized retarded children and in children of average intellect.* Unpublished manuscript, Yale University, 1979.

MacMillan, D. L. Motivational differences: Cultural-familial retardates versus normal subjects on expectancy for failure. *American Journal of Mental Deficiency*, 1969, *74*, 254-258.

MacMillan, D. L., & Keogh, B. K. Normal and retarded children's expectancy for failure. *Developmental Psychology*, 1971, *4*, 343-348.

MacMillan, D. L., & Knopf, E. D. Effect of instructional set on perceptions of event outcomes by EMR and nonretarded children. *American Journal of Mental Deficiency*, 1971, *76*, 185-189.

MacMillan, D. L., & Wright, D. L. Outerdirectedness in children of three ages as a function of experimentally induced success and failure. *Journal of Educational Psychology*, 1974, *68*, 919-925.

McCarver, R. B., & Craig, E. M. Placement of the retarded in the community: Prognosis and outcome. *International Review of Research in Mental Retardation*, 1974, *7*, 145-207.

McCormick, M., & Balla, D. Self-image disparity and attachment to ethnic subculture. *The Journal of Psychology*, 1973, *84*, 97-104.

Ollendick, T., Balla, D., & Zigler, E. Expectancy of success and the probability learning of retarded children. *Journal of Abnormal Psychology*, 1971, *77*, 275-281.

Ollendick, T., & Gruen, G. Level of n achievement and probability in children. *Developmental Psychology*, 1971, *4*, 486.

Penrose, L. S. *The biology of mental deficiency*. London: Sidgwich & Jackson, 1963.

Phillips, D., & Zigler, E. Children's self-image disparity: Effects of age, socioeconomic status, ethnicity, and gender. *Journal of Personality and Social Psychology*, 1980, *39*, 689-700.

Phillips, L., & Rabinovitch, M. Social role and patterns of symptomatic behaviors. *Journal of Abnormal and Social Psychology*, 1958, *57*, 181-186.

Phillips, L., & Zigler, E. Social competence: The action-thought parameter and vicariousness in normal and pathological behavior. *Journal of Abnormal and Social Psychology*, 1961, *63*, 137-146.

Plenderleith, M. Discrimination learning and discrimination reversal learning in normal and feebleminded children. *Journal of Genetic Psychology*, 1956, *88*, 107-112.

Ruble, D. N., & Nakamura, C. Outerdirectedness as a problem-solving approach in relation to developmental level and selected task variables. *Child Development*, 1973, *44*, 519-528.

Sanders, B., Zigler, E., & Butterfield, E. C. Outerdirectedness in the discrimination learning of normal and mentally retarded children. *Journal of Abnormal Psychology*, 1968, *73*, 368-375.

Sarason, S. B. *Psychological problems in mental deficiency*. New York: Harper & Row, 1953.

Seitz, V., Abelson, W. D., Levine, E., & Zigler, E. Effects of place of testing on the Peabody Picture Vocabulary Test scores of disadvantaged Head Start and non-Head Start children. *Child Development*, 1975, *46*, 481-486.

Shallenberger, P., & Zigler, E. Rigidity, negative reaction tendencies, and cosatiation effects in normal and feebleminded children. *Journal of Abnormal and Social Psychology*, 1961, *63*, 20-26.

Shultz, T., & Zigler, E. Emotional concomitants of visual mastery in infants. *Journal of Experimental Child Psychology*, 1970, *10*, 390-402.

Spitz, R. A., & Wolf, K. M. Analytic depression. In A. Freud et al. (Eds.), *The psychoanalytic study of the child* (Vol. II). New York: International Universities Press, 1946.

Stevenson, H. W., & Zigler, E. Discrimination learning and rigidity in normal and feebleminded individuals. *Journal of Personality*, 1957, *25*, 699-711.

Stevenson, H. W., & Zigler, E. Probability learning in children. *Journal of Experimental Psychology*, 1958, *56*, 185-192.

Tizard, J. The prevalence of mental subnormality. *Bulletin of the World Health Organization*, 1953, *9*, 423-440.

Turnure, J. E. Reactions to physical and social distractors by moderately retarded institutionalized children. *Journal of Special Education*, 1970, *4*, 283-294. (a)

Turnure, J. E. Distractibility in the mentally retarded: Negative evidence for an orienting inadequacy. *Exceptional Children*, 1970, *37*, 181-186. (b)

Turnure, J. E., & Zigler, E. Outerdirectedness in the problem solving of normal and retarded children. *Journal of Abnormal and Social Psychology*, 1964, *69*, 427-436.

Weaver, S. J. *The effects of motivation-hygiene orientation and interpersonal reaction tendencies in intellectually subnormal children*. Unpublished doctoral dissertation, George Peabody College for Teachers, 1966.

Weaver, S. J., Balla, D., & Zigler, E. Social approach and avoidance tendencies of institutionalized retarded and noninstitutionalized retarded and normal children. *Journal of Experimental Research in Personality,* 1971, *5,* 98-110.

Weaver, T. R. The incidence of maladjustment among mental defectives in military environments. *American Journal of Mental Deficiency,* 1946, *51,* 238-246.

Werner, H. *Comparative psychology of mental development.* New York: Follett, 1948.

White, R. W. Motivation reconsidered: The concept of competence. *Psychological Review,* 1959, *66,* 297-333.

Whittenborn, J., & Myers, B. *The placement of adoptive children.* Springfield, Ill.: Charles C. Thomas, 1957.

Windle, C. Prognosis of mental subnormals. *American Journal of Mental Deficiency,* 1962, *66* (Monograph Supplement).

Witkin, H. A., Dyk, R. R., Faterson, H. F., Goodenough, D. R., & Karp, S. A. *Psychological differentiation: Studies of development.* New York: Wiley, 1962.

Yando, R., & Zigler, E. Outerdirectedness in the problem solving of institutionalized and noninstitutionalized normal and retarded children. *Developmental Psychology,* 1971, *4,* 277-288.

Zigler, E. *The effect of preinstitutional social deprivation on the performance of feebleminded children.* Unpublished doctoral dissertation, University of Texas, 1958.

Zigler, E. Social deprivation and rigidity in the performance of feebleminded children. *Journal of Abnormal and Social Psychology,* 1961, *62,* 413-421.

Zigler, E. Rigidity in the feebleminded. In E. Trapp & P. Himelstein (Eds.), *Readings on the exceptional child.* New York: Appleton-Century-Crofts, 1962.

Zigler, E. Bruner and the Center for Cognitive Studies: Discussion. In M. Garrison (Ed.), *Cognitive models and development in mental retardation. American Journal of Mental Deficiency,* 1966, *70,* 118-126 (Monograph Supplement). (a)

Zigler, E. Research on personality structure in the retardate. In N. R. Ellis (Ed.), *International review of research in mental retardation* (Vol. 1). New York: Academic Press, 1966. (b)

Zigler, E. The retarded child as a whole person. In H. E. Adams & W. K. Boardman, III (Eds.), *Advances in experimental clinical psychology* (Vol. I). New York: Pergamon Press, 1971.

Zigler, E., & Abelson, W. *Is an intervention program necessary in order to improve economically disadvantaged children's IQ scores?* Unpublished manuscript, Yale University, 1975.

Zigler, E., & Balla, D. Developmental course of responsiveness to social reinforcement in normal children and institutionalized retarded children. *Developmental Psychology,* 1972, *6,* 66-73.

Zigler, E., Balla, D., & Butterfield, E. C. A longitudinal investigation of the relationship between preinstitutional social deprivation and social motivation in institutionalized retardates. *Journal of Personality and Social Psychology,* 1968, *10,* 437-445.

Zigler, E., Balla, D., & Watson, N. Developmental and experimental determinants of self-image disparity in institutionalized and noninstitutionalized retarded and normal children. *Journal of Personality and Social Psychology,* 1972, *23,* 81-87.

Zigler, E., & Butterfield, E. C. Motivational aspects of changes in IQ test performance of culturally deprived nursery school children. *Child Development,* 1968, *39,* 1-14.

Zigler, E., Butterfield, E., & Goff, G. A measure of preinstitutional social deprivation for institutionalized retardates. *American Journal of Mental Deficiency,* 1966, *70,* 873-885.

Zigler, E., & Child, I. Socialization. In G. Lindzey & E. Aronson (Eds.), *The handbook of social psychology* (2nd ed.). Reading, Mass.: Addison-Wesley, 1969.

Zigler, E., & de Labry, J. Concept switching in middle-class, lower-class, and retarded children. *Journal of Abnormal and Social Psychology,* 1962, *65,* 267-273.

Zigler, E., & Harter, S. Socialization of the mentally retarded. In D. A. Goslin & D. C. Glass (Eds.), *Handbook of socialization theory and research.* New York: Rand McNally, 1969.

Zigler, E., Hodgden, L., & Stevenson, H. The effect of support on the performance of normal and feebleminded children. *Journal of Personality,* 1958, *26,* 106-122.

Zigler, E., Levine, J., & Gould, L. Cognitive challenge as a factor in children's humor appreciation. *Journal of Personality and Social Psychology,* 1967, *6,* 332-336.

Zigler, E., & Unell, E. Concept switching in normal and feebleminded children as a function of reinforcement. *American Journal of Mental Deficiency,* 1962, *66,* 651-657.

Zigler, E., & Yando, R. Outerdirectedness and imitative behavior of institutionalized and noninstitutionalized younger and older children. *Child Development,* 1972, *43,* 413-425.

3 Learned Helplessness and the Retarded Child

John R. Weisz
University of North Carolina, Chapel Hill

The developmental-difference controversy is fundamentally a debate about cognitive processes. Yet, one of its richest legacies is in the noncognitive realm. Here, I refer to the detailed account of metaintellectual and personality factors that influence the performance of retarded children. Factors such as outerdirectedness, low expectancy of success, wariness of adults, high levels or motivation for social reinforcement, and atypical hierarchies of reward preference (all discussed in a chapter by Zigler and Balla, in this volume) can taint performance on even the "purest" of our cognitive measures. Thus, many of the performance deficits manifested by retarded children are not necessarily a direct, inherent, or inexorable result of their lowered intellectual abilities. This suggests the hopeful possibility that a number of performance deficiencies may be remediable, or preventable, by means of interventions focused on problematic motivational and personality factors.

I first had an opportunity to observe some of these noncognitive factors when, as a graduate student, I pilot tested procedures for a study with retarded children. In particular, I was struck by the children's uneasy vacillation between wariness of a strange adult (me) and prepotent dependence on any praise or encouragement I could offer. I also sensed another phenomenon that differed somewhat from those described previously—a rather fatalistic passivity, an apparent resignedness, that seemed to set many of the retarded children apart from their nonretarded schoolmates. The research took place in the days of self-contained classrooms for retarded students, and under these circumstances group differences seemed particularly vivid. Once children from the regular classes had figured out why I was in their school, my entry into their classroom often triggered unconcealed excitement; raised hands waved and beckoned, and whispers of "take *me*" could be heard from various quarters. Children even cornered me outside of class with special requests to "try the games."

Such behavior contrasted noticeably with the demeanor of the retarded children in special-education classes, where hand waving and other signs of eagerness were rare indeed. One of these youngsters did approach me outside of class and ask to participate; this was a boy with cerebral palsy, who was anxious to show that he did not belong in a "special" class. Despite the lack of volunteers, the retarded children did not appear unwilling to participate in the activities. Instead, they seemed equally content either to go or to remain at their desk, whatever *others* decided they should do. My clinical assessment was that many of these children felt they were unlikely to exert much control over events in their lives, and they had to come to accept this state of affairs.

The passive, resigned orientation displayed by the retarded children resembled a syndrome that Seligman and his colleagues labeled "learned helplessness" (Abramson, Seligman, & Teasdale, 1978; Seligman, 1975). The syndrome involves a perception that one cannot exercise control over outcomes, with concomitant deficits in efforts to exert control (e.g., failure to initiate actions to influence one's environment, or lack of perseverance in problem solving following difficulty, failure, or failure feedback). Behavior that takes these general forms has been mentioned to me frequently by teachers of mentally retarded children. For example, some special educators have described what might be called the "pencil down" syndrome, in which children react to a problem they cannot solve quickly by placing pencil on desk and sitting passively, making no effort to persist at the puzzling problem, go on to another, or request assistance. One experienced teacher explained that these children "go into any new situation expecting to fail; when the going gets tough, they quit trying."

One obvious problem with such generalizations, and with the supporting anecdotes, is that they derive from unstructured observations that are subjectively interpreted. The extent to which they are influenced by stereotypes regarding mentally retarded persons is unknown, as is the degree to which they actually distinguish between retarded and nonretarded children's behavior. A few, more objective comparative assessments have come from experiments designed to test the applicability of the learned helplessness paradigm to the behavior of retarded persons. The twofold purpose of this chapter is to survey these efforts and to suggest prospects for future research. In doing so, I do not attempt a comprehensive review of all potentially relevant evidence but focus on studies that fit rather precisely within the learned helplessness paradigm.

RESEARCH ON LEARNED HELPLESSNESS IN RETARDED POPULATIONS

The Incidence of Helpless Behavior and Attributions

The Floor–Rosen Study. Perhaps the first attempt to link the helplessness model to the behavior of retarded persons was Floor and Rosen's (1975) study of young adults. The investigators employed four measures of helplessness. According to Floor and Rosen (1975), one was a "passive-dependency scale" (adapted from Kessler, 1953), designed to assess the individual's concept of self: "as an action-oriented and independent or a passive and dependent personality [p. 567]." The scale included such items as "Do you prefer to start something yourself rather than wait and let someone else do it?" and "Do you wish you were still a child?" A second measure was the "coping behavior questionnaire," which related verbal solutions to problems of living. Respondents were asked, for example, what they would do if their wallet were stolen, and how they would go about looking for a job if they had no one to help them. Third was a locus of control scale (adapted from Bialer, 1961). A fourth general operational definition was what might be called *response initiation,* assessed by actual responses to five mildly aversive circumstances. For example, at one point the experimenter left the testing room, and shortly thereafter a telephone on the desk began to ring. Participants were scored for the number of times they allowed the phone to ring before answering it. In another contrived situation, each person discovered upon leaving that his or her coat was not on the rack where it had been left; scores were based on the actions they took to locate the missing coat.

Floor and Rosen tested both institutionalized and noninstitutionalized retarded adults, as well as a group of college students who were about the same age ($\bar{x}$ CA for the entire sample was about 21 years). In general, the two retarded groups showed no marked differences, and both scored significantly more helpless than the nonretarded group on almost all items. These results, however, pose a major problem of interpretation. If passive behavior is to conform to the definition of learned helplessness, it must be manifest by individuals who are capable of exercising active control in a given situation. For, group differences in passivity to be interpreted as differences in learned helplessness, the groups must have the same general ability to exert appropriate controlling responses. The retarded and nonretarded groups in the Floor–Rosen experiment were matched for CA, but they differed markedly in IQ and thus in MA. Consequently, group differences in knowledge of, say, how to look for a job, or what to do when one's coat is missing, may have reflected only varying degrees of intellectual maturity. Although the Floor-Rosen study represents a useful beginning for good comparative research in learned helplessness, the design may have confounded group differences in passive behavior with those in actual ability.

Weisz's Developmental Study. Building on the theoretical foundation laid by Seligman and his colleagues, and on the empirical foundation laid by Floor and Rosen, I conducted a study (Weisz, 1979) of learned helplessness in retarded and nonretarded children matched at three general levels of ability (MAs 5½, 7½, and 9½ years). In an effort to survey a broad spectrum of intellectual ability, each MA level included retarded, average, and "gifted" children.

Four operational definitions of helplessness were used. To assess *perseverance following failure*, children were first given enough time to complete a puzzle successfully. Next, they were presented a second puzzle and stopped short of completion, in an apparent failure. They were then given a choice of returning to the failure puzzle or repeating the one at which they had succeeded. Using a similar procedure, Dweck and Bush (1976) found that children who attributed their failures to uncontrollable factors (a defining characteristic of learned helplessness) were less likely to persevere at the failed task than those who felt their failures were due to controllable factors.

A second operational definition was a set of four *response initiation* measures patterned in part after measures used by Miller, Seligman, and Kurlander (1975) and those by Floor and Rosen (1975) described earlier. For example, children were trained to turn off a buzzer in an ostensible reaction time task; later, the experimenter left the testing room and surreptitiously activated the buzzer with a remote control switch. The length of time the child tolerated the unpleasant noise before initiating a controlling response was scored and combined with the three other measures into an overall response initiation score.

Two questionnaires were also used to assess helplessness. In one, teachers estimated the likelihood that each child would initiate controlling responses in a variety of classroom situations. For example, the child was described as facing a new activity that *looks* difficult but is actually within the child's range of ability; the teachers estimated the likelihood that each child would "feel that he/she can do it and be eager to try." In a second questionnaire, children selected causal attributions for various favorable and unfavorable outcomes that they might experience at school and at home. On a similar measure, Diener and Dweck (1978) found that children who attributed unfavorable outcomes to insufficient effort on their own part, presumably regarding their failures as reversible through increased effort, evidenced low levels of helpless behavior.

All three of the children's measures revealed IQ-MA interactions. In general, all showed the retarded children to be more helpless than children in the two nonretarded groups, but only at one or both of the upper MA levels. The pattern was most pronounced with respect to the response initiation measure, where the MA 9½ retarded group was more helpless than all three of the MA 5½ groups. This pattern of findings suggests that retarded children learn helplessness gradually, over years of development. If this developmental hypothesis is borne out in future research, it would then be important to unearth causal factors that might operate in the life of the retarded child to promote the development of helplessness. Later in this chapter, I suggest a few causal possibilities that merit further examination.

Weisz's Study of Performance Deterioration in Response to Failure. Studying causes, however, would be premature in the absence of firmer evidence on helplessness in retarded persons. Although Weisz's (1979) data suggest that retarded children at relatively mature MA levels may be more susceptible to helplessness then their nonretarded MA peers, this evidence must be regarded as preliminary because of the experimental measures employed. A more commonly used and probably more definitive procedure to assess learned helplessness involves creating a series of uncontrollable aversive experiences that can elicit various types of response. In previous research, these experiences have generally taken the form of problem-solving activities in which the problems appear to defy solution. The individual's perseverance at the task, or at subsequent activities, indicates degree of helplessness.

One of the most revealing paradigms of this type involves a simple, two-choice discrimination-learning problem, where performance feedback is given only periodically, (Levine, 1966; Weisz, 1977). Performance during the no-feedback trials is used to infer the degree to which useful strategies are being employed. Children who continue to search for solution in the absence of "help" from the experimenter are thought to be less helpless than those who abandon the challenge of this simple problem. Under conditions of extended *negative* feedback, the use of strategies has been found to decline markedly in helpless children (those who are unlikely to attribute failures to their own insufficient effort). Nonhelpless children, by contrast, persevere in the application of useful strategies despite the disappointments that must accompany the ongoing feedback indicating that their responses are wrong (Diener & Dweck, 1978).

In my study (Weisz, in press-b), retarded and nonretarded children (MAs about 9½ years) were given a series of concept formation problems; on four sucessive test problems every instance of feedback was negative.[1] These problems followed a series of structurally similar training problems involving veridical feedback that was frequently positive. The two groups of children performed similarly on the training problems (suggesting similar ability), but they diverged markedly when the feedback became negative. Retarded children showed a highly significant decline in their use of strategies from early to late test prob-

---

[3.1]This experience was followed by a set of problems involving a high density of positive feedback. Afterward, the children were told that the problems in the middle (the four "failure" problems) "are *very hard,* even for adults," and that on problems made for kids their age they had done very well. Overall, the experience of learning a skill, applying it despite difficulty and negative feedback, and finally succeeding seemed to leave children feeling pleased, and in some cases proud.

lems, whereas nonretarded children actually showed a slight increase in their search for effective strategies.[2] The pattern of results suggests that negative feedback may indeed provoke something like the "giving up" phenomenon described by special education teachers, and that this response may be more prepotent in retarded than in nonretarded children at similar levels of ability.

Two other aspects of this study should be noted here. A new measure to assess teachers' judgments, the *Helpless Behavior Checklist,* was employed to remedy a number of weaknesses in a previous questionnaire (Weisz, 1979), which did not reveal significant group differences. The new checklist followed the much simpler format of a widely used child behavior checklist (Achenbach, 1966). Teachers were presented a series of brief behavior descriptions and asked to indicate whether each was "not true," "somewhat or sometimes true," or "very true or often true" of each child. Some of the items involved helpless *attributions* (e.g., "Says, 'I can't do it,' when s/he has trouble with her/his work"); some involved helpless *behavior* (e.g., "When s/he runs into difficulty, s/he gives up and quits trying"). On both components of the checklist, teachers rated the retarded children significantly more helpless than their nonretarded peers.

Another aspect of the procedure was notable for its failure to reveal group differences. Diener and Dweck (1978) trained helpless children to "think aloud" as they worked at the discrimination-learning trials, and they found that only helpless children made substantial numbers of causal attributions for their negative feedback. Most of these were attributions to the uncontrollable factor of low ability. Intrigued by the Diener–Dweck results, I included similar "think aloud" training in the procedure for Weisz (in press-b). The results, however, did not reveal even a marginally significant main effect for IQ group. So, although the groups differed strikingly in their *performance* under negative feedback, their comments shed little light on the underlying thought processes that may have led retarded children to show performance deterioration, whereas nonretarded children did not.

Gibson's Attributional Study. Helplessness-related differences in verbalizations about task performance were again examined in a carefully executed experiment by Barry Gibson (1980). Retarded and nonretarded boys, both at MAs of about 9½ years, performed a pursuit rotor activity. The experimenter secretly controlled outcomes on the task such that half of each group succeeded and half failed. Afterward, each boy explained his outcome by judging the causal importance of ability, effort, task difficulty, and luck.

In earlier research (Diener & Dweck, 1978; Weisz, 1979), the attribution of unfavorable outcomes to insufficient effort was regarded as an important con-

---

[3.2]The results also revealed a potentially important interaction of IQ level (retarded versus nonretarded) and race. Black retarded children appeared to be more susceptible to learned helplessness than their white counterparts. For further details on this aspect of the findings, see Weisz (in press-b).

traindicator of helplessness. In Gibson's study, although retarded children were less likely to blame insufficient effort than their nonretarded MA peers, this theoretically important difference did not attain significance. Nonetheless, the overall pattern of Gibson's findings was consistent with the view that mentally retarded children are particularly susceptible to helplessness. Compared to nonretarded children of similar ability, the retarded children were more likely to ascribe success to the variable, uncontrollable factor of luck and less likely to make causal ascriptions to ability. In accounting for failure, the retarded children were more likely to indict the stable, uncontrollable factor of low ability and less likely to blame bad luck. Such a pattern of attributions would seem to give the retarded child little reason to persevere in the face of failure, because the perceived cause is beyond control; and success, if it comes, may well occur by dint of luck anyway. Children with such a perspective might be *expected* to show the kind of performance deterioration under failure feedback that was reported by Weisz (in press-a).

Although the helpless attributions and behavior of retarded children may have a certain logical consistency, I must stress that they represent fundamentally inappropriate judgments and behavior. In the studies surveyed here, retarded and nonretarded children were rather carefully matched for general level of ability, as defined by MA. Thus, ability should play a similar causal role for both the retarded and the nonretarded child. Moreover, when the children are also similar in performance on the target task (as in the training problems used by Weisz, in press-b), perseverance in the face of failure at that task is about equally likely to pay off for either intellectual group. Thus, the debilitating attributions and the performance deterioration seen in retarded children are quite inappropriate. Why then do they occur? Are retarded children exposed to a disproportionate share of helplessness-inducing experiences in life? In what follows, I offer a few speculations and survey a few studies in an effort to begin answering this question.

The Etiology of Helplessness

Most research on the etiology of helplessness has involved short-term experimental manipulations with infrahuman species and with nonretarded people (Abramson et al., 1978; Maier & Seligman, 1976). In general, this research has identified two factors that can lead to helpless behavior. One is the experience of repeated failure to exercise control; this has ranged in form from failures to terminate an aversive noise to failures to solve a series of anagram problems (Dweck & Bush, 1976; Hiroto & Seligman, 1975). Some research in the area of mental retardation gives the impression that the retarded child's life may be something of a macrocosm of the helplessness-induction experiment, in that it involves repeated exposure to failure. Zigler (1971) has stated that retarded children are likely to experience: "a lifetime characterized by frequent confrontations with tasks with which they are intellectually ill-equipped to deal [p. 83]."

As a result, they come to anticipate failure—a view supported by a large body of evidence (see reviews by Cromwell, 1963; Zigler, 1971). On the other hand, some investigators (Spitz, 1979) have argued that retarded children are actually sheltered from failure. This is certainly suggested by the fact that special education literature often urges teachers to emphasize success experiences and positive feedback with retarded children in order to bolster their confidence (Bigelow, 1972; MacMillan, 1971). To determine whether retarded children actually experience more or less failure and negative feedback than do nonretarded children, we will need careful observational research in natural settings like the classroom. One preliminary step in this direction is described in the following section.

A second factor that has been shown to predispose people to helplessness is performance feedback that suggests failure is due to uncontrollable factors. Apparently, even feedback patterns that are quite subtle in their implications can be quite powerful in their impact. For example, Dweck, Davidson, Nelson, and Enna (1978) linked helplessness in elementary schoolgirls to a pattern of teacher-to-child feedback, where a relatively high proportion of negative evaluations concerned the intellectual quality of the child's work (as opposed to intellectually irrelevant aspects such as misconduct). Such a pattern evidently leads children to read negative feedback in general as a reflection of their ability—a stable, uncontrollable cause of the outcomes they experience. As a result, Dweck et al. reasoned, these children are more likely to show helplessness (performance debilitation) in response to feedback suggesting failure. They also reasoned that such a feedback pattern, in combination with relatively low frequencies of negative feedback overall, would make susceptibility to helplessness even more pronounced, because the negative feedback would be difficult to attribute to other circumstances, such as the habits or personality of the teacher.

The Raber-Weisz Study of Classroom Feedback. In an effort to build on this analysis and generate causal hypotheses, Suzanne Raber and I (1981) investigated both the frequency and contingencies of actual negative feedback in the classroom. Retarded and nonretarded children, all roughly matched for reading ability (fourth-grade level), were observed during their reading groups for a total of about 3 to 9 hours. Our observers coded every instance of evaluative feedback from teacher to child, noting whether it was positive or negative and categorizing it according to the child's activity that precipitated it.

We found, first, that retarded children received much more feedback per unit of time than did nonretarded children. The groups did not differ in rates of positive feedback, but the retarded children received a significantly higher proportion of negative feedback than the nonretarded children. This finding, based on a modest sample of only eight reading groups, is certainly not conclusive. However, it does reveal at least one context in which retarded children may encounter failure in the form of negative evaluations more often than nonretarded children of similar ability.

A second focus of our analyses was the pattern of contingency that governed feedback to the two groups. The proportion of negative feedback directed to the intellectual quality of the child's performance was found to be significantly higher for the retarded than the nonretarded groups. According to the Dweck et al. (1978) analysis discussed earlier, this pattern of feedback should make retarded children more likely to show helplessness in the form of performance deterioration under negative feedback. However, Dweck et al. regard intellectually relevant negative feedback as particularly helplessness-inducing when it occurs within the context of generally positive feedback. The retarded children we observed received a disproportionate amount of *negative* feedback, both intellectually relevant and otherwise. Thus, there is reason to believe that, contrary to the Dweck et al. reasoning, frequent negative feedback can exacerbate susceptibility to helplessness.

Studies of Adult Attributions for Retarded Children's Performance. In addition to direct performance feedback, other ways adults interact with retarded children may foster the development of helplessness. In particular, certain stereotypes and connotations of the label "mental retardation" may lead adults to tolerate, or even expect, failure by a retarded child. The logical impact of this attitude will be deficits in the child's perseverance.

To illustrate this process, consider adult attributions for failure by a child labeled "mentally retarded." A defining characteristic of a retarded child is *low ability*, relative to nonretarded children of similar CA. Because "low ability" is such a salient characteristic, the contribution of alternative factors to the child's behavior is likely to be "discounted" (Jones, Davis, & Gergen, 1961; Kelley, 1973). When the retarded child fails, emphasis on the ability deficit could lead attributors to discount the role of other important causal factors, notably low effort. Furthermore, lack of ability may be emphasized in causal attributions, even in cases where retarded and nonretarded children differ in CA but are functioning at the *same* level of ability. Such erroneous reasoning illustrates what I have called *attributional overextension*—the extension of a salient causal ascription (e.g., low ability) beyond its logical limits (Weisz, in press-a).

Could such an attributional pattern translate into behavior that fosters helplessness? To answer this question, consider an adult—perhaps a parent or teacher—who observes several children failing the same task. If the adult believes that most failed because of insufficient effort but that one child's failure resulted from insufficient ability, that child is less likely than the others to be encouraged to persist and more likely than the others to be allowed to give up the task.

There is some evidence that adults do interpret failure by retarded persons in this manner. For example, findings by Severance and Gasstrom (1977) and Gibbons, Sawin, and Gibbons (1979) indicate that adults rate low ability as a more important cause of failure and predict lower levels of ultimate success for people labeled "mentally retarded" than for unlabeled individuals. In both studies, however, the retarded and unlabeled individuals were described to respondents as being the same age. This makes the findings difficult to evaluate, because the retarded person would be lower in mental age; thus, low ability would indeed be more important and ultimate success less likely.

In an effort to clarify these issues, I conducted a set of studies (Weisz, in press-a) in which adults gave causal attributions for failure in problem solving and estimated probability of future success for a hypothetical mentally retarded and an unlabeled child *of equal mental age*. In the first study, the adults made these judgments about *either* the retarded *or* the unlabeled child (i.e., a between-groups design). In the second study, the judgments were made about *both* children concurrently (a repeated measures design). In both studies, low ability was rated a more important cause of failure for the retarded child; insufficient effort was rated more important for the unlabeled child, who was also deemed more likely to succeed in the future. In a third study, I discovered that adults would be less likely to urge the retarded child to persevere following failure than they would the unlabeled child.

These findings suggest an important possibility that bears future study: The simple knowledge that a child is mentally retarded may lead adults into an illogical pattern of attributions and expectancies. This pattern may stimulate adult behavior that implicitly condones and perhaps even encourages helplessness and perseverance deficits in retarded children.

SOME THOUGHTS ON FUTURE DIRECTIONS FOR RESEARCH ON HELPLESSNESS IN RETARDED CHILDREN

The evidence reviewed previously has many limitations, but it does suggest an overall picture that may be useful as a stimulus for future research. First, pronounced helplessness has only been found in relatively mature retarded youngsters—generally those at MA levels or 9 years and above. Only one study (Weisz, 1979) made comparisons with lower MA levels, where there was no evidence that young retarded children were more susceptible to helplessness than were nonretarded children. One interpretation for these findings is that retarded children learn helplessness over the course of time, but this developmental hypothesis has yet to be tested. One problem that will confront the investigator who wishes to do so will be the relative unavailability of good operational definitions of learned helplessness that are appropriate across a broad spectrum of developmental levels. Recently, Rholes, Blackwell, Jordan, and Walters (in press) developed an embedded-figures task that may be useful at various ages. With additional work, other available measures of learned helplessness can be adapted for use at higher or lower MAs, and or course we can always learn from past mistakes which measures are *not* appropriate.

The literature also suggests that relatively mature retarded children make attributions for their performance that predispose them to helpless behavior. In interpreting unfavorable outcomes, they seem unlikely to accuse controllable factors such as insufficient effort (Weisz, 1979). Instead, they see failure as resulting from the stable, uncontrollable factor of low ability (Gibson, 1980). To make matters worse, they seem likely to ascribe their successes to the whims of luck (Gibson, 1980), hardly a factor that one would seek to influence by perseverance or increased effort. As might be expected from this pattern of causal attributions, when retarded children encounter prolonged difficulty or failure at a problem-solving task, they are less likely than nonretarded children of similar ability to persevere in applying their abilities (Weisz, in press-b). These rather bold generalizations emerge from the present limited body of data, but each needs to be cross validated in new experimental contexts, and with the rich variety of new helplessness measures that have emerged from research with children (reviewed in Dweck & Goetz, 1978) and adults (reviewed in Abramson et al., 1978).

Findings concerning causal factors can also be summarized boldly, because the available evidence is not yet voluminous enough to offer much in the way of contradiction. Retarded children appear to experience more failure in the form of negative feedback (at least in reading groups) than do nonretarded children of roughly similar ability (Raber & Weisz, 1980). In addition, the negative feedback received by the retarded children is more often relevant to the intellectual/academic quality of their performance—a fact that one analysis (Dweck et al., 1978) suggests should make them particularly susceptible to helplessness. Other "feedback effects" bear examination in future research. For example, the undiplomatic comments of nonretarded peers, and even the diplomatic institutional feedback implied by assignment to a "special program" or "resource room" may suggest to retarded children that others regard their failures as due to unalterable factors.

A related area concerns how institutional categories and labels, such as "mentally retarded" or "special education," can bias adults' attributions and expectancies, and how this can affect the child's behavior. There is some evidence that such labels make adults more likely to attribute failure to low ability and less likely to expect eventual success (Weisz, in press-a). As a consequence, the retarded child may receive little encouragement to persevere at a failed task, and this may contribute to "learning" helplessness.

A significant limitation of the preceding findings, save those of Raber and Weisz (1980), is that they provide no direct information on the ways children and adults behave in everyday life. Laboratory analog studies are useful devices, particularly at early stages in the development of a field (Weisz, 1978), but the findings they yield will have much greater credence if they are supported in naturally occurring contexts. To underscore this point, I should emphasize that at the present time there is actually *no* evidence that retarded children (at any MA level) show more helplessness than nonretarded children in the routines of their daily lives. To generate such evidence will require ingenuity on the part of investigators. But developing observational measures of helplessness would be an extremely useful service to this laboratory-bound field of inquiry.

Another useful direction for future research comes from Abramson et al.'s (1978) suggestion that learned helplessness may assume a number of forms, some more devastating than others. Helplessness may be broadly generalized ("I expect to be helpless in many situations") or specific to particular problems or contexts. It may be chronic or acute. It may also be personal ("I am helpless, but others in this situation would not be") or universal ("Everyone would be helpless here"). These dimensions carry important implications for other aspects of human functioning. For example, individuals who believe that everyone in the same situation would be helpless might feel depressed, but those who perceive their helplessness as personal are apt to suffer a general loss of self-esteem. What particular forms of helplessness do retarded children suffer, and how do these affect their emotional responses to failure and other adversities? A question this broad could form the basis for a lifetime of research.

Ultimately, of course, a key focus of research will be prevention and remediation, and a number of approaches to alleviate helplessness have already shown promise (Andrews & Debus, 1978; Chapin & Dyck, 1976; Dweck, 1975). But such applications should probably await further evidence on the situations in which retarded children are particularly susceptible to helplessness, and on the forms of helplessness to which they are most likely to fall prey. If research continues to indicate that preventive and therapeutic interventions are needed, it would be difficult indeed to imagine a more significant task for psychologists than that of refining and testing such efforts.

There can be little doubt that retarded children draw from a more limited reservoir of cognitive potential than do nonretarded children. For this reason it is important to promote, in whatever ways we can, optimum expression of the abilities retarded children do possess. One means of doing this is to identify noncognitive factors that may undermine expression of those abilities, and the evidence reviewed here suggests that one such factor may be learned helplessness. Thus, continued efforts to understand, and ultimately to minimize, susceptibility to helplessness may hold significant benefits for retarded children in their pursuit of competence and independence.

REFERENCES

Abramson, L. Y., Seligman, M. E. P., & Teasdale, J. D. Learned helplessness in humans: Critique and reformulation. *Journal of Abnormal Psychology,* 1978 *87,* 49–74.

Achenbach, T. M. The classification of children's psychiatric symptoms: A factor analytic study. *Psychological Monographs,* 1966, *80,* 1–37.

Andrews, D. R., & Debus, R. L. Persistence and the causal perception of failure: Modifying cognitive attributions. *Journal of Educational Psychology,* 1978, *70,* 154–166.

Bialer, I. Conceptualization of success and failure in mentally retarded and normal children. *Journal of Personality*, 1961, *29*, 303-320.

Bigelow, G. The behavioral approach to retardation. In T. Thompson & J. Grebowski (Eds.), *Behavior modification of the mentally retarded*. New York: Oxford University Press, 1972.

Chapin, M., & Dyck, D. G. Persistence of children's reading behavior as a function of N length and attribution retraining. *Journal of Abnormal Psychology*, 1976, *85*, 511-515.

Cromwell, R. L. A social-learning theory approach to mental retardation. In N. R. Ellis (Ed.), *Handbook of mental deficiency*. New York: McGraw-Hill, 1963.

Diener, C. I., & Dweck, C. S. An analysis of learned helplessness: Continuous changes in performance, strategy, and achievement cognitions following failure. *Journal of Personality and Social Psychology*, 1978, *36*, 451-462.

Dweck, C. S. The role of expectations and attributions in the alleviation of learned helplessness. *Journal of Personality and Social Psychology*, 1975, *31*, 674-685.

Dweck, C. S., & Bush, E. S. Sex differences in learned helplessness: (I) Differential debilitation with peer and adult evaluators. *Developmental Psychology*, 1976, *12*, 147-156.

Dweck, C. S., Davidson, W., Nelson, S., & Enna, B. Sex differences in learned helplessness: (II) The contingencies of evaluative feedback in the classroom, and (III) an experimental analysis. *Developmental Psychology*, 1978, *14*, 268-276.

Dweck, C. S., & Goetz, T. E. Attributions and learned helplessness. In J. H. Harvery, W. Ickes, & R. F. Kidd (Eds.), *New directions in attribution research* (Vol. 2). Hillsdale, N. J.: Lawrence Erlbaum Associates, 1978.

Floor, L., & Rosen, M. Investigating the phenomenon of helplessness in mentally retarded adults. *American Journal of Mental Deficiency*, 1975, *79*, 565-572.

Gibbons, F. X., Sawin, L. G., & Gibbons, B. N. Evaluations of mentally retarded persons: "Sympathy" or patronization. *American Journal of Mental Deficiency*, 1979, *84*, 124-131.

Gibson, B. J. *An attributional analysis of performance outcomes and the alleviation of learned helplessness on motor performance tasks: A comparative study of educable mentally retarded and nonretarded boys*. Unpublished doctoral dissertation, University of Alberta, 1980.

Hiroto, D. S., & Seligman, M. E. P. Generality of learned helplessness in man. *Journal of Personality and Social Psychology*, 1975, *31*, 311-327.

Jones, E. E., Davis, K. E., & Gergen, K. J. Role playing variations and their informational value for person perception. *Journal of Abnormal and Social Psychology*, 1961, *63*, 302-312.

Kelley, H. H. The process of causal attribution. *American Psychologist*, 1973, *28*, 107-128.

Kessler, S. *The Kessler passive dependency scale*. Unpublished manuscript, 1953 (available from S. Kessler, Encino Counseling Center, 18075 Ventura Boulevard, Encino, Calif. 91316).

Levine, M. Hypothesis behavior by humans during discrimination learning. *Journal of Experimental Psychology*, 1966, *71*, 331-338.

MacMillan, D. L. The problem of motivation in the education of the mentally retarded. *Exceptional Children*, 1971, *37*, 579-586.

Maier, S. F., & Seligman, M. E. P. Learned helplessness: Theory and evidence. *Journal of Experimental Psychology: General*, 1976, *105*, 3-46.

Miller, W. R., Seligman, M. E. P., & Kurlander, H. M. Learned helplessness, depression, and anxiety. *Journal of Nervous and Mental Disease*, 1975, *161*, 347-357.

Raber, S. M., & Weisz, J. R. Teacher feedback to mentally retarded and nonretarded children. *American Journal of Mental Deficiency*, 1981, *86*, 148-156.

Rholes, W. S., Blackwell, J., Jordan, C., & Walters, E. A developmental study of learned helplessness. *Developmental Psychology*, in press.

Seligman, M. E. P. *Helplessness*. San Francisco: W. H. Freeman, 1975.

Severance, L. J., & Gasstrom, L. L. Effects of the label "mentally retarded" on causal explanations for success and failure outcomes. *American Journal of Mental Deficiency*, 1977, *81*, 547-555.

Spitz, H. *Personal communication*, 1979.

Weisz, J. R. A follow-up developmental study of hypothesis behavior among mentally retarded and nonretarded children. *Journal of Experimental Child Psychology*, 1977, *24*, 108–122.

Weisz, J. R. Transcontextual validity in developmental psychology. *Child Development*, 1978, *49*, 1–12.

Weisz, J. R. Perceived control and learned helplessness in mentally retarded and nonretarded children: A developmental analysis. *Developmental Psychology*, 1979, *15*, 311–319.

Weisz, J. R. Effects of the "mentally retarded" label on adults' attributions and expectancies concerning children's failure. *Journal of Abnormal Psychology*, in press. (a)

Weisz, J. R. Learned helplessness in black and white children identified as retarded and nonretarded. *Developmental Psychology*, in press. (b)

Zigler, E. The retarded child as a whole person. In H. E. Adams & W. K. Boardman (Eds.), *Advances in experimental clinical psychology*. Elmsford, N. Y.: Pergamon Press, 1971.

4 Impact of Institutional Experience on the Behavior and Development of Retarded Persons*

David Balla
Edward Zigler
Yale University

In this chapter we discuss the impact of institutional experience on the behavior and development of retarded persons. In some cases the findings discussed in this chapter overlap those discussed in Chapter 2, "Personality Factors in the Performance of the Retarded," but the vantage point is that of the effects of institutions, not that of personality development in retarded persons. As soon becomes clear, much less is known about the impact of institutions than would be expected, considering the importance of the issue. Reliable knowledge concerning the effects of institutions is important for several reasons. At a theoretical level, many investigations of retarded persons' behavior have involved comparisons of noninstitutionalized nonretarded individuals and institutionalized retarded individuals. In this kind of study it is impossible to determine which effects are attributable to institutionalization as contrasted to mental retardation per se (Baumeister, 1967; Hagen & Huntsman, 1971; Katz & Rosenberg, 1969). Indeed, several of our colleagues are now trying to separate these two factors.

Secondly, increased knowledge about the effects of institutions would be extremely helpful to parents and professionals. The decision of whether to institutionalize a retarded person is one of the most painful that parents can face. Many professionals hold strong views on this subject, but they are often contradictory or too simplistic. Depending on the expert approached, a parent might be informed that: (1) the degree of retardation is such that institutionalization is the only possible solution; (2) institutionalization is necessary so the development of the other children in the family will not be prejudiced; or (3) in-

---

*Portions of this article appeared in *American Journal of Mental Deficiency*, 1977, 82(1), 1-11. Reprinted by permission.

stitutionalization should be avoided at all costs because it is either unnecessary or so demeaning to the retarded persons that no parent should permit it. If the effects of institutionalization were known, a great deal of parental conflict and pain would be alleviated.

Perhaps of greatest importance, though, is that reliable knowledge concerning institutionalization effects—especially differences between large central institutions versus community-based regional centers or group homes—would be extremely helpful when formulating social policy in the field of mental retardation. For almost 15 years, the predominant thrust of social policy in the mental retardation area has been a movement away from large central institutions to a community-based regionalization model in which retarded persons are treated in small, residential, community settings. This social policy has evolved almost completely without an empirical base. The lack of data on what constitutes the most adequate care setting for retarded individuals is potentially disastrous for those involved in the creation of social policy, whatever their persuasions as to what is the best care setting. For example, in this day of drastic budget cutting at all levels of government, it is entirely possible that the large central institution will be rediscovered: Expensive professional services can be consolidated, there would be savings in administrative costs, and the economies of scale would operate. If policy makers cannot demonstrate that regional centers or group homes are cost effective, it would be difficult to resist such arguments for central institutions.

With this background as to the importance of the issue, we discuss research that has been conducted for the past 20 years. To anticipate, we have become convinced that any comprehensive understanding of the effects of institutionalization must require a consideration of three classes of variables. The first is the characteristics of the person. The effects of institutionalization have been found to be different as a function of such factors as the person's gender, diagnosis, developmental level, and chronological age (CA). Of particular importance is the preinstitutional life experience of the individual. It has been found again and again that a retarded person's response to institutionalization is partially determined by the nature of his/her experiences prior to institutionalization.

The second important class of variables concerns the nature of the institution. Discussions of the nature of institutions have typically focused on the issue of size, the assumption being that the larger the size of the institution, the poorer the quality of care. Such an assumption may lie on rather tenuous grounds. Balla (1976) reviewed the existing literature on the relationship of institution size to quality of care and concluded that, whereas there was some evidence that the quality of life is better in smaller than in larger facilities, there was no evidence that behavioral functioning of residents differed in institutions of different sizes. There was also very little evidence that parental and community involvement may be enhanced in small community-based facilities. Thus, it is crucial that we go beyond the simple question of size when discussing institutional adequacy. We must look at other demographic variables (e.g., cost, number of staff per resident, and employee-turnover rate). We must go even further than this examination of multiple demographic variables and investigate the social-psychological characteristics of institutions—administrative structure, employee attitudes, and the actual way in which the residents are cared for. We consider this class of variables to be especially important. The view that institutions with enlightened administrators, employees with positive attitudes concerning retarded persons, and humane caretaking practices will promote more adequate adaptation and competence in the residents is certainly a plausible one. However, we feel that investigations concerned with the quality of life of retarded persons are valuable in and of themselves. Retarded individuals have a right to humane care and treatment whether or not such care ultimately results in greater behavioral growth. The final class of variables of importance is, of course, measures of the behavioral status and growth of retarded individuals, including both cognitive and motivational factors.

Our own work on institutional effects can be traced back to the second author's doctoral dissertation (Zigler, 1958) concerning the phenomena of perseveration and dependency so often seen in institutionalized retarded persons. Based on the work of Lewin, it was widely believed at the time that this perseveration was somehow an inherent characteristic of retarded individuals (Kounin, 1941a, b; Lewin, 1936). In this study, an alternate view was proposed. Zigler (1958, 1961) hypothesized that many institutionalized retarded persons had been deprived of supportive contacts with adults both before they were institutionalized and while they were in the institutions. Consequently, it seemed reasonable to assume that they would be extremely responsive to supportive contacts with adults when such contacts were available. In this context perseveration was viewed as being a consequence of such a heightened responsiveness to social reinforcement. To test this idea, a group of retarded individuals who had been institutionalized for approximately 2 years played an extremely boring and repetitive game involving simply dropping marbles in the hole of a box. However, when they dropped the marbles they were frequently told that they were doing very well, with additional frequent reinforcement in the form of nods and smiles. Two experienced clinical psychologists were asked to rate the social histories of the individuals as to how much social deprivation they had experienced before coming to the institution. It was found that people who had been rated as more deprived persevered longer on the Marble-in-the-Hole game than individuals rated as less deprived. It seemed that the perseveration so often seen in retarded persons was due to a lack of contact with supportive adults rather than somehow being intrinsic to mental retardation. Additional support for this view was found in a study of responsiveness to social reinforcement in institutionalized and noninstitutionalized nonretarded and retarded children (Zigler, 1963). The institutionalized nonretarded children were just as responsive to social reinforcement as the institutionalized retarded children. There were also no differences between the noninstitutionalized nonretarded and retarded groups.

At this point, our own interest in institutionalization led us in several different directions. Probably, the most important was the choice of a research strategy that has been characteristic of our work for many years—the longitudinal study. It is apparent that there are difficulties in any study involving institutionalized persons on a one-time basis. If the behavior of institutionalized retarded individuals is found to be different from that of noninstitutionalized retarded persons, we really have difficulty in saying that these differences are solely due to the effects of institutionalization. It may be that institutionalized individuals are different in many crucial respects from those who remain in their homes. Consequently, we came to believe early, along with others, that longitudinal studies are necessary in order to understand fully the effects of institutions. When the growth of a group of individuals is mapped over time, we can be on more confident grounds in attributing any changes to the effects of institutional experience.

The first longitudinal study was conducted by Zigler and Williams (1963). In this study, the individuals tested in a previous study (Zigler, 1961) were retested after 3 additional years of institutional experience. In addition to changes in responsiveness to social reinforcement, we also looked at changes in intelligence test scores. We found that, over the 3-year period, individuals become significantly more motivated to receive the attention and support of a friendly adult. However, the increase in motivation for social reinforcers was related to the amount of preinstitutional deprivation that the individuals had experienced. Individuals who came from relatively good homes showed a much greater increase in their motivation for social reinforcers than did individuals coming from more socially deprived homes. It seemed that the effects of institutionalization depended on the preinstitutional history of the individual, with such institutionalization being more socially depriving for individuals from relatively good homes than for individuals from extremely deprived backgrounds.

We were surprised to find a general decrease in IQ between the first and second testing. We also found that this finding was reminiscent of those in a study done in England by Clarke and Clarke (1954). They discovered that individuals coming from extremely poor homes showed an increase in IQ following institutionalization, with no increase observed in individuals coming from relatively good homes. Indeed, in the Zigler and Williams (1963) study, the only persons showing increase in IQ were in the highly deprived group, as defined by the clinical psychologists who had rated the social histories.

Zigler, Butterfield, and Capobianco (1970) studied these same individuals after 7 and after 10 years of institutional experience. After both 7 and 10 years of institutionalization, highly deprived individuals became much less responsive to social reinforcement than did less-deprived individuals. This finding certainly supported the view that institutionalization was less depriving for individuals from poor homes than for those from good homes. Even more important was our discovery that the effects of preinstitutional social deprivation were still in evidence after 10 years of institutionalization. The importance of this point cannot be overemphasized. Social deprivation is a phenomenon that, once experienced, is built into the motivational structure of the individual and subsequently mediates his interactions with his environment.

At about this time, we conducted another longitudinal study of changes in responsiveness to social reinforcement and IQ in a group of institutionalized retarded persons (Zigler, Balla, & Butterfield, 1968). We tested individuals approximately 3 weeks following institutionalization and then again approximately 3 years after institutionalization. The individuals were residents in what was considered to be one to the finest public institutions in the country. In contrast to the findings in the Zigler and Williams (1963) study, the individuals in this institution became less responsive to social reinforcement over 3 years and increased in IQ. Furthermore, individuals from relatively good homes showed a smaller decrease in responsiveness to social reinforcement than did individuals from relatively poor homes. It seemed most reasonable to conclude that the differences in findings between the two studies were due to the differences in the quality of the two institutions. It seemed that the institution employed in the first study was a depriving one, whereas the one employed in the second study actually ameliorated the effects of preinstitutional deprivation. In a further study of this group of individuals, we found that after 6 years of institutional life the tendencies toward psychological growth found after 3 years were still in evidence (Balla & Zigler, 1975). There was a further significant increase in IQ, whereas the individuals' responsiveness to social reinforcement stabilized. Just as in the Zigler et al. (1970) study, the effects of preinstitutional life experience were still in evidence after 6 years, in that organically retarded subjects who came from homes characterized by marital discord and/or mental illness were more responsive to social reinforcement over all 6 years than less-deprived organically retarded subjects.

As in our previous studies, we found that those individuals who had experienced greater preinstitutional social deprivation were more responsive to social reinforcement than less-deprived children. Of special interest was our finding that the retarded individuals who maintained contact with their parents or parent-surrogates either by being visited at the institution or by going home on vacations were more likely to display the type of autonomous behavior characteristic of nonretarded children. Thus, we found empirical evidence that an institutional policy of encouraging many contacts with the community does promote psychological growth.

By this time, we were demonstrating in our research that the effects of institutionalization are extremely complex, dependent on the individuals' preinstitutional life experience and the particular institution under consideration.

Although this point should almost be self-evident, it is all too often overlooked. Institutions for retarded persons continue to be seen as uniform entities producing monolithic behavioral consequences.

As it became increasingly apparent that there were important differences among institutions, we planned cross-institutional studies. The first of these was conducted by Butterfield and Zigler (1965). Two nearby large central institutions with which we were familiar impressed us as having very different social climates. In the first institution, every effort was made to provide a home-like atmosphere: No buildings were locked, and all the residents could freely move around the grounds. It was organized on a cottage system with a large number of relatively small residential units. In the second institution, little effort was made to provide a home-like atmosphere. The residents ate in a large central dining room with virtually no individual supervision; all the buildings were locked, and an individual could not move around the grounds unattended by an employee. The institution was organized on a dormitory system with very large living units. We expected and found that the second institution was much more socially depriving than the first one, and the effects of such deprivation would be seen in the responsiveness to social reinforcement of the individuals.

The next cross-institutional study was a good deal more ambitious (Balla, Butterfield, & Zigler, 1974). We used a longitudinal design and investigated four institutions in different parts of the country. In this study, we tried to take a much more fine-grained look at the nature of the institutions: size, number of residents per living unit, cost per resident per day, employee-turnover rate, number of direct-care personnel per resident, number of professional staff per resident, and number of volunteer hours per resident per year. We felt that an examination of these factors, in conjunction with our general impressions, would provide a reasonable framework from which to evaluate residents' behavior change. Indeed, the institutions varied in size from approximately 400 to 2000 residents. There was also considerable variation in cost, number of aides per resident, and employee-turnover rate.

Residents in each of the institutions were examined within 6 months of their admission date and again after 2.5 years of institutional experience. In addition to the measure of responsiveness to social reinforcement used in previous studies, we also obtained measures of MA, IQ, verbal dependency, extent of imitation of adults, and variability in behavior. Contrary to our most pessimistic views concerning the effects of institutionalization, we found considerable evidence of psychological growth on the part of the residents. Over the course of 2.5 years, in all of the institutions the residents became less verbally dependent, less imitative, and more variable in their behavior. IQ level did not change and MA level increased. To our surprise, very few of the findings were related to any of the characteristics of the institutions. Residents in the largest of the institutions were more responsive to social reinforcement than residents in the other three institutions. With this exception, none of the other demographic characteristics of the institutions were found to be related to the behavior or development of the residents. Our subjective impressions were equally inaccurate in relating to the behavior of the development of the residents. At this point, it seemed clear to us that an even more detailed measure of institutional characteristics was needed.

We were extremely fortunate in that King, Raynes, and Tizard (1971) had conducted extensive and sensitive cross-institutional studies of resident-care practices in institutions for retarded persons in England. They developed a Resident Management Practices Inventory that was an excellent measure of the social–psychological characteristics of the institutions. This inventory was conceptualized as tapping institution-oriented care practices, at one extreme, versus resident-oriented practices at the other. In their view, the items in the inventory could be grouped along four dimensions. The first dimension was called Rigidity of Routine and concerned the inflexibility of management practices, so that at one extreme, neither individual differences among residents nor unique circumstances are taken account by the staff in their interactions with residents. The second dimension was called Block Treatment and concerned the regimentation of residents before, during, and after specific activities (e.g., meal time). The third dimension was referred to as Depersonalization, a measure of the presence or absence of opportunities for residents to have personal possessions, privacy, or situations allowing self-expression and initiative. The fourth dimension was referred to as Social Distance and concerned the limitation of interaction between staff and residents to formal and specific activities and the use of physically separate areas of congregation between the staff and those they cared for.

Using this inventory, King et al (1971) investigated three types of facilities for retarded persons: mental deficiency hospitals, ranging in size from 121 to 1650 residents; voluntary homes, from 50 to 93 residents; and local authority hostels (group homes), from 12 to 41 residents.

The care practices were found to be more resident than institution oriented in the group homes and more institution oriented in the mental deficiency hospitals, with the voluntary homes falling between. Of particular interest was the finding that, once type of institution was taken into account, there was no tendency for management practices to be associated with institution size. In other words, type rather than size of institution was the important determinant of care practices. The importance of this point is underscored when it is recalled that the mental deficiency hospitals ranged in size from approximately 100 to 1600 residents, yet no differences in care practices were found within this type of institution. When type of institution was taken into account, no association was found between the number of residents in each living unit and the care practices observed nor was a relationship found between resident-to-staff ratios and care practices. Finally, King et al. (1971) found that the level of retardation of residents in the individual living units was not an overriding determinant of care practices. This result was of some surprise in view of the findings that child-rearing practices are as much determined by the characteristics of the child as by the characteristics of the adult

(Bell, 1968; Yarrow, Waxler, & Scott, 1971). More severely retarded children are less responsive and provide less feedback than children of higher cognitive competence. It would seem quite easy to become mechanical and unresponsive while caring for children when responsiveness to such care is not immediately evident.

We felt that the investigations by King et al. (1971) were important for several reasons. Firstly, they studied different types of institutions at a time when far too little attention had been paid to the relative adequacy of central institutions, regional centers, and group homes. Secondly, they were directly concerned with the quality of life of institutionalized retarded persons, a matter that has been grossly neglected in empirical research. Finally, they underscored the importance of the living unit as a unit of analysis.

We decided that just such a study was needed for institutions in the United States and were also quite fortunate in having the opportunity to study institutions in a Scandinavian country world-renowned for its humane care of retarded persons. We studied the resident-care practices in 166 living units from 19 institutions in the United States and 11 institutions in the Scandinavian country (McCormick, Balla, & Zigler, 1975). A number of institutional demographic variables were examined: institution type (i.e., large, central, regional center and group home); institution size; average number of residents per living unit; cost per resident per day; number of aides per resident; number of professional staff per resident; annual employee-turnover rate; volunteer hours per resident per year; and mean institutional IQ. We also obtained additional information on level of retardation in each unit (i.e., mild, moderate, or severe–profound)—and the age level of the residents in each unit (i.e., child, adolescent, or adult).

We found that living units in the Scandinavian country were more resident oriented than were living units in the United States. In both countries, large central institutions were characterized by the most institution-oriented care practices and group homes by the most resident-oriented care practices, with regional centers falling between. This finding was consistent with that of King et al. (1971). Living units for more severely retarded residents were found to be more institution oriented. We then determined which of the demographic variables were most closely associated with care practices by employing multiple regression analyses, with the demographic characteristics of both institution and individual living unit as predictor variables and the Resident Management Practices Inventory as the dependent variable. The findings of these analyses were particularly interesting. Large living-unit size and level of retardation were found to be predictive of institution-oriented care practices. Cost per resident per day, number of aides per resident, or number of professional staff per resident *did not* predict care practices.

The lack of association of either financial or human factors—as measured by cost per resident per day and by number of aides and professional staff per resident, respectively—came as a considerable surprise to us. Apparently, simply increasing expenditures or personnel will not necessarily guarantee better care for retarded persons. Rather, it is how these personnel are utilized in the settings. The finding that living-unit size was predictive of care practices is of special practical interest. One way of creating more humane settings for institutionalized retarded persons may well be to design living units small enough so that each resident is, of necessity, seen as an individual. It is encouraging to note that it may be possible to pursue such a policy with existing resources. The reader recalls that the most resident-oriented care practices were found in group homes, which were operated at less cost than either the regional centers or the large central institutions. It may well be that part of the lower cost for group homes can be accounted for by the fact that these facilities, for the most part, serve mildly retarded residents who require less care and supervision. However, as mentioned earlier, number of aides or professional staff per resident were not found to be predictive of care practices.

In the McCormick et al. (1975) study, we also found that living units for more severely retarded residents were characterized by more institution-oriented care practices. Level of retardation was highly predictive of care practices in large central institutions, relatively large regional centers, and small regional centers. These findings were inconsistent with those of King et al. (1971), who did not find differences in care practices as a function of the average level of retardation of living-unit residents but were intuitively quite plausible to us. More severely retarded individuals are less responsive and provide less feedback than individuals of higher cognitive competence. It would seem quite easy to become mechanical and unresponsive while caring for individuals when responsiveness to such care is not immediately evident.

Howell and May (1980) also investigated resident care practices in small institutions (range 130-250) and group homes (range 11-24) in England, using the Resident Management Practices Inventory. Consistent with the findings of McCormick et al. (1975) and King et al. (1971), they found that the group homes were generally more resident oriented in their care practices than were the small central institutions. However, these authors did find that care for mildly and moderately retarded residents was as resident oriented in the institutions as in the group homes.

Although there may be some support from the preceding data on resident care practices that large may be bad, one cannot conclude that small is good. The mere placement of a retarded person in a small community-based facility will not necessarily insure more adequate care practices. This point has been well illustrated by Edgerton (1975) in a study of family-care homes with six or fewer residents and board and care facilities (group homes) in California. Edgerton stated:

> Some board and care facilities are 'open' settings which provide more nearly normalized experiences than large institutions typically do. Most, however, are

closed, ghetto-like places, whose residents are walled-off from any access to community life. Such places frequently lack most medical, psychological, and recreational services and their amenities are few indeed. Perhaps more significant still, the residents of such facilities are given to understand, in no uncertain terms, that they can hope for nothing different in the future... The quality of life in the alternative care facilities we have studied is highly variable, with evidence here and there of exciting progress toward the goal of normalization. For most mentally retarded people in this system, however, the little institutions where they now reside appear to be no better than the large ones from which they came, and some are manifestly worse [pp. 130–131].

In the McCormick et al. study (1975), we did find one exception to the general lack of association of such "human variables" as number of aides per resident and employee-turnover rate and care practices. In group homes in the United States, low employee-turnover rate and a high ratio of professional staff per resident were found to be predictive of more resident-oriented care practices. It may well be that such human factors as continuity of staffing can only become operative in certain settings.

In some recent studies, a direct observational approach has been used to assess the quality of life in different types of residential facilities for retarded persons. Bjaanes and Butler (1974) investigated directly observed behavior, time use patterns (i.e., active leisure, passive leisure, work and chores, personal activity, social interaction), and characteristics of behavior in two group homes (range 24–30) and two home-care facilities (range 4–6). They found more independent behavior in the group homes than in the home-care facilities. They also concluded that the group homes examined were closer to the goal of normalization than were the home-care facilities. Landesman–Dwyer, Sackett, and Kleinman (1980) found that, in group homes ranging in size from six to 20 residents, the residents in the larger facilities engaged in more social behavior and were more likely to have intense reciprocal friendships than were residents in smaller facilities. Thus, there is a possibility that extremely small residential settings for retarded persons may actually hinder growth and development. However, in an observational study of social interactions in two institutions of approximately 300 to 600 population, Grant and Moores (1977) found both more positive and total interactions in the smaller facility.

In our own work, the results of the McCormick et al. (1975) study, as well as the findings of King et al. (1971), convinced us that we had a sensitive method of characterizing the social–psychological milieu or residential settings for retarded persons. What was lacking in both our work and that of King et al. (1971) was a study in which both care practices and the actual behavior of the residents were investigated. We decided to conduct just such a study (Balla, Kossan, & Zigler, 1980). A total of 114 retarded persons in 20 living units in seven institutions were examined. Five of the facilities were regional centers and two were large central institutions. In each living unit, King et al.'s Resident Management Practices

Inventory was administered to the charge aide. We also obtained a measure of attitudes concerning the retarded residents from each aide in each living unit. We looked into such institutional demographic variables as cost per resident per day, employee-turnover rate, and number of aides per resident. The association of preinstitutional life experience, CA, MA, IQ, gender, and length of institutionalization with behavior was also examined. On the behavioral side, we obtained indices of responsiveness to social reinforcement or dependency, wariness of adults, and imitation. Our previous work has suggested that these three factors are particularly important in retarded individuals' daily competence.

Before discussing the findings concerning the determinants of the behavior of the subjects in the study, one major result with the demographic institutional variables should be mentioned. Large institution size was found to be very significantly related to larger living-unit size, high employee-turnover rate, low cost per resident per day, a low ratio of aides to residents, a low proportion of professional staff to resident, a low number of volunteer hours per resident per year, more adverse opinions concerning retarded persons, and more institution-oriented care practices. This pattern of interrelationships is especially important in discussions concerning social policy and residential facilities, which most often focus solely on institution size. If our findings have generality beyond the state in which the study was conducted, discussions could as easily focus on lack of professional staff, lack of aides, or lack of continuity of care, as measured by turnover rate. We should certainly display considerable caution when interpreting relationships between institution size and some other variable, because any such empirically discovered relationship may be due to the common relationship that these two measures have with a third measure.

Turning now toward findings concerning behavior, there were no differences between persons residing in central institutions and persons residing in regional centers on any of our behavioral measures. This lack of findings was of some surprise in view of the fact that the average size of the large central institutions was 1633, whereas the average size of the regional centers was 111. The central institutions also housed more residents per living unit and had a higher employee-turnover rate. The cost per resident per day was twice as high in the regional centers as in the central institutions. The number of aides per resident was twice as high in the regional centers as in the central institutions. The proportion of professional staff per resident and number of volunteer hours per resident per year was almost six times as great in the regional centers as in the central institutions. Such findings lend credence to the view that simply increasing cost and/or increasing staff will not, in and of itself, ensure greater behavioral competency on the part of residents in institutions. The findings also suggest that more intensive efforts need to be made to discover what particular kinds of programs enhance the behavioral competency of residents in institutions. The mere placement of a retarded person in a regional center did not seem to suffice as a means for increasing competency.

With one exception, no behavioral differences were found between persons residing in the two central institutions or five regional centers. There were also no behavioral differences between persons residing in the largest regional center (population 290) and the smallest regional center (population 12). It seems most reasonable to conclude that the behavior of the residents in all the institutions was similar.

A series of multiple-regression analyses were performed in which all the characteristics of the residents (e.g., MA or length of institutionalization) and all the institutional characteristics (e.g., cost per resident per day or Resident Management Practices Inventory score) were used to predict the scores on our measures of behavior. We should note that in this kind of analysis, the effect found for any one variable is independent of the effects of all other variables.

We found that several of the characteristics of the institutions were associated with the behavior of the residents. The larger the size of the institution, the greater the motivation of the individuals to receive adult attention and support, a finding reminiscent of Balla et al. (1974), that individuals in the largest of four institutions studied were most responsive to social reinforcement. Thus, in large institutions, individuals appear to be relatively deprived of this class of social reinforcer. This finding was the single instance in which institution size was predictive of the resident's behavior. To this point, we had been assuming that depriving socializing experiences lead retarded individuals to be excessively dependent on adults, when the adults are reinforcing their behavior by making supportive comments. However, there is a body of work in the tradition of Spitz (Spitz, 1945; Spitz & Wolf, 1946) and Bowlby (1951) suggesting that extreme forms of deprivation can result in apathy, withdrawal, and a lack of responsivity to supportive adults. In order to develop attachments to adults and thus become responsive to their attention and support, it seems as if the child must have some minimal number of positive encounters with them. Children extremely deprived of such encounters would be expected to show greatly attenuated responsivity to adult attention and support. On the other hand, if children experience some minimum of support and attention at the hands of adults within a general socializing history of deprivation, we would expect these children to show atypically high responsivity to attention and support. We found some support for this formulation: Large professional staffs and active volunteer programs were associated with higher responsiveness to social reinforcement.

We found considerable evidence that depriving socializing conditions produce wariness of adults. The larger the number of individuals in a living unit, the greater the wariness of the individuals who lived in the unit. Increased wariness was found in settings with high employee-turnover rates and a high proportion of aides to residents. Thus, it would seem that the response to a large number of noncontinuous adult caretakers—and, therefore, nonpredictable adult caretaking—is the development of wariness. We also found that aides' adverse attitudes concerning retarded persons was related to greater wariness on the part of the residents.

There was evidence suggesting that some institutions socialize their residents in the direction of reduced behavioral spontaneity and/or conformity. We found high levels of imitation in individuals institutionalized a relatively long period of time and in individuals who were the recipients of institution- as opposed to resident-oriented care practices. Thus, many institutionalized retarded persons appear to live in a highly predictable environment that emphasized conformity, a finding consistent with that of Lustman, Zigler, and Balla (1979), who found higher levels of imitation in a group of institutionalized as compared to noninstitutionalized retarded persons. Such conformity may be a form of adjustment to the institution. The value of living in a well-organized and predictable environment can be seen in a finding that less wariness was displayed by residents receiving institution- as opposed to resident-oriented caretaking practices. However, such conformity was probably purchased at too high a psychological cost. The conforming and imitative child distrusts spontaneous solutions to problems and may be ill equipped to function in the much less organized and predictable environment outside the institution.

We have come to view either too little or too much imitation as negative psychological indicators, with some intermediate level of imitation being viewed as a positive developmental phenomenon reflecting a person's healthy attachment to adults and responsivity to cues adults emit that can be used in problem-solving efforts. Consistent with this view was our finding that retarded individuals whose caretakers had negative attitudes concerning them were less imitative. Persons consistently reacted to in a negative manner may respond by ignoring the cues provided by adults and thus become less imitative.

In addition to these effects of institutions upon behavior, we found several characteristics of the persons to be predictive of their behavior. Consistent with earlier findings (Balla et al., 1974; Zigler & Balla, 1972), residents of high MA were found to be less motivated for social attention and support than were residents of low MA. Thus, retarded children, like their peers of average IQ, seemed to move from dependency to autonomy as their cognitive level became higher. Evidence was also found indicating that the higher the MA level, the greater the wariness. Consistent with earlier findings, MA was negatively related to imitation (Balla et al., 1974; Balla, Styfco, & Zigler, 1971; Ruble & Nakamura, 1973; Yando & Zigler, 1971; Zigler & Yando, 1972). This finding was in keeping with two facets of our outerdirectedness formulation (Zigler, 1972; Zigler & Balla, 1976). The higher the cognitive level of the child, the less he employs imitation in problem-solving efforts, and the lower the IQ of the child, the more failure experiences he has when employing his own cognitive resources and, thus, the greater tendency for imitativeness.

Finally, we found that individuals who had experienced frequent changes of parenting figures before they were institutionalized were both more motivated to attain the attention and support of an adult and more wary of doing so. These findings provided additional evidence for our view that deprived retarded individuals have both atypically high positive and negative reaction tendencies (Zigler, 1971; Zigler & Balla, 1976). The subjects in this study had been institutionalized for an average of over 8 years, and the fact that the effects of preinstitutional life experience were still in evidence after so long a time is consistent with our general position that social deprivation experienced relatively early in life can affect the behavior of retarded persons when it is assessed many years later (Balla & Zigler, 1975; Zigler et al., 1968; Zigler et al., 1970).

There has been another series of studies where the social-psychological characteristics of residential settings for the retarded were related to the growth and development of the residents (Eyman, Demaine, & Lei, 1979; Eyman, Silverstein, McLain & Miller, 1977; McLain, Silverstein, Hubbell, & Brownlee, 1977). Typically, in these studies two measures of institutional characteristics have been used. The first, the Characteristics of the Treatment Environment developed by Jackson (1969) consists of two dimensions: *Autonomy,* the amount of independence allowed; and *Activity,* the amount and type of programs and program involvement in the facility. The second has been the Resident Management Practices Inventory described earlier. A version of the Adaptive Behavior Scale of the American Association on Mental Deficiency has been used to measure behavioral development.

In these studies, it was first demonstrated that these scales differentiated different types of residential facilities: large central institutions, skilled nursing facilities, group homes (range 7-50), and family homes (less than six residents). The large institutions were generally least adequate and the family homes the most adequate (McLain et al., 1977, 1979). One 3-year longitudinal study (Eyman et al., 1977) involved residents in two large central institutions and in community care facilities (skilled nursing homes, group homes, and foster care homes) in two western states. Differential change in adaptive behavior did occur over the period of the study, with the changes being related to level of retardation, age, and type of facility. The less-retarded residents in the foster care and group homes improved most in adaptive behavior, although the younger, less-retarded residents in one of the large institutions also showed improvement. The older, profoundly retarded residents generally showed regression. In general, residents in the foster care and group homes did evidence more positive change than did residents in the other residential settings. These results again demonstrate the impossibility of speaking of institutions as having monolithic effects on their residents.

In another study, the PASS measure of the quality of residential facilities (Wolfensberger & Glenn, 1975) was related to changes in adaptive behavior over a 3-year time period for a group of 245 residents in 87 family-care homes and 11 group homes. A general improvement in overall adaptive behavior was found for the older, less-retarded residents. The location and proximity of community services and the comfort and appearance of the residents was associated with improvement in all aspects of adaptive behavior, whereas administrative policies and environmental blending with the neighborhood were selectively related to the cognitive and self-help aspects of adaptive behavior. In sum, then, evidence seems to be accumulating that the quality of life in residential settings for retarded persons is related to behavioral growth and development.

There is some evidence concerning the effects of transfer from a large central institution to a smaller facility on the adaptive behavior of retarded persons (Cohen, Conroy, Frazer, Snelbecker, & Spreat, 1977). A group of 92 residents who were transferred were compared in changes in adaptive behavior with a matched group of residents who remained in a central institution. The adaptive behavior measures were obtained immediately prior to transfer, immediately after transfer, and 6 to 8 weeks after transfer. The less-retarded residents demonstrated a pattern of lowered functioning and withdrawal following relocation. Relative to the comparison group, they became more withdrawn and demonstrated regression in language. However, more retarded residents demonstrated increases in both adaptive and disruptive behavior. Of course, these adverse effects may have been due to the stress of relocation, but the findings suggest that we cannot assume that placement from a large institution to a smaller community-based facility will inevitably lead to positive change in behavior. Such a conclusion is consistent with the position of Balla & Klein (1981), that the specific characteristics of treatment environments for retarded persons, on a variety of dimensions, must be identified before we can make any firm conclusions about the relative adequacy of different types of residential settings.

CONCLUSIONS

The previous discussion of the effects of institutionalization has important implications for the developmental-difference controversy. As mentioned earlier, many of our theories of retarded behavior are based on the comparison of nonretarded individuals living at home and institutionalized retarded individuals, making it difficult to disentangle the effects of institutionalization on behavior from the effects of retardation per se. In addition, it is clear from the research cited previously that institutionalized retarded individuals often come from homes characterized by extreme poverty, parental histories of significant psychopathology, and a higher prevalence of abuse and neglect than nonretarded individuals. If psychologists interested in nonretarded development had limited their investigations to children in orphanages with a high probability of extremely adverse social histories, few would deny that our theory of normal development would be badly distorted. In this context it is perhaps not surprising that Weisz, Yeates, and Zigler (Chapter 14), in their comprehensive review of Piagetian evidence relevant to the developmental-difference controversy, found that the difference position was likely to be supported if the institutionalization variable was not considered, whereas the developmental position was likely to be supported if it was.

Finally, if there is a persistent theme in our own work on the effects of institutionalization on retarded persons, it is a continuing and increasing emphasis on the social-policy implications of our research. We believe that those of us who investigate the effects of institutions must also be advocates on behalf of the people who live there. We must try to translate our research findings into direct ways to improve the daily lives and competence of retarded citizens. We are convinced that one important way of meeting this goal is through a comprehensive research program that takes into account not only the behavioral functioning of residents but the quality of life they experience, the extent to which they maintain contact with their community, and whether they are discharged to progressively more nearly independent placements. We believe that only by means of such multifacted research will it be eventually possible to determine empirically the optimal residential setting for each person at the optimal cost.

REFERENCES

Balla, D. A. Relationship of institution size to quality of care: A review of the literature. *American Journal of Mental Deficiency*, 1976, *81*, 117–124.

Balla, D., Butterfield, E. C., & Zigler, E. Effects of institutionalization on retarded children: A longitudinal cross-institutional investigation. *American Journal of Mental Deficiency*, 1974, *78*, 530–549.

Balla, D., & Klein, M. Labels for and taxonomies of environments for retarded persons. In R. Newbrough & H. C. Haywood (Eds.), *Community placement for retarded persons*. Baltimore: University Park Press, in press.

Balla, D., Kossan, N., & Zigler, E. *Effects of preinstitutional history and institutionalization on the behavior of the retarded*. Unpublished manuscript, Yale University, 1980.

Balla, D., Styfco, S. J., & Zigler, E. Use of the opposition concept and outerdirectedness in intellectually average, familial retarded, and organically retarded children. *American Journal of Mental Deficiency*, 1971, *75*, 663–680.

Balla, D., & Zigler, E. Preinstitutional social deprivation and responsiveness to social reinforcement in institutionalized retarded individuals: A 6-year follow-up study. *American Journal of Mental Deficiency*, 1975, *80*, 228–230.

Baumeister, A. A. Problems in comparative studies of mental retardates and normals. *American Journal of Mental Deficiency*, 1967, *71*, 869–875.

Bell, R. A reinterpretation of the direction of effects in studies of socialization. *Psychological Review*, 1968, *75*, 81–95.

Bjaanes, A. T., & Butler, E. W. Environmental variation in community care facilities for mentally retarded persons. *American Journal of Mental Deficiency*, 1974, *78*, 429–439.

Bowlby, J. *Maternal care and mental health*. Geneva: WHO, 1951.

Butterfield, E. C., & Zigler, E. The influence of differing institutional social climates on the effectiveness of social reinforcement in the mentally retarded. *American Journal of Mental Deficiency*, 1965, *70*, 48–56.

Clarke, A. D. B., & Clarke, A. M. Cognitive changes in the feebleminded. *British Journal of Psychology*, 1954, *45*, 173–179.

Cohen, H., Conroy, J. W., Frazer, D. W., Snelbecker, G., & Spreat, S. The effects of interinstitutional relocation of mentally retarded residents. *American Journal of Mental Deficiency*, 1977, *82*, 12–18.

Edgerton, R. B. Issues relating to the quality of life among mentally retarded persons. In M. J. Began & S. S. Richardson (Eds.), *The mentally retarded and society: A social science perspective*. Baltimore: University Park Press, 1975.

Eyman, R. K., Demaine, G., & Lei, T. Relationship between community environments and resident changes in adaptive behavior: A path model. *American Journal of Mental Deficiency*, 1979, *83*, 330-338.

Eyman, R., Silverstein, A., McLain, R., & Miller, C. In P. Mittler & J. deJong (Eds.), *Research to practice in mental retardation: Care and intervention* (Vol. I). Baltimore: University Park Press, 1977.

Grant, G. W. B., & Moores, B. Resident characteristics and staff behavior in two hospitals for mentally retarded adults. *American Journal of Mental Deficiency*, 1977, *82*, 259-265.

Hagen, J. W., & Huntsman, N. J. Selective attention in mental retardates. *Developmental Psychology*, 1971, *5*, 151-160.

Howell, H. H., & May, A. E. Resident-care practices in the county of Somerset, England. *American Journal of Mental Deficiency*, 1980, *84*, 393-396.

Jackson, J. Factors of the treatment environment. *Archives of General Psychiatry*, 1969, *21*, 39-45.

Katz, P., & Rosenberg, S. Effects of labels on the perception and discrimination learning of retardates. *Journal of Abnormal Psychology*, 1969, *74*, 95-99.

King. R. D., Raynes, N. V., & Tizard, J. *Patterns of residential care: Sociological studies in institutions for handicapped children*. London: Routledge & Kegan Paul, 1971.

Kounin, J. Experimental studies of rigidity: I. The measurement of rigidity in normal and feebleminded persons. *Character and Personality*, 1941, *9*, 251-272. (a)

Kounin, J. Experimental studies of rigidity: II. The explanatory power of the concept of rigidity as applied to feeble-mindedness. *Character and Personality*, 1941, *9*, 273-282. (b)

Landesman-Dwyer, S., Sackett, G. P., & Kleinman, J. S. Relationship of size to resident and staff behavior in small community residences. *American Journal of Mental Deficiency*, 1980, *85*, 6-17.

Lewin, K. *A dynamic theory of personality*. New York: McGraw-Hill, 1936.

Lustman, N., Zigler, E., & Balla, D. *Imitation in institutionalized and noninstitutionalized retarded children and in children of average intellect*. Unpublished manuscript, Yale University, 1979.

McCormick, M., Balla, D., & Zigler, E. Resident-care practices in institutions for retarded persons: A cross-institutional, cross-cultural study. *American Journal of Mental Deficiency*, 1975, *80*, 1-17.

McLain, R., Silverstein, A., Brownlee, L., & Hubbell, M. Attitudinal versus ecological approaches to the characterization of institutional treatment environments. *American Journal of Community Psychology*, 1979, *7*, 159-165.

McLain, R., Silverstien, A., Hubbell, M., & Brownlee, L. Comparison of the residential environment of a state hospital for retarded clients with those of various types of community facilities. *Journal of Community Psychology*, 1977, *5*, 282-289.

Ruble, D., & Nakamura, C. Outerdirectedness as a problem-solving approach in relation to developmental level and selected task variables. *Child Development*, 1973, *44*, 519-528.

Spitz, R. Hospitalism: An inquiry into the genesis of psychiatric conditions in early childhood. In Anna Freud et al. (Eds.), *The psychoanalytic study of the child* (Vol. 1). New York: International Universities Press, 1945.

Spitz, R., & Wolf, K. Anaclytic depression. In Anna Freud et al. (Eds.), *The psychoanalytic study of the child* (Vol. II). New York: International Universities Press, 1946.

Wolfensberger, W., & Glenn, L. *Pass 3, a method for the quantitative evaluation of human services*. Toronto: National Institute on Mental Retardation, 1975.

Yando, R., & Zigler, E. Outerdirectedness in the problem solving of institutionalized and noninstitutionalized normal and retarded children. *Developmental Psychology*, 1971, *4*, 277-288.

Yarrow, M., Waxler, C., & Scott, P. Child effects on adult behavior. *Developmental Psychology*, 1971, *5*, 300-311.

Zigler, E. *The effect of preinstitutional social deprivation on the performance of feebleminded children.* Unpublished doctoral dissertation, University of Texas, 1958.

Zigler, E. Social deprivation and rigidity in the performance of feebleminded children. *Journal of Abnormal and Social Psychology*, 1961, *62*, 413-421.

Zigler, E. Rigidity and social reinforcement effects in the performance of institutionalized and noninstitutionalized normal and retarded children. *Journal of Personality*, 1963, *31*, 258-269.

Zigler, E. The retarded child as a whole person. In H. E. Adams & W. K. Boardman, III (Eds.), *Advances in experimental clinical psychology* (Vol. I). New York: Pergamon Press, 1971.

Zigler, E. Rigidity in the retarded: A re-examination. In E. Trapp & P. Himelstein (Eds.), *Readings on the exceptional child: Research and theory* (2nd ed.). New York: Appleton-Century-Crofts, 1972.

Zigler, E., & Balla, D. Developmental course of responsiveness to social reinforcement in normal children and institutionalized retarded children. *Developmental Psychology*, 1972, *6*, 66-73.

Zigler, E., & Balla, D. Motivational factors in the performance of the retarded. In R. Koch & J. C. Dobson (Eds.), *The mentally retarded child and his family: A multidisciplinary handbook* (2nd ed.). New York: Brunner-Mazel, 1976.

Zigler, E., Balla, D., & Butterfield, E. C. A longitudinal investigation of the relationship between preinstitutional social deprivation and social motivation in institutionalized retardates. *Journal of Personality and Social Psychology*, 1968, *10*, 437-445.

Zigler, E., Butterfield, E. C., & Capobianco, F. Institutionalization and the effectiveness of social reinforcement: a 5- and 8-year follow-up study. *Developmental Psychology*, 1970, *3*, 255-263.

Zigler, E., & Williams, J. Institutionalization and the effectiveness of social reinforcement: A 3-year follow-up study. *Journal of Abnormal and Social Psychology*, 1963, *66*, 197-205.

Zigler, E., & Yando, R. Outerdirectedness and imitative behavior of institutionalized and noninstitutionalized younger and older children. *Child Development*, 1972, *43*, 413-425.

II THE DIFFERENCE POSITIONS

5 Rigidity— A Resilient Concept*

Edward Zigler
David Balla
Yale University

Few views in the area of mental retardation have had the influence and the staying power of the formulation that retarded persons are inherently more rigid. This position was originally advanced by Lewin (1936) over 40 years ago and subsequently elaborated by Kounin (1939, 1941a, b, 1948). In the 3 decades following the original statements of the position, numerous empirical investigations on the issue were conducted. Perhaps even more importantly, it had a great deal of influence on the care, treatment, and training of retarded individuals (Sarason & Gladwin, 1958). In recent years the rigidity position has been seen as being little more than a relic, of interest only in the context of the history of the mental retardation movement. It is our view that the view of rigidity as only a matter of history is inaccurate and that variants of the rigidity position, phrased in the current language of cognitive psychology, are still very much a part of the psychology of mental retardation. The current variants of the rigidity position are discussed following a presentation of the original position.

Although the rigidity position as advanced by Lewin and Kounin was widely accepted as a major theoretical breakthrough for the understanding of the behavior of retarded persons, it should be noted that the formulation has been surrounded by controversy since its inception. Much of the early controversy seems to have stemmed from a failure of investigators to deal adequately with both the definitional and methodological demands of the rigidity formulation. A

---

*Portions of this article appeared in Zigler, E. "Rigidity in the Retarded: A Reexamination," in *Readings on the Exceptional Child*: *Research and Theory*, E. Trapp & P. Himelstein (Eds.), copyright 1972, 2nd ed., pp. 123-160. Reprinted by permission of Prentice-Hall, Englewood Cliffs, N.J.

particular source of this confusion was the failure of some critics and defenders of the view to grasp fully the theoretical formulation of the rigidity position as advanced by its original proponents, Kurt Lewin and Jacob Kounin. As is discussed later, the failure to grasp the theoretical demands of a rigidity position, in either its original form or its later reincarnations, has persisted to the present day.

In this chapter we present an historical overview of the rigidity issue. In the context of this historical perspective we review some empirical work related to the rigidity issue, beginning with the work of Lewin and Kounin. Finally, we discuss some aspects of the motivational work done by the authors and their colleagues, more fully reviewed in Chapter 4, from the perspective of the rigidity position.

THE LEWIN–KOUNIN FORMULATION

In Lewin's general theory, the person is treated as a dynamic system with individual differences derivable from differences in: (1) structure of the total system; (2) material and state of the system; or (3) its meaningful content. The first two factors play the most important role in Lewin's theory of mental retardation. In respect to structure, Lewin viewed the retarded child as being cognitively less differentiated (i.e., having fewer regions in the cognitive structure) than a nonretarded child of the same CA. Thus, in respect to the number of regions in the cognitive structure, the retarded child resembles a nonretarded younger child. However, in relation to the material and state of the system, Lewin stated that even though retarded children corresponded to nonretarded younger children in degree of differentiation they were not to be regarded as entirely similar. He (Lewin, 1936) explicitly stated that he conceived: "the major dynamic difference between a feebleminded and a normal child of the same degree of differentiation to consist in a greater stiffness, a smaller capacity for dynamic rearrangement, in the psychical systems of the former [p. 210]."

Lewin presented a considerable amount of observational and anecdotal material as well as the findings of one experiment to support his theoretical position concerning the rigidity of retarded persons. Lewin's experimental procedure consisted of having groups of nonretarded and retarded children of differing CAs draw moon faces until they were satiated on this activity. The persistence (i.e., longer satiation time) displayed by the 10-year-old retarded children as compared to the 10-year-old nonretarded children was used by Lewin as evidence of the greater rigidity of the retarded.

A serious difficulty in Lewin's study was that comparisons were made between groups having different MAs, thus varying in their degree of differentiation. This placed Lewin in the position of being faced with a behavioral manifestation of rigidity without being able to ascribe it solely to the principle that the 10-year-old retarded children were less differentiated than the 10-year-old nonretarded children, or to the principle that, differentiation notwithstanding, retarded as compared to nonretarded individuals are characterized by a lessened fluidity between regions of the dynamic system. Thus, in accounting for his results, Lewin vacillated between an explanation in terms of degree of differentiation and one in terms of fluidity of the system.

Although Lewin undoubtedly felt that lack of differentiation could lead to rigid behaviors (e.g., pedantry, fixation, stereotypy, inelasticity, concreteness, etc.), he was quite clear that this lack of differentiation was not what he meant by rigidity. To Lewin, lack of differentiation referred to the number and hierarchy of regions within the total system, whereas rigidity was defined in terms of the fluidity existing between regions. It follows from Lewin's theory that, if an individual's system is characterized by lack of differentiation or by rigidity or both, that individual is more more likely to emit behaviors commonly referred to as rigid. Lewin's failure to draw a clear distinction between the meaning of rigidity, as he employed it, and rigid behaviors, as such, appears to be a major factor leading to the subsequent controversy in this area. This difference between rigidity, as defined by Lewin, and the concept of rigidity, as employed to characterize a particular class of phenotypic behaviors, must be kept firmly in mind.

Lewin also suggested a motivational explanation, centered around the high incidence of failure experiences, for the rigid behaviors observed in the retarded. However, he quickly dismissed it as inadequate. In addition, Lewin issued a warning that psychologically comparable situations must be employed if differences in rigidity are to be assessed correctly. Lewin here was suggesting that a particular situation may constitute a conflict situation for a retarded individual, whereas presenting no conflict for a nonretarded individual.

An examination of Lewin's work thus discloses at least four factors that must be taken into consideration when assessing differences in the occurrence of rigid behaviors in nonretarded and retarded individuals. These four factors may be summarized as follows:

1. Degree of differentiation. Of two individuals of the same CA, one nonretarded and one retarded, it is assumed that the retarded individual is less differentiated (i.e., has fewer regions) than the nonretarded individual. Owing to this lesser degree of differentiation, the retarded individual will manifest more rigid behaviors over a wide range of tasks than will the nonretarded individual of the same CA.

2. Rigidity. Of two individuals having the same degree of differentiation, one a younger nonretarded and one an older retarded, the boundaries between the regions in the retarded individual will be less permeable, thus making the total system less fluid and more rigid. Owing to this rigidity within the system, the retarded individual will manifest more rigid behaviors over a wide range of tasks than will the chronologically younger nonretarded individual possessing an equal degree of differentiation.

3. History of the individual. Any individual who is frequently faced with problems beyond his capacity and who experiences an inordinate number of failures may adopt a life style characterized by rigid behaviors. Such behaviors would not be considered the result of the innate rigidity of the individual but rather the product of a unique history of environmental events.

4. The psychological situation. In assessing differences in the amount of rigid behaviors between any two individuals, care must be taken that the overall assessment situation be psychologically equivalent for both individuals. Otherwise, differences in the amount of rigid behaviors may be due to the individuals operating in phenomenally different situations rather than to actual differences in the amount of rigidity possessed by the two individuals.

In any individual, these factors would interact, the interaction of factors 3 and 4 being especially obvious. Although the last two factors played a relatively minor role in the early efforts to analyze the high incidence of rigid behaviors in the retarded, factors of this type have been prominent features in studies aimed at elucidating experiential factors in rigid behaviors (see Chapter 4).

The clearest experimental support for the position that retarded individuals are more rigid than nonretarded individuals having the same degree of differentiation is contained in the work of Kounin (1939, 1941a, b, 1948). Kounin, building upon Lewin's work, advanced the view that rigidity is a positive, monotonic function of CA. Again, it is imperative to note that by "rigidity" Kounin, like Lewin, was referring to "that property of a functional boundary which prevents communication between neighboring regions" and not to phenotypic rigid behaviors as such. Thus, with increasing CA, the individual was seen to become more differentiated (i.e., has more cognitive regions), which results in a lower incidence of rigid behaviors, whereas the boundaries between regions become less and less permeable. Furthermore, although this lack of permeability in the boundaries between regions might often result in behaviors that would be characterized as rigid, in some instances it was seen to lead to behaviors that could be characterized as indicative of "flexibility." (For an example of the latter possibility, see the results of Kounin's lever-pressing task following.)

Kounin offered the findings of five experiments in support of his formulation. In these experiments he employed three groups: older retarded individuals, younger retarded individuals, and nonretarded individuals. (It should be noted that the two retarded groups resided in an institution, whereas the nonretarded children did not.) In view of the inadequacies of Lewin's satiation study, Kounin instituted certain experimental controls. He defined the degree of differentiation as the MA of an individual and controlled for this factor by equating the three groups on MA. He (Kounin, 1948) also attempted to reduce what he later referred to as: "motivational factors (such as low success expectation, hesitance to enter unfamiliar regions, etc.) that might produce those varied types of behavior that are sometimes lumped together in the pseudo-descriptive category of 'behavioral rigidity' [p. 163].'' Kounin attempted to control for these factors by having his subjects engage in each of the activities prior to the experiment proper, thus attempting to make each subject feel confident and secure during the experimental tasks.

As Kounin predicted, the three groups differed in certain instruction-initiated tasks (e.g., drawing cats until satiated and then drawing bugs until satiated) and lowering a lever to release marbles and then raising the lever to release marbles. As predicted from the Lewin-Kounin hypothesis, the nonretarded children showed the greatest amount of transfer effects from task to task, the younger retarded a lesser amount of transfer, and the older retarded children the least amount of transfer; that is, on the drawing task, the retarded individuals drew longer on the second task following satiation on the first task than did nonretarded individuals, with the least cosatiation effects being observed in the older retarded group. On the lever-pressing task, the greatest number of errors, lowering rather than raising the lever on task 2, was made by the nonretarded children, the least number of errors by the older retarded, with the younger retarded children falling between these two groups. One should note that on this task the lesser ''rigidity,'' as defined by Lewin and Kounin, of the nonretarded children resulted in a higher incidence of a behavioral response often characterized as rigid (i.e., perseverative responses). One should further note that this lack of influence of one region on another in the performance of the retarded children would only be predicted in these cases where the retarded individual is ''psychologically'' placed into a new region by employing an instructional procedure. In those instances where the individual must on his own move from one region to another, the Lewin-Kounin formulation would predict that such movement would be more difficult for the retarded than for the nonretarded individual. This prediction was also confirmed by Kounin in his concept-switching experiment, in which the child was given a deck of cards that could be sorted on the basis of either one (form) or another (color) principle. In this experiment the subject, after voluntarily sorting the cards on the basis of either color or form, was asked to put the cards together some other way. Here, the nonretarded children evidenced the least difficulty in shifting, the older retarded individuals the most difficulty in switching, with the younger retarded children again falling between these two groups. Thus, in the instance where a movement to a new region is self-initiated, it is the retarded individuals who evidence the higher incidence of perseverative responses.

The Lewin-Kounin theory of rigidity is a conceptually demanding one in that it sometimes predicts a higher and sometimes a lower incidence of phenotypically rigid behaviors in retarded as compared to nonretarded individuals. However, the fact that the theory generates specific predictions as to when one or the other state or affairs will obtain is a tribute to this theory. Kounin thus offered impressive experimental support for the view that, with MA held constant, the older and/or more retarded an individual is, the more will his behaviors be characterized by dynamic rigidity (i.e., greater rigidity in the boundaries between regions).

THE CRITICISMS OF GOLDSTEIN AND WERNER

Both Lewin's and Kounin's positions on rigidity in the retarded were soon criticized by Goldstein (1942-43). Although taking issue with those earlier investigators on several points, Goldstein clearly stated that he did not deny that rigidity was an important symptom of mental retardation. He disagreed with Kounin that rigidity was a positive monotonic function of chronological age and with both Kounin and Lewin on their conception of rigidity. He offered in its place a two-factor theory of rigidity that differentiated between primary and secondary rigidity.

A comparison of the views of Goldstein with those of Lewin and Kounin presents certain difficulties. Lewin implicitly and Kounin explicitly applied their theory only to the familial retarded. Goldstein treated mental retardation as a homogeneous entity having a common organic etiology, drawing no distinction between the organic and the familial retarded. Another problem lies in Goldstein's use of the term *rigidity*. He sometimes employed it as a physiological construct having organic referents, whereas at other times he uses it to describe the behaviors themselves. As noted earlier, failure to make this differentiation explicit has caused considerable difficulty. Goldstein's failure to comprehend fully Kounin's definition of rigidity led him to what appears to be a misdirected criticism of Kounin's satiation experiment, in which the subjects drew pictures of animals.

Goldstein argued that the four tasks in this experiment were in reality just one task, drawing four objects one after the other, which required but a single *Einstellung*. He noted the ease with which the retarded individuals shifted from drawing one animal to another and used this fact as indicating that all the drawings comprised one task, for Goldstein felt that "if it were a new task, rigidity would appear." Thus, Goldstein treated Kounin's concept of rigidity as involving no more than ease of shifting. However, Kounin (1948) had clearly pointed out that in this experiment he was not measuring the ease of shifting but was instead measuring the degree to which the satiation of one need cosatiated a neighboring need. Kounin further pointed out that no predictions concerning the ability to shift in this particular experiment could be derived from his concept of rigidity. Once again, Goldstein's error appears to lie in his insistence on interpreting Kounin's concept of rigidity as referring to a type of behavior, rather than a hypothesized quality of the boundaries between cognitive regions.

One aspect of Goldstein's criticism of the satiation experiment does merit further consideration. Goldstein stated, in effect, that Kounin's four drawing tasks did not require the person to move from one region to another. It would appear that anyone who uses a theory that employs such concepts as "degree of differentiation," "region," "overlapping situation," "restructuring a given field," *"Einstellung,"* "mental set" to predict behaviors must make an effort to define these concepts independently of the operations that constitute the predicted behaviors.

With the exception of Kounin's defining the degree of differentiation as the MA of the individual, this has never been clearly done. It is true that to the extent that one employs his theory, implements such concepts in any single experimental procedure, and obtains positive results, not only is the general theory supported but the implication is that the implicit requirements of the concepts have been fulfilled. It is, however, only to the extent that these requirements be made explicit and the concept divorced from any single experimental procedure, as such, that one can unequivocally state that the demands of the concept have been met. Goldstein's criticism of Kounin's satiation experiment stands as evidence on this point. It is difficult for Kounin to show that drawing bugs after drawing cats requires the individual to "move to a new region." Goldstein's criticism further illustrates that not dealing with this problem invites different interpretation of positive results.

The issue becomes even more critical in respect to negative findings. A requirement of any theory is that it produce testable hypotheses that are open equally to both proof and disproof. Because the concepts referred to previously are not independently defined, any negative results obtained employing them can be explained by stating that the demands implied in the concepts were not met. For example, had Kounin found no differences between the three groups in the satiation experiment, these results could have been discarded on the grounds that this particular experimental procedure did not really involve movement to a new region. In this respect, the theory is receptive only to positive results and not to findings that may constitute a disproof. This shortcoming is a serious one and must be kept in mind when evaluating the various positions being discussed.

Returning to Goldstein's distinction between primary and secondary rigidity, Goldstein (1942–1943) felt that primary rigidity involved: an abnormality of the *Einstellung* mechanism, frequently observed in lesions of the subcortical ganglia. Goldstein advanced the position that primary rigidity is independent of an impairment of higher mental processes, manifesting itself in a lack of ability to change from one "set" to another. This deficiency becomes apparent only when the individual attempts to shift from one task to a second unrelated task. The difficulty is not related to the various tasks themselves, for Goldstein felt that an individual suffering from primary rigidity is quite capable of solving individual tasks, even if such tasks demand a high level of abstraction. This variant of the rigidity position has persisted, in various forms, until the present day.

Goldstein (1942–1943) viewed secondary rigidity as being "due to a primary defect of the higher mental processes occurring in cortical damage and cortical malformations, such as feeblemindedness." Underlying secondary rigidity is an impairment of abstract thinking. The ability to think abstractly can be positively related to the concept of degree of differentiation. In a manner reminiscent of Kounin's equating degree of differentiation with MA, Goldstein equated ability to think abstractly with "mental capacity." Indeed, at one point, Goldstein made the translation and placed lack of differentiation at the center of the problem of rigidity in retarded individuals. Goldstein, thus, agreed with Lewin and Kounin that lack of differentiation results in a high incidence of rigid behaviors but disagreed with them concerning their assumption of a primary abnormality in the boundaries between regions. Goldstein suggested that all differences in the incidence of rigid behaviors in the retarded stemmed from their relative lack of differentiation and from this factor alone. To Goldstein, secondary rigidity is a result of an individual's dealing with a problem beyond his mental capacity. Rigid behaviors, such as perseveration, are adaptive mechanisms that allow the individual to escape frustration. Retarded individuals emit more of such behaviors, because they encounter problems beyond their capacity more frequently than do nonretarded individuals.

Goldstein, feeling that Kounin had not considered this problem, tried to explain away Kounin's findings. He attributed Kounin's positive results to Kounin's experimental tasks varying in the intellectual demands they made on the three groups of subjects. This criticism of Kounin's work by Goldstein would only be appropriate if Kounin had either given tasks differing in complexity to three groups of individuals having the same mental capacity or had given the same task to three groups differing in mental capacity. Actually, Kounin did neither. In each experiment, all subjects performed the same task. As to mental capacity, not only did Kounin equate his three groups on MA, but he made a further effort to see that his three groups were equated in ability to perform the specific experimental task employed. Therefore, as interesting as Goldstein's concept of secondary rigidity is, it can in no way explain the differences found by Kounin.

There appears to be another difficulty in Goldstein's distinction between primary and secondary rigidity. One wonders exactly how his secondary rigidity is any more "secondary" than his primary rigidity. Primary rigidity implies subcortical damage, which results in an inability to change "sets," from which ensue certain definite behaviors (i.e., inability to shift to a new task). Secondary rigidity implies cortical damage, which results in an inability to think abstractly, from which ensue certain behaviors (i.e., perseveration or distractibility). How, then, is one "primary" and one "secondary" unless these terms have as a referent only the level of the central nervous system involved? It is only to the extent that secondary rigidity is divorced from organic involvement that the distinction "secondary" becomes meaningful. If this were done, then Goldstein's secondary rigidity would become simply a general behavior mechanism, unrelated to retardation, that appears when any individual is confronted with a problem beyond his capacity. It is of interest to note that such a general behavior mechanism has indeed been utilized to account for the appearance of certain rigid behaviors when individuals are faced with difficult or insoluble tasks (see Chapter 4).

Werner (1940, 1948) has also advanced the view that retarded individuals are rigid. He has, however, taken exception to Kounin's concept of rigidity and especially to Kounin's hypothesis that rigidity is a positive monotonic function of CA. Werner ascribed differences in behavior between nonretarded and retarded persons to lack of differentiation in the retarded and to descriptive generalizations like retarded children are less easily satiated than nonretarded children, those familiar with retarded children have noticed the stereotypy even of their free activity, and, retarded children are not opposed to monotonous work; they rather enjoy it. Werner felt that Kounin's hypothesis on the relationship of rigidity and age was erroneous, because, as a person grows older he becomes more differentiated, with his behavior becoming less stereotyped, less perseverative, less concrete, more plastic, etc. As Kounin (1948) has noted in a reply to Werner, this controversy appears to be the result of Werner's failure to distinguish between "behavioral rigidity" (rigid behaviors) and "dynamic rigidity" as Kounin defined it.

Werner's attempt to relate the differences obtained by Kounin between his normal and retarded subjects to differences in degree of differentiation also appears inadequate. As noted earlier, Kounin obtained these differences after equating the groups on degree of differentiation (MA). Werner nowhere stated that Kounin's equating procedure failed to achieve its purpose. It thus appears that Werner's criticisms of Kounin's work suffer from some of the same shortcomings as did those of Goldstein. One can only conclude that Goldstein's and Werner's critiques of Kounin's work have cast very little doubt on Kounin's position that retarded persons display more rigid behaviors than do nonretarded subjects of the same MA, and that the older and/or more retarded an individual is the more will his behavior be characterized by rigidity as defined by Kounin.

However, this review of the Goldstein-Werner criticisms does allow for the clarification of certain issues. It is clear that all investigators agree that the greater the degree of differentiation (i.e., mental capacity or MA of the individual) the lower will be the incidence of rigid behaviors manifested across tasks. There is thus no argument that the mentally retarded child will emit more rigid behaviors than a nonretarded child of the same CA. The issue, stated in its simplest form, is that, with the degree of differentiation (i.e., MA, held constant), a difference in the incidence of rigid behaviors will be found between nonretarded and familial retarded individuals.

It is also clear that Lewin and Kounin felt that their formulation applied only to familial retarded individuals. It therefore becomes difficult to evaluate the pertinence of studies (see Chapter 17) that investigate the relative flexibility of retarded individuals without considering the etiological variable. It would appear that much work must be done before the Lewin-Kounin formulation can be extended to the organically retarded.

This review of the work of the early rigidity theorists reveals an awareness that motivational factors (e.g., fear of failure, comfort in the experimental situation) can lead to behaviors labeled "rigid." Thus, we find in the work of Lewin, Goldstein, Werner, and especially Kounin the seeds of the position that, with MA controlled, it is motivational factors rather than inherent rigidity that result in the greater incidence of rigid behaviors in retarded individuals. This motivational position was the original impetus to much of the work discussed in Chapter 4 and is discussed in the context of the rigidity position in the final section of this chapter.

EMPIRICAL TESTS OF THE LEWIN-KOUNIN FORMULATION

In Kounin's work, MA was employed as a general measure of the individual's cognitive differentiation. However, even though equated on this measure, Kounin's three groups differed on several tasks. Thus, within the Lewin-Kounin position, MA is viewed as an adequate referent of one important developmental dimension (i.e., differentiation) but is not seen as a very good predictor of tasks sensitive to cognitive rigidity, defined in terms of the permeability in boundaries between cognitive regions. The very procedure by which an MA score is obtained makes the Lewin-Kounin view of the MA a perfectly reasonable one. An individual's overall MA is obtained by employing a heterogeneous collection of test items and summing across those items that the individual passes. Thus, two individuals may obtain identical MAs, although one has succeeded at certain items, and the other person has succeeded at different items. The Lewin-Kounin formulation would, therefore, lead us to expect that retarded and nonretarded individuals having the same MA will pass different items on the intelligence test, with the retarded doing expecially poorly on those test items sensitive to cognitive rigidity.

An empirical test of this expectation was conducted by Thompson and Magaret (1947). These investigators examined the Stanford-Binet test performance of nonretarded and retarded individuals equated on MA. Consistent with the Lewin-Kounin expectation, they found that the nonretarded did significantly better on a number of the subtests than did the retarded, whereas the retarded did significantly better on a number of the other subtests than did the nonretarded. However, Achenbach (1969) found that retarded and nonretarded individuals of the same MA did not differ on nearly as many Stanford-Binet subtests as reported by Thompson and Magaret. Most relevant to the Lewin-Kounin expectation is not that retarded and nonretarded individuals of the same MA differ, but that the retarded would be inferior on those subtests sensitive to cognitive rigidity. Thompson and Magaret tested this specific prediction by having two judges well versed in the Lewin-Kounin formulation (Jacob Kounin and Roger Barker) rate the items for their sensitivity to cognitive rigidity. No support for the prediction was obtained inasmuch as the rigidity ratings of those items on which the nonretarded excelled were strikingly similar to the ratings for those items on which the retarded excelled.

Viewed historically, the negative findings of Thompson and Magaret do not appear to have unduly impeded the popularity of the Lewin-Kounin rigidity formulation. It was shortly after the report of the Thompson and Magaret findings that Kounin and Werner engaged in the controversy reported in the previous section. There can be little question that Kounin got the better of this particular exchange of theoretical papers. One is tempted to conclude that by simply pointing out the error in Werner's view of the Lewin-Kounin formulation, Kounin further convinced workers of the validity of this particular formulation. In any case, almost a decade passed before the rigidity hypothesis was subjected to another rigorous empirical test.

This test was conducted by Plenderleith (1956), and her findings contradicted the Lewin-Kounin formulation. In her experiment, subjects were required to learn to choose one of two stimuli. After this discrimination was learned, the stimuli were reversed and the subjects were required to shift their response to the previously incorrect stimulus. Contrary to the predictions derived from the Lewin-Kounin formulation, the retarded children did not differ from the nonretarded children in learning the discrimination nor in reversal trials that were given after 24 hours.

Stevenson and Zigler (1957) conducted a study that was similar to Plenderleith's, in that it was also designed to test the validity of the Lewin-Kounin theory of rigidity, and in that it also investigated the ability of nonretarded and retarded subjects to acquire one response and then to switch to a new response in a discrimination and reversal learning situation. Moving from Kounin's postulate that the boundaries within the life space are more rigid in the retarded than in the nonretarded, they (Stevenson & Zigler, 1957) hypothesized: "that the solution of a reversal problem would require movement to a new region of the life space and that such movement would be more difficult for the feebleminded subject because of the more rigid boundaries separating the regions of the life space [699]." As to the actual rigid behavior resulting from such rigidity in a reversal problem, Stevenson and Zigler chose as their measure the relative incidence of perseverative responses, in which the subject continues during the solution of the second problem to make the response that was previously correct but is no longer appropriate. It would appear that such a perseverative response following the switch is the most direct evidence that the subject has remained in a prior region and has not moved to a new region.

Three groups of subjects were used: an older retarded group, a younger retarded group, and a group of nonretarded children, of equivalent MA. The results indicated a striking equivalence in performance among the three groups. They did not significantly differ on the number of trials required to learn the initial discrimination problem, the number of correct choices on the reversal problem, the number of subjects in each group who learned the reversal problem, or on the direct measure of rigidity employed—the frequency with which subjects of each group made the response on the reversal problem that had been correct for them on the initial discrimination problem.

Although the switching problem employed by Stevenson and Zigler was more difficult than Plenderleith's reversal problems, the possibility still remained that the switching problem they employed was too easy to allow differences among the groups to become manifest. In order to investigate this possibility, Stevenson and Zigler conducted a second experiment, designed to investigate the performance of nonretarded and retarded individuals on a more difficult reversal problem than that employed in their first experiment. On the basis of the findings of the first experiment, Stevenson and Zigler rejected the Lewin–Kounin hypothesis, assuming instead the hypothesis that rigidity is a general behavior mechanism, from which it may be deduced that the frequency with which rigid behaviors are shown is a function of the complexity of the problem. Stevenson and Zigler then predicted that the frequency of rigid responses (perseverations) would be greater for both the nonretarded and retarded groups in the second experiment than in the first experiment, but that there would be no differences between the groups in the number of such responses. All predictions made for the second experiment were confirmed.

The reversal learning tasks employed by Plenderleith (1956) and Stevenson and Zigler (1957) have become relevant for theories concerning mental retardation other than that proposed by Lewin and Kounin. O'Connor and Hermelin (1959), employing Luria's (1961) formulation that the retarded suffer from a dissociation between the motor and verbal systems, generated and confirmed the prediction that nonretarded individuals would have greater difficulty on a discrimination reversal learning task than would retarded children (see Chapter 7 for a more complete discussion of this issue). This prediction is antithetical to that derivable from the Lewin–Kounin formulation. Balla and Zigler (1964), in an effort to resolve contradictory findings of earlier studies, failed to replicate the O'Connor and Hermelin findings, finding instead a general similarity between the performance of nonretarded and retarded children of the same MA. The findings of Balla and Zigler were, thus, generally consistent with those reported by Plenderleith and Stevenson and Zigler. A number of other studies involving comparisons of nonretarded and retarded subjects on discrimination reversal learning tasks have now been conducted and these studies have been reviewed by Wolff (1967). The findings of these studies led Wolff to conclude that, with MA held constant, there is no consistent evidence indicating that performance on reversal learning tasks is related to IQ. This failure to find consistent differences between nonretarded and retarded individuals of the same MA thus calls into question the Lewin–Kounin rigidity formulation.

In spite of the failure to find consistent support for the Lewin–Kounin formulation in a number of early studies employing a variety of tasks, the type of difference in perseverative behavior between the nonretarded and the retarded that is in keeping with the general views of Lewin and Kounin has been reported. Thus, Kaufman and Peterson (1958) found that retarded, as compared to nonretarded, children made a significantly greater number of stimulus-perseveration errors on a learning set task, leading these investigators to conclude that stimulus perseveration was a characteristic of the learning approach of retarded, but not of nonretarded, children. Greater perseveration by retarded than by nonretarded children was found by Siegel and Foshee (1960) on a task quite different from that employed by Kaufman and Peterson. These investigators presented nonretarded and retarded children with a task in which pushing any one of a number of buttons could turn on a light. The nonretarded children displayed much greater variability in their selection of buttons than did the retarded children. Perseveration by the retarded of a somewhat different sort was also found by Terdal (1967). This investigator compared the performance of nonretarded and retarded children when confronted with the task of attending to designs projected alternately on the left and the right of the subject. The results indicated that, compared with nonretarded, retarded subjects showed marked position (spatial) preferences. Greater perseveration in retarded than in nonretarded children was also found by Penney, Croskery, and Allen (1962) on a habit-reversal task, leading these investigators to conclude that the retarded were more rigid than the nonretarded. Greater perseveration of habit in retarded than in nonretarded children in drawing tasks was found by Carkhuff (1962, 1966).

An interesting study specifically designed to test the Lewin–Kounin formulation was that conducted by Kern (1967). In this study, nonretarded and retarded children were required to perform three sorting tasks: sorting first by shape, then by color, and, finally, by color and shape. The children did not have to generate the sorting concept but merely had to comply with the instructions to sort in a particular way. Thus, Kern's series of sorting tasks was a parallel to Kounin's lever-pressing task. The Lewin–Kounin formulation would generate the prediction that the nonretarded as compared to the retarded children would make more errors on second and third sorting tasks due to the greater negative transfer. The degree of negative transfer was found to be related to the MAs of both the nonretarded and retarded children, but not to the IQs of the two groups. The performance of the nonretarded and retarded children was found to be quite comparable, and, thus, Kern's study provides no support for the Lewin–Kounin formulation. Another explicit test of the rigidity hypothesis was conducted by Corter and McKinney (1968), who compared the performance of nonretarded and retarded children on five tests of cognitive flexibility. The findings of this study did lend some support to the Lewin–Kounin rigidity hypothesis. Nonretarded children were found to be superior to retarded children on an object-sorting test reminiscent of the concept-shifting task employed by Kounin. However, the support for the Lewin–Kounin formulation provided by the Corter-

McKinney study must be considered equivocal in that no significant differences between nonretarded and retarded subjects were found on any one of the other four cognitive flexibility tasks.

A sorting task similar to that used by Kounin and Corter and McKinney was employed by Backer (1966). Becker employed five card-sorting tasks and analyzed the performance of nonretarded and retarded subjects on these tasks several ways. His overall findings were rather complex. Although there were certain findings consistent with the Lewin-Kounin rigidity formulation, the bulk of Backer's findings were not consistent with the rigidity hypothesis and led Backer to conclude that the inherent rigidity position was not capable of encompassing the complex findings revealed in his study.

In an effort to directly investigate the replicability of Kounin's original findings, Zigler and Butterfield (1966) compared the performance of younger and older retarded individuals in two institutions and a group of noninstitutionalized nonretarded individuals (all groups equated on MA) on three of Kounin's tasks, the cosatiation drawing task, the lever-pressing transfer-of-habit task, and the card-sorting task involving the switching of concepts. The general findings of this study were not consistent with those reported by Kounin. On the drawing task, the one significant finding obtained was in a direction opposite to that reported by Kounin. On the lever-pressing task, no significant differences were found between the groups. There was a trend of borderline significance indicating that the older retarded made more errors than the younger retarded. This trend was in opposition to the rigidity formulation and to the findings of Kounin. On the concept-switching task, the young retarded did not differ significantly from the nonretarded. The one result of the Zigler and Butterfield study consistent with the rigidity formulation was the finding that the older retarded had more trouble switching concepts than did the other groups. In view of the tendency of the older retarded to manifest the least rigidity on the transfer-of-habit task, it is difficult to interpret their performance on the concept-switching task as clearly indicating greater rigidity. Making any straightforward interpretation of the concept-switching findings even more difficult was Zigler and Butterfield's discovery, that the retarded residing in the instiution with a poor social climate did better on the concept-switching task than did the retarded residing in the institution having a better social climate.

THE MOTIVATIONAL ALTERNATIVE
TO THE RIGIDITY FORMULATION

The great majority of the research relevant to motivational factors in retarded behavior has been reviewed in Chapter 4. In this section, we discuss some early studies that indicated that rigid behaviors exhibited by retarded persons can often be attributed to motivational differences between retarded and nonretarded individuals of the same MA rather than to differences in cognitive rigidity.

As noted earlier, Stevenson and Zigler (1957) obtained findings inconsistent with those of Kounin. In an effort to reconcile these disparate findings, Stevenson and Zigler directed their thinking at the differences in tasks employed across the two sets of experiments and, probably more importantly, the characteristics of the subjects, over and above their formal cognitive characteristics, which could have influenced their performance. In respect to the retarded groups, their most obvious characteristic was that they were residing in institutions. Thus, Stevenson and Zigler hypothesized that the performance of such subjects on tasks like those employed by Kounin could, at least in part, be attributed to the social deprivation experienced by institutionalized subjects. Stevenson and Zigler noted that, in their experiments, the subjects were required to learn two successive discriminations in which there was minimal interaction with the experimenter, whereas in Kounin's task, the response had been made primarily on the basis of instructions. Thus, differences in rigid behaviors between normal and retarded individuals of the same MA in the instruction-initiated tasks may be related to differences in the subjects' motivation to comply with instruction and interact with supportive adults rather than to differences in rigidity.

The first test of this motivational hypothesis was contained in a study of Zigler, Hodgden, and Stevenson (1958). In an effort to employ tasks comparable to Kounin's instruction-initiated satiation task, they constructed three simple motor tasks, each having two parts and each allowing the experimenter to secure a satiation, cosatiation, and error score. The study deviated from Kounin's procedure in that two conditions of reinforcement were used. In one, the experimenter maintained a nonsupportive role and did not reinforce the subject's performance; in the second, the experimenter made positive comments and in general reinforced the subject's performance.

Two specific hypotheses were advanced: (1) support has a reinforcing effect that results in an increment in performance over that found in nonsupport conditions; and (2) interaction with an adult and adult approval provide a greater reinforcement for the responses of institutionalized retarded subjects than they do for those of normal subjects. Two retarded groups (a support and a nonsupport) equated on CA and two normal groups (a support and a nonsupport) equated on CA were employed. All four groups were equated on MA. Six predictions were derived from the two hypotheses. Five of the six predictions were fully or partially confirmed.

It was found that:

1. Retarded subjects spent a significantly greater amount of time playing the games under the support than under the nonsupport condition, whereas nonretarded subjects did not.

2. Retarded subjects spent more time on the games than the nonretarded subjects in both reinforcement conditions.

3. There was a significantly greater difference in length of performance between support and nonsupport conditions for the retarded than for the nonretarded subjects.

4. There was little difference in the cosatiation scores for nonretarded subjects between support and nonsupport conditions. However, for retarded subjects, support not only resulted in lower cosatiation scores but in scores that were negative in value (the subject played longer on part 2 of the game than on part 1).

5. Cosatiation effects were generally less for retarded than for nonretarded subjects under both conditions of support and nonsupport.

The marked sensitivity of the retarded as compared to the nonretarded to variations in the degree of social reinforcement, as well as the marked shift by the retarded from one social reinforcement condition to another in behavioral indices thought by Kounin to reflect cognitive rigidity, lent a certain amount of support to the social-deprivation hypothesis. However, the findings of the study by Hodgden, Zigler and Stevenson were not of the sort that would lead one to abandon totally the Lewin–Kounin inherent rigidity formulation. In fact, certain of the Zigler, Hodgden, and Stevenson findings were reminiscent to those found by Kounin. Consistent with Kounin's results, they found that, regardless of social reinforcement condition, their retarded subjects performed an inordinately long time on relatively boring and monotonous tasks. As Kounin surprisingly found with his older group of retarded, they found that their retarded subjects in the support condition played the second part of a two-part cosatiation task longer than they did the first part, even though both parts of the task were extremely similar. In light of this, the Zigler, Hodgden, and Stevenson findings hardly constitute any death blow to the Lewin–Kounin rigidity formulation. At most, these findings indicate that the production of phenotypically rigid behaviors is also influenced by motivational effects, a view not very much at variance with Lewin and Kounin's own stance concerning motivational factors. At this point, what appeared to be in order was a more convincing test of the view that the Lewin–Kounin rigidity formulation lent little to the understanding of the grossly observable high incidence of rigid behaviors emitted by the retarded.

In what was hoped to be a more definitive test of the view that the rigid behaviors emitted by the retarded were a result of the social deprivation they had experienced rather than a product of any inherent cognitive rigidity, Zigler (1958, 1961) did a study in which it was hypothesized that, within an institutionalized retarded population, a relationship should exist between the degree of deprivation experienced and the amount of rigidity manifested. The specific hypothesis tested was the following: The greater the amount of preinstitutional social deprivation experienced by the retarded child, the greater will be his motivation to interact with an adult, making such interaction and any adult approval or support that accompanies it more reinforcing for his responses than for the responses of a retarded child who has experienced a lesser amount of social deprivation.

On the basis of preinstitutional social deprivation ratings (described in Chapter 4), retarded children were divided into two groups. The groups did not differ significantly on either MA, CA, or length of institutionalization. The study employed a social reinforcement to those used in earlier studies. The majority of the predictions derived from the hypothesis were confirmed. The more socially deprived subjects: (1) spent a greater amount of time on the game; (2) more frequently made the maximum number of responses allowed by the game; and (3) evidenced a greater increase in time spent on part 2 over that spent on part 1 of the game.

Results consistent with these were obtained by Zigler, Balla, and Butterfield (1968). These findings would appear to call into question the Lewin–Kounin rigidity formulation, because it is difficult to derive from this formulation an explanation of differences in rigid behaviors between groups of retarded children equated on both CA and MA. The findings offered further support for the view that the rigid behavior observed in retarded individuals is a product of higher motivation to maintain interaction with an adult and to secure approval from him through compliance and persistence. These results also offered evidence that the institutionalized retarded subjects' higher motivation to interact with an adult is related to the greater preinstitutional social deprivation such subjects have experienced. Furthermore, individual differences among the retarded in persistent and/or compliant behavior can be related to differences in the amount of social deprivation experienced.

Another test of the view that the incidence of rigid behaviors is a function of the greater social deprivation experienced by the institutionalized retarded child rather than a function of his inherent rigidity was carried out by Green and Zigler (1962). The investigators used three groups of subjects: institutionalized retarded, noninstitutionalized retarded, and nonretarded individuals. It was assumed that the noninstitutionalized retarded child has suffered less social deprivation than the institutionalized retarded child. All three groups were equated on MA, and the two retarded groups were also equated on CA. As in the earlier studies, only familial retarded children were employed. Again, a two-part satiation-type task was used.

The Lewin–Kounin rigidity formulation would generate the prediction that the performance of the two retarded groups would be similar and that their performance would differ from that of the nonretarded group. The social-deprivation hypothesis would generate the prediction that the performance of the nonretarded and the noninstitutionalized retarded would be similar and that their performance would differ from that of the institutionalized retarded. The latter hypothesis was supported with no significant differences in performance found between the noninstitutionalized retarded and the nonretarded. Both of these groups differed significantly from the institutionalized retarded. Again, it was the institutionalized retarded who showed the relatively long satiation times, a perseverative behavior that has been employed as evidence for the inherent rigidity of the retarded.

Zigler (1963) conducted a further test of the view that perseveration on an open-ended satiation-type task is a result of an enhanced effectiveness of social reinforcers stemming from the greater social deprivation experienced rather than a product of an inherent cognitive rigidity. This study differed from that conducted by Green and Zigler primarily in that it included a group of institutionalized nonretarded children. In this study, institutionalized children of both nonretarded and retarded intellect were found to play a socially reinforced satiation-type task longer than did groups of noninstitutionalized nonretarded and retarded of the same MA. This greater effectiveness of social reinforcement for both institutionalized nonretarded and retarded children as compared with noninstitutionalized nonretarded and retarded children has also been found by Stevenson and Fahel (1961).

The studies outlined previously indicate that certain behaviors of institutionalized retarded persons that have been attributed to their inherent rigidity can more parsimoniously be viewed as a product of the greater social deprivation experienced by the institutionalized retarded child.

CONTEMPORARY VARIANTS OF THE RIGIDITY POSITION

Although, as aforementioned, the rigidity position is often seen as little more than an historical relic, the view that retarded individuals are less flexible in their approaches to problem solving than nonretarded individuals has recurred to the present day. In discussing the current variants of the rigidity position, though, it is important to note one factor. It might be argued that Lewin and Kounin emphasized structural aspects of the cognitive system, whereas more contemporary views tend to emphasize process or "control" aspects (Sternberg, in press). Although a comprehensive discussion of the distinction between structural and process features of the cognitive system is beyond the scope of this chapter, it is our view that both aspects are implicitly included in the Lewin–Kounin position.

Brown and her colleagues (Brown, 1973, 1974, 1978; Campione & Brown, 1977) have done a series of investigations on short-term memory functioning in retarded individuals. They have attempted to provide some evidence of a trained strategy in retarded persons that shows some transfer or generalization. Brown (1974) has been extremely explicit in the specification of the steps necessary to demonstrate the generalization of training: task analysis; the need to test for the spontaneous use of the necessary strategies for performing the task; the need to demonstrate that retarded persons can maintain the acquired strategy over time; and finally that retarded persons show transfer of the strategy to a variety of tasks. From her own research and her review of the American and Soviet literature she (Brown, 1974) reached a conclusion remarkably close to that of Lewin and Kounin:

> so far, the prognosis for training a generalized skill in retarded children is not optimistic as there is little evidence in the literature to date of generalization of an

acquired strategy. Indeed, both American and Soviet investigators have suggested that one of the main difficulties in training mildly retarded children is that they tend to acquire information which is "welded" to the form in which it was acquired (Shif, 1969, p. 347), thus depriving them of an indispensable flexibility [p. 102].

Budoff and his colleagues (Budoff, 1968; Budoff & Pagell, 1968) have presented still another variant of the rigidity position. They noted considerable heterogenity of ability to learn and to reason when instructed as to how to solve a series on nonverbal reasoning problems (Koh's Blocks). Budoff speculated that those individuals who could profit from the instructional procedure may well be suffering from the inhibiting motivational factors discussed earlier and in Chapter 4, whereas those who could not were excessively rigid. However, the design of Budoff's study did not permit the discovery that nonretarded individuals may also show considerable heterogeneity in reasoning, when instructed as to how to solve a series of nonverbal reasoning problems; that is to say "rigidity" may be a characteristic of some nonretarded, as well as some retarded individuals. In our laboratory we conducted a study in which we attempted to separate instructional and motivational components of capacity to improve on the Koh's Blocks task employed by Budoff. We were especially interested in determining whether similar proportions of retarded and nonretarded children would not profit from instruction, thereby showing the same rigidity. One group each of retarded and nonretarded children were initially tested, given the instructional procedure as described by Budoff, and retested. Additional groups of retarded and nonretarded children were tested, then retested in an extremely supportive situation where a high level of success was assured. Additional groups were simply tested and retested. We found that essentially the same proportion of nonretarded as retarded children failed to change in their performance. Further, it was found that gains made by both nonretarded and retarded children were as striking in the motivational condition as in the instructional condition.

Using a research strategy highly similar to that of Budoff and his colleagues, Field (1974, 1975, 1977a, b) has attempted to train familial retarded and nonretarded children in Piagetian conservation tasks. Essentially, a pretest, training, posttest, and delayed posttest design was used. In the pretest, all children were assessed for conservation of number, length, mass, liquid, and weight. Naturally, conserving children were identified and eliminated from the training procedure. Children were then given three training sessions in the conservation of number and length. At these training sessions, all children were given a total of about 1½ hours of individual attention, tangible and intangible reinforcement, and verbal instruction in conservation rules. At both initial and delayed posttest, the children were assessed for conservation of number, length, mass, liquid, and weight, thus making it possible to test for generalization of training. Control groups where no training was given were also employed. All groups were matched on MA and gender.

Reminiscent of our own findings discussed previously, the proportions of children in the retarded and nonretarded groups who profited from conservation training did not differ. Perhaps more relevant to the rigidity position, in whatever form it takes, were the findings that the retarded and nonretarded groups did not differ in the extent to which they generalized their conservation mastery to quantities that were not trained, even though none of the children were conservers at the start of the training. The retarded and nonretarded groups were also highly similar at the delayed posttest, given after 2½ to 16 months, maintaining their conservation mastery. The groups that received training also were superior in conservation performance to the control groups both at posttest and delayed posttest.

REFERENCES

Achenbach, T. M. Cue learning, associative responding, and school performance in children. *Developmental Psychology,* 1969, *1,* 717-725.

Backer, M. H. An experimental investigation of the motivational hypothesis of rigidity in retardates: A comparison of retarded and normal performance on a series of card-sorting tasks. *Dissertation Abstracts,* 1966, *26,* 4068-4069.

Balla, D., & Zigler, E. Discrimination and switching learning in normal, familial retarded, and organic retarded children. *Journal of Abnormal Social Psychology,* 1964, *69,* 664-669.

Brown, A. L. Conservation of number and continuous quantity in normal, bright, and retarded children. *Child Development,* 1973, *44,* 376-379.

Brown, A. L. The role of strategic behavior in retardate memory. In N. R. Ellis (Ed.), *International review of research in mental retardation* (Vol. 1). New York: Academic Press, 1974.

Brown, A. L. Knowing when, where, and how to remember: A problem of metacognition. In R. Glaser (Ed.), *Advances in instructional psychology* (Vol. 1). Hillsdale, N. J.: Lawrence Erlbaum Associates, 1978.

Budoff, M. Learning potential as a supplementary strategy to psychometric diagnosis. In J. Hellmuth (Ed.), *Learning Disorders* (Vol. 3). Seattle: Special Child Publications, 1965.

Budoff, M., & Pagell, W. Learning potential and rigidity in the adolescent mentally retarded. *Journal of Abnormal Psychology,* 1968, *73,* 479-486.

Campione, J. C., & Brown, A. L. Memory and metamemory development in educable retarded children. In R. V. Kail, Jr. & J. W. Hagen (Eds.), *Perspectives on the development of memory and cognition.* Hillsdale, N. J.: Lawrence Erlbaum Associates, 1977.

Carkhuff, R. R. Perseveration of habit in drawing tasks as a characteristic distinguishing mental defectives from normals. *Journal of Clinical Psychology,* 1962, *18,* 413-415.

Carkhuff, R. R. Variations in performance of noninstitutionalized retardates. *Journal of Clinical Psychology,* 1966, *22,* 168-170.

Corter, H. M., & McKinney, J. D. Flexibility training with educable retarded and bright normal children. *American Journal of Mental Deficiency,* 1968, *72,* 603-609.

Field, D. Long-term effects of conservation training with educationally subnormal children. *Journal of Special Education,* 1974, *8,* 237-245.

Field, D. *Studies in conservation training with retarded and normal school-children.* Unpublished doctoral dissertation, University of London, 1975.

Field, D. How children in educationally subnormal schools in London learn conservation skills. In *Proceedings of the seventh annual interdisciplinary conference on Piagetian theory and its implications for the helping professions.* Los Angeles: University of Southern Calif., 1977. (a)

Field, D. The importance of the verbal content in the training of Piagetian conservation skills. *Child Development*, 1977, *48*, 1583-1592. (b)
Goldstein, K. Concerning rigidity. *Character and Personality*, 1942-1943, *11*, 209-226.
Green, C., & Zigler, E. Social deprivation and the performance of retarded and normal children on a satiation type task. *Child Development*, 1962, *33*, 499-508.
Kaufman, M. E., & Peterson, W. M. Acquisition of a learning set by normal and mentally retarded children. *Journal of Comparative and Physiological Psychology*, 1958, *51*, 619-621.
Kern, W. H. Negative transfer on sorting tasks, MA, and IQ in normal and retarded children. *American Journal of Mental Deficiency*, 1967, *72*, 416-421.
Kounin, J. S. *Experimental studies of rigidity as a function of age and feeblemindedness.* Unpublished doctoral dissertation, State University of Iowa, 1939.
Kounin, J. Experimental studies of rigidity: I. The measurement of rigidity in normal and feebleminded persons. *Character and Personality*, 1941, *9*, 251-272. (a)
Kounin, J. Experimental studies of rigidity: II. The explanatory power of the concept of rigidity as applied to feeblemindedness. *Character and Personality*, 1941, *9*, 273-282. (b)
Kounin, J. The meaning of rigidity: A reply to Heinz Werner. *Psychological Review*, 1948, *55*, 157-166.
Lewin, K. *A dynamic theory of personality*. New York: McGraw-Hill, 1936.
Luria, A. R. Study of the abnormal child. *American Journal of Orthopsychiatry*, 1961, *31*, 1-16.
O'Connor, N., & Hermelin, B. Discrimination and reversal learning in imbeciles. *Journal of Abnormal and Social Psychology*, 159, *59*, 409-413.
Penney, R. K., Croskery, J., & Allen, G. Effects of training schedules on rigidity as manifested by normal and mentally retarded children. *Psychological Reports*, 1962, *10*, 243-249.
Plenderleith, M. Discrimination learning and discrimination reversal learning in normal and feebleminded children. *Journal of Genetic Psychology*, 1956, *88*, 107-112.
Sarason, S. B., & Gladwin, T. Psychological and cultural problems in mental subnormality: A review of research. *Genetic Psychology Monographs*, 1958, *57*, 3-290.
Shif, Z. I. Development of children in schools for the mentally retarded. In M. Cole & I. Maltzman (Eds.), *A handbook of contemporary Soviet psychology*. New York: Basic Books, 1969.
Siegel, P. S., & Foshee, J. G. Molar variability in the mentally defective. *Journal of Abnormal and Social Psychology*, 1960, *61*, 141-143.
Sternberg, R. J. Cognitive-behavioral approaches to the training of intelligence in the retarded. *Journal of Special Education*, in press.
Stevenson, H. W., & Fahel, L. S. The effect of social reinforcement on the performance of institutionalized normal and feebleminded children. *Journal of Personality*, 1961, *29*, 136-147.
Stevenson, H. W., & Zigler, E. Discrimination learning and rigidity in normal and feebleminded individuals. *Journal of Personality*, 1957, *25*, 699-711.
Terdal, L. G. Complexity and position of stimuli as determinants of looking behavior in retardates and normals. *American Journal of Mental Deficiency*, 1967, *72*, 384-387.
Thompson, C., & Magaret, A. Differential test responses of normal and mental defectives. *Journal of Abnormal and Social Psychology*, 1947, *42*, 285-293.
Werner, H. *Comparative psychology of mental development*. New York: Harper & Row, 1940.
Werner, H. *Comparative psychology of mental development*. New York: Follett, 1948.
Wolff, J. L. Concept shift and discrimination-reversal learning in humans. *Psychological Bulletin*, 1967, *68*, 369-408.
Zigler, E. *The effect of preinstitutional social deprivation on the performance of feebleminded children*. Unpublished doctoral dissertation, University of Texas, 1958.
Zigler, E. Social deprivation and rigidity in the performance of feebleminded children. *Journal of Abnormal and Social Psychology*, 1961, *62*, 413-421.
Zigler, E. Rigidity and social reinforcement effects in the performance of institutionalized and noninstitutionalized normal and retarded children. *Journal of Personality*, 1963, *31*, 258-269.

Zigler, E., Balla, D., & Butterfield, E. C. A longitudinal investigation of the relationship between preinstitutional social deprivation and social motivation in institutionalized retardates. *Journal of Personality and Social Psychology,* 1968, *10,* 437-445.

Zigler, E., & Butterfield, E. C. Rigidity in the retarded: A further test of the Lewin-Kounin formulation. *Journal of Abnormal Psychology,* 1966, *71,* 224-231.

Zigler, E., Hodgden, L., & Stevenson, H. The effect of support on the performance of normal and feebleminded children. *Journal of Personality,* 1958, *26,* 106-122.

6. Psychological Studies of Mental Deficiency in the Soviet Union*

A. R. Luria (*deceased*)

Dynamic Approach to the Mental Development of the Abnormal Child

Child psychiatry, just as the science that is engaged in the education of abnormal children, is now confronted with a fundamental task; it must learn to *qualify the basic defect* and still more to approximate to the analysis of *its underlying mechanisms*.

Any more or less marked advance in the accomplishment of this task will enable us to diagnose the defect with much greater exactitude, to discern between externally similar but in essence profoundly different states, to place the therapy of these diseases on a scientific basis, and finally to find proper methods and ways for corrective training and education of abnormal children.

There is no doubt that child psychiatry, like special pedagogics dealing with abnormal children, both being very young branches of science, has attained notable successes during the last decades.

Considerable headway has been made in the clinical description of certain forms of anomalous development; one of the indisputable achievements of modern psychiatry is its special study of such forms as primary mental deficiency, anomalies in development resulting from traumas, inflammatory processes, or other retarding factors, as well as anomalies connected with partial defects (local lesions of the brain). Another achievement is the now widespread description of cases of anomalous mental development connected with reactions

---

*This article first appeared in *Journal of Mental Deficiency Research*, Volume 2, Part 2, December, 1958.

of the child to complex life situations; the valuable contribution to the study of this problem made by a number of scientists engaged in dynamic psychology and psychosomatics is beyond doubt.

However, it is quite clear that many fundamental problems of child psychiatry still remain unsolved, and that the future decisive successes of this young branch of science will be connected with the analysis of *the causes that are responsible for the emergence of this or another form of anomalous development, as well as with the study of the underlying initial defect.*

There is no need to trace here the entire intricate course of anomalous development formed under the influence of mental conflicts and difficult situations (in recent years these facts have already been repeatedly discussed in European and American literature); here, we dwell on the analysis of *some forms of anomalous development arising as a result of organic disturbances in the activity of the central or peripheral nervous apparatus.* In this field Soviet researchers (physicians and psychologists) have applied some special methods and attained certain results, which clarify the nature of anomalous development and its neurophysiological mechanisms.

In the present communication, we dwell on two fundamental problems. We try first to show the extensive systematic consequences that may be called forth by particular defects arising at early stages of the child's development; then, we try to show that the study of the neurodynamic mechanisms that characterize various forms of anomalous development may furnish essential material to the researcher.

In the theory of the abnormal child there often still persist erroneous conceptions that lag far behind the level of modern scientific knowledge and greatly hamper the practical work of educating abnormal children. These conceptions consist in a naive, extremely simplified *symptomatic approach* to the defect exhibited by the child; they disregard the complexity of the child's mental development and stop the genuinely scientific analysis of the symptoms just when such analysis should be started; this often leads to errors that impede the proper comprehension of the causes of anomalous development and do not allow us to find adequate ways for its correction.

The narrow-mindedness of the naive symptomatic approach is equally manifested in the analysis of general disturbances observed in the child's development and in the interpretation of its particular defects.

When describing backward schoolchildren or children with considerably retarded mental development, many psychologists and teachers up to now have drawn the flat conclusion that such cases of subnormal development, or "dullness," are always accounted for by inborn mental deficiency, often by a hereditary deterioration of "mental abilities," and that the derangement of "general ability" (in the terminology of the British authors), which is observed in these cases, is of a primary and irreversible character. On the other hand, when describing particular defects often observed in children, such as derangements in writing, reading, and arithmetical operations, or defects in the child's character, psychologists and psychiatrists not infrequently confine themselves to the statement that these defects are due to the underdevelopment of "special abilities" and refer to such phenomena of particular disturbances as *dyslexia* and *dysgraphia* but do not attempt to disclose the very essence of these disturbances and to trace the considerably more extensive consequences that they may entail.

This naive symptomatic approach, which is, unfortunately, not uncommon in the analysis of the abnormal child, lags far behind both the conceptions of modern psychology and the views firmly established in the neurological and psychiatric clinic.

Already more than a quarter of a century ago, the outstanding Russian psychologist, L. S. Vygotsky, expressed the idea that the principal mental functions, such as complex perception or intelligent memorization, voluntary attention or logical thinking, do not represent inborn properties of personality. By a series of important observations and experiments, subsequently carried on by his collaborators and pupils, he showed that all these complex processes are formed in the course of the child's development, and that they are accounted for by the methods and means of organization of activity that arise and are adopted by the child in the course of its manipulations with real objects and in its intercourse with adults, rather than by inborn capacities (that are, of course, of great importance as well).

The mother shows the child a cup and pointing to it says: "This is a cup." With the help of this gesture and these words she singles out the given object from other objects, renders this stimulus more powerful and essential, and attaches to it, according to our terminology, a new "signaling sense." Then the child begins to reproduce the mother's gesture and to repeat the same word; thus, it organizes its own perception. Such perceptive processes are formed in the child in a social way: Intelligent perception and voluntary attention result from the intercourse of the child; the function that was previously divided between two persons gradually turns into an internal psychological method of organization of the child's own activity.

Subsequent investigations carried out by A. N. Leontiev, A. V. Zaporozhetz, and P. Y. Galperin, of Moscow University, show that other mental processes, like active memorization, voluntary action, and abstract thinking, are formed in a similar way.

What for many decades have been regarded as inborn properties of the human mind, or as inborn "abilities," actually pass through a long process of formation. As shown by the aforementioned investigations, such faculties as active memorization or logical thinking are derived from the extensive material activity that is adopted by the child in the process of its intercourse; later, this activity gradually diminishes, becomes curtailed, relies more and more on external and internal speech, and finally turns into these mental functions that seem so simple but, in reality, have their own long and intricate story of development.

Also similar is the course of development of those faculties that were usually considered manifestations of inborn "special gifts," such as a good ear for music. *What were erroneously regarded in psychology as inborn and elementary "properties" of the mind actually represent complex functional systems* formed during the long process of the child's development; therefore, we should commit a great mistake if we overlooked this; if we naively assumed that active attention and insight are inborn properties of the child's mind that can be interpreted as direct manifestations of natural general ability.

There is no doubt that many natural inclinations constitute a very important prerequisite for the development of these complex systemic functions, and when they become deranged, the entire further development of the child assumes an abnormal character. However, it would be the height of carelessness to ignore this entire course of development, to disregard the highly complicated methods and means with the help of which the child, during its intercourse with adults, forms its complex system of functions, and to interpret any retardation of mental development or any defects in behavior as a direct manifestation of innate dullness, or of an inborn deficiency of abstract thinking. Such assertions would hardly differ much from the judgments of Moliere's physician, who felt that the soporific action of opium was a result of its inherent "soporific force" and explained derangements in speech by saying that the patient's tongue did not move properly.

It is quite natural that this concept of the nature of complex mental abilities, regarded by us as a result of intricate development, impels us radically to change our attitude toward anomalous development in children and toward the tasks that confront us in the diagnosis of children with these or other forms of mental anomalies.

The peculiar features of abnormal children are no longer interpreted as direct manifestations of some general deficiency; they are regarded as a result of complex and anomalous development, accounted for by the fact that a definite link indispensable to the normal development of mental activity becomes deranged, owing to an early (more often intrauterine) disease and sometimes to an inborn defect. This deranged or defective link that is responsible for the anomalous development of the child may relate to various stages of its formation and be highly diverse in nature. In some cases it is the elementary nervous processes that constitute this defective link; the disorganization of the force, equilibrium, and mobility of these nervous processes may from the very onset greatly impede the further development of the activity of the child. In other cases this defective link, hindering the further mental development of the child, is formed by a certain defect in a particular mental function, for example, in the visual or auditory analysis of the signals perceived; in these cases a particular defect may entail considerable systemic consequences and markedly retard the general mental development of the child. Finally, in still other cases a retardation of the development of cognitive processes and of the higher psychological systems may be caused by defects in the intercourse of the child with adults, as well as by defects in training. Indeed, the formation of complex mental activity always requires strict consistency and a succession of individual operations; sometimes, if only a single link of training is missed, if a certain stage in the development of the necessary operation is not properly worked out, the entire process of further development becomes retarded, and the formation of higher mental functions assumes an abnormal character.

It is quite clear that such an approach to abnormal childhood complicates, and at the same time enriches, the course of clinical and psychophysiological analysis of the child. In the place of the naive symptomatological approach, which unjustifiably ascribes intellectual defects to the underdevelopment of certain "primary abilities," a new approach arises and takes definite shape; it consists in the qualification of symptoms, that is, in a more precise ascertainment of the structure of the defect under observation, and in the analysis of the various causes that are responsible for the retardation and distortion of the mental development of the child.

About 30 years ago, Kurt Goldstein expressed the idea that in any analysis of a syndrome it is, above all, necessary to disclose the *basic disturbance* that entails a number of *secondary symptoms* arising from it and that requires no special explanation. This proposition remains true also for the analysis of any abnormal child, being even more complicated on account of the systemic development of mental processes. Any researcher who does not confine his research to a mere ascertainment of the defect in the abnormal child must always attempt to reveal the basic, primary disturbance and deduce from it the secondary systemic consequences that, in the course of the mental development of the child, may assume quite an extensive character.

A researcher proceeding from such a causal-dynamic approach must be ready to face the fact that serious, sometimes fundamental, changes in development may be called forth by disturbances of very particular and seemingly insignificant functions, if these particular functions are of great importance for the further formation of the complex mental activity of the child. *The effect produced by an early disturbance of a certain function depends primarily on the role played by this function in the general mental development of the child, as well as on the period of development during which the given disturbance occurred.* Therefore, as stated by L. S. Vygotsky, one and the same localization of a lesion may evoke quite different consequences, depending on whether the lesion occurred in early childhood or at a mature age. In the first case, along with the derangement of a particular function (for example, hearing) there takes place a derangement of a whole system of functions created on its basis. In the second case, when the formation of all these complex processes has already been fully completed, this primary disturbance may remain a particular defect, which is more or less easily compensated by the already developed speech and intellect of the adult. In all cases, only such causal-dynamic analysis, which thoroughly considers the structure of the syndrome and discloses its basic source, can comply with the principal task—and overstep the limits of formal description of the defect to impart to the diagnostics of anomalous development a truly scientific character.

This genetic and systemic analysis of defects in abnormal children may contribute to the proper solution of the problem concerning the nature of the anomaly under observation and the correlation between particular and general disturbances; it may facilitate the highly complicated task of the differential diagnosis of various externally similar, but in essence profoundly different, disturbances. Finally, it may help the physician correctly to formulate the prognosis of the given disturbance and, what is most important, to find proper methods of therapy as well as appropriate corrective pedagogical methods, which prove to differ considerably, depending on the nature of the anomalous development of the child.

Thus, our task can be quite clearly formulated. When approximating to the clinical and psychophysiological analysis of the abnormal child, we must put before ourselves the following question: *What is the nature of the psychophysiological structure of the defect, and precisely what constitutes the basic (sometimes inconsiderable by itself) disturbance* arising even at the earliest stages of development? On the other hand, we must realize *how this disturbance influenced the further mental development of the child*, what its effect was on the formation of mental processes conditioned by it.

It is quite natural that the aforementioned task should render the clinical investigation of the abnormal child much more complicated; it requires decisive renunciation of the simplified descriptive symptomatological approach that disregards the many-sided development of the child; it presupposes the application of special, sometimes experimental, psychological and physiological methods of investigation, which disclose the nature of the basic defect and of its systemic consequences. But, will not this new approach be of benefit to the accomplishment of our principal humane task—to reveal the essence of anomalous development and to find adquate means of compensating the defect?

We begin our analysis of systemic anomalies of development with cases in which a relatively insignificant defect causes considerable changes in the entire mental development; only then, we pass to those various forms where the anomalous development of the child is due to causes that bear a more general character and require special physiological investigation.

Let us first dwell on *defective hearing*; owing to the frequency of this defect, the analysis of its influence on the general mental development of the child may present considerable interest.

Defective hearing, in its grave and mild forms, is well-known to otologists and teachers of ordinary schools; the specific nature of this defect is beyond any doubt.

However, two facts arrest our attention at once: they are connected with the peculiarities of general intellectual development as well as development of speech in children with defective hearing.

Statistical data collected by Sir Cyril Burt and relating to British children show that, whereas in ordinary schools the number of children with severe defects of hearing does not exceed 1% and the number of children with slight defects of hearing amounts to 4%, in schools for mentally backward children the respective figures are 6 and 18% (Burt, 1951). This means that almost one-quarter of all the children who cannot attend ordinary schools and are compelled to enter schools for backward children suffer from these or other defects of hearing.

The second fact relates to the development of speech in children with defective hearing. Experience shows that if this defect arises at a mature age, in practice it does not lead to any gross derangements of speech; but as shown by investigations carried out at the Moscow Institute of Defectology, even a relatively inconsiderable derangement of hearing, even a decline in its intensity by 20 to 25 decibels, if it occurs at a very early stage of development, is almost invariably accompanied by a serious defect of speech.

How should the two facts be interpreted? Do they mean that each of these phenomena has its own particular cause and that, whereas in the first group of children the defect of hearing is accompanied by organic mental deficiency, in the second group, along with the derangement of hearing, there are additional defects of speech of the aphasic or alalic type caused by the presence of a special local lesion in the cerebral cortex? If this supposition is correct, then it is quite reasonable that children of the first group should attend schools for the feeble-minded, and that children of the second group should be treated as those who suffer from residual phenomena of severe cerebral lesions.

However, such a conclusion, which is typical of the simplified symptomatological approach, is profoundly wrong.

Thorough observations carried out by a number of Soviet psychologists, physicians, and teachers (R. M. Boskis, T. A. Vlasova, L. V. Nieman, and others) have shown that derangements of speech and retardation of intellectual development in children suffering from defects of hearing since early childhood are *inevitable systemic consequences of the auditory defect* and need not be explained by any other additional causes.

It is a well-known fact that the development of speech, as well as of intellectual activity, takes place in the child in the process of its intercourse with the adult: the child first accumulates a rather extensive "passive" vocabulary and only then begins to speak, adjusting its speech to the system of phonemes and of their combinations adopted from the adult. Active articulations are formed by the child on the basis of differentiated perception of the speech of others or, using physiological terminology, are afferented by the child's auditory perception. A habitual conversation seldom proceeds at high intensities of sound; the intensity of sound is particularly low in the articulation of certain unaccented vowels, as well as suffixes and inflexions that are often pronounced very faintly or almost omitted.

In order to be able clearly to perceive oral speech and to form the necessary system of language, the child must, naturally, possess a keen, irreproachable ear. Therefore, a relatively slight deterioration of the sense of hearing, which in the adult is easily compensated by his guessing, owing to his good knowledge of the language, and which thus remains practically imperceptible, proves to be fatal to speech formation if it occurs in early childhood. In this case the child perceives only insufficiently differentiated sounds that do not group into distinct systems of phonemes; the child does not discern the phonetic cues (sometimes very delicate), which are of signaling importance; the words that the child does perceive prove to be greatly distorted and inarticulate; words having a like phonetic contour (for example, "whiskers" and "whispers") are mixed up; thus, the necessary system of language is not assimilated.

Early disturbances of hearing entail one more consequence: The deranged formation of a strictly differentiated phonemic system inevitably causes a retardation in the development of active articulated speech. Not being afferented by this distinct auditory system, the child's own speech may for a long time remain at the level of babbling, or it assumes an inarticulate character that is a natural consequence of the hearing defect, and the explanation of which should not be sought for in any additional local lesion affecting the speech areas of the cerebral cortex. In this case *a relatively inconsiderable, purely peripheral defect leads to extensive functional consequences.*

The secondary disturbance evoked by defective hearing is not confined to external defects of speech but manifests a number of additional symptoms.

A thorough study of the mental development of children with hearing defects has been carried out for a number of years in special schools created for such children in the Soviet Union. This study has shown that in the course of training a considerable majority of such children exhibit distinct phenomena of *agrammatism* and that special efforts are required to overcome it. For a considerable length of time these children confuse the case inflexions, omit the prefixes and suffixes, and reveal, in their speech, elements of the "telegraphic style" that is so familiar to researchers dealing with the clinic of motor aphasias.

However, it would be erroneous to ascribe such agrammatism of these children to any additional factors or, as was often the practice, to interpret these cases as a combined manifestation of hearing defects and motor (or sensory) aphasia. The impossibility of clearly discerning all the phonetic elements of speech, which particularly manifests itself in the impeded perception of indistinctly articulated suffixes and inflexions, hinders the mastery of the grammatical system of the language and at the same time makes it difficult to learn the abstract meanings expressed in the linguistic combinations of words. This is why a child with hearing defects for a long time exhibits phenomena of agrammatism and has great difficulties in mastering the categories of quality, number, tense, and passage of the action to an object, which in inflected languages (such as Russian and German) are expressed by special grammatical forms.

Thus, from a primary, limited defect, which, however, hampers the normal intercourse of the child and thereby retards its normal development, there arise distinct secondary consequences; as a result, a child suffering from an inconsiderable and purely peripheral defect begins to show a highly peculiar, anomalous development that leads both to a retardation of speech and to substantial disturbances in intellectual activity.

However, to confuse such a child with an aphasic or with a real feebleminded, oligophrenic child and to place it in a clinic or school for the feebleminded would be to commit a fatal mistake. Secondary defects arising in such a child prove to be quite surmountable, but this requires a number of specially organized measures. To eliminate the defect of the child it is not sufficient to seat the child in the front row of desks or to supply it with a sound-intensifying device; it is necessary to work out a special system of corrective training that must be based on conscious learning of those grammatical forms of the language that normal children have practically mastered before they enter school. Such systematic corrective influence on the secondary defects must have the attention of the teacher and physician; precisely, this sytem of corrective measures directed against the systemic consequences of the primary defect, rather than against the defect itself, can fully restore the normal thinking and speech of the child.

This is why special schools for children with defective hearing have been established in the Soviet Union; the system of training in these schools is aimed at conscious learning of the grammatical system of the language, as well as of the system of notions that is connected with it. And this is why the fundamental pedagogical principle—to act upon the systemic consequence produced by the primary defect rather than upon the defect itself (that yields to influences with difficulty)—proves its value in the practice of work with these children.

Up to now we have dealt with cases clearly showing that a relatively inconsiderable, particular defect may evoke essential changes in the general mental development of the child, which often gives grounds for erroneously regarding them as inborn deficiencies of mental development.

Now we should like to approach the same question from the opposite direction and to dwell on cases in which the causal-genetic analysis of mechanisms responsible for the given defect may help to explain the nature of the obscure defect and to determine proper methods for its compensation.

In school practice, children are frequently encountered who have keen vision and hearing and who make relatively good progress in other disciplines, but who exhibit great difficulties in mastering *writing* and *reading*. They make dozens of incomprehensible mistakes in dictation so that their writing is often deciphered with great difficulty. Usually, these children give no cause for regarding them as mentally backward, and teachers and psychologists used to refer to their difficulties as an underdevelopment of the special ability for writing and reading or to defects of a "special factor," which was designated by different letters (s, special, or p, partial) but whose nature remained to a considerable degree obscure.

However, these cases of dysgraphia or dyslexia prove to be particularly accessible to analysis if we interpret them as secondary, systemic disorders and are able to break them down into component elements so as to disclose the underlying primary defect; of great importance is the fact that if this is done these cases will likewise become accessible to corrective training.

What is, then, the cause of this disturbance that, at first sight, seems so astonishing? To answer this question it is necessary, first of all, to understand the psychophysiological structure of the process of writing (of reading) and to know precisely in which of its links this process may become deranged; otherwise, we shall be unable to analyze it and shall be compelled to explain the phenomena of dysgraphia and dyslexia in a tautological way, as the "underdevelopment of the ability for writing or reading."

In all languages having phonetic transcription (such are, for example, the Russian and German languages and, with the exception of some conventional forms of spelling, also the English and French languages), the process of writing does not represent an act of direct graphic representation of notions (as is the case with the Chinese language); it presupposes the preliminary acts of separation of sounds from the living speech, decomposition of the fluent sequence of its phonation into individual phonetic elements, and designation of these elements by respective letters. The complexity of this process is best proved by the strained efforts that a little child exerts when trying to master it; the child not only listens attentively to the words offered but reinforces the sound analysis by his/her own articulation, carefully repeating separate sounds and singling them out from the general flow of sounds. In the course of one of our researches it was demonstrated that *if such repetition is excluded, as when the pupil is compelled to write the dictation with his mouth open, the number of mistakes in his dictation increases sixfold.*

From the point of view of modern phonology, this process of separating individual sounds from the living language and designating them by letters is quite clear. *It consists in the transformation of certain unstable variants of the pronounced sounds into distinct and stable phonemes*; in other words, it consists in the act of inhibiting those properties that are inessential to speech sounds (intensity, pitch, timbre, etc.) and marking out those essential (or phonemic) properties whose modification immediately changes the meaning of the word (for example, "ball" and "pall," "dome" and "tome"), and without which it is impossible to make speech distinct and articulate. To perform all this work, which precedes the act of writing, it is insufficient to possess a keen ear; a human being must not only discern diverse and delicate nuances of the sounds but also mark out in them the essential properties, separate these from the inessential ones, and relate the sounds possessing essential properties to that stable group whose phonation, irrespective of the intensity and timbre of pronunciation, is invariably designated by the letters "d" or "t," "b" or "p," etc. This complicated work, which physiologically may be denoted, in accordance with Pavlov's term, the process of "differentiation of sounds" based on the phonemic properties of the language (for example, based on such properties as the voicefulness and voicelessness essential to these sounds), requires a number of auxiliary means. The decisive role in this work belongs to the processes of excitation and inhibition in the *auditory analyzer* (in particular, in the cortex of the left temporal lobe), but the articulatory or *kinesthetic* analysis that adds new subsidiary means facilitating the accomplishment of the task of differentiation between related sounds may also be of considerable help.

Only when the required sounds are quite distinctly separated and their sequence firmly preserved does the next stage come into play—the very act of writing, during which the auditory phoneme is converted into a visual symbol, and this receives graphical expression in a motor act.

What happens to the act of writing if a link of this complex process becomes deranged? In this case we witness a process very similar in nature to that which has already been described previously; a minor derangement will bring about sizable secondary consequences, and the entire functional system will become disturbed owing to this, even though minor, primary defect.

In order to get the clearest possible idea of the concrete consequences that a particular disturbance may entail, we have to digress for a few minutes from the sphere of abnormal childhood and turn to the analysis of the question: How does an already developed process of writing disintegrate when this or some other particular defect arises in an adult? Such analysis of more elementary stages of development, through the investigation of disturbances arising in more perfect and already fully developed forms, proves to be sometimes very helpful.

During World War II we were in a position to analyze a considerable number (amounting to many hundreds) of cases of bullet and shell-splinter wounds in the brain; they were supplemented by numerous cases of operatively verified local lesions of the brain by tumors. The results of these observations found a partial reflection in special researches (Luria, 1947a, b, 1950).

The observations showed that derangements in the act of writing were particularly often met with in cases of wounds in the left (predominating) hemisphere; they accompanied, as particular symptoms, those phenomena of aphasia, which inevitably arose when the wound (or tumor) destroyed also this or some other section of the so-called "speech zones" of the cerebral cortex. However, the nature of the derangement of writing (just as that of speech) proved to be absolutely dissimilar in different cases and was obviously dependent on which link of this complex process was in each case deranged.

If the wound destroyed the brain tissue in the area of the posterior part of the superior temporal convolution in the left hemisphere, the patients exhibited pronounced phenomena of disturbances of the auditory cortex. These disturbances did not necessarily lead to a decline in the hearing acuity (the keeness of hearing in many cases remained fully preserved); of essential importance was the fact that the activity of the temporal cortex, which is the central part of the auditory analyzer, proved to be disturbed: the process of excitation in it became so diffuse and the processes of inhibition so weakened that the cortex could no longer cope with the complex task of singling out the necessary phonemic cues and of differentiating some related phonemes (and in more serious cases also phonemes of remote likeness). As a result, the overwhelming majority of patients with such wounds could not discern the so-called correlating (or oppositional) phonemes (that are distinguished only by one property, for example, by voicefulness or voicelessness) and wrongly repeated them pronouncing "b-p" as "b-b" or "p-p" and "d-t" as "d-d" or "t-t"; naturally, they likewise confused these sounds in their spelling, feeling that there was a certain difference between them, but being unable to qualify it and to relate the sounds to definite groups. This disturbance (that could be also observed in the course of elaboration of more elementary sound differentiations)[1] led to the manifestation of complete helplessness in the separation of the required sounds from complexes of consonants (for example, in the word 'strike''). The phonation of words containing more or less complex combinations of sounds assumed the character of inarticulate noises.

All this, naturally, led to a marked derangement of writing that manifested itself in the inability to separate individual sounds from their complexes, in omitting certain sounds, in their displacement, sometimes in their anticipation or perseveration. I do not dwell here on the fact that all these derangements of writing were developed as a particular symptom of sensory aphasia that was accounted for by the same primary disturbance of the analyzing and synthesizing activity of the auditory cortex.

Derangements of writing of a similar character could develop in cases when the wound destroyed other areas of the cortex located within the central parts of the *kinesthetic analyzer*, which plays an important role in the regulation of complex motor processes. However, these derangements greatly differed in nature from those that have just been described, and the underlying primary mechanisms called forth marked differences in the structure of the symptoms.

Lesions of the kinesthetic parts of the cortex in the left hemisphere invariably caused substantial derangements in the differentiation of kinesthetic impulses; the planning of movements proved to be disturbed, the motor impulses lost their strictly established directions and became diffused, excitation did not take the proper course at once and spread to inadequate groups of muscles. Owing to this, the act of proper coordination of movements greatly suffered, and there arose the

---

[1]This has been carried out in the researches of the Institute of Neurology of the U.S.S.R. Academy of Medical Sciences.

phenomena of "afferent motor apraxia" that manifested themselves in both the derangement of the delicate movements of the arm and (what is particularly important) the delicate movements of the articulatory apparatus. A patient with such a lesion lost the ability to differentiate the pronunciation of the necessary sounds and confused those sounds that are closed as regards their articulation (for example, substituting "m" or "p" for the labial "b" and "d" or "l" for the linguopalatal "n").

This quite peculiar derangement of articulemes (when sounds were confused because of the likeness of their pronunciation and not their acoustic properties) led, in its turn, to a peculiar derangement of writing. A patient deprived of distinct articulatory means, necessary for the separation of individual sounds from speech, was unable to write down these sounds properly; such derangements of writing, caused by this primary defect and expressed in the confusion of closed articulemes, made it possible to ascertain logically the nature of their underlying primary defect.

We are in a position to advance our investigation of defects in writing somewhat further. If the lesion affects one more area of the cerebral cortex and destroys the central parts of the visual-spatial analyzer situated within the parieto-occipital parts of the cerebral hemispheres, the ensuing changes in the behavior of the patient will be of a different nature. Being deprived of strict spatial differentiation of excitation, the patient will confuse the right and left sides, will be unable to coordinate properly the movements of the hand, and will confuse the disposition of the cardinal geographical points; these principal disorders will inevitably be reflected in his writing. In this case the analysis of the sound composition of speech will remain unchanged, but the handwriting will be substantially deranged: the patient will be unable to differentiate the direction of the strokes when tracing the contours of a letter, preserving only elements of the letter, but not its spatial orientation and synthesis, so that it will become quite unrecognizable.

We do not continue our analysis by dwelling on cases in which derangements in the act of writing are caused not by limited local disorders but by a *defect of the general neurodynamics*. These are defects connected with the weakness of the inhibitory process, owing to which the child is unable to inhibit its direct impulses, and each excitation at once reaches its motor end deranging the normal *order* of tracing letters and imparting to the act of writing an impulsive character. In these cases, as shown by our experience, the defects in the child's writing can be easily eliminated by placing the child in a condition of constant control that inhibits the impulsive character of his reactions.

From the preceding analysis it is quite clear that *a primary derangement of any particular link may inevitably lead to the disintegration of the whole system*, and that genuine analysis of the nature of derangements in this system is possible only *if we disclose this primary disorder, as well as the systemic consequences that it entails*.

There is no need to emphasize that such analysis of the symptom considerably oversteps the bounds of mere references to a derangement of the ability for writing and brings us close to scientific diagnosis of the given derangement.

We have deliberately cited a few examples of such analysis borrowed from the clinic of local cerebral lesions in the adult. These examples enable us to solve with particular exactness the problem arising before us in the clinic of abnormal childhood; the only difference is that in conditions of anomalous development these defects may manifest themselves with still greater intensity and if the defect arises early enough, it may bring about severe disturbances in the entire mental development of the child.[2] A child with central lesions or underdevelopment of corresponding cortical systems, accompanied by disturbances of the auditory, kinesthetic, or spatial analyzing and synthesizing activity, just as a child with serious defects of general neurodynamics, will inevitably exhibit marked derangements in the mastery of the process of writing, but in different cases these derangements have different foundations, are components of different syndromes, and bear a different character.

We have dwelt only on the causal-dynamic analysis of phenomena of dysgraphia (and of the related phenomena of dyslexia); however, we could with equal success apply this analysis to the phenomena of disorders of speech and derangements of motor processes or, what is of particular interest, to various forms of anomalous behavior (for example, resulting from early encephalitis). In all such cases, the approach to the symptom under observation in respect to a secondary consequence of a definite primary defect, a consequence that has taken shape in the course of development, proves to be effective and makes it possible not only to understand the structure of the derangement better but also to approximate the scientific analysis of the anomalous development as a whole.

Our exposition of the way that we consider most effective in the analysis of anomalous development of children would not be complete if we did not dwell on the *practical results* of the systemic or, in other words, causal-dynamic approach to the phenomena under investigation.

The formal symptomatological approach, describing only those defects of the abnormal child that most of all arrest our attention, and attempting to explain them by an underdevelopment of certain inborn (general and special) abilities, not only lags far behind the level of modern scientific knowledge but also proves to be practically inefficient. Being unable to reveal the primary cause of the derangement and to interpret the symptoms under observation as its systemic consequences, it is useless in finding any proper, scientifically grounded methods for its compensation.

Indeed, what is the practical use of a mere assertion that the given child

---

[2]We had the opportunity to observe it when specially analyzing a case of underdevelopment of speech in twins. In A. R. Luria and Y. C. Yudovich, *Speech and Development of Mental Processes in the Child*, Moscow, 1956.

exhibits general intellectual deficiency or suffers from primary derangements of the ability to write and to read, which is expressed as inborn dysgraphia and dyslexia?

At best, such an assertion does not lead to any distinct results nor does it open any definite ways for correcting the defect. At worst, it leads to an erroneous approach and to such recommendations that cannot be of any practical help in devising corrective work for the abnormal child. What could be practically achieved if we placed a child who does not speak and suffers defects of hearing in a school for feebleminded or alalic children, and if we attempt to teach him according to a program designed for such children? Could we attain any sizable results if, upon establishing a derangement of writing in a child with a primary defect of the auditory or kinesthetic analysis or synthesis, we began (as, unfortunately, is often the case) to have such a child copy letters, thereby compelling him to perform absolutely unnecessary work?

The causal-dynamic analysis of the abnormal child, aimed at disclosing its primary defect and deducing from it the secondary systemic consequences, simultaneously enables us to find adequate means of compensating this defect and, in the case of adults, adequate ways of corrective training. This corrective training—in cases of organic lesions of the peripheral and central apparatus—must be only to an inconsiderable degree aimed at the direct elimination of the primary cause underlying the anomalous development. Primary defects of hearing, just as a primary derangement of the auditory or kinesthetic analysis and synthesis, can be eliminated only to a small extent, and the effect of treatment (such as administration of stimulating substances) is usually of limited use.

However, corrective training directed against the *systemic consequences of this defect* and, as a rule, consisting in a *functional readjustment of the deranged system* may produce a tremendous, decisive effect and to a considerable degree restore the deranged (or underdeveloped) function.

It would be senseless to direct all efforts exclusively to the elimination of severe defects of hearing; but children with such defects can successfully cope with the normal program of general 10-year education (though in a somewhat longer period), if special attention is paid to the compensation of those secondary difficulties in their mastery of the grammatical system of speech and the forms of abstract thinking, which arise as a result of their primary defects.

Nor would it be reasonable to attempt directly to eliminate the defects of the form of sound and kinesthetic analysis and synthesis that suffered as a result of a cerebral lesion; but a series of rational methods aimed at the readjustment of the functional system may lead to complete elimination of the secondary defects caused by the primary derangement.

I cannot forget a well-known engineer and designer who, having been wounded in the temporal area, preserved his abilities as a designer but fully lost the ability of writing; he was brought to our clinic after unsuccessful attempts to restore his ability to write with the help of protracted exercises in copying texts.

After an adequate 4 months' course of training in sound analysis based on the intact visual and articulatory analysis, this patient, like many others, left our clinic with a fairly well restored writing ability. Similar positive results were obtained in cases when the derangement of the kinesthetic analysis of articulations was supported by the auditory and visual oral analysis of speech.

A special clinic of speech disorders in Moscow created at the Institute of Defectology of the Academy of Pedagogical Sciences and headed by R. E. Levina has worked out an elaborate system of such corrective training of alalic children and convincingly proved the effectiveness of those practical methods that are engendered by a correct theoretical analysis of the symptom.

There is no doubt that a thoughtful approach to the analysis of the defect and the ability to disclose its real nature will be of great practical use and provide a scientific foundation for the corrective training of abnormal children, which is the most humane branch of our medical and pedagogical sciences.

REFERENCES

Burt, C. *The backward child*. London, 1951.
Luria, A. R. *Traumatic aphasia*. Moscow, 1947. (a)
Luria, A. R. *Recovery of cerebral functions after wounds*. Moscow, 1947. (b)
Luria, A. R. *Essays on the psychophysiology of the act of writing*. Moscow, 1950.

7 The Developmental-Difference Controversy in Verbal Mediation of Behavior

Rosa Cascione
Yale University

Alexander Luria's studies in mental retardation can best be understood and appreciated within the context of his whole life's work. During a career that spanned over 50 years, Luria devoted himself to the study of higher mental processes in human beings. He examined the development of cognitive functioning in nonhandicapped and intellectually handicapped children, the development of writing and voluntary movements, disturbances of intellectual capacities in patients with brain lesions, eye-movement mechanisms, mnemonic disorders, and variations in thinking across different cultures. As broad and varied as was the scope of Luria's work, his thinking in all of these areas was unified under a single conceptual framework, which derived from his collaboration with Lev S. Vygotsky in the 1920s and 30s. This framework inspired the goals, hypotheses, and methodology of most of Luria's lifetime research, including his studies in mental retardation (Luria, 1979).

In this chapter I discuss Luria's investigations and views concerning mental retardation from two different perspectives. The first is a developmental perspective, tracing the evolution of Luria's thought and work in mental retardation from Vygotsky's conceptual framework. The second is a comparative perspective, relating Luria's difference and Zigler's developmental views on mental retardation. It is my belief that a better understanding of both of these viewpoints and indeed of mental retardation can be gained from examining the underlying assumptions, models, and goals of the theorists. The fact that the developmental-difference controversy has been a lively and viable one for over 15 years indicates that both viewpoints have particular merits. Thus, by focusing on the underlying conceptual sources of the controversy, it is hoped that the strengths and weaknesses of each viewpoint are uncovered, thereby providing a structural framework that could lead to a more complete and better understanding of mental retardation.

Development of Luria's Position on Mental Retardation

Both Vygotsky and Luria were disenchanted with the two prevailing approaches of the 1920s to the study of higher mental functions. According to Luria (1979), the reductionistic approach of Wundt, Ebbinghaus, and others attempted to reduce complex psychological processes to elementary mechanisms that could be studied in the laboratory. Vygotsky and Luria believed, however, that in the process of simplification the functions being studied became totally devoid of any significant relationship to complex human behavior. The phenomenological approach of Dilthey and Spranger, on the other hand, was descriptive and holistic and careful not to lose any of the complexity of psychological processes. For this very reason, however, the proponents of this approach claimed that higher mental processes could not be studied by objective laboratory methods.

As their primary goal, Vygotsky and Luria wished to create a new science of psychology to study higher mental activities by objective methods. At the same time, they were caught up in the excitement and enthusiasm of a new social order brought about by the Bolshevik revolution in the Soviet Union. Their new scientific framework, therefore, was designed not only to gain insight into psychological processes but to yield practical benefits to society as well. There is very little separation between basic and applied research in Luria's work. These two aims of serving science and serving society lend a unique character to all of Luria's work. This goal is reflected in the typical clinical orientation of Luria's studies. Research questions were derived largely from clinical observation and experience; the methods of inquiry were, like Piaget's, basically clinical.

The theoretical underpinnings of the new science, the most original aspect of the conceptual framework, came from Vygotsky (Luria, 1979). According to Vygotsky, higher forms of human conscious behavior develop not as an inevitable process of maturation nor as a disconnected process of acquisition of new links and associations, but through the individual's social relations with the external world. Influenced by Marx, Vygotsky believed that the social nature of people becomes their psychological nature as well. Thus, socially organized experiences, which are transmitted primarily through language, determine the structure of human conscious activity. By means of language, the historical and cultural experiences of a society are passed on to the child. Assimilation of these experiences brings about new knowledge, new ways of organizing mental activities, and new forms of behavior.

The Role of Speech in the Regulation of Behavior

The essence of human higher mental activity, according to Vygotsky and Luria, is dependent on speech. Language serves two fundamental functions: It changes and organizes the individual's perception of reality, and it exerts a higher level of control over behavior.

The ability of speech to modify perception of the world develops first in the child. The mother, for example, points to objects and names them for her child, saying such words as "cup" or "spoon." This interaction between mother and child will actually change the child's perception. As Luria (1961a) explains it:

> By the laws of temporary links, the mother's gesture and the word designating the object become secondary signals causing marked changes in the range of stimuli acting on the child. In isolating the object from its environment, the action of pointing reinforces the stimulus, making it a figure set in a ground. The word designating the object delineates its essential functional properties and sets it within the category of other objects with similar properties; it serves a complex task of analysis and synthesis for the child [p. 19].

Soon the child begins to mark given objects off from the environment and names them by himself. By using speech to alter the relative strength of stimuli acting on him, the individual becomes capable of actively modifying the environment that influences him. When the person responds or adapts his behavior to the external environment, he does so to an environment that has first been modified perceptually by himself. According to Luria (1961a), this is the first step by which speech comes to regulate behavior.

The notion that language brings about perceptual changes and thereby behavioral changes was illustrated in an experimental demonstration cited by Luria (1961a). Both animals and humans typically react to the strongest component of a complex stimulus. If complex stimuli, such as a red circle on a gray ground and a green circle on a yellow ground, are presented to a 3-to-5-year-old child who is asked to press a bulb with his/her right or left hand, respectively, when one or the other stimulus appears, the child will after a short period of time respond correctly on every trial. To demonstrate which element of the complex stimulus determines the required response, the child was presented with a red circle on a yellow ground instead of gray, and a green circle on a gray ground instead of yellow. In this altered situation, the child still squeezes with his/her right hand for the red circle and his/her left for the green, indicating that the circle is decisive in determining the response. Luria's colleague, Abramyan (cited by Luria, 1961a), demonstrated that by means of speech it was possible to alter the relative natural strength of the figure and ground in these visual stimuli.

Abramyan replaced the circles by colored airplanes on the same yellow or gray grounds. The child was now asked to squeeze the bulb with his/her right hand for a red airplane on a yellow ground because "the plane can fly when the sun is shining and the sky is yellow," and with his left hand for a green airplane on a gray background because "when it's raining the plane can't fly and has to be stopped." When these verbal instructions were given, the colored backgrounds of the two figures, which had been the weaker elements in the compound stimuli, became the stronger signals, and even most children of 3 or 4 reacted to the backgrounds instead of the figures.

Other studies in Luria's laboratory have shown that speech may also modify human involuntary reactions to stimuli of different strengths. When a new stimulus is presented to an individual, it elicits a system of orienting reflexes, including involuntary vascular, skin-galvanic, and EEG reactions. The intensity of these reactions is related roughly to the intensity of the stimuli and declines gradually as the stimuli are repeated. Sokolov and Vinogradova (cited by Luria, 1961a) demonstrated that verbal instructions can influence the intensity of orienting reactions. They told subjects to press a button in response to weak acoustic signals or to keep count of such signals and measured the vascular component of the orienting reflex to these stimuli. Surprisingly, they found that subjects continued to produce stable vascular reactions to the physically weak acoustic signals but failed to respond to any extraneous stimuli—that is, stimuli not included in the verbally defined signal system—not even to loud noises such as the clang of sheet metal thrown down outside the window. This experiment as well as others demonstrated that by changing perception speech gives human beings a certain control over their own behavior, whether voluntary or involuntary. Individuals need not remain merely passive recipients of environmental inputs. Language provides a tool permitting a transactional relationship with their environment.

In severely retarded persons, studies in Luria's laboratory showed that speech failed to influence the perception process. Regardless of the verbal instructions given, these subjects oriented to stimuli in a reflexive manner; that is, the intensity of their response always correlated with the intensity of the stimuli.

The second major function of speech, that of regulating behavior, is closely related to its first function. The potential regulatory influence of speech was mentioned, though not examined and elaborated, by Ivan Pavlov. Pavlov believed (Luria, 1961a) that speech introduced: "a new principle in nervous activity, that of abstracting and generalizing innumerable signals coming in from the external envirnoment [p. 42]." According to Luria, when fully developed, the regulatory power of speech proceeds from its ability to alter the basic laws of the formation of temporary links.

As discovered by Pavlov, a temporary link is formed when a conditioned signal is accompanied by a constant unconditioned reinforcement. The development of the link is gradual, with initial generalization of reactions to similar stimuli and only later differentiation to a particular stimulus. The link becomes established only gradually; without constant reinforcement in the early stages of its development, the link will be readily disrupted. In addition, a well-established system of temporary links is quite inert in the sense of being very difficult to convert into an opposite system of links. The new connections can be made only by applying new reinforcements. For example, without new reinforcements an animal will not learn that the previous negative stimulus is now the positive one and vice versa. Finally, temporary links can be established in animals only in response to concrete signals. It is almost impossible for an animal to learn to respond to abstract properties of the presented stimuli, as for example to every third positive stimulus.

Although the preceding characteristics describe accurately the formation of conditioned responses in animals, they do not apply completely to the formation of temporary links in human beings. The reason, of course, is language. Language, or the "second-signalling system," as Pavlov termed it, abstracts and systematizes the external stimuli acting on the person and thereby (Luria, 1961a): *"creates a new information-system within which each signal presented to the subject now operates* [p. 43-44]." The different quality that language imparts to the formation of a conditioned reflex in the human being is illustrated in the following example. If an individual is shown a neutral stimulus such as a blue light paired with the reinforcement to "Press the bulb," and if he is then shown a red light without any accompanying reinforcement, his behavior is never as immediate as that of an animal. He may ask, "Shall I press for that one, too?" or he may formulate a hypothetical rule for himself, "I am to press for a blue light and not for a red," or "I am to press for a light of any color." Once such a verbal rule or system of verbally formulated links is adopted, reactions to all subsequently presented stimuli will depend more on the system into which they are taken than on their physical properties.

Man's ability to formulate verbal rules modifies considerably the basic laws of formation of temporary links. Whereas temporary links develop gradually in animals, in humans they usually form quickly by virtue of incorporating or excluding the given stimulus from an existing system of reactions. In animals, eliminating the reinforcement results in the gradual extinction of the link. Man, however, having formulated a verbal rule, no longer needs constant external reinforcement. According to Luria, the reinforcement now becomes the coincidence of the response and the behavior rule. In animals it is very difficult to reshape a firmly established link. In humans, on the other hand, the reinforcement need be changed only once, for example by saying "Before you pressed for a red light, from now on don't," and the whole system is instantly modified. Finally, language enables the human being, unlike the animal, to form systems of reactions to abstract attributes, as for instance to the sequence of signals or to alternate signals.

According to Luria, it is the meaning or significative function of speech that comes to exert a regulatory role over the formation of conditioned responses, and thus of all of behavior as well. Luria described the process by which language gains control over behavior as one of coupling of the verbal and motor systems.

This coupling is the culmination of a developmental process that takes place over the first 6 or 7 years of life. In young children, when speech is just beginning to develop, it is not coupled or actively incorporated in the formation of new links. Rather, temporary links are formed without speech participation—much as the process occurs in animals—going through initial generalization to gradual differentiation, needing continual reinforcement, extinguishing when the reinforcement is eliminated, and linking only concrete, physical aspects of stimuli.

Development of the Regulatory Role of Speech

As we have seen, Luria showed that speech is an integral part of the structure of the cognitive apparatus, and that it is a powerful means of regulating human behavior. By a series of simple but ingenious studies, he demonstrated the existence of four stages in the developmental process, whereby speech becomes the main mechanism of conscious voluntary behavior. During the first stage, speech is not developed sufficiently to play any regulatory role in behavior. During the second stage, the child's own speech begins to regulate behavior. In this stage, however, the regulation stems not from meaningful or significative connections of the verbalization but from the direct, "impellant" or initiating action of speech. In the third stage, the impellant action of speech subsides, whereas the main regulatory influence passes to the significative connections produced by speech. In the final stage, the need for regulation from external speech becomes reduced, and control is assumed by internal speech, which becomes the most significant component of both thought and volitional action.

Luria traced this development experimentally by employing a simple model, which he believed embodied all the principle characteristics of conscious voluntary regulation of behavior and which could be analyzed in precise psychophysiological terms. This model was based on the assumption that accomplishing a simple action on verbal instruction could be viewed as the core of voluntary behavior regulated by speech.

Luria found that prior to the age of 1½ or 2 years, speech cannot control the child's actions. The child will not respond to any verbal instructions. Beginning at approximately the age of 2, however, speech begins to serve an *impellant* or *initiating* function. At this stage, the child will respond to simple verbal instructions, such as "Clap your hands," or "Give me your hands." However, speech at this early stage is unable to inhibit an action already begun by the child or to switch the action from one to another. For example, the instruction to "Take your socks off" while the child is putting them on will result not in the child's stopping and then taking his socks off but in intensifying the action in which he was already engaged, that is, putting on the socks. What Luria called the regulatory role proper of speech, the regulation imparted by the meaning of speech, is not developed in this early stage. This was demonstrated by having children at this stage respond to the verbal instruction, "When you see the light, squeeze the balloon." Upon hearing the first part of the instruction, the children would orient to the light. Then, upon hearing the second part, "squeeze the ballon," they would immediately begin to obey these words. Thus, although the child in the second developmental stage is able to respond properly to the separate parts of the instructions, he cannot yet carry out the essence or significative function of the instructions—in this case, a demand for synthesis of the two verbal elements.

At approximately the age of 3 or 4, while still in the second stage, the child begins to use his own speech to regulate behavior. If a 3½-year-old child is asked to "Press the bulb when the light goes on," he/she will respond to each presentation of the light. However, he/she will also press the bulb when the light is not presented. Luria attributed these intersignal reactions to a diffuseness of the motor excitation produced by the verbal instruction in the nervous system. At this age the excitatory part of the verbal instruction is still stronger than the inhibitory. By having the child make use of his/her own speech by asking him/her to say "Go" and press the bulb simultaneously when the light goes on, the child will no longer exhibit extra reactions. Thus, the use of the child's own speech eliminates the diffuseness of the motor process and coordinates the motor reactions with the signals. The child, as described by Luria, begins to subordinate his/her movements to his/her own command "Go," which becomes a link between the conditioned stimulus, the light signal, and the reaction that controls the movements.

It is clear, however, that at this stage the child is reacting merely to the nonspecific, impellant function of his own speech rather than to its significative function. This was demonstrated by O. K. Tikhomirov in Luria's laboratory (cited by Luria, 1961a) by having children react to a light flash either by the verbal command "I shall press twice" or by saying "Go! Go!" as they pressed two times to its presentation. Although the command "Go! Go!" was able to regulate successfully the motor reactions, the command "I shall press twice"—in children who knew the meaning of twice perfectly well—failed to bring about the correct motor reactions. Rather, the child usually responded by multiple responses or a single protracted movement. Thus, the regulatory influence of the first command derived from two impulses—Go! Go!, whereas the correct regulatory influence of the second command stemmed from the significative side of the instruction. Indeed, the impulse side of the latter command conflicted with the significative side, because the words "I shall press twice" contain only a single, protracted signal.

Beginning with the third stage of development, at approximately the age of 4½ to 5½, it becomes possible to elicit a stable system of motor reactions by means of verbal instruction. Children at this stage are able to understand and respond correctly to such complicated instructions as "Press when you see one signal and do not press when you see the other," to regulate their behavior according to the internally retained verbal rule, and to refrain from inappropriate impulsive reactions to inhibitory signals. However, if the investigator complicates the conditions of the experiment, by increasing the rate of stimulus presentation or by reducing the discrimination between stimuli, the child will continue to produce impulsive reactions. In such cases, if the child begins to verbalize the instructions out loud, such as "Don't press," the impulsive reactions are inhibited. Similarly, a 5-year old can respond appropriately to such complex instructions as to press twice in response to two successive similar signals but not to a similar third signal, if he is allowed to verbalize what he is to do but not if he attempts to carry out the instructions in silence. This finding indicates that the child at this stage is not yet capable of following the traces of the preliminary verbal instruction in silence. The child is able to carry out these complicated instructions correctly only by verbalizing parts or all of the instructions himself.

When the child reaches the fourth and final stage of development, the decisive regulatory role passes from the child's external to internal speech. At this stage, it is no longer necessary for the child to verbalize the instructions out loud so as to achieve better regulation. Rather, the child's internal speech alone becomes capable of regulating motor actions.

In summary, the development of the regulatory function of speech, according to Luria, is characterized by a progression along two dimensions: The first is a transferring of regulation from the impulsive, initiating side of speech to the analytic system of significative connections that are produced by speech; and the second, which occurs simultaneously with the first, is a shift of the regulatory power from the external to the internal speech of the child.

Studies with Mentally Retarded Persons

Luria's belief that higher human cognitive processes, such as complex perception or intelligent memorization, logical thinking, voluntary attention, or volitional activity, are not exclusively inborn capabilities of the human being but develop gradually during the course of growth as the child manipulates objects and interacts with adults influenced how he regarded and studied mental retardation. Rather than being a manifestation of some general deficiency, he (Luria, 1963) viewed the cognitive features of retarded children as being the result of anomalous development due to: "the fact that a definite link indispensable to the normal development of mental activity becomes deranged owing to an early (more often intrauterine) disease and sometimes to an inborn defect [p. 357]." The deranged link could, according to Luria, be a general abnormality in the functioning of the nervous system, a specific defect in a particular neurological function, such as visual or auditory analysis, or a defective pattern of interrelationship between the child and adults.

Luria focused his studies predominantly on two groups of children who fail in regular schools, although he recognized other groups of children who have difficulties in school (Luria, 1961b). The first, called *cerebro-asthenic* or weak children, were believed to suffer from either a metabolic disturbance, general infection, or malnutrition early in life. These children can be very clever, but they become exhausted rather quickly. They can work for no longer than 10-15 minutes and then become either very excited and restless or quite lethargic. They generally fail in their school work. In U.S. nomenclature, these children might be similar to the group we call learning disabled. The second abnormal group Luria studied was the group he considered truly *feebleminded* or intellectually retarded. This designation was applied to children who, on the basis of evidence provided by several researchers (M. S. Pevzner, V. I. Lubovsky, A. I. Mescheriakov, E. N. Martsinovskaya, cited by Luria, 1963), were thought to have suffered brain injury either prenatally, neonatally, or in the earliest years of development. The feebleminded children Luria studied would be comparable to children designated as moderately, severely, or profoundly retarded according to the current U.S. classification system.

In studying these children who display abnormalities in cognitive functioning, Luria was interested primarily in discovering the basic psychophysiological disturbance and elucidating the anomalous developmental course that gave rise to the abnormal features. He believed that such an analysis would contribute to an understanding of the nature of the abnormality, facilitate the differential diagnosis of various seemingly similar, but in reality very different disturbances, and finally aid in finding proper methods of therapy and corrective pedagogical practices (Luria, 1963).

In his analysis of the mental difficulties of abnormal children, Luria and his colleagues employed the same experimental model he used in tracing normal cognitive development. He demonstrated, for example, how different are the psychophysiological mechanisms responsible for cerebro-asthenia and feeblemindedness.

Experiments by E. D. Homskaya (cited by Luria, 1963) revealed the physiological disturbance characteristic of the cerebro-asthenic syndrome. In one study, he observed the reactions of a 9-year-old cerebro-asthenic child instructed to press the bulb in response to red signals but not to press to green signals. The asthenic child produced inappropriate impulsive reactions to the inhibitory green signals, particularly when the presentation of signals was accelerated. If, however, the child was asked to respond verbally to the signals, saying "Yes" to the positive red signal and "No" to the negative green signal, he/she performed this task most accurately. Thus, although the motor system of the cerebro-asthenic child was characterized by a deterioration of the inhibitory processes, the verbal system remained relatively intact. Indeed, Homskaya found that the child recognized the errors he/she made but was unable to stop making them. The normal verbal system was utilized by the investigator in order to compensate for the presumed neurodynamic defects in the motor processes of the child. The child was asked to say "Yes" and simultaneously to press the bulb in response to the appearance of the positive signal and to say "No" and not to press in response to the inhibitory signal. In testing a large number of cerebro-asthenic children this method of compensation proved to be remarkably effective. Whereas under conditions of silence, cerebro-asthenic children displayed 60-70% impulsive reactions to inappropriate negative signals, when verbal and motor responses were combined, the number of impulsive reactions dropped to 0-15%.

Some cerebro-asthenic children displayed marked motor inhibition rather than excitation. Instead of responding inappropriately to negative signals, these children failed to respond to positive stimuli. Luria found that even in these children a compensatory effect could be obtained by utilizing the regulatory role of their normal verbal system.

The abnormal behavior of cerebro-asthenic children, apparently due to the inability of internal speech mechanisms to regulate behavior, resembled the behavior of younger nonretarded children in the third stage of cognitive development described by Luria. In both cerebro-asthenic and third-stage children, externally verbalized speech was able to adequately control behavior. However, internal speech did not exert a regulatory role because it had not achieved a hierarchical control over the motor system (Luria, 1979).

In retarded children, Luria and his colleagues discovered a different pattern of neurological dysfunction. In contrast to the cerebro-asthenic children, retarded children were found to suffer defects in their speech processes that severely impaired the regulatory function of speech. These defects consisted of an inertness of the verbal processes and an impairment of the significative function of speech.

By inertness of the verbal processes, Luria referred to the inability of the individual to pass quickly from one system of connections to another. According to Luria, inertness is characteristic not only of the retarded individual's verbal system but of his motor system as well, although the degree of inertness is greater in the verbal system. Inertness of the motor and verbal system is illustrated in the following examples of behavior of retarded children.

A 12- or 14-year-old retarded child, asked to press the bulb upon presentation of the red light but to refrain from pressing upon presentation of the green light, learned this task and subsequently also learned the reverse task—to press to the green light but not to the red. If, however, while performing the second task a strong bell was rung or the task was interrupted for 2 or 3 minutes, the child would resume responding as in the first task—pressing to red but not to green. Thus, the child's motor responses reverted to those based on older, more stable connections. Continuing the experiment, the child would next be asked to press in response to a long light signal but not to a short light signal. When this other task was well-learned, the experimenter would ask the child to describe the action he/she was performing. Typically, the child would insist that he/she was pressing the bulb in response to a red signal and not pressing in response to a green signal. The latter finding indicates in a most striking way the greater degree of pathological inertia in the verbal system than in the motor system. Although the child had already modified successfully his motor pattern of reactions, he/she continued to retain the older verbal system of connections or explanation.

The disparity in degree of inertia of the verbal and motor systems has serious pathological consequences. Neurologically, it leads to a dissociation of the motor and verbal system of connections. As a result of the dissociation, the verbal system can make very little contribution to the formation of motor reactions. Thus, the child accomplishes most tasks in a largely unconscious manner. The correct links are formed very slowly, by a process of gradual differentiation out of the generalized motor excitation. The formation of the link needs constant reinforcement, and the link will disappear if the reinforcement is discontinued. The development of behavior, therefore, seems to obey the basic laws of the formation of temporary links without the aid of the second-signalling system. It is perhaps for this reason that Luria (1963) believed that the dissociation of the verbal and motor system: *"prevents the child from any creative, intellectual activity* [p. 383]."

In addition to pathological inertia, the other major disturbance of the verbal system in retarded children occurs in its significative function. The ability to abstract and generalize signalling properties is characteristically impaired in these children. Retarded children have great difficulty in generating response systems consisting, for example, of positive reactions to a long signal and inhibitory reactions to a short signal of the same color, or of positive reactions to every third signal of a series of similar signals. Though the retarded child may, after a prolonged training process, learn to respond correctly, Luria (1961a) demonstrated that the child's behavior was not really based on a system of appropriate verbal connections. In one study the child was trained to press to every third stimulus presentation. Once the child was performing perfectly on this task, the rate of stimulus presentation was accelerated such that four stimuli then appeared in the same time interval in which three had appeared previously. With this alteration in the experimental situation, the child began to respond to every fourth signal rather than every third, thus indicating that he/she was responding to the physical aspect of the time interval rather than to the abstract element of the number of signals.

As a result of the impairment in the significative function of speech, the more primitive, nonspecific, impellant function of speech tends to predominate. In certain experimental conditions, the child may even succeed in elaborating a simple, correct verbal response, but, as Luria (1961a) showed, the meaning of the verbal response does not exert a higher regulatory influence over behavior. For example, the child who has learned to say "Don't press" when the red light appears will actually press the bulb in response to his/her utterance rather than inhibit his/her motor reactions. Thus, the child's speech affects his/her behavior through its initiating, activating function, not through its meaning or significative function.

The defective verbal system of the retarded individual not only makes higher regulatory control of behavior impossible but may actually impede the elaboration of behavior by the lower level system of motor connections. An example was provided by O. K. Khomirov in Luria's laboratory (cited by Luria, 1961a). A 10½-year-old-retarded child was tested under three conditions. In the first, the child was asked to press the bulb upon seeing the red signal but to refrain from pressing upon seeing the green signal. In the second condition, the child was asked to verbalize "Yes" to the positive red signal and "No" to the negative green signal. In the third condition, the child was required to combine the motor and verbal responses to the signals, that is, to press the bulb and simultaneously say "Yes" when the red light appeared and not to press and say "No" when the green light appeared. The child performed fairly well in the first—motor—condition and more poorly in the second—verbal—condition. Most significantly, however, Khomirov found the worst performance in the third condition in which motor and verbal responses were combined. According to Luria, the reason for the deteriorated performance lies in the dissociation of the verbal and motor systems. Because language and action do not form a single functional system, the two isolated series of reactions—the verbal and motor—inhibit each other due to a process of neurological negative induction. Thus, unlike in cerebro-asthenic children, the verbal system of retarded children cannot be employed to overcome deficiencies of their motor nervous processes.

Although not mentioned in his writings, the findings of Luria and his colleagues on the regulation of behavior in retarded and cerebro-asthenic individuals appear to be similar to their findings in children at lower stages of cognitive development. Indeed, the major features of cognitive structure of the retarded children, as revealed in Luria's studies, correspond to those of younger nonretarded children. The behavior displayed by the retarded children tested in Luria's laboratory, who ranged in age between approximately 10 and 16 years, may be characterized as typical of the second stage of development, where the main regulatory role of speech stems from its impellant rather than its significative function and from external speech rather than internal speech. The behavior of cerebro-asthenic children, on the other hand, resembles that typical of the third stage of development, where the significative function of speech is established but internal speech is not yet able to exert adequate control over behavior. Whatever the brain lesion or physiological disturbance primarily responsible for retardation or cerebro-asthenia, the consequences appear to be manifested ultimately as arrested development in verbal regulation of behavior.

Comparison of Luria's and Zigler's Views

Luria characterized retarded individuals as suffering from a major defect in the ability of the verbal system to regulate behavior. This defect was seen to arise from two major neurodynamic abnormalities in the functioning of the verbal system. The first consists of considerable inertness of the verbal system relative to the motor system, leading to a functional dissociation of the two systems. Normally, these two systems are unified in a hierarchical arrangement whereby the verbal system may exert control over the motor (Luria, 1979). The second abnormality relates to a qualitative weakness in the verbal system such that the significative function of speech—the ability to abstract and generalize—is severely impaired, leaving its impellant function relatively intact.

As we have seen, Luria's experimental findings may also be interpreted as indicative of a developmental halt in the verbal regulation of behavior in retarded persons. The major features of cognitive functioning of retarded individuals studied by Luria typify those of young children in the second stage of cognitive development delineated by Luria.

Luria's defect interpretation and the latter developmental interpretation appear to be simply two different ways of characterizing the same phenomena. What is of greater importance is that the same phenomena—the same set of behavioral observations—may be characterized both in difference and developmental language. Why then did Luria choose to describe his findings as indicating the existence of a particular defect in mentally retarded persons? And why did Zigler, in studying Luria's work, not consider it as corroborating evidence for his own developmental view of retardation? The answers to these questions may be gained by examining the underlying conceptual differences reflected in the work and thought of these two investigators.

At least two conceptual differences form the basis for the development-difference controversy in mental retardation. These conceptual differences apply not only to the contrast between Zigler's developmental view and Luria's defect view but also between the developmental and other difference theories. These differences concern the *categorization* of phenomena and the *level of analysis*.

The first difference between Luria's and Zigler's orientation, that of categorization, refers to the issue of definition of mental retardation. It is this fundamental issue that is addressed by the developmental position. According to Zigler (1967), there should be a two-group approach to the study of mental retardation. This recommendation is based on the fact that the distribution of intelligence test scores in the human population is actually bimodal. The overwhelming majority of persons fall within the group having a normal distribution of intelligence with a mean IQ score of 100 and a range of 50 to 150. This distribution may be generated theoretically from a polygenic model of the inheritance of intelligence. A small fraction of the population has scores that fall outside this general distribution into a second independent distribution. The mean IQ of the latter is 35 and the range 0 and above, with the vast majority having IQs below 50. According to Zigler (1967), this distribution contains those persons whose very low intelligence stems from an organic lesion or disturbance in their physical makeup.

The group of individuals that society chooses to label as mentally retarded—persons having an IQ score below 70 with a concomitant deficit in adaptive behavior—fall either in the lower end of the general population distribution of intelligence or within the smaller distribution of persons whose low IQ has an organic basis. Zigler's developmental theory is an attempt to account for the apparent retardation of the subgroup of retarded individuals that falls within the general population distribution of intelligence, that is, whose members presumably have never sustained any organic damage. This subgroup has traditionally been called cultural-familial retarded but more recently has come to be known as mentally retarded due to psychosocial disadvantage.

In Zigler's view, the subnormal intellectual level of cultural-familial retarded persons is due to their lower rate of cognitive development and lower asymptote of development reached, as compared to more intelligent persons in the population. The cognitive processes and development of cultural-familial retarded individuals are believed to be qualitatively similar to those of more intelligent individuals. The difference between the more and less intelligent lies in the rate of cognitive development and the ultimate level of cognitive functioning attained.

Luria did not develop his theoretical formulations from an analysis of the shape of the distribution of intelligence of the total human population. Rather, he began with observations of children who do well in school and those who fail in school. Within the latter group, he distinguished five main subgroups (Luria, 1961b, 1963): the cerebro-asthenic, the true feebleminded, the emotionally disturbed, those having a single, specific defect such as a visual or auditory defect that leads to secondary impairment in cognitive functioning, and children retarded in cognitive development due to faulty social interactions with adults or faulty training.

Luria reported no experimental studies on the group of children whose retardation could be attributed to deficiencies in social experiences, children that might be comparable to those whose retardation is designated as originating from psychosocial disadvantage. The retarded children that Luria did study, on the other hand, were believed to have suffered cerebral lesions in the intrauterine or early developmental period. Thus, Luria's defect theory of mental retardation applies specifically to that category of children having organic derangements in their neurological processes. Zigler's developmental theory, in contrast, refers explicitly only to the category of retarded children not having any organic disturbances. Thus, at least according to the authors' own intentions, the two theories address nonoverlapping segments of the retarded population.

Whether or not all the retarded children studied by Luria had indeed incurred a brain lesion, Luria (1963) assumed that all "true" feebleminded individuals have defective neurological functioning. He criticized the developmental view indirectly in the following statement:

> We contest the viewpoint—incompatible with modern science—which is inclined to deduce peculiarities of development from different inborn abilities. The assertion of some authors that a considerable part of the population is hereditarily 'subnor-

mal,' or exhibits traits of 'constitutional psychopathy' can be hardly regarded as a worthy contribution to science [pp. 368-369].

In this quote Luria alludes to the conceptual difficulty of the notion that *normal* variations in the genetic endowment of intellectual characteristics could be responsible for *abnormal* or *subnormal* processes of intellectual functioning. If a major proportion of mentally retarded persons—cultural-familial retarded individuals constitute about 75% of the total retarded population—are, according to the developmental view, considered normal variants of the total human population, then they should not be labeled mentally retarded. If they are labeled mentally retarded, then, in Luria's view (1963), the developmental explanation would be an inadequate account of their abnormal functioning. The developmental explanation that retarded persons are characterized by a slower rate of cognitive development would be regarded by Luria as explanation by labeling of symptoms, much as the inability to read and write are attributed to inborn dyslexia and dysgraphia. Instead, a more satisfactory explanation for Luria would derive from an answer to the following question: What is the *cause* of the slower rate of cognitive development in retarded children?

This question reveals a difference in the *level of analysis* of the developmental and difference orientations. Zigler's explication of cultural-familial retardation is based on a factorial level of analysis. His focus, as can be seen in other parts of this book, is on discovering and elucidating the role of the various factors that influence the behavior of cultural-familial retarded persons, the rate of cognitive development being only one of the important factors. Zigler also points to the necessity of considering heredity, socialization experiences, and emotional and motivational characteristics in explaining the behavior of retarded individuals. Luria, on the other hand, carried out a reductive analysis, seeking to discover the primary cause of the abnormal behavior of retarded persons at the biological level. Having assumed that retardation originates from a pathological physical makeup, he sought an explanation of the behavior at the biological level.

Interestingly, Luria and Zigler's different levels of analysis were determined in part from their different schema of categorization of normal and abnormal intellectual functioning. If cultural-familial retarded persons are part of the normal distribution of intelligence, no single biological or psychological factor is likely to account for differences between an IQ above 70 and one below 70. This is true because a normal distribution arises through the operation of multiple, independent factors. A single factor or cause, however, is more likely to account for differences between discrete groups, whether different age groups, pathological groups, or normal and abnormal groups.

Zigler's appreciation of the graduated changes in intellectual functioning in the human population, as well as of the arbitrariness of an IQ score of 70 as the line of demarcation between mentally retarded and nonretarded persons, led to his view of cognitive continuity between nonretarded and physiologically intact retarded individuals. His view that a difference exists in rate of cognitive development between retarded and nonretarded individuals is actually a description of the continuity of distribution of IQ scores between the retarded and nonretarded limits rather than an explanation for it. No single underlying factor could account for the continuity, or differences, between these two arbitrarily divided groups of individuals. Luria, on the other hand, perceived clear evidence for discontinuity between retarded and nonretarded individuals and thus could attempt to seek an underlying primary cause that led to the divergence of the two groups.

The Developmental-Difference Controversy in Verbal Mediation

There is no doubt from Luria's work and that of other investigators (Milgram, 1973) that retarded individuals have an IQ-related deficiency in employing the verbal system in cognitive tasks. Does this deficiency persist, however, once differences in cognitive level between retarded and nonretarded individuals are controlled? This is the question that is addressed in the developmental-difference controversy in verbal mediation of behavior. Although Luria did not examine this question directly, other researchers have attempted to do so.

O'Connor and Hermelin (1959) compared the performance of retarded and nonretarded children on two-choice size discrimination learning and reversal shift. The two groups of children had MAs of 5 years. The retarded group had an IQ range of 33–50 and CA range of 9–15 years. No attempt was made to distinguish type of retardation, although the IQ and CA ranges suggested that the group consisted of some organically retarded children.

Both the retarded and nonretarded children learned the original discrimination in about the same number of trials. In the reversal task, however, the retarded children required fewer trials to reach criterion. O'Connor and Hermelin repeated this experiment with another group of retarded children matched in age and IQ to the previous retarded group, but this time the children were asked to give a verbal account of correct responses during the discrimination trials. This group of children required a greater number of trials to learn the reversal than the previous group of retarded children. Their performance on the reversal shift was not significantly different from that of the normal children in the previous experiment.

O'Connor and Hermelin interpreted these results as evidence for Luria's notion of a dissociation between the verbal and motor systems in retarded children. The nonretarded children learned both a motor habit and verbal habit in the original discrimination. In the reversal task, they had to break both habits and learn two new ones. The retarded children in the first experiment took fewer number of trials to learn the reversal, because they had learned only a motor habit. But having to learn a verbal response impaired the reversal learning of the retarded children in the second experiment. It should be noted that the nonretarded children in this study, with a mean CA of 5.1, were probably still in the third stage of development in Luria's scheme, when internal speech does not yet have a regulatory role over behavior. Thus, the verbal and motor systems of the nonretarded children were also dissociated, though probably to a lesser degree than those of the retarded children. Older nonretarded children, with their better developed verbal system, would probably have adapted their verbal behavior with greater ease and efficiency in the reversal task.

Balla and Zigler (1964) attempted to replicate O'Connor and Hermelin's first experiment, employing separate groups of cultural-familial, organically retarded, and nonretarded children of MAs of 5 and 6 years. In contrast to O'Connor and Hermelin's findings, the nonretarded children in this study performed better on the reversal task than either of the retarded groups of children. There were no differences among the groups in the original discrimination learning. In addition, no differences among the groups were found in discrimination learning and switching involving three choices and in performance on a transposition task. In reflecting upon their findings and those of O'Connor and Hermelin (1959), Balla and Zigler (1964) concluded that the overall results did not lend support to Luria's position.

Another study examining the relationship between verbal ability and cognitive ability was conducted by Milgram and Furth (1963). These investigators examined concept attainment, or the discovery of a conceptual principle of solution, by educable retarded and nonretarded children of comparable MA on problems thought to differ along the dimension of language investment in the concept. Three tasks assessed the discovery of the concepts of sameness, symmetry, and opposition. They hypothesized that the concepts of sameness and symmetry are not language relevant; that is, the amount of a child's language experience and his ability to process that experience would not affect his discovery of those concepts. The concept of opposition, however, would be language relevant, because our language commonly uses word pairs as opposites (e.g., boy-girl, hot-cold). Thus, a child's verbal experiences and processing would affect his/her discovery of the opposition concept. The retarded children, aged 9 through 17, had an IQ range of 50-75. They were divided into four groups with mean MAs of 6, 7, 8, and 10 and compared with nonretarded children having the same mean CAs as the MAs of the retarded children.

In the sameness task, pairs of cards were presented on which either two identical or two different geometrical figures were drawn. For the symmetry task, the cards illustrated either a symmetrical figure or an asymmetrical figure. The correct solutions in these tasks were the cards with identical and symmetrical figures, respectively. The opposition task was carried out by presenting the child with four discs out of a series of eight having varying diameters. The experimenter pointed to either the largest or smallest disc, and the solution was the disc most different in size from that pointed to by the experimenter.

Milgram and Furth found that a smaller percentage of the retarded than the nonretarded children discovered the opposition concept. No differences were found in discovery of the sameness concept by the two groups of children. However, a greater percentage of retarded children discovered the symmetry concept. These findings were comparable to those obtained by Furth (1961) with deaf children.

Balla, Styfco, and Zigler (1971) attempted to replicate Milgram and Furth's (1963) study for the opposition concept. In addition to some methodological improvements, Balla et al. obtained independent estimates of how well the concept of opposition had been acquired by the children prior to the experiment and also examined the influence of an outerdirected style of problem solving on their performance. Retarded children have been found to be more outerdirected, relying to a greater extent on external cues in problem-solving situations, than nonretarded children (Balla & Zigler, 1979). For this reason, Balla et al. investigated the usage of the opposition concept under three different conditions, varying in the type of external cue provided to indicate the opposite of the correct response. One was a human-pointing condition, similar to that used by Milgram and Furth. The second was a color condition, in which the cue was a green circle, whereas the remaining circles from which the subject had to choose the correct response were red. The third was an external cue condition, in which the cue was a circle external to the four circles presented to the subject. The subjects were intellectually average, cultural-familial, and organically retarded children of MAs 6, 7, 8, and 10 years.

The findings across all conditions were consistent with those of Milgram and Furth (i.e., significantly fewer of the retarded children used the concept of opposition than the intellectually average children). The nonretarded children attained criterion in the fewest number of trials, whereas the organically retarded required the most and the cultural-familial an intermediate number. The intellectually average children and familial retarded children learned more easily in the human-pointing and external conditions than in the color condition, whereas the organically retarded children learned more easily in the human-pointing condition than in the color and external conditions. Another assessment of outerdirectedness was made by examining the number of errors next in size and next in position to the cue. Both of these types of errors were made most frequently by organically retarded children, least frequently by the intellectually average children, and intermediate in frequency by the cultural-familial retarded children. By these measures of outerdirectedness, therefore, the three groups of children differed in their reliance on an outerdirected style of problem solving. On two verbal tests of the opposition concept, which the investigators employed to assess the extent to which the subjects possessed the concept prior to the experiment, the intellectually average children performed best, the familial retarded children next best, and the organically retarded children worst. These findings indicated that the three groups of children had unequal access to the concept prior to the experimental testing. When differences in possession of the concept and degree of outerdirectedness were controlled, however, significant differences in the performance of the three groups of children remained. The results of this study, therefore, suggested the existence of an impairment in the verbal system of retarded children compared to nonretarded children of the same MA. Furthermore, this deficit may be observed in cultural-familial retarded as well as organically retarded children.

In spite of some positive findings from their own laboratory, Zigler and Balla (1971) have disputed the notion that a verbal mediation deficit over and above a lower level of verbal ability associated with their lower MA exists in mentally retarded individuals. They have pointed to the contradictory findings of many studies comparing retarded and nonretarded children of the same MA on efficiency of concept usage. In discussing O'Connor and Hermelin's, Milgram and Furth's, and their own studies, Zigler and Balla emphasized that a verbal deficiency in retarded children should have led to impaired performance in the tasks of three-choice size discrimination and reversal, transposition, and discovery of the concepts of sameness and symmetry. This criticism raises a controversial issue over the relationship between language and cognition that has been discussed by Milgram (1973). In their criticism, Zigler and Balla revealed their assumption that conceptual activity is fundamentally verbal activity. Milgram (1973) questioned this assumption and presented evidence that conceptual activity is not equivalent to verbal activity.

It is clear from Luria's writings that he recognized two different conceptualization systems during the period of development. These were the first-and second-signalling systems, which at first are dissociated but with increasing development become fully integrated in the normal individual. The first-signalling system is the perceptual-motor system underlying the "primitive" cognition of animals and young children. The second-signalling system, based on language, gradually comes to predominate over the first-signalling system and lends richness and flexibility to normal adult cognition.

Of importance in the developmental-difference controversy is the question whether the development of the verbal and motor systems and the degree of dissociation between them are equal in retarded and nonretarded children of equal MA. The answer depends largely on what psychological processes constitute conceptual ability, and which of these processes are reflected in the MA score. If conceptual activity is equated with verbal processing, as Zigler and Balla seem to believe, then no differences between retarded and nonretarded children of equal MAs would be expected on cognitive tasks. If conceptual activity is more than verbal processing, as Milgram (1973) suggested, and the equal MAs of the retarded and nonretarded children do not reflect the extra ingredient, then differences on some types of conceptual tasks between the groups would be expected. Thus, the type of conceptual demand made by the task as well as the subject's level of cognitive functioning would determine whether the results favor the defect position or the developmental position regarding verbal mediation ability in retarded children.

According to Luria, retarded children function fairly normally on the basis of the first-signalling system and thus would be expected to do well on tasks not requiring verbal processing. They would compare favorably particularly in relation to nonretarded children of low CA, who also rely predominantly on perceptual–motor processing for problem solving. The predominance of perceptual–motor processing might account for the similarities observed in the retarded and nonretarded groups of equal MA in discrimination learning, the three-choice reversal and transposition tasks, and the usage of the sameness concept in the studies discussed earlier. Because the stimuli employed in these studies were pictorial and the response required of the 5- and 6-year MA children was pointing, the exact nature of the conceptual demands made by these tasks is uncertain. The equality of performance by the retarded and nonretarded children on these tasks does not unequivocally speak of their respective verbal conceptual abilities.

When definite verbalization is involved in a task, on the other hand, we have a somewhat clearer idea of the verbal demands of the task. In a series of interesting studies in which cultural–familial and nonretarded children of comparable MA were verbally trained on acquisition of conservation in Piagetian-type problems, Dorothy Field (1977, 1979) found that retarded children were able to acquire conservation through verbal training as well as children of average intelligence. Children with MAs greater than 5 years trained by means of verbal rules learned to conserve the quantities that were trained, generalized to other quantities, gave adequate verbal justifications for their responses, and retained their conservation understanding for long periods of time, as shown by posttests given up to 16 months after training. Interpreted according to Luria's scheme, Field's results indicate that cultural–familial retarded children can reach the third stage of development, in which external speech is able to exert analytic and synthetic functions in cognition. Moreover, retarded children appear to be able to perform these cognitive functions at the same MA level as nonretarded children.

As we have seen, even on tasks that involve some type of verbal conceptual ability, as in the processing of verbal rules to acquire conservation or in the discovery of the concept of opposition, retarded children do not perform consistently. They demonstrate either equal ability or inferior ability compared to more intelligent children of the same MA. The reason for this inconsistency may lie in differing cognitive demands of the tasks. In terms of Luria's developmental framework, for example, the discovery of the opposition concept involves the abstractive function of internal speech that is not evident until the child reaches the fourth stage of cognitive development. Field's task, on the other hand, involves processing that is characteristic of the third-stage level of development, in which external speech is able to exert regulatory control over behavior.

These contradictory findings on verbal mediation ability of retarded children also suggest that greater clarity and refinement of our notions of verbal mediation, conceptual processing, and cognition are needed. Luria viewed cognitive development as a progression from regulation by an impellant function of external speech to regulation by a significative function of internal speech. He devoted considerable attention to studying the earlier stages of speech's regulation of behavior but relatively little attention to the last stage, in which the significative function of internal speech predominates. Although Vygotsky and Luria believed that internal speech forms the basis for all types of intellectual activity in the average adult, this view has been criticized by Milgram (1973) and Piaget (1962), who believe that cognitive processing does not depend exclusively on verbal functioning.

Perhaps the most significant contribution made by Luria is the notion that verbal processing undergoes a gradual evolution during the developmental period. Unfortunately, he did not examine all the aspects of this evolution in as great detail as we might wish. It remains for others to build upon the framework laid down by Luria and reshape it as necessary. Only as this is accomplished, as we gain a greater understanding on the exact nature of verbal mediation and its relationship to cognition throughout the developmental period, can we begin to answer the question of whether the verbal processing impairment of retarded children is related only to their level of cognitive development, or whether it represents a qualitatively different disorder in cognitive functioning.

REFERENCES

Balla, D., Styfco, S. J., & Zigler, E. Use of the opposition concept and outerdirectedness in intellectually average, familial retarded, and organically retarded children. *American Journal of Mental Deficiency*, 1971, *75*, 663-680.

Balla, D., & Zigler, E. Discrimination and switching learning in normal, familial retarded, and organic retarded children. *Journal of Abnormal and Social Psychology*, 1964, *69*, 664-669.

Balla, D., & Zigler, E. Personality development in retarded individuals. In N. R. Ellis (Ed.), *Handbook of mental deficiency* (2nd ed.). Hillsdale, N.J.: Lawrence Erlbaum Association, 1979.

Field, D. The importance of the verbal content in the training of Piagetian conservation skills. *Child Development*, 1977, *48*, 1583-1592.

Field, D. A. *Comparison of the Acquistion of Mentally Retarded and Nonretarded Children*. Paper presented at the NATO International Conference on Intelligence and Learning, York, England, July 19, 1979.

Furth, H. G. The influence of language on the development of concept formation in deaf children. *Journal of Abnormal and Social Psychology*, 1961, *63*, 386-389.

Luria, A. R. *The role of speech in the regulation of normal and abnormal behavior*. New York: Liveright (Pergamon Press), 1961. (a)

Luria, A. R. An objective approach to the study of the abnormal child. *American Journal of Orthopsychiatry*, 1961, *31*, 1-16. (b)

Luria, A. R. Psychological studies of mental deficiency in the Soviet Union. In N. R. Ellis (Ed.), *Handbook of mental deficiency*. New York: McGraw-Hill, 1963.

Luria, A. R. *The making of mind* (M. Cole & S. Cole, Eds.). Cambridge, Mass.: Harvard University Press, 1979.

Milgram, N. A. Cognition and language in mental retardation: Distinctions and implications. In D. K. Routh (Ed.), *The experimental psychology of mental retardation*. Chicago: Aldine, 1973.

Milgram, N. A., & Furth, H. G. The influence of language on concept attainment in educable retarded children. *American Journal of Mental Deficiency*, 1963, *67*, 733-739.

O'Connor, N., & Hermelin, B. Discrimination and reversal learning in imbeciles. *Journal of Abnormal and Social Psychology*, 1959, *59*, 409-413.

Piaget, J. Comments. In L. S. Vygotsky, *Thought and language*. Cambridge, Mass.: The MIT Press, 1962.

Zigler, E. Familial mental retardation: A continuing dilemma. *Science*, 1967, *155*, 292-298.

Zigler, E., & Balla, D. Luria's verbal deficiency theory of mental retardation and performance on sameness, symmetry, and opposition tasks: A critique. *American Journal of Mental Deficiency*, 1971, *75*, 400-413.

8 Research Perspectives in Mental Retardation

Norman R. Ellis
University of Alabama

Albert R. Cavalier
*Partlow State School
and Hospital
University of Alabama*

The behavioral sciences commitment to mental retardation began in earnest after World War II. The preceding years had witnessed only scattered, nonsystematic research efforts, most of which had been in the psychometric tradition—the development of tests, intercorrelations of tests, measures to detect "organicity," and the like. Few of these studies had the earmarks of experimental psychology, including experimental designs in which variables are manipulated; the study of topics such as learning, memory, discrimination, transfer, or perception; and rigorous quantitative methods. McPherson (1948) found only nine laboratory studies on learning in the retarded during the period 1904 to 1948. In a review covering the next decade, she uncovered 14 additional studies (McPherson, 1958). Behavioral theories fared little better. Most of the literature described comparative studies contrasting retarded persons with normal persons, or retarded persons of differing IQ or MA levels. A few studies tested theories from general psychology, merely using retarded persons as convenient organisms. A notable exception is Kounin's work (1941a, b), in which Lewin's Theory (1936) was applied to the retarded and the "Kounin-Lewin theory" about the behavior of the retarded was developed. Perhaps, the position of Strauss and his associates (see Strauss & Lehtinen, 1947) could be described as a theory developed, in part, about retarded children. Before the 1950s, however, both research and theory pertaining to the behavior of retarded persons were scarce.

Beginning in the late 1950s, research in mental retardation burgeoned and theory in the area soon followed. The *Handbook of Mental Deficiency* published in 1963 collated the major research efforts and theories of the time. These included the sophisticated and influential attention theory of Zeaman and House, the insightful deductions from field theory by Herman Spitz, and the extensive application of social learning theory by Rue Cromwell. Most of the research with the retarded supporting these theories was conducted in the 5-year period antedating the book's publication. The theories of Luria, Piaget, and Hull were also invoked to "explain" the inadquate behavior of the retarded. The stimulus trace theory (Ellis, 1963) was presented in this volume. Another important theory appearing in the early 1960s was the developmental theory of Edward Zigler (See Zigler, 1966a, b). The initial impetus for Zigler's work was his rejection of the rigidity notion advanced by Lewin and Kounin. Zigler and his associates have since conducted a systematic series of studies that show that social-motivational variables are especially important in the behavior of retarded persons.

Zigler has also been concerned with the issue of research strategies and the orienting attitudes toward research in mental retardation. In 1969, Zigler classified theories in mental retardation as "developmental" and "difference or defect" theories. The last two were similar in some respects. Other issues pertaining to research and theory testing were addressed. Two other articles in the same journal, by Milgram (1969) and by Ellis (1969), described other approaches to research and offered rebuttal to some of Zigler's criticisms of difference and/or defect theories. The debate has continued.

Our purpose here is to review the approach we have adopted for our own research and to respond to some of the issues raised by Zigler and others. In particular, we review the logic of the research strategy reflected in the stimulus trace theory (Ellis, 1963) and in the rehearsal deficiency theory (Ellis, 1970) as prototypic "defect" theories; analyze the assumptions and central tenets of the developmental theory; review selected contemporary studies bearing on the stimulus trace theory; provide an interface for the stimulus-trace and the rehearsal deficiency theories; and discuss in general the IQ/short-term memory (STM) relationship. We adopt Zigler's (1969) terminology and refer to these positions as "defect" theories, but it later becomes clear that these positions do not have all the characteristics Zigler attributes to defect theories.

The Logic of the Defect Approach

We perceive organisms as developing, changing over time, the nature and extent of change being determined by heredity and environment. Development may be, and usually is, both physical and behavioral (or mental). Children grow larger and become capable of more difficult and complex behaviors. At one age, they are capable of behaviors they could not perform at an earlier age, but definitive evidence on whether development occurs in stages or is continuous is not in hand. We can only be sure that it develops, becoming more varied and complex. Those aspects of behavior labeled *cognitive* also change over time, and some of the changes are measurable with intelligence tests. It is generally agreed that all cognitive behaviors are not measured by any one intelligence test, and some insist that intelligence tests merely reflect achievement that is in turn dependent on underlying cognitive processes. In any case, most accept mental age (MA) as a measure of cognitive developmental level. Growth in MA presumably becomes asymptotic at around 18 years of age. Although older adults may score higher on mental tests, presumably it is due to further acquisition of knowledge and not to continuing maturation of cognitive processes.

Children defined as mentally retarded develop at a slower rate than normal children, and as adults they never catch up. (We adopt the American Association on Mental Deficiency definition of mental retardation; see Grossman, 1977.) In other cases the condition seems to be familial and/or associated with lowered opportunity to learn. The "damage" may occur at or before birth or at any age in the developmental years. It may be mild and hardly noticeable, or it may be devastating, even resulting in early death. Whether the insult to the organism is a result of genetic mechanisms, disease, injury, or learning environment, we assume that the nervous system is affected. That is, low intelligence (IQ) is presumptive evidence of a "damaged" nervous system (Baumeister & MacLean, 1979). No doubt a number of variables are important in determining the behavioral sequelae of central nervous system (CNS) pathology—the number of areas affected; the particular areas affected; the age of the organism and level of cognitive development at the time of insult; and the postinsult environment. But, behavior theories of the difference or defect type that seek to establish nomothetic laws of retarded behavior assume that insult to the CNS, however and whenever it occurs, produces common defects or deficiencies in all the organisms studied. Typically, in research deriving from these theories, equal MA or chronological age (CA) retarded persons are compared with nonretarded persons, and it is expected that members of the retarded group will exhibit deficits in attention, learning, memory, discrimination, or some other process. Although the deficit may not be reflected in every group member, or it may appear in varying degrees in different members, these variations are assumed to reflect imprecision in procedure, differing degrees of CNS insult, or experimental error. A statistically significant group mean difference in the dependent variable leads to the conclusion that retarded persons, similar to those studied, have deficient STM, attention, or another process deficit. In support of this approach, deficiencies are pervasive, their absence quite rare. Groups of retarded persons representing diverse etiological conditions may exhibit STM or attention deficits; if all group members do not show the deficit, increasing task difficulty (i.e., increasing the demand on the process being studied) usually will result in inadequate performance on the part of the retarded subjects. There are a few exceptions.

The notion of common behavioral deficits reflects both a strength and a weakness of the difference/defect position. Certainly, if retarded persons have common behavioral characteristics, it is important to know what they are. An enormous advance toward understanding, and possibly, ameliorating retarded behavior would be made in identifying the deficiencies. On the other hand, if each investigator who seeks to identify a deficiency finds one, the concept of specific inadequacy in a context of adequate (normal) processes is invalid. The retarded would simply be inadequate generally (i.e., deficient in all cognitive processes). There is some evidence to the contrary, however. For example, serial position curves in memory tasks apparently show the retarded to be deficient in the primacy portion of the curve but not in the recency section (Belmont & Butterfield, 1971; Ellis, 1970). If this finding is genuine (i.e., not due to measurement artifacts), it is supportive of the deficiency concept. Zeaman and House (1979) demonstrate attention deficits in the retarded but normal rates of learning once learning begins. To demonstrate that some behavioral processes are normal in the retarded whereas others are inadequate would, as noted, be of tremendous importance. Our understanding would become more precise, and remediation attempts could capitalize on cognitive process strengths and offer grounds for training in the deficient areas.

It should be clear to the reader that a "defect" or "difference" refers to the contemporary behavior of the person. If a retarded person in the laboratory performs below "normal" on a STM task, we conclude that the individual has a defect in STM. *Defect* is a term descriptive of subnormal behavior. We make no assumptions about the origins of the deficit. With rare exceptions, the study of the retarded is ex post facto, and clinical histories are quite unreliable. Although we may speculate about the ultimate etiology of a cognitive deficit, the determination of such causes in the history of the individual is not a scientific objective of our approach. Not only do we recognize the serious limitations in establishing such information, we also question its usefulness from a behavioral-theory standpoint. Constructs based in behavior seem to have far greater value in understanding, predicting, and changing behavior. This is not to deny that at some later time a rapprochement may occur between neurophysiological and behavioral studies, allowing prediction from one to the other. We have not yet reached such a state, however. Instead, our approach attempts to establish behaviorally defined logical constructs that carry the explanatory burden.

In search of differences/defects, we compare retarded and normal persons of similar CA. This approach reflects the fundamental distinction between retarded and nonretarded persons. The mother compares her child with a neighbor's of the same age and notes that hers is not yet walking, talking, or keeping up in class. Retarded adults are defined, not by comparison with nonretarded children, but with other adults. These are the differences that the behavioral sciences must explain—why one child learns to talk, read, socially interact, and another does not or does so at a later age. Our research strategy is to compare equal CA retarded and nonretarded persons in experimental situations that may identify the process(es) underlying various aspects of the deficient behavior. Our initial research sought to identify rather broad areas of deficit, memory, for example. Later efforts have attempted more fine-grained analyses, and memory research with the retarded has been divided into short- and long-term memory and into acquisition, storage, and retrieval. Currently, various conceptual approaches have elaborated these cognitive functions, including a host of metaprocesses (Borkowski & Cavanaugh, 1979; Campione & Brown, 1977; Evans & Bilsky, 1979; Glidden, 1979).

Because we study contemporary behavior as presented in the laboratory, we may choose to view deficits from a developmental point of view. Indeed, one of the assumptions by Ellis (1963) of the stimulus trace theory was that: "the young child has a stimulus trace deficit, and the establishment of the adult form of the short-term memory function will show a developmental trend [p. 140]." Whether or not developmental variables are singled out for study, the stimulus trace theory and our other notions of human memory (Ellis, 1970) are based firmly in the belief that behavioral/cognitive processes *develop*.

We turn now to issues that have been raised by Zigler and others that pertain to defining difference/defect theories and to the distinctions between these theories and Zigler's developmental theory. Hopefully, these comments further clarify the difference/defect position and communicate our own orientation to research and theory construction in this area.

The Two-Group Issue

Zigler (1969) posits that there are two etiological groups of retarded persons: those retarded as a result of polygenic inheritance and those with definite organic pathology. His developmental theory applies to the first group but not to the second. These "cultural-familials" are presumed to develop cognitively at a slower rate and to reach a lower final level of development. Intellectually average and retarded persons at the same stage of development, as determined by MA on an intelligence test, are similar in cognitive processes. They may differ in motivation and other attributes, but cognitively they should perform equally on "cognitive" tasks. The organically retarded are not addressed in Zigler's theory. In fact, he does not object to difference/defect theories of the "organically" retarded.

In our view, defining subjects for research because they seem to fit the polygenic model of the inheritance of intelligence is a highly tenuous procedure. The polygenic model itself is a hypothesis. From this hypothesis a model is derived, and from this model it is predicted that certain percentages of the population will have certain IQs. Retarded persons, mainly those with IQs in the mild range, are judged to derive from this type of inheritance, presumably in combination with a poor environment. Typically, these persons with higher IQs yet still in the retarded range, with parents and/or siblings with similar IQs, and without neurological signs of brain injury are classified as "cultural-familial." These are the subjects of Zigler's research and the basis for his developmental theory.

Firstly, in the vast majority of cases, it is impossible to know the full past history of the retarded person. In public institutions, from which most subjects are recruited, records are especially poor and the etiology of the condition in most cases is quite difficult to determine. Sorting potential subjects into those retarded as a result of polygenic inheritance (even if we could be sure that such mechanisms exist) and those retarded as a result of other conditions is highly risky at best. In practice, the distinction is often made on the basis of IQ alone. We believe that the present technology of diagnostic procedures does not provide a reliable basis for sorting the retarded into "organics" and "cultural-familials."

Secondly, behavioral research has not differentiated organic and cultural-familial retarded persons (i.e., behavioral studies taken as a whole have failed to find distinctive and reliable behavioral correlates of these etiological categories. See Baumeister & MacLean, 1979, and Belmont, 1971, for further discussion of this issue). Even easily diagnosed clinical types such as Down Syndrome do not display behavioral characteristics that set them apart.

Finally, there is increasing evidence that most retarded persons have brain "damage." Baumeister and MacLean (1979) summarize a number of studies to illustrate this point: Crome (1960) found neuropathology in "most" of the 282 institutionalized retarded persons at autopsy; Jellinger (1972) found organic pathology in over 90% of 1000 cases at postmortem examination; Malamud (1964), in 1410 autopsies, found only 2.5% without definite neuropathology. As Baumeister and MacLean point out, these autopsies were performed on persons who had been institutionalized and therefore more likely to have been severely affected, some were mildly retarded and examination techniques may have overlooked many with organic damage. Furthermore, "brain damage" may be quite subtle, affecting the structure and function within neurons or at synaptic junctures.

It has long been recognized that structural changes in the brain may involve such subtle differences as the growth of nerve endings or the size of individual neurons (Hebb, 1949). It seems likely that subtle differences in brains may result from differences in environment and the opportunity to learn. With advances in brain assay techniques, the identification of morphological correlates of cultural-familial mental retardation may be expected. This projection stems from a recognition of the intimate relationship between the brain and behavior. Because the behavior of retarded persons is abnormal, we expect that brain correlates that are also abnormal will be found.

Baumeister and MacLean (1979) have taken a somewhat similar approach. They state:

> If we make the assumption that intelligent behavior is mediated through the central nervous system, then one may conclude that, to the extent that behavior is impaired, defects of the central nervous system are inevitably implicated [p. 199].

They cite findings by Tredgold and Soddy (1963) and by Masland (1958) that tend to support this notion. Baumeister and MacLean conclude:

> unless otherwise shown, brain injury (in its broadest sense) is always present in cases of mental retardation. This perspective then requires that brain damage be ruled out and that is very difficult to do, rather like proving a null hypothesis. Nevertheless, it is our impression that the role of brain pathology is greatly underestimated as a feature of mental retardation [p. 199].

These authors view degree of brain injury as being continuous, with some persons very mildly affected, requiring careful study to uncover aberrations, and others barely alive with profound neurological damage. Differing labels, ranging from minimal brain dysfunction or learning disability to profound mental retardation, are applied to persons along this continuum. A vast range of behavioral symptoms may occur at any point along the continuum.

We concur with the Baumeister and MacLean position. As a working hypothesis, we assume that behavioral deficits definable as mental retardation are presumptive evidence of CNS pathology. Those who seek behavioral evidence for CNS pathology in terms of "neurological signs" in retarded persons are ignoring the most obvious sign, low IQ.

For these reasons, we reject the strategy of dividing the retarded into "organic" and "culturally-familially" retarded. Of course, selecting groups for study on the basis of symptoms that presumably distinguish these groups would be an entirely legitimate procedure. Unfortunately, it has not yet been a productive one. Behavioral theories of differences between these hypothesized types should follow some substantive evidence of *behavioral* differences. Our research approach will not succeed or fail on the basis of the previous assumptions regarding brain-behavior relationships. Moreover, it will also be able to handle behavioral differences among etiological types, should they occur.

Physiological-Behavioral Theory

Throughout Zigler's critique of defect theories, he seems to equate defect with a physiological and/or morphological state of affairs and to demand that these defects be point-at-ables. Zigler (1969) notes:

> use of organic retardates presents an almost insurmountable problem when one attempts to evaluate the degree to which any differences in behavior support the

major theoretical premise which underlies most difference approaches. This premise, clearly seen in the work of Luria, Spitz, and Ellis, is that all retardates, familials and organics alike, suffer from one specifiable deficit. However, until the etiological issue is attended to in the research design, there is no way of assessing how much of the difference between normals and retardates of the same MA is a product of the gross organic pathology known to exist in the retarded group and how much is a product of the deficiency thought by the difference theorists to exist in all retardates [p. 552].

Some confusion exists in this last sentence. We hypothesize that whatever differences exist in all retarded persons are products of the behavioral constructs we devise. It would not seem meaningful to attempt to explain some behavioral deficits as due to "organic pathology" and some as due to logical construct X or Y. Philosophically, we feel that all deficiencies stem from organic pathology but in terms of understanding and predicting behavior, such information, even if factually established, would be of little use. Instead, we wish to devise all the explanatory constructs from the observable behavior.

In view of the language in which the original presentation of the stimulus-trace theory is couched, it is understandable that it might be viewed as a physiological or "quasineurological" theory. On the contrary, the theory is entirely a behavioral theory. The concept of neurological integrity is a logical construct inferred from the relationship between the stimulus complex and the consequent behavior. The manipulated variables in the various studies are nonphysiological. (If one chooses to define EEG alpha blocking as physiological, this constitutes one exception.) Of course, we elaborated possible underlying neurophysiological correlates of the behavioral phenomena and summarized substantial work in neurophysiology which identified processes that tended to parallel stimulus trace, but this was not required by the theory. In sum, the defect we suspected is behavioral, not physiological.

Structural Features Versus Control Processes

An issue closely related to the physiological/behavioral issue is the differentiation of structural features and control processes in cognitive functioning, first proposed by Atkinson and Shiffrin (1968) and adopted by many others. Based on a computer analogy, structural features are similar to the hardware (and firmware), fixed and unmodifiable. Control processes, on the other hand, are like the software, docile and at the option of the organism. Campione and Brown (1977) note:

The essential difference between structural and control failures lies in their susceptibility to training: control deficiencies are, by definition, trainable, while structural features are not... Empirically, the question of whether a retardate deficiency reflects structural or control features rests on the effectiveness of training procedures. If the deficiency responds to training, control failures are implicated; if training is unsuccessful, the inference is that structural difference is involved [p. 369].

Campione and Brown point out difficulties with these concepts. Foremost among these is the fact that to label a failure "structural" would require exhausting all possible training approaches (i.e., proving the null hypothesis).

Stimulus trace has usually been treated as a structural feature, fixed and invariant within the organism (Campione & Brown, 1977). The question has not been settled, however. To our knowledge, no studies have attempted to "cognitively" influence the magnitude and duration of the stimulus trace. Although such studies might be important from an applied standpoint, we see little value in attempting the conceptual distinction between structure and control. Instructions to subjects, induced changes in cognitive strategy, or other manipulations that lead to changes in the dependent variable (and to defining a process as "control") demonstrate that a once-asymptotic behavior can be modified by changing the test conditions. With this distinction, uncovering the appropriate manipulations would necessitate changing the classification from structural feature to control process. However, the distinction might discourage such investigations in the first place. It seems very doubtful that there are very many molar behaviors of human beings that cannot be modified to some extent.

A logic somewhat similar to the structure/control distinction leads to the conclusion that a deficit does not really exist in retarded behavior, if it can be modified or caused to occur spontaneously as a result of training. Of course, training and instruction may well bring a retarded child up to the functional level of a normal child on a particular task. But, this does not negate the proposition that the retarded child had a deficiency. Because external assistance was needed to bring performance to normal levels, some deficit(s) had been identified. This is similar to the view of Resnick and Glaser (1976) that a major component of intelligence is the ability to derive solutions under conditions in which they have not been specifically trained or are not directly prompted. Certainly, the notion of overcoming a cognitive deficit through training would be much stronger if it could be shown that the training generalizes to other dissimilar tasks and situations that make similar cognitive demands. Unfortunately, this has not been the case. In regard to this point, Campione and Brown (1977) state: "we would argue that the vast majority of the studies have been concerned with *maintenance* rather than generalization. That is, the format of the transfer task is the same as that employed during training [p. 380]."

Typically, when retarded persons are taught to use a process that they did not previously use, they are said to have had a "production deficiency" (Flavell, 1970). For example, having been taught to organize the items of a to-be-remembered word list into associated clusters, memory of retarded subjects is improved more than that of nonretarded subjects. If it could be shown that instruction in organizational strategies generalizes to other *dissimilar* tasks, a firmer basis for contending that a deficit had been ameliorated would have been established. To be sure, task-specific training should not be confused with the training of *cognitive processes*.

The Developmental Theory

Zigler's (1969) developmental theory proposes that children at the same cognitive levels, as measured by MA on an intelligence test, are similar cognitively and will not differ in performance on cognitive tasks. Exceptions would occur when motivation or some other noncognitive variable produced differences. Figure 8.1 presents his "model of cognitive growth." Obviously, to the extent that groups are equated on cognitive level and the comparison task measures cognitive skills, the groups should perform similarly. Of course MA does not perfectly measure all cognitive skills, and, also, there may be noncognitive components in the criterion task. In such cases, differences in the MA matched groups can be expected. From our view, if the measuring instruments were perfect, MA would be a perfect measure of all cognitive skills: One of these skills would constitute the dependent variable in studies of cognitive development. Such studies would confirm the obvious.

In practice, both IQ and MA are less than perfect, and, therefore, we cannot decide whether older retarded persons are cognitively similar to younger normal persons. Thus, the developmental theory remains a theory. This is not to disparage the developmental theory; it is empirically testable and tests of it continue to be made. Its confirmation or refutation would be an enormously important advance in knowledge.

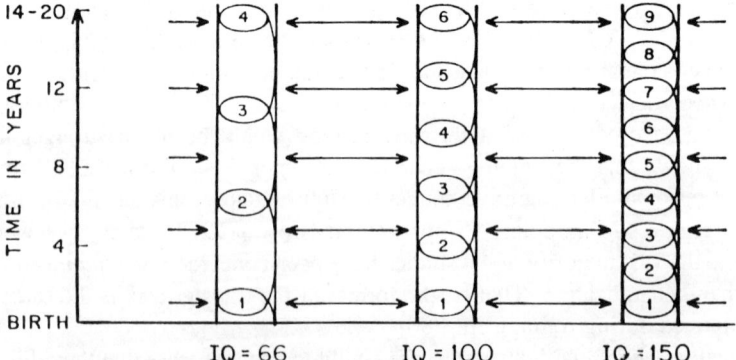

FIG. 8.1. Zigler's developmental model of cognitive growth (modified version). The vertical arrow represents chronological age. The horizontal arrows represent environmental influences on the individual, who is represented by a pair of vertical lines. Cognitive development is represented by an internal ascending spiral, with the numbered loops representing successive "stages."

We do have misgivings about certain aspects of the theory. It may be seen in Fig. 8.1 that a 100-IQ child of about 6 years of age has reached level 3 of cognitive development, a level reached by the IQ-66 child about 5 years later. Yet, these two children are assumed to be cognitively the same. This implies a trade off between experience and organic potential. Five additional years is equivalent, quantitatively and qualitatively, to the "organic" inadequacy. We view the rich variety of complex cognitive processes as deriving from the interaction of past environmental experiences and inheritance. Ten units of inheritance and 20 units of environmental experience may result in a cognitive structure similar to that produced by 20 units of inheritance and 10 of environmental experience, but we have serious doubts about this.

In describing the developmental theory, Balla and Zigler (1979) state:

"for the cultural-familial group, we endorse the general developmental approach to the understanding of their development (e.g., Zigler, 1969). Stated most simply, the developmental theorist views the culturally-familially retarded person as an essentially normal individual in the sense that he falls within the normal variation dictated by the gene pool. Thus, we believe that the behavior of this group of retarded persons is best understood by the principles found to be generally applicable to nonretarded persons. Finally, we believe that the most relevant nonretarded comparison group in most personality studies are nonretarded persons of equivalent developmental levels, most typically assessed by mental age (MA). This is the best way to separate clearly experiential from developmental determinants of personality. We do think, however, when the interest of the study is in delineating both cognitive and experiential determinants of performance, both MA and chronological age (CA) retarded comparison groups are most relevant [p. 143]."

We find this position puzzling. To assume that we separate "experiential from developmental determinants of personality" by equating groups on MA is to assume that experience is not a contributor to MA (i.e., to cognitive development). To match nonretarded and retarded persons on MA merely equates them on *some* aspects of contemporary behavior. This same behavior has been determined *by experience* and organic maturational variables. Actually, this state of affairs is depicted in Zigler's model shown in Fig. 8.1.

Further, Balla and Zigler attempt to delineate "both cognitive and experiential determinants of personality." Because we assume that experience is a central determinant of cognitive processes, it is not meaningful to view them both as determinants of behavior or personality. They are at different levels of analysis, and the degree to which one produces the other cannot be determined.

Finally, we recognize the experimental "convenience" of MA-matched studies. Moreover, to know that retarded persons are like younger nonretarded persons would be of immense practical, perhaps even theoretical, value. However, data from such designs are not open to clear interpretation. Moreover, the assumption that cognitive abilities and experience can be isolated in such studies is even contradicted by the developmental theory.

Criticisms of Difference and Defect Theories

Over the years, the publications of Zigler and his associates (see for example, Balla & Zigler, 1979; Butterfield, 1968a, b; Zigler, 1966a, b, 1969) have presented various characterizations of the theories they labeled "difference or defect" theories. We review and respond to some of these comments in the hope that our own position becomes clearer.

With reference to the stimulus trace theory, Zigler (1966a) states:

> With respect to his own experimental tests, Ellis' reliance on the IQ as the measure of neural integrity has produced two types of comparisons: retardates and normals of the same CA, and retardates and normals of the same MA. In either comparison, Ellis' model would predict that the retardates would be inferior on tasks involving short-term retention because of their lower IQ.

He further notes:

> However, little evidence has come out of the Ellis work indicating that retardates and normals of the same MA differ on tasks involving short-term memory [pp. 139–140].

These comments reflect a misinterpretation of the trace theory. In the original presentation of the theory, Ellis (1963) stated:

> Although n_i has been defined as an intelligence test score, the IQ is nothing more than a sampling device for selecting populations which vary in level of adaptation. Other indices could be used: success in school, institutionalization, and non-institutionalization, or other criteria which reflect degree of adaptation.... the immature organism, the human infant, possesses behavioral characteristics which are similar to the defective [p. 140].

Because others have also treated equal MA comparisons as tests of trace theory, perhaps there is some ambiguity in the preceding statements. Let us clarify this point. Organisms of differing intelligence levels, that is, those differing in adaptive behavior, may be expected to differ in stimulus trace functioning. Because most of our original work, upon which the theory was based, dealt with adult retarded persons, we emphasized IQ as a measure of intelligence level. Surely, MA is another: a retarded or nonretarded person with a higher MA is viewed as being more intelligent (i.e., he/she is more capable of performing successfully on cognitive problems and exhibits more adaptive commerce with the environment). Therefore, the trace theory predicts superior trace functioning in higher IQ or higher MA persons. Those of similar IQ or MA should have comparable trace functioning. Then we must ask what will be the relative trace functioning of a 16-year-old retarded person with an MA of 8 and an IQ of 50 and a nonretarded child of 6 years with an MA of 6 and an IQ of 100? In this case, we tentatively suggest MA as the better indicator of adaptive behavior and predict that trace functioning will be greater in the retarded person. Because, to our knowledge, no such comparisons have been made, the prediction is conjectural. We feel on much safer ground predicting that retarded persons of equal CA will differ or that nonretarded persons of differing MA will differ. We do not feel that problems of "whether to use MA or IQ" are serious, if one bears in mind the intent of the notion. Oganisms differ in cognitive abilities: The stimulus trace is hypothesized to vary with level of cognitive ability, "docility," as Tolman (1932) might have put it.

On a related point, Zigler (1966a) stated: "it should be pointed out that the discovery of a difference between normals and retardates of the same CA is just as amenable to a general developmental interpretation as to the view that all retardates suffer from CNS pathology since the MA of such retardates is necessarily lower than the MA of the normals [p. 141]." It is agreed that such differences are interpretable as "developmental." We do not view "development," however, as an *explanatory* construct except in a limited sense. "Explaining" a behavioral difference by invoking the retarded person's slower rate of development still leaves unspecified, at the behavioral level, the reason for the slower rate of development. To "explain" STM differences between cultural–familial retarded persons and nonretarded persons of the same CA in terms of the developmental theory allows us to state only that: (1) The retarded person had reached a developmental level comparable to a particular level in a nonretarded person but lower than the level of the control persons; and (2) the relative performance on other trace tasks would also be lower. One must first know how a nonretarded person of equal MA would perform under similar circumstances, before anything could be said about the retarded. The developmental theory does not provide a clear basis for predictions based on differing experimental situations or tasks. Nor does it provide an obvious basis for the derivation of measures that may lead to improvement or the amelioration of the deficient behavior.

It is incorrect to depict development and CNS pathology as opposing or alternative interpretations of behavioral phenomena. Pathology is a central aspect of development in retarded persons. A stimulus trace deficit may be a product of cerebral trauma and *subsequent changes in environmental experiences*. Zigler and his associates imply that defect theorists equate behavioral defects with organic defects. Instead, we view defects such as stimulus trace in a developing, experiencing, and learning organism. The defect is a product of complex interactions among many variables in a developing organism.

In defining difference/defect theorists, Zigler (1969) comments: "I have classified, as difference or defect theorists, all workers who assume that the IQ is a reflection of certain features of the physiological or cognitive functioning of the individual and thus, must affect cognitive functioning over and above that predicted by the general cognitive level attained by the individual [p. 541]." It should now be clear to the reader that this statement does not characterize the stimulus trace theory. We make no predictions based on differential IQ of MA-matched subjects. Zigler (1969) goes on to state: "The crucial factor lies in the theorist's explanation of the etiology of the process thought to be producing the differences in behavior associated with IQ. In order for a formulation to be of the difference type, the etiology of the postulated defect or difference must inhere in the low IQ itself [p. 548]." Because stimulus trace is a molar behavior theory, its constructs refer only to behavior and the related stimulus conditions. Other etiological explanations are neither sought nor necessary. We do not understand the meaning of the phrase "defect or difference must inhere in the low IQ." Defect or difference refers to a part of the organisms's contemporary behavior and *therefore is a part of IQ* (i.e., a part of the organism's intelligent behavior).

Although Zigler and his colleagues initially did not distinguish difference and defect theories, he later came to do so. Zigler (1969) states: "The distinction rests completely on whether or not the theorist considers the particular shortcomings to vary across the entire range of intelligence [p. 549]." Those attributing shortcomings, varying in degree, to the whole intelligence range are difference theorists. Defects, on the other hand, apparently refer to qualitative differences between normal and retarded persons. Using this distinction, Zigler correctly classifies stimulus trace as a defect theory. We should note, however, that we expect persons with any downward deviation from average intellectual funtioning to exhibit trace deficits. This includes persons variously labeled as MBD, brain-injured, hyperactive, Strauss syndrome, autistic, dyslexic, or retarded.

Summary

Before turning to a review of the stimulus trace theory, and some of the pertinent research, we summarize the preceding comments:

1. Behavioral theories designed to provide a better understanding of retarded persons developed mainly in the late 1950s and early 1960s. During this period, notable changes occurred in the quality and quantity of research. Research interests shifted to topics relating to experimental, and away from traditional clinical psychology.

2. Some of the theories that have led to systematic research efforts were the attention theory of Zeaman and House, the cortical satiation theory of Spitz, the social learning theory of Cromwell, the stimulus trace theory of Ellis, the verbal mediation theory of Luria, and the developmental theory of Zigler.

3. Zigler and his associates have divided these theories into defect or difference theories and developmental theories. He and others have attempted to characterize differences in the approaches of the various theorists.

4. Here, we have attempted to analyze these presumed differences, as described by Zigler and others, and to describe our own approach to research and theory. We have found that a part of this controversy rests on misperceptions and misunderstanding.

5. Our analysis of the various theories leads us to conclude that it is incorrect to classify some as developmental and others as not. Some merely stress developmental variables more than others. All recognize, or implicitly assume, the importance of development in the history of the organism.

6. The stimulus trace theory is a defect theory. However, the "defect" is a molar behavioral construct and does not depend on physiological defects to establish its validity. The theory allows predictions based on differences in intelligence in equal CA persons, and in nonretarded persons of differing intellectual maturity, as measured by MA, for example.

The Stimulus Trace Theory

Since the publication of the trace theory 19 years ago, a number of experimental tests of the theory have been made. Some have found supportive evidence, some negative. A number were based on misinterpretations of the theory and many are flawed methodologically, with results that resolve nothing. We review the theory because it has served as a prototype of defect theories. Although there are slight differences between the present description and that of 1963, no substantive changes are intended. Instead, the intent is to clarify aspects of the theory that apparently have been misunderstood. Finally, we review selected studies that relate most directly to the theory.

Figure 8.2 depicts the model. n_i, neurological integrity, is defined by some index of intelligence. IQ is presented in the diagram but MA, DQ (development quotient), or some other measure that reflects varying levels of adaptive ability would serve equally well. n_i is a hypothetical or logical construct. Although we suspect that it has substantive existence in the underlying neurophysiology of the brain, it is a molar behavioral construct. Even if it were identified in the organic structure of the brain, its usefulness as a physiological construct in understanding, predicting, and controlling behavior would probably be less than that of its molar behavioral counterpart; that is, if we knew for a fact the n_i is due directly to the number and complexity of reverberatory circuits present in the brain, such information would be of little use at the present time.

S_t is the hypothetical construct "stimulus trace." It too is a molar behavioral construct, defined entirely in terms of environmental events, the stimulus complex and the organism's behavior. The stimulus trace is hypothesized to be the intraorganism representation of a stimulus or stimulus complex. With some limitations, the stimulus trace is presumed to vary in amplitude and duration as a function of stimulus characteristics. In the organism with diminished neurological integrity, it is hypothesized to be of less amplitude and shorter in duration. Therefore, for situations in which behaviors are separated in time from their

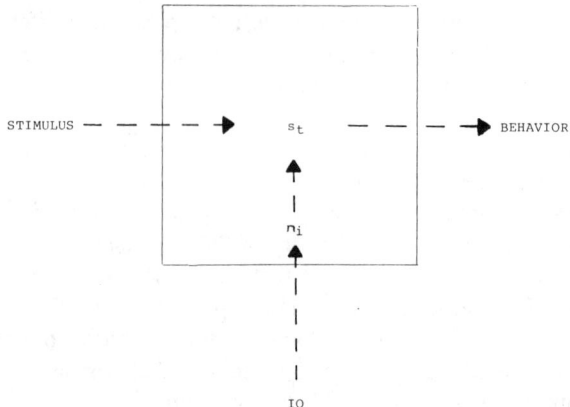

FIG. 8.2. The stimulus trace model. s_t represents stimulus trace, and n_i, central nervous system integrity.

eliciting, associated, or controlling stimuli, the stimulus trace will play an important bridging role. The less-intelligent organism with an impoverished stimulus trace can be expected to exhibit inadequate behaviors in such situations.

In the original formulation, a number of differing test paradigms were suggested, ranging from classical conditioning to serial recall. Tests of the trace theory using some of these more complex tasks have not been supportive, nor should we have expected them to be. In retrospect, the theory should have been offered as an explanation only for behaviors depending on passive, or primary memory, a minimally cognitive process. No doubt stimulus traces are present and necessary in the most complex behaviors, but many other variables influence those behaviors, and unambiguous predictions cannot be made. Some general predictions can be made for test situations in which the dependent behavior reflects the operation of passive, noncognitive memory:

1. Persons of equal CA differing in intelligence (IQ, MA, or similar measures) will differ in stimulus traces, with the less intelligent having diminished traces and therefore poorer primary memory, as defined by Waugh and Norman (1965), for example.

2. Persons of differing MA, irrespective of CA or IQ, will exhibit stimulus trace differences, with those of lower MA having traces of lower amplitude and duration, and, therefore, poorer primary memory.

3. Stimulus characteristics that increase the duration and amplitude of the trace will have a greater facilitating effect in less-intelligent persons, therein improving their primary memory relative to that of more intelligent persons.

4. Stimulus traces are expected to show a developmental trend in normal persons and also in those with CNS pathology. Consequently, primary memory

should improve with age in normal children. Retarded persons will also exhibit developmental changes in stimulus-trace functioning, but improvements will be less pronounced. Whether trace deficits are permanent in any persons is an empirical issue. Trace deficits may not be present in *all* persons with CNS pathology; however, we anticipate finding such deficits in most such persons.

There is some degree of criterion contamination in any experiment that selects subjects on the basis of intelligence tests and then analyzes some cognitive behavior as a dependent variable. In the case here, most intelligence tests include memory measures, and, of course, the dependent variable in a test of trace theory must reflect memory. We see no way to avoid this dilemma. If the memory subtest(s) are omitted in the subject selection process, essentially the same persons will be found in the subject sample, because the subtest scores are usually intercorrelated. This dilemma is more apparent than real, however. We already know that the subjects exhibit absolute differences in memory, for memory is a part of intelligence. We do not seek to establish absolute differences in the dependent variable, however, but rather to investigate the underlying memory *process*. The process is expected to be revealed by manipulating variables that *differentially* influence the process in persons of differing intelligence levels (Baumeister, 1967). Moreover, we expect to break the process down into subprocesses and to determine which of these relate to intelligence. Intelligence tests, by their global and static nature, do not provide the information we seek. However, misunderstanding of the objectives of behavioral research seems to be widespread. For example, Schonebaum and Zinober (1977) noted that:

> the distinction between 'defect' and 'developmental' interpretations of differences between retarded and normal people on learning and memory tasks has become controversial in recent years ... and seems to have diverted attention away from a more central issue. It has raised the question of whether performance differences indicate that retarded individuals are cognitively less efficient than normal persons, but it has obscured the question of how they are less efficient

Further:

> The experimental literature provides amply evidence that normal subjects outperform retarded subjects on a variety of learning and memory tasks ... therefore, the issue is not whether retarded individuals are less efficient in learning and memory, but how the steps taken by an individual who learns readily and remembers well differs from the responses which comprise the behavioral pattern of the less efficient person.

These statements are made even more puzzling by recognition later in Schonebaum and Zinober's article that the attention studies of Zeaman and House and the memory work of Belmont and Butterfield do seek "to evaluate the component processes." We fail to see how the other approaches of Luria, Spitz,

Ellis, Milgram, and others are not process oriented. Surely, research in this area has more lofty goals than to demonstrate "efficiency differences" in nonretarded and retarded persons.

Studies Bearing on Trace Theory

We now comment on selected studies that are relevant to the trace theory. No exhaustive review is attempted. The studies considered serve mainly to review the issues addressed by the trace theory. To anticipate the findings: The trace conditioning studies of Ross and associates and Lobb and coworkers generally support predictions from the theory. The Ferretti dissertation might be interpreted as negative evidence for the theory, but it along with the Cavalier dissertation raises fundamental questions about the nature of the deficit in persons with lowered intellectual functioning. The data collected by Cohen and his colleagues seriously challenge the current belief that passive or primary memory is comparable in persons of differing intelligence levels.

In keeping with the notion of stimulus trace as a brief passive memory process, classical trace conditioning provides a paradigm that seems minimally contaminated by cognitive variables. In the original trace theory, it was stated by Ellis (1963): "Classical trace conditioning is a case in point. The deleterious effect of increasing CS–UCS interval, that is, beyond the optimal value, should be more pronounced in the mentally defective [p. 145]." Ross and Ross (1976) have published a careful analysis of trace conditioning studies, including their own, and we do not redescribe these dozen or so studies here. In addition to the work of Ross and Ross, Lobb and his associates have conducted systematic studies on this issue, which are also included in the Ross and Ross analysis. (Lobb, 1968; Lobb & Nugent, 1966).

After reviewing these studies, Ross and Ross (1976) state:

> In 1969 Belmont and Butterfield summarized the literature comparing the trace and delay classical conditioning performance of normal and retarded subjects and concluded that trace conditioning involving varying demands upon retention does not differentiate Ss of different intellectual levels [p. 47]. However, since the time of their review additional data have been collected, and these data, as well as a reexamination of the data reviewed by Belmont and Butterfield (1969), indicate that their generalization may have been incorrect [p. 183-184].

They conclude:

> Thus it appears that there is a reliable retardate trace deficit in both EDR and eyelid conditioning. Under conditions similar to those used in these experiments, the critical trace interval length seems to be between 400 and 450 msec, although the EDR conditioning data in this trace interval range are limited. It is possible that further EDR conditioning research using trace intervals between 400 and 900 msec will reveal a somewhat different critical value for the EDR [p. 190].

These authors offer a number of caveats that should be heeded if other investigators attempt to demonstrate the trace deficit in conditioning studies.[1]

Although the trace conditioning findings are supportive of trace theory and in keeping with the original a priori predictions, on the face, trace conditioning seems unrelated to other paradigms used for the study of STM. To our knowledge, there have been no studies empirically establishing a relationship between trace conditioning and more conventional measures of memory. Although we believe that the trace conditioning studies uncover important information about behavioral inadequacy in the retarded, we have misgivings about the usefulness of labeling trace conditioning "memory."

In a recent doctoral dissertation, Ferretti (1979) compared primary memory in CA-matched retarded and normal adults. His study was modeled after those of Reitman (1971, 1974). The experimental paradigm combined a Brown-Peterson-type STM task and a signal detection-retention interval filler task. Subjects were presented sets of consonants to be recalled. Prior to the main study, individual subject "storage loads" were determined in order to equate acquisition at 70% correct recall at 0 sec. Retarded subjects were initially exposed to a 3-consonant set and normal subjects to a 4-consonant set. The exposure duration was 4 sec for both. Subjects read aloud the consonants and at the end of the 4-sec interval attempted to recall the consonants. Each time recall was perfect the exposure duration was reduced by .5 sec, until exposure time and reading time were approximately equal. Then, set size was increased in 1-consonant steps, with .5 sec added exposure duration for each. These adjustments resulted in an average memory load of 7.04 consonants and an exposure duration of 2.94 sec for normal subjects. For retarded subjects, these values were 4.96 consonants and 3.21 sec. The signal detection task interpolated during the 9 or 27 sec retention intervals consisted of listening for and signalling the occurrence of a tone. The loudness of the tones was adjusted on an individual basis to be equally difficult for all subjects. Following the retention interval, subjects recalled aloud.

Subjects were instructed not to rehearse. The signal detection task was designed to prevent rehearsal or to identify those who did rehearse. Using several indices of detection performance, Ferretti was able to identify 6 normal subjects who rehearsed, 18 normal nonrehearsers, 9 retarded rehearsers, and 15 retarded nonrehearsers within the two 24-subject groups. Normal nonrehearsing subjects were superior in recall to the retarded nonrehearsers, and there was a significant, approximately linear, decay of recall over the retention intervals. The comparison of rehearsers and nonrehearsers was marginally significant (.06). The interaction of intelligence level and retention interval was not significant: Forgetting curves for the normal and retarded subjects were parallel.

---

[1]Bolles (1979) interprets classical conditioning as dependent on anticipatory cognitive processes (see pages 153 ff). In a similar vein, Hall (1976) notes: "the bulk of experimental findings supports the position that awareness plays an important role in conditioning; however, further research is necessary to identify its appropriate contribution [p. 170]."

These results demonstrate that differential forgetting does not occur in normal and retarded adults under conditions in which memory loads are different. Despite Ferretti's adjustment procedure, performance levels at 0 sec were not equated. The retarded acquired an average of about 3.42 consonants, or 69% of those presented to them; the normals acquired about 5.20 consonants, or 74% of those presented to them. Under these conditions, forgetting did not differ in these subjects. We cannot be sure, however, that forgetting for *equal* storage loads would follow a similar course. Another recent dissertation comparing normal and "learning disabled" (LD) children bears directly on this issue.

Cavalier (1979) compared 36 normal (CA = 10.5 years, IQ = 103) and 36 LD children (CA = 10.1 years, IQ = 97) under highly motivating conditions on recall of consonant trigrams after retention intervals of 0, 3, 6, 12, 18, and 30 sec, using the Brown-Peterson paradigm. Retention intervals were either unfilled or filled with a task that required subjects to say aloud the names of single digits as they were randomly (visually) presented. The rate of digit presentation was determined in pilot work to be such that subjects would be maximally occupied but would not make a substantial number of errors. Unlike the Ferretti dissertation, Cavalier was not concerned with detecting and eliminating rehearsers. The intent was to present a demanding cognitive task, plot the course of forgetting, and compare the effects of encoding strategies. Subgroups of intellectually average and LD children were instructed in one of three encoding strategies that they were to use during the presentation interval: vocalization, in which they were to say the letters out loud twice; elaboration, in which they were to vocalize any words that began with the three consonants and that were conceptually related; and control, in which they were to "study" the trigram. After completing the task, children were asked if they did anything during either the presentation or the retention interval to aid in remembering the letters. Behavioral observations of active strategy usage (lip movements, whispering, vocalizing) during unfilled retention intervals were recorded.

The groups did not differ significantly at 0 sec recall. During the unfilled retention intervals, there was no appreciable forgetting for either group in any condition. Across filled retention intervals, the different encoding strategies had different effects on recall: the vocalization strategy had a suppressive effect on recall as compared to the other strategies, which did not differ from each other. These effects were similar in intellectually average and LD children. LD children showed significantly faster rates of forgetting than intellectually average children across filled intervals, regardless of encoding strategy. LD children also had lower levels of recall after 30 sec than intellectually average children. To approximate equal acquisition in both groups, the data of children who did not have perfect recall at 0 sec were eliminated. The significantly faster rate of forgetting and lower final level of recall for LD children were still in evidence.

The lack of any forgetting across unfilled retention intervals suggests that both intellectually average and LD children used cognitive strategies to retain the information. That the strategy manipulation produced similar effects across filled retention intervals in both groups is further evidence that intellectually average and LD children used these strategies. This is supported by postexperimental inquiries, in which all the LD children reported active strategy usage. Behavioral observations of such activity were recorded for 25 of the 36 LD children, including all 12 in the control condition. Assuming that rehearsal did not occur, or occurred minimally, during the filled retention interval, the faster rate of forgetting by the LD children suggests more fragile memory traces. More fragile memory traces have descriptively been referred to by others as "more susceptible to interference." The faster rate of forgetting and lower final level of recall in LD children reflect a more rapid loss from primary memory and possibly less transfer into or retrieval from secondary memory. Cavalier's results are contrary to a rehearsal-deficiency explanation. If nonretarded children are more mnemonically active, their performance should be more adversely affected by interpolating a rehearsal-distracting task in the retention interval when compared to recall after unfilled intervals, than that of LD children. Consequently, when nonretarded and LD children have the same amount of information to remember, the more fragile traces of the LD children should result in poorer primary memory. In addition, because of this reduced amount of available time in primary memory to employ cognitive strategies, poorer secondary memory should also result.

The LD children in Cavalier's study scored no lower than one standard deviation below the mean on intelligence tests, performed at least one year below grade expectancy in reading, one half year below grade expectancy in mathematics, and qualified for special class placement. Interpretation of the results in terms of stimulus trace is somewhat clouded, if IQ scores are taken as evidence of neurological integrity. The IQ scores are slightly lower, however, and these children have intellectual deficits, as we define them, indicated by their need for special services (Baumeister & MacLean, 1979; Resnick & Glaser, 1976).

Cohen and his associates have performed a series of studies that we interpret as suggestive evidence for primary memory deficits in subjects of low intelligence and, therefore, provide some support for a passive memory-trace deficiency. In the first study (Cohen & Sandberg, 1977), 9-digit numbers were presented auditorily at either 1 or 4 digits per sec. The letter A, B, or C, also presented orally, followed the ninth digit, indicating to the subject whether to recall the first, middle, or last three digits, respectively. The most reliable correlation coefficient was between C-digit recall and IQ. The other clear-cut finding was the absence of correlation between A digits and IQ. Some less-dependable relationship was found between B digits and IQ, which varied from group to group. Significantly, the subjects in this study apparently were all within the normal range of intelligence (i.e., with IQs of about 75 and above).

In Experiment II, in this same article, Cohen and Sandberg reported a replication of the first study and also a modified running memory-span experiment. In the latter, two series of 10 auditory digit sequences were presented, each varying in length from 9 to 20 digits. Subjects attempted to recall the last three digits in a sequence under conditions in which they could not anticipate the end of the series. Two presentation rates were used, 6 and 9 digits per sec.

The C-digit scores from the probe task correlated substantially, .62 and .53 (for 6 and 9 sec rates) with the running memory-task performance. The B-digit scores were also correlated, .34 and .34, with running memory; and, A-digit scores were unrelated to running memory, .07 and .17. IQ and running memory correlated .59 and .56 for 6- and 9-digit rates, respectively. For the probe task, A digits and IQ correlated $-.03$, B digits and IQ .30, and C digits and IQ .46. Cohen and Sanberg further noted that increasing presentation rate in the running memory task did not differentially affect low and high IQ subjects. Therefore, it would appear that IQ/STM correlations for recency items did not depend on encoding differences.

In Experiment III, Cohen and Sandberg made several minor modifications in the running memory-span task. They also included a visual presentation mode in the probe task, in addition to the auditory mode. The findings were quite similar to those in the previous studies, and Cohen and Sandberg (1977) concluded that: "maintenance rehearsal, chunking, and perceptual encoding do not appear to play a part in producing the IQ/STM correlations [p. 551]." The authors favored an "availability" explanation, based on individual differences in decay rate.

Cohen and Gowen (1978) attempted to determine whether or not the differences between the Cohen and Sandberg findings, particularly the IQ-recency correlation, and those of Ellis (1970) and Belmont and Butterfield (1971) could be due to the "ordered recall" requirement in the Cohen and Sandberg studies as compared to the recall of item information in the others. In their Experiment I, children ranging in IQ from 84 to 137 were studied. A running memory model was again used, in which 16 sequences of digits of varying length were presented at the rate of 4 digits per sec. A tone sounded at the end of a sequence, and subjects were instructed to recall the last three digits. In a serial recall condition, recall had to be in the order presented; in a free recall condition, ordered recall was not required. Free recall and IQ correlated .56; serial recall correlated .73 with IQ. In a later part of the study, serial recall was tested again, and the correlation dropped to .60. Cohen and Gowen found that subjects generally recalled in serial order in both conditions, regardless of the instructions. This led them to doubt that different processes were being measured by the free and serial recall tasks.

In Experiment II, Cohen and Gowen structured the task so that subjects were more likely to remember order in one condition and item information in another. The running memory task was modified so that subjects tried to *recognize* correct answers. In the order information condition, three digits were presented to the subjects, and they gave a yes or no response. The three digits were always the same as the last three presented, but some were in the correct order and some were not. In the recognition test for item information, the digits were never in the order presented; on some trials the test set contained the correct three digits, on others only two of the digits were the same. The correlation between IQ and order information was only .14, but that for item information was .48. Item and order information correlated only .17. Cohen and Gowen favored an explanation of these findings that depended on "accessibility" rather than the availability of items in memory.

Cohen and Netley (1978a) compared nonretarded and LD children on seven experimental tasks, two of which directly investigated STM. On the probed serial recall task, LD subjects performed worse on the A, B, and C digits. On a probed paired-associate task with items differing on meaningfulness, LD subjects recalled significantly less than intellectually average subjects at the primacy positions, whereas their recency performance was comparable. Meaningfulness yielded significant differences, regardless of the group. This time the authors preferred a "flexibility of processing system" explanation. LD children are said to have a less-flexible system, in which overloading causes a breakdown. No real explanation was offered for the disparate recency effects on the two tasks. Cohen and Netley (1978b) found STM deficits in reading disabled children under conditions in which rehearsal probably could not have played a role. In a running memory task, the deficits were most evident at presentation rates too high for rehearsal to be of any importance. The authors offered "sluggish subvocalization" in reading disabled children as an explanation.

In a study comparing retarded and MA- and CA-matched groups of nonretarded subjects, Cohen and Nealon (1979) presented six 6-digit lists and then six 7-digit lists for either total serial recall, or in a probed condition, recall of the first or last three digits in serial order. The primacy digits (first three) and the recency digits (last three) were the objects of analysis in both conditions. The retarded subjects were significantly lower on primacy performance than the two nonretarded groups. The latter two did not differ. In the analysis of recency, the two nonretarded groups were significantly higher than the retarded group, but again the nonretarded groups did not differ. The probed/nonprobed conditions produced significant differences in the nonretarded subjects but not in the retarded. List length also yielded significant differences. None of the interactions were significant.

The Cohen and Nealon results differ from those of the previous Cohen studies in that IQ and primacy performances are related (i.e., nonretarded subjects retain more primacy items than the retarded subjects). Curiously, no individual IQ/primacy or IQ/recency memory correlations were reported. Unlike the findings by Ellis (1970) and Belmont and Butterfield (1971), recency performance was also lower in retarded subjects. Of course, this is in agreement with the finding in previous Cohen studies of an IQ/recency memory correlation in nonretarded subjects. Cohen and Nealon prefer "reduced availability" in the retarded as an explanation of their poorer primacy performance and both reduced availability and "access difficulty" in the retarded as an explanation of their poorer recency performance.

This series of studies by Cohen and his associates seems quite important. Although we have reservations about Cohen's many interpretations, one conclusion is clear: The notion that deficits in STM in subjects of lower intelligence are due solely to their failure to rehearse is seriously challenged. Cohen and his associates find intelligence level (above about 70 IQ) unrelated to primacy performance as reflected in serial position curves. One study of retarded and nonretarded subjects found differences between these subjects in both primacy and recency, but for some reason they did not compute IQ/STM correlations on an individual score basis. A second finding of importance is that IQ is related to recency performance. It seemed well-established (see Belmont & Butterfield, 1971; Ellis, 1970) that recency in serial position curves represented primary memory *that did not vary with intelligence level*. Whereas we have some question about Cohen's probed recall tasks as a pure measure of primary memory, running memory has face validity as a measure of passive, noncognitive memory. Therefore, most of the Cohen findings appear to support the notion of a primary memory deficit in persons of low intelligence, a state of affairs predicted by trace theory.

The studies reviewed here raise interesting and challenging questions. In 1969, Belmont and Butterfield, after reviewing studies investigating the intelligence/STM relationship, stated:

> Ellis (1963) stimulated the majority of these studies when he proposed that retention would be found deficient in retardates and suggested that the deficiency might also be found in children as contrasted with adults. The latter hypothesis is clearly not supported by research, and the former fares little better, only four of the studies of retardate retention gave reliable evidence for deficient retention processes in retardates.... A fifth study... appeared to be reliable, but we were unable to confirm his results in our replication [p. 53].

If the four studies are reliable, as Belmont and Butterfield indicate, we hardly see how they could be ignored in arriving at their conclusions. Belmont and Butterfield (1969) agree that a relationship exists between IQ and performance on STM tasks. But, following the lead of Melton (1963), they divided STM into the subprocesses of acquisition, storage, and retrieval and then proceeded to attribute IQ-related STM deficits to acquisition and/or retrieval rather than to storage. This conclusion is based on their failure to find slope differences in retention curves for retarded and nonretarded persons and for intellectually average persons of differing maturity levels. As we have noted, failures to find slope differences in forgetting curves typically are found in studies comparing retarded and nonretarded persons remembering different amounts of information. In our view, their strong conclusions were premature. In fact, even now the evidence is not in hand for drawing firm conclusions about the relationship, or lack of, between intelligence and storage.

Ellis (1970), Belmont and Butterfield (1969), and Brown (1974), among others, have presented studies that suggest that rehearsal deficiencies are responsible for STM deficits in retarded persons. This work seemed to have served to focus research in this direction and to deemphasize the issue of whether or not storage differences existed. Most of the rehearsal-deficit research analyzed serial position effects as dependent variables, and quite early it was assumed that primacy was related to intelligence and recency was not. Primacy quickly became the object of study, and the issue of recency and primary memory differences received very little attention.

Now, in reviewing stimulus trace theory, a theory of primary memory, a number of old issues provide new challenges. Firstly, the rehearsal-deficiency hypothesis, coupled with the equal storage notion of Belmont and Butterfield, assumes that subjects rehearse during an arbitrarily defined acquisition period but *not* during the immediately following retention interval (i.e., rehearsal during this interval either does not occur or is not effective). Ferretti's (1979) findings of parallel forgetting curves in rehearsing and nonrehearsing retarded and normal subjects suggest that rehearsal is unrelated to forgetting. For if rehearsal were occurring in some subjects, as his data indicate, the slopes of the curves should have differed. They did not. Roediger, Knight, and Kantowitz (1977) have conducted three experiments that they claim call into question the use of nonverbal interpolated tasks to consume processing capacity in Reitman-type paradigms. We believe their interpretation is not conclusive, however, if rehearsal were occurring undetected in the Ferretti experiment, as the Roediger et al. study implies, slope differences again should have obtained. Cavalier (1979) found differences in slopes of retention curves when, unlike the Ferretti study, storage loads were equivalent in normal and LD subjects. Significantly, slopes of these curves are unrelated to attempts to train encoding strategies. Interpretation is somewhat clouded, however, because Cavalier's LD subjects had average *measured* intelligence.

A second issue is defined by contrasting the studies of Ferretti and Cavalier. In the Ferretti study, storage loads were adjusted so that the proportions of information acquired were equal for the two groups. In fact, these adjustments did not equalize performance in the memory task, not even for the 0-sec retention interval. Only the stimulus reading times were actually equalized. There were differences in the proportion, and absolute number, of items correctly recalled at 0, 9, and 27-sec, between the retarded and nonretarded subjects. No slope differences means that nonretarded subjects retained an average of 5.20 items and the retarded 3.42 items equally well over the 27 sec interval.

On the other hand, Cavalier presented his subjects with the same amount of information and found not only absolute differences between LD and nonretarded subjects at most retention intervals but also a more rapid loss in the retention of

LD subjects. Cavalier almost succeeded in testing retention under equal storage loads. The nonretarded subjects retained an average of 3.0 items at the 0-sec interval; LD subjects retained an average of 2.92 items. The point we wish to make is that even when investigators attempt to measure retention under conditions of equal storage load, rarely is this achieved. We are not aware of a retention study that attempts to adjust storage loads with complete success. Almost without exception, retention studies compare intellectually average and retarded persons under conditions in which the amounts to be retained are not equal.

A third issue derives from the work of Cohen and his associates. Their failure to find a clear relationship between primacy in serial probe and serial recall tasks and intelligence is clearly damaging to rehearsal as a comprehensive explanatory construct for the memory deficit in subjects of low intelligence. Their evidence for memory deficits in lower-IQ subjects on running memory tasks with rates that would seem to preclude rehearsal is also in opposition to the rehearsal-deficiency hypothesis. Although they did find nonretarded-retarded differences in primacy on a probe task, which is compatible with the rehearsal hypothesis, they did not relate individual IQ scores to the primacy scores, and we cannot be sure that IQ is related. Moreover, they found both lower primacy and lower recency in this study (Cohen & Nealon, 1979). In view of this, attention, motivation, or some other variable(s) would appear to be a more plausible explanation.

Studies by other investigators have obtained results with nonretarded children and adults that are difficult to reconcile in terms of the rehearsal-deficiency hypothesis. Primacy effects in serial recall have been found with simultaneous tachistoscopic presentation of items (Harcum, 1967) and with very fast auditory presentation rates (Aaronson, 1968; Yntema, Wozencraft, & Klem, 1964), conditions that seem to preclude rehearsal. Frank and Rabinovitch (1974) varied the opportunity for rehearsal and found no interaction with age. Lyon (1977) found individual serial recall differences in adults to be unrelated to rehearsal, grouping, or chunking strategies. Huttenlocher and Burke (1976) found experimenter-imposed grouping strategies produced comparable effects on span performance across three age levels. Primacy effects were obtained in all age groups. They doubted that primacy effects were valid indices of rehearsal. Cole, Frankel, and Sharpe (1971) have shown that serial position effects in children are more a result of the order of output than of rehearsal, and Berch (1978) and Siegel, Allik, and Herman (1976) showed in serial probe recall that they often are a function of spatial distinctiveness.

In the general memory literature, the multistore model of memory, which underlies much of the rehearsal deficiency research in the field of mental retardation, has received a good deal of criticism. This is based primarily on findings that the amount of rehearsal contributes little to the memory trace, but that the "depth of processing" is crucial (Craik & Tulving, 1975; Craik and Watkins,

1973; Rundus, 1977; Woodward, Bjork, & Jongeward, 1973). More recently, serious problems with the levels of processing model have been brought to light. These center on a lack of conceptual clarity, and results showing that shallow (nonsemantic) processing may produce durable memory traces and deep (semantic) processing will not always produce such effects (Baddeley, 1978; Dark & Loftus, 1976; Morris, Bransford, & Franks, 1977; Nelson, 1977; Nelson & Vining, 1978; Postman, Thompkins, & Gray, 1978; Stein, 1978; Stein, Morris, & Bransford, 1978). More generally, the adequacy of multistore/multiprocess models of memory have been called into question (Gruneberg, 1970, 1972; Melton, 1963; Rakover, 1977; Wickelgren, 1973).

Still another issue is raised by the Cohen data: Memory for *recently* presented items, in serial recall tasks, serial recognition tasks, serial probe tasks, and in running memory, is related to intelligence. Poorer performances on more recently presented information, generally viewed as an index of primary memory, characterizes the person with lower intelligence. In view of the scope of these studies, this finding cannot be dismissed lightly.

Finally, we submit that the problems of memory deficits in persons of low intelligence are far from being fully understood. The stimulus trace theory still seems to be an viable explanation for certain types of memory deficits, in particular, those that may be described as deficits in primary memory. In our view, some of the data presented here points to possible primary memory deficits in persons of low intelligence. Coupled with these findings is evidence against rehearsal deficiency as a comprehensive explanation of the poorer STM performance in persons of low intelligence. But, even compelling evidence for the rehearsal deficiency hypothesis should not deter us from a more careful analysis of primary memory processes in the retarded. Traces of old issues and theories persist.

Summary and Concluding Comments

The rapid development of behavioral research on retarded persons after World War II was accompanied by a number of theories designed to explain behavioral differences between retarded and nonretarded persons. Among the more systematic approaches were the investigations and theories of Zeaman and House, Spitz, Luria, Cromwell, Zigler, and Ellis. Zigler characterized his own approach as developmental, and a number of others as reflecting a difference and/or defect research orientation. The present analysis of these attempts to characterize and categorize these theories shows many of the alleged differences to be more apparent than real. To us, all the theories derive from a developmental orientation. All of those reviewed are basically molar behavior theories, and none are physiological. None, excepting those of Zigler and the social learning studies of Cromwell and his associates, attempts to establish the cause of retardation within the past history of the organism. Instead, in most of these theories, cause is related to a logical construct, a cognitive or behavioral construct, in the contemporary behavior of the organism.

The stimulus trace theory was, according to Zigler, judged to be a defect theory, even though it did not meet all the criteria established by Zigler for defect theories. Also, reduced stimulus trace is not a physiological defect, not something that "inhered" in a low IQ, not an "innate" or "immutable" defect. Nor was stimulus trace viewed as classifiable within the structural feature/control process dichotomy. Control processes were merely seen as processes with different behavioral manifestations under changed stimulus situations.

Serious doubts were cast on the two-group approach to the study of mental retardation. The hypothesis that some retarded persons seem to fit the polygenic inheritance model did not seem to constitute grounds for subject diagnosis and selection. Behavioral research has failed to reliably differentiate "brain-injured" and "cultural-familial" retarded persons, and there is increasing evidence of different brain structure and function in all retarded persons.

The assumption of the developmental theory that retarded and nonretarded persons of equal MA, as measured by an IQ test, are equal in cognitive level seemed of doubtful validity. The developmental theory would have to posit a trade off between organic maturation and environmental experience for this to be true. Moreover, the developmental theory offers little in terms of experimental predictions. For example, most of the exemplary research of Zigler and his colleagues may be philosophically guided by his developmental theory. But, most of his research supports the theory only by yielding findings that support a null hypothesis, for most of Zigler's research compares persons of equal MA. Because the developmental theory predicts equal cognitive performance for such subjects, it is the failures to find equal performance that are not compatible with the theory and must be explained in terms of noncognitive variables. Thus, the main thrust of the support for the developmental theory is based on accepting the hypothesis of no cognitive differences between intellectually average and retarded subjects.

Because the stimulus–trace theory was one of the prototypic defect theories, it was reviewed, and some of the research that seemed to provide tests of the theory was summarized. Hindsight indicated that the original formulation of the theory was too ambitious. The explanatory power of the notion was considerably over-extended. The research on classical trace conditioning reported findings that generally supported predictions from the theory. But, trace conditioning and STM did not have face validity as measures of a common process. Dissertation studies of Ferretti and Cavalier highlighted the fact that forgetting is rarely, if ever, measured in persons differing in intelligence, under conditions in which both groups must recall the same amount of information. Parallel forgetting curves were found in retarded and nonretarded persons in the Ferretti study but with different storage loads in the two groups. The presence or absence of rehearsal in these subjects could not be related to memory. In the Cavalier study, storage loads were not equated, though more nearly so than in the Ferretti study, but differences in the slopes of retention curves were found, with LD (average IQ) subjects showing more rapid memory loss. Finally, a series of studies by Cohen and associates provided evidence against a rehearsal deficit explanation of STM inadequacy in persons of low intelligence. Moreover, his studies point to *primary* memory deficits in persons of low intelligence, which is in agreement with the basic premise in the stimulus trace theory.

The more recent evidence, and a reexamination of the evidence presented by Belmont and Butterfield in their 1969 review, does not warrant the conclusion that IQ and STM are unrelated, as they contended. The evidence presented here invites a reexamination of the notions that:

1. Memory deficits in the retarded are due solely to acquisition or retrieval deficiencies, and not to storage.
2. Rehearsal deficiencies (or failure to "decide" to rehearse) are the cause of "acquisition" deficiencies in the retarded on STM tasks.
3. Primary memory is normal in retarded persons.

In our view, the available evidence on these issues does not warrant firm conclusions.

REFERENCES

Aaronson, D. Temporal course of perception in an immediate recall task. *Journal of Experimental Psychology*, 1968, *76*, 129–140.

Atkinson, R. C., & Shiffrin, R. M. Human memory: A proposed system and its control processes. In K. W. Spence & J. T. Spence (Eds.), *The psychology of learning and motivation: Advances in research and theory* (Vol. 2). New York: Academic Press, 1968.

Baddeley, A. D. The trouble with levels: A reexamination of Craik and Lockhart's framework for memory research. *Psychological Review*, 1978, *85*, 139–152.

Balla, D., & Zigler, E. Personality development in retarded persons. In N. R. Ellis (Ed.), *Handbook of mental deficiency, psychological theory and research* (2nd ed.). Hillsdale, N.J.: Lawrence Erlbaum Associates, 1979.

Baumeister, A. A. Problems in comparative studies of mental retardates and normals. *American Journal of Mental Deficiency*, 1967, *71*, 869–875.

Baumeister, A. A., & MacLean, W. E., Jr. Brain damage and mental retardation. In N. R. Ellis (Ed.), *Handbook of mental deficiency, psychological theory and research* (2nd ed.). Hillsdale, N.J.: Lawrence Erlbaum Associates, 1979.

Belmont, J. R. Medical-behavioral research in retardation. In N. R. Ellis (Ed.), *International review of research in mental retardation* (Vol. 5). New York: Academic Press, 1971.

Belmont, J. M., & Butterfield, E. C. The relations of short-term memory to development and intelligence. In L. P. Lipsitt & H. Reese (Eds.), *Advances in child development and behavior* (Vol. 4). New York: Academic Press, 1969.

Belmont, J. M., & Butterfield, E. C. Learning strategies as determinants of memory deficiencies. *Cognitive Psychology*, 1971, *2*, 411–420.

Berch, D. B. The role of spatial cues in the probe-type serial memory task. *Child Development*, 1978, *49*, 749-754.

Bolles, R. C. *Learning theory*. New York: Holt, Rinehart, & Winston, 1979.

Borkowski, J. G., & Cavanaugh, J. C. Maintenance and generalization of skills and strategies by the retarded. In N. R. Ellis (Ed.), *Handbook of mental deficiency, psychological theory and research* (2nd ed.). Hillsdale, N.J.: Lawrence Erlbaum Associates, 1979.

Brown, A. L. The role of strategic behavior in retardate memory. In N. R. Ellis (Ed.), *International review of research in mental retardation* (Vol. 7). New York: Academic Press, 1974.

Butterfield, E. C. Serial learning and the stimulus-trace theory of mental retardation. *American Journal of Mental Deficiency*, 1968, *72*, 778-787. (a)

Butterfield, E. C. Stimulus trace in the mentally retarded: Defect or developmental lag? *Journal of Abnormal Psychology*, 1968, *73*, 358-362. (b)

Campione, J. C., & Brown, A. L. Memory and metamemory development in educable retarded children. In R. V. Kail & J. W. Hagen (Eds.), *Perspectives on the development of memory and cognition*. Hillsdale, N.J.: Lawrence Erlbaum Associates, 1977.

Cavalier, A. R., Jr. *An analysis of primary and secondary memory and the effects of encoding strategies in learning disabled and normal children*. A doctoral dissertation, Department of Psychology, University of Alabama, 1979.

Cohen, R. L., & Gowen, A. Recall and recognition of order and item information in probed running memory, as a function of IQ. *Intelligence*, 1978, *2*, 343-352.

Cohen, R. L., & Nealon, J. An analysis of short-term memory differences between retardates and nonretardates. *Intelligence*, 1979, *3*, 65-72.

Cohen, R. L., & Netley, C. Cognitive deficits, learning disabilities, and WISC verbal-performance consistency. *Developmental Psychology*, 1978, *14*, 624-634. (a)

Cohen, R. L., & Netley, C. *Short-term memory deficits in reading disabled children*. Paper presented at the Canadian Psychological Association Meetings, Ottawa, June 1978. (b)

Cohen, R. L., & Sandberg, T. Relation between intelligence and short-term memory. *Cognitive Psychology*, 1977, *9*, 534-554.

Cole, M., Frankel, F., & Sharpe, D. Development of free recall learning in children. *Developmental Psychology*, 1971, *4*, 109-123.

Craik, F. I. M., & Tulving, E. Depth of processing and the retention of words in episodic memory. *Journal of Experimental Psychology: General*, 1975, *104*, 268-294.

Craik, F. I. M., & Watkins, M. J. The role of rehearsal in short-term memory. *Journal of Verbal Learning and Verbal Behavior*, 1973, *12*, 599-607.

Crome, L. The brain and mental retardation. *British Medical Journal*, 1960, *1*, 897-904.

Dark, V. J., & Loftus, G. R. The role of rehearsal in long-term memory performance. *Journal of Verbal Learning and Verbal Behavior*, 1976, *15*, 479-490.

Ellis, N. R. The stimulus trace and behavioral inadequacy. In N. R. Ellis (Ed.), *Handbook of mental deficiency*. New York: McGraw-Hill, 1963.

Ellis, N. R. A behavioral research strategy in mental retardation: Defense and critique. *American Journal of Mental Deficiency*, 1969, *73*, 557-567.

Ellis, N. R. Memory processes in retardates and normals. In N. R. Ellis (Ed.), *International review of research in mental retardation* (Vol. 4). New York: Academic Press, 1970.

Evans, R. A., & Bilsky, L. H. Clustering and categorical list retention in the mentally retarded. In N. R. Ellis (Ed.), *Handbook of mental deficiency, psychological theory and research* (2nd ed.). Hillsdale, N.J.: Lawrence Erlbaum Associates, 1979.

Ferretti, R. P. *An analysis of passive memory in normal and mentally retarded persons*. A doctoral dissertation, Department of Psychology, University of Alabama, 1979.

Flavell, J. H. Developmental studies of mediated memory. *Advances in child development and behavior* (Vol. 5). New York: Academic Press, 1970.

Frank, H. S., & Rabinovitch, M. S. Auditory short-term memory: Developmental changes in rehearsal. *Child Development*, 1974, *45*, 397-407.
Glidden, L. M. Training of learning and memory in retarded persons: Strategies, techniques, and teaching tools. In N. R. Ellis (Ed.), *Handbook of mental deficiency, psychological theory and research* (2nd ed.). Hillsdale, N.J.: Lawrence Erlbaum Associates, 1979.
Grossman, H. (Ed.) *Manual on terminology and classification in mental retardation* (1977 revision). Washington, D.C.: American Association on Mental Deficiency, 1977.
Gruneberg, M. M. A dichotomous theory of memory—unproved and unprovable? *Acta psychologica*, 1970, *34*, 489-496.
Gruneberg, M. M. The serial positon curve and the distinction between short- and long-term memory. *Acta Psychologica*, 1972, *36*, 221-225.
Hall, J. F. *Classical conditioning and instrumental learning*. New York: Lippincott, 1976.
Harcum, E. R. Parallel functions of serial learning and tachistoscopic perception. *Psychological Review*, 1967, *74*, 51-62.
Hebb, D. O. *The organization of behavior*. New York: Wiley, 1949.
Huttenlocher, J., & Burke, D. Why does memory span increase with age? *Cognitve Psychology*, 1976, *8*, 1-31.
Jellinger, J. Neuropathological features of unclassified mental retardation. In J. B. Cavanagh (Ed.), *The brain in unclassified mental retardation*. Baltimore: Williams & Wilkins, 1972.
Kounin, J. Experimental studies of rigidity: I. The measurement of rigidity in normal and feebleminded persons. *Character Personality*, 1941, *9*, 251-272. (a)
Kounin, J. Experimental studies of rigidity: II. The explanatory power of the concept of rigidity as applied to feeblemindedness. *Character Personality*, 1941, *9*, 273-282. (b)
Lewin, K. *A dynamic theory of personality*. New York: McGraw-Hill, 1936.
Lobb, H. Trace GSR conditioning with benzedrine in mentally defective and normal adults. *American Journal of Mental Deficiency*, 1968, *73*, 239-246.
Lobb, H., & Nugent, C. M. Interaction between intelligence level and interstimulus trace interval in electrodermal conditioning. *American Journal of Mental Deficiency*, 1966, *70*, 548-555.
Lyon, D. R. Individual differences in immediate serial recall: A matter of mnemonics? *Cognitive Psychology*, 1977, *9*, 403-411.
Malamud, N. Neuropathology. In H. A. Stevens & R. Heber (Eds.), *Mental retardation: A review of research*. Chicago: University of Chicago Press, 1964.
Masland, R. L. The prevention of mental subnormality. In R. L. Masland, S. B. Sarason, & T. Gladwin, *Mental subnormality*. New York: Basic Books, 1958.
McPherson, M. W. A survey of experimental studies of learning in individuals who achieve subnormal ratings on standardized psychometric measures. *American Journal of Mental Deficiency*, 1948, *52*, 232-254.
McPherson, M. W. Learning and mental deficiency. *American Journal of Mental Deficiency*, 1958, *62*, 870-877.
Melton, A. W. Implications of short-term memory for a general theory of memory. *Journal of Verbal Learning and Verbal Behavior*, 1963, *2*, 1-21.
Milgram, N. A. The rational and irrationale in Zigler's motivational approach to mental retardation. *American Journal of Mental Deficiency*, 1969, *73*, 527-532.
Morris, C. D., Bransford, J. D., & Franks, J. J. Levels of processing versus transfer appropriate processing. *Journal of Verbal Learning and Verbal Behavior*, 1977, *16*, 519-533.
Nelson, T. O. Repetition and depth of processing. *Journal of Verbal Learning and Verbal Behavior*, 1977, *16*, 151-171.
Nelson, T. O., & Vining, S. K. Effect of sematic versus structural processing on long-term retention. *Journal of Experimental Psychology: Human Learning and Memory*, 1978, *4*, 198-209.
Postman, L., Thompkins, B. A., & Gray, W. D. The interpretation of encoding effects in retention.

Journal of Verbal Learning and Verbal Behavior, 1978, *17*, 681-705.
Rakover, S. S. Does interpolated interference affect only the short-term store in a free recall task? *Memory and Cognition*, 1977, *5*, 453-456.
Reitman, J. S. Mechanisms of forgetting in short-term memory. *Cognitive Psychology*, 1971, *2*, 185-195.
Reitman, J. S. Without surreptitious rehearsal, information in short-term memory decays. *Journal of Verbal Learning and Verbal Behavior*, 1974, *13*, 365-377.
Resnick, L. B., & Glaser, R. Problem solving and intelligence. In L. B. Resnick (Ed.), *The nature of intelligence*. Hillsdale, N.J.: Lawrence Erlbaum Associates, 1976.
Roediger, H. L., III, Knight, J. L., Jr., & Kantowitz, B. H. Inferring decay in short-term memory: The issue of capacity. *Memory and Cognition*, 1977, *5*, 167-176.
Ross, S. M., & Ross, L. E. The conditioning of skeletal and autonomic responses: Normal-retardate stimulus-trace differences. In N. R. Ellis (Ed.), *International review of research in mental retardation* (Vol. 8). New York: Academic Press, 1976.
Rundus, D. Maintenance rehearsal and single-level processing. *Journal of Verbal Learning and Verbal Behavior*, 1977, *16*, 665-681.
Schonebaum, R. M., & Zinober, J. W. Learning and memory in mental retardation: The defect-developmental distinctions reevaluated. In I. Bialer & M. Sternlicht (Eds.), *The psychology of mental retardation: Issues and approaches*. New York: Psychological Dimensions, 1977.
Siegel, A. W., Allik, J. P., & Herman, J. F. The primacy effect in young children: Verbal fact or spatial artifact? *Child Development*, 1976, *47*, 242-247.
Stein, B. S. Depth of processing reexamined: The effects of the precision of encoding and test appropriateness. *Journal of Verbal Learning and Verbal Behavior*, 1978, *17*, 165-174.
Stein, B. S., Morris, C. D., & Bransford, J. D. Constraints on effective elaboration. *Journal of Verbal Learning and Verbal Behavior*, 1978, *17*, 707-714.
Strauss, A. A., & Lehtinen, M. A. *Psychopathology and education of the brain-injured child*. New York: Grune & Stratton, 1947.
Tolman, E. C. *Purposive behavior in animals and man*. New York: Century, 1932.
Tredgold, R. F., & Soddy, K. *Textbook of mental deficiency*. Baltimore: Williams & Wilkins, 1963.
Waugh, N. C., & Norman, D. A. Primary memory. *Psychological Review*, 1965, *72*, 89-104.
Wickelgren, W. A. The long and the short of memory. *Psychological Bulletin*, 1973, *80*, 425-438.
Woodward, A. E., Jr., Bjork, R. A., & Jongeward, R. H. Recall and recognition as a function of primary rehearsal. *Journal of Verbal Learning and Verbal Behavior*, 1973, *12*, 608-617.
Yntema, D., Wozencraft, F., & Klem, L. *Immediate serial recall of digits presented at very high rates*. Paper presented at Psychonomic Society, Niagara Falls, Ontario, 1964.
Zeaman, D., & House, B. J. A review of attention theory. In N. R. Ellis (Ed.), *Handbook of mental deficiency, psychological theory and research* (2nd ed.). Hillsdale, N.J.: Lawrence Erlbaum Associates, 1979.
Zigler, E. Mental retardation: Current issues and approaches. In L. W. Hoffman & M. R. Hoffman (Eds.), *Review of child development research* (Vol. 2). New York: Russell Sage, 1966. (a)
Zigler, E. Research on personality structure in the retardate. In N. R. Ellis (Ed.), *International review of research in mental retardation* (Vol. 1). New York: Academic Press, 1966. (b)
Zigler, E. Developmental versus difference theories of mental retardation and the problem of motivation. *American Journal of Mental Deficiency*, 1969, *73*, 536-556.

III THE DEVELOPMENTAL-DIFFERENCE CONTROVERSY

9 The Rationale and Irrational in Zigler's Motivational Approach to Mental Retardation*

Norman A. Milgram
Catholic University of America

ABSTRACT

This chapter acknowledges the important theoretical and practical contributions of Edward Zigler's motivational approach to mental retardation but criticizes his characterization of a dichotomy between a motivational approach and a cognitive or so-called "defect" or "difference" approach. His view that differences in performance between retardates and MA-matched normals are to be attributed to motivational rather than cognitive factors is questioned. It is suggested that the notion of mutually exclusive explanations for differences in MA-matched groups is not intrinsic to Zigler's work and could be discarded without jeopardizing any of his major theoretical formulations.

During the past decade in a series of research studies and reviews, Edward Zigler has marshalled evidence and argument about the importance of motivational factors in the performance of retarded persons. He has contributed to the field of mental retardation by asserting that retardates suffer adverse social and emotional deprivation experiences both in the community and in residential institutions, and demonstrating that these experiences generate social expectancies and task expectancies that affect acquisition of skills and other performance parameters. He has proposed that retardates differ from normals in the hierarchy of reinforcers

---

*This article is reprinted with permission from *American Journal of Mental Deficiency*, 1969, 73, 527–532.

for which they expend effort, and that a judicious choice of reinforcer may improve retardate performance; that retardates tend to be outerdirected rather than innerdirected in their problem-solving ability, looking to external cues rather than to their own frames of reference or fund of information for solutions to problems (Zigler, 1966a, b).

These theoretical contributions possess heuristic significance, are generating important research, and may modify practices in the field of mental retardation. Greater attention, for example, will be paid to the milieu in which retarded persons live, learn, work, and play. For several decades we have been aware that the mental hospital is a social institution whose structural and functional characteristics may facilitate or impede the rehabilitation of the emotionally disturbed patient. The field of mental retardation could also profit from this insight and from the innovations in practice that would follow from an application of the knowledge accumulated about mental institutions. The fact that ideas about the mental hospital as a social community have not yet penetrated into the thinking, much less the practice, of men and institutions in the field of mental retardation is a sad commentary on the unfortunate communication gap between the two fields. Zigler's motivational approach and his focus on the social and emotional climate of the settings, past and present, in which the retardate develops and learns may contribute to bridging this gap.

This writer does not take issue with the case that Zigler has made *for motivational factors* in retardate performance, but rather with the case that Zigler has made *against cognitive factors*. Zigler has attempted to dichotomize the theoretical approaches of researchers in the field as falling at two extremes, his own motivational position and that of cognitive theories that he terms a "defect" or "difference" position. Commenting on the repeated finding that even when normal and retarded groups are matched on MA, the retardate does less well, or at least behaves differently, than the normal control, he states that two distinctly different explanations have been advanced for this phenomenon; the one view asserting that these performance differences reflect a variety of experiential or motivational differences, the other that the cultural–familial retardate is really not a normal individual developing at a slower rate but rather is an inherently different type of organism, who, at every level of development, is suffering from some defect in his physiological or cognitive structure. These hypothesized differences are then viewed as producing differences in behavior even in those instances in which MA is equated (Zigler, 1966b). Under defect approaches he subsumes such theories as stimulus trace (Ellis, 1963), verbal mediational deficiency (Luria, 1963), and attention deficit (Zeaman & House, 1963). Zigler characterizes the so-called defect approach as asserting that there is an innate, if not immutable, difference between normals and all mental retardates; that retardates are relatively homogeneous with respect to this defect; and that this defect adequately accounts for retardate performance.

The present chapter discusses this characterization of cognitive theories, proposes an explanation for Zigler's erecting an unfortunate and false dichotomy, and cites inconsistencies in his approach.

A starting point for this discussion and probably also the starting point in the theoretical development of Zigler's views is the two-group approach toward etiology in mental retardation. Ample evidence, genetic, statistical, and behavioral, has documented a dichotomy between: (1) *biomedical* mentally defective persons, generally trainable or requiring intensive custodial supervision, whose subnormal intelligence is the result of genetic anomalies, biochemical imbalances, infection, trauma, etc., in short a biological defect or pathological condition; and (2) the larger group of *cultural–familial* retarded persons, almost invariably educable or borderline, whose mental subnormality is: (a) the reflection of inherited capacities and the result of large numbers of genes operating in a normal nonpathological manner; or (b) a reflection of the adverse social, psychological, and educational experiences that characterize the lives of many children growing up in so-called culturally disadvantaged homes; or (c) both of the foregoing conditions. If intelligence is normally distributed throughout the entire population, then a certain percentage of children born normal and without biological defect will score below 70 on standardized IQ tests and more important will fall short of the academic, vocational, and social norms set by a technologically advanced society. Moreover, if children are malnourished, physically and/or cognitively in their formative years, their performance will fall short of their optimal potential, whatever level it may be. Whereas all dichotomies are somewhat artificial, the biomedical defective is likely to be handicapped in any society, advanced or primitive, even when his own immediate environment was conducive to his optimal development. The cultural–familial retardate is likely to be handicapped only in an advanced society, and when his immediate environment was not conducive to optimal development.

Zigler goes to great lengths in stressing this dichotomy between retarded groups. His eloquent and well-documented exposition of the two-group approach is laudable because of the confusion of these groups in the minds of lay and professional people alike. Extending the notion of organic pathology from the biomedical mental defectives to the cultural–familial retardates is unwarranted and unfortunate. Unfortunate, because it directs a disproportionate amount of research funds into biomedical research that is irrelevant to the majority of the mentally retarded and away from the educational, social, and psychological research that is relevant. Unfortunate also, because it justifies a medical model characterized by medical hegemony of the research, training, and service programs designed for the retarded.

In many respects, the confounding of the biomedical defectives and the cultural–familial retardates in the field of mental retardation is analagous to the confounding of the mentally ill (whose emotional disturbance is based on biochemical imbalance or some other pathological process) and persons with emotional problems of living in the field of mental health. Lay and professional societies in America have been taught two myths that are contrary to objective reality: a myth of mental illness and a myth of mental retardation. Common to both myths is the assumption that because some people designated as mentally ill or mentally retarded suffer from a demonstrable pathological condition, that all do. Even though an organic or pathological condition has yet to be demonstrated in the vast majority of persons in either field, faith in a pathological defect persists and justifies predominantly biomedical research and medically oriented, if not directed, evaluation and treatment. This writer is in complete agreement with Zigler's characterization of *this* dichotomy, and with the importance of accentuating the dichotomy in discussion.

Dichotomizing mental retardates in two groups does not require us, however, to dichotomize theories of retardation, but apparently for Zigler, the two dichotomies are interrelated. In his view, cognitive theories and theorists either obscure, ignore, or reject the two-group dichotomy when they conceptualize about the relationship of cognitive processes to MA, IQ, and other variables, without regard for the etiology or precise level of subnormal mental functioning. The Russian investigator, Luria, would appear to reject the two-group approach and to classify all retardates as brain damaged, but the majority of cognitive investigators in America do not. There is nothing inherent in cognitive investigations that is antithetical to the fundamental polarities associated with the two-group dichotomy: pathological versus nonpathological, every social class versus lowest social class, and trainable versus educable.

Cognitive theorists prefer, however, to use a common set of concepts in investigating cognitive functioning across the entire IQ range from below average to above average and to disregard etiology or other differing subject parameters. This is a legitimate research strategy, if we control for the nonintellective subject or task variables, or if we demonstrate that these variables do not affect the task performance being investigated. An alternate research or theoretical strategy, which would generate one theory of cognitive functioning for biologically damaged trainable defectives, a different theory to handle the functioning of cultural–familial retardates, and possibly a third for the average or superior intelligence group, is neither parsimonious nor necessary. Not only do cognitive investigators argue for continuity between trainable and educable retardates but also for continuity among retarded, normal, and superior-intelligence groups. If Zigler agrees that the same principles of cognitive development apply throughout the educable retarded–gifted range, an extension downward to the trainable defective should be logically acceptable.

Because Zigler draws the unwarranted conclusion that cognitive theories inherently obscure, ignore, or reject the two-group dichotomy, the logic of this position dictates that he maintain, as stated earlier in this chapter, that all performance differences between retardates and normals of comparable MA are the result of motivational rather than cognitive factors. This position is as untenable as it is unnecessary for him to maintain. It is untenable because there is insufficient evidence that *all* performance differences can be attributed to motivational and experiential differences, and because there is sufficient grounds for attributing many performance differences to cognitive considerations. Research has demonstrated that equating people of different IQ levels on MA scores based upon a particular test or series of tests in no way guarantees that they are comparable on problems outside the universe of items tapped by the equating measures. Frequently, MA-matching is based on a single homogeneous scale, a pictorial or verbal vocabulary test that has a correlation with other cognitive variables that falls far short of 1.0. Even when a heterogeneous scale is used (Stanford–Binet, Form LM, or the Wechsler Intelligence Scale for Children), equating on the composite MA score only averages in the differences between retardates and their MA controls on the component items or subtests, so that one might expect group differences to emerge on tasks similar to those test items on which the groups differed.

It is precisely these differences between groups comparable on MA that intrigue some cognitive investigators. No effort is made here to present a defense or exposition of the major theories referred to by Zigler under the rubric of the defect approach. If we take, however, one position with which this writer is familiar, the verbal mediation position, we find a conceptualization of cognitive process that is developmental in character and continuous in distribution, rather than a discrete distribution with the defect restricted to retardates. Rather than argue that all retardates are characterized by a verbal mediational deficiency, and normals by a verbal mediational efficiency, the various formulations of this position assume that verbal mediational ability is developmental in character, and that with increasing MA, there is a corresponding increase in mediational facility or efficiency. Moreover, at least one formulation of this position (Milgram, 1968; Milgram & Furth, 1967) allows for differences in mediational facility above and beyond MA level. This view would argue that at any given MA, there is a range of performances based on this cognitive process, the range being somewhat narrower than in a group comparable only in CA, but a range nonetheless related to IQ level. This position allows not merely for a verbal mediational deficiency in retardates versus children of average IQ but also in children of average IQ when compared with children functioning in the gifted range. Recent work by Harter (Harter, 1965; 1968) with children of superior, average, and retarded IQs on discrimination learning tasks supports this line of reasoning.

This view runs counter to the assumption that groups who differ in CA and are MA-matched in some performance tasks are equivalent in the qualitative and/or quantitative features of the cognitive processes utilized to solve the problem or perform the task on which the MA-matching was based. This assumption of equivalent process because of equivalent MA score does not follow, because the intelligence test items on which the MA scores are based tell us more about content than process. Whereas MA is a content or performance variable, it is not necessarily a process variable. It tells us merely how well a person performed in solving a set of homogeneous items differing in level of difficulty or a series of different sets of homogeneous items. It does not tell us what cognitive processes were utilized by the testee or problem solver to earn a correct score on the set of test items, so that even if normal S's and retardates were genuinely matched on all subitems or subtests constituting the MA composite score (which as mentioned earlier is not the case), there would still be an opportunity for Ss to utilize different cognitive processes to achieve the same end result. When we attach a descriptive label to a problem, we do not know if one cognitive process or another was employed to yield the same quantitative performance on the problem. One person may achieve solution via one cognitive operation, another person by a less-complex operation. Zigler himself discusses the distinction between content and process fully (Zigler, 1966b) and praises those Piagetian investigators that purport to elucidate the cognitive processes or operations employed by mental retardates.

Parenthetically, it is observed that of the research methodologies utilized to test for cognitive differences between MA-matched or CA-matched groups differing in IQ level, the one that recommends itself to this writer is equating of groups on performance on a given task that is relevant to, if not the counterpart of, the criterion comparison task; in the latter task, however, we introduce an experimental variation (e.g., a change of stimulus parameters, introduction of new instructions, training on some interpolated task). When we then observe differences in performance on the criterion task, we can safely attribute these differences to an experimental variation for which the range of explanations is circumscribed.

In summary, Zigler appears to equate the cognitive defect–motivational dichotomy with the biomedical cultural–familial dichotomy and to invest the polarities of the former dichotomy with the characteristics attributed to the polarities of the latter. If the biologically mentally handicapped suffer from a pathological condition or defect that is innate or acquired early in development and if it is generally considered irreversible, then theories emphasizing the continuity of cognitive functioning across a broad IQ range are alleged to make the same assumptions. Zigler states that there is a continuity in cognitive functioning between normal and cultural–familial retardates but balks at incorporating the moderately and severely biomedically handicapped retardates in an overall conceptualization for fear of obscuring the two-group etiological distinction. He then appears constrained to argue that the performance differences between cultural–familial retardates and MA-matched normals on some performance task must be attributed to a motivational difference between the two groups, rather than to cognitive factors associated with IQ level above and beyond MA. Nothing prevents an investigator from having the best of possible worlds, allowing *both* for cognitive and motivational factors to interact in determining the performance of *all* retardates, whether biomedical or cultural-familial, but this has not been the dominant theme of Zigler's presentation.

At times Zigler implies that the difference approach is pessimistic and the motivational approach optimistic, with reference to maximizing the performance of retarded persons. This is both an oversimplification of the problem and an unwarranted generalization. One of the applications of cognitive research has been to recommend techniques to shore up relatively inefficient cognitive abilities by special training or to circumvent the relatively weak abilities and capitalize on the stronger ones by packaging the stimulus input or teaching method, so as to permit retardates to achieve a desired result by alternate routes that are more readily available to them. In other words, cognitive theories may contribute to a maximization of the modest innate intellectual ability whether of educable retardates or of biomedical defectives. On the other hand, although knowledge of the environmental contingencies of motivational expectancies and the effect of the latter on retardate performance is valuable for establishing preventive programs to reduce the psychological disabilities exacerbating the problems of educable retardates in a complex technological society, there is no guarantee that once these motivational histories have been internalized in adolescent or adult retardates that they are easily modifiable. These generalized expectancies may be relatively impervious to anything but intensive and long-term modification of milieu.

To be entirely fair to Zigler, toward the end of one major review (Zigler, 1966a), he states that his position is suggestive rather than definitive; he asserts that the behavior of a retarded child on a given task is a complex and multiply-determined phenomenon influenced by both cognitive or intellectual factors and motivational or emotional factors. Nevertheless, his characterization of the cognitive-motivational dichotomy and his position with regard to performance differences in MA-matched group differing in IQ level are untenable and are not really called for by his own motivational position.

ACKNOWLEDGMENT

This paper was written in part through the support of VRA Grant No. 2569-P.

REFERENCES

Ellis, N. R. The stimulus-trace theory and behavioral inadequacy. In N. R. Ellis (Ed.), *Handbook of mental deficiency.* New York: McGraw-Hill, 1963.

Harter, S. Discrimination learning set in children as a function of IQ and MA. *Journal of Experimental Psychology,* 1965, 2, 31-43.

Harter, S. Paper read at Gatlinburg Conference, March 1968.

Luria, A. R. Psychological studies of mental deficiency in the Soviet Union. In N. R. Ellis (Ed.), *Handbook of mental deficiency.* New York: McGraw-Hill, 1963.

Milgram, N. A. The effects of MA and IQ in verbal mediation in paired-associate learning. *Journal of Genetic Psychology,* 1968, *113,* 129-143.

Milgram, N. A., & Furth, H. G. Factors affecting conceptual control in normal and retarded children. *Child Development,* 1967, *38,* 531-543.

Zeaman, D., & House, B. J. The role of attention in retardate discrimination learning. In N. R. Ellis (Ed.), *Handbook of mental deficiency.* New York: McGraw-Hill, 1963.

Zigler, E. Research on personality structure in the retardate. In N. R. Ellis (Ed.), *International review of research in mental retardation* (Vol. 1). New York: Academic Press, 1966. (a)

Zigler, E. Mental retardation: Current issues and approaches. In L. W. Hoffman & M. L. Hoffman (Eds.), *Review of child development research* (Vol. 2). New York: Russell Sage Foundation, 1966. (b)

10 Developmental Versus Difference Theories of Mental Retardation and the Problem of Motivation*

Edward Zigler
Yale University

ABSTRACT

The point is made that the essential controversy concerning mental retardation in which Zigler has been engaged is not one between motivational and cognitive viewpoints. The theoretical argument is rather between two cognitive approaches: a developmental position, on the one hand, and a difference position, on the other. Both of these positions are described, and the differential predictions stemming from them are noted. The relevance to the developmental-difference controversy of the MA measure, motivational factors, and the two-group approach to mental retardation is discussed.

I have read Milgram's critique of my work with great care and am most grateful for the compliments he has bestowed upon my efforts. I must confess, however, that in certain respects, Milgram does not appear to be sufficiently conversant with my point of view concerning mental retardation to either praise it or condemn it. Many of my views, as presented by Milgram, are so distorted as to be totally unrecognizable. Milgram has insisted on erecting differences between us where none exist and has, throughout his chapter, confounded methodological and theoretical issues. The title of Milgram's critique led me to expect that he would present a brief overview of my general theoretical position (i.e., its

---

*This article is reprinted with permission from *American Journal of Mental Deficiency*, 1969, 73(4), 536–556.

"rationale") and then go on to point out the inconsistencies or shortcomings (much more polite words than "the irrational") of this general position. This Milgram has failed to do. I am very much afraid that any irrationality, rather than residing in the general approach to mental retardation that I have developed over the years, inheres only in Milgram's misstatement of my position. Indeed, the bulk of Milgram's criticism of my position is based on an erroneous premise. Milgram's critique is continuously couched in terms of a controversy between a motivational approach (attributed to me) and a cognitive approach (espoused by Milgram and his colleagues).

Milgram, along with others (Zeaman, 1968) who have attributed to me a motivational theory of mental retardation, appear to have restricted their focus to those research articles that have demonstrated that motivational variables play a role in the performance of the retarded. They have not attended sufficiently to my theoretical views concerning the essential nature of familial mental retardation, which have now been presented in a number of sources (Zigler, 1967a, b, 1968a, b), and which was further explicated in an exchange of letters in *Science* between Weir (1967) and myself (Zigler, 1967c). For the sake of others who may have been misled by the lack of clarity in my previously written presentations, let me unequivocally declare that I have never advanced a motivational theory of mental retardation. I have been specific in asserting that the essential problem in mental retardation is an intellectual or cognitive one. In respect to familial mental retardation, I have espoused a developmental theory that is essentially cognitive in nature, not motivational. Contrary to Milgram's critique, the controversy in which I am engaged is between a developmental-cognitive theory and a collection of theories that I have referred to as difference or defect theories. As becomes clear later, resolution of this controversy may require a consideration of motivational factors in the performance of the retarded. The controversy, however, is essentially between two viewpoints that are both cognitive in nature.

Stated most simply, I have, in agreement with others, asserted that variation in cognitive development is determined in large part by polygenic considerations and that within the variation of intelligence dictated by these considerations the familially retarded represent the lower end of the distribution. (It is amusing that, whereas some criticize me for being too motivational and thus too experiential in my orientation, others have taken me to task for being too genetic in my approach [Wortis, 1967].) Within such a formulation, the familially retarded would be viewed as essentially normal individuals, in the sense that they fall within the normal variation dictated by the gene pool. At this point, the reader is referred to Hirsch (1963) for a discussion of normalcy, which has been most influential in my thinking concerning the retarded. Employing a stage or levels approach to cognitive development (an approach hardly unique to me), the normal variation viewpoint generated in my thinking the rather parsimonious view that the cognitive development of the familially retarded is characterized by a slower progression through the same sequence of cognitive stages (a rate phenomenon) and a more limited upper stage of cognition (a levels phenomenon) than is characteristic of the individual of average intellect. What must be emphasized, however, is that the relationship just posited concerning the cognitive development of individuals of retarded and average intellect also obtains if the comparison is made between individuals of average and superior cognitive development.

DEVELOPMENTAL THEORY AND A MODEL OF COGNITIVE DEVELOPMENT

I think that the similarities between my approach to mental retardation and that of the Geneva group are quite apparent. These relationships can easily be seen in Fig. 10.1, which depicts the developmental theory that I have been advancing. Represented in Fig. 10.1 are three individuals of different IQs, each of whose cognitive development is taking place at a different rate, and whose cognitive ability asymptotes (somewhere between ages 14 and 20) at a different level. The approach to cognitive development represented by this model is essentially an interactionist one, in which experience (represented by the horizontal arrows) impinges or interacts in the development of the intellect with a variety of nativistic or autochthonous factors, some of which are probably of the biological read-out type whose manifestations are minimally influenced by environmental events. (See Lenneberg, 1967, for a cogent argument that one of man's most impressive cognitive accomplishments, namely language, is in many ways a cognitive phenomenon of this latter sort.)

Within this model, a cognitive level or stage represents all the formal cognitive processes investigated by such cognitive theorists as Piaget, Vygotsky, Werner, Luria, Bruner, and Milgram. I have argued that it is this collection of cognitive processes that constitutes the intellect and is, therefore, the only appropriate referent for the construct of intelligence, which is, of course, not to be confused with the Intelligence Quotient. In keeping with general developmental-cognitive thought, a cognitive stage within this model represents the totality of *formal* cognitive processes and not the specific contents of behavior or phenotypic achievements of the individual. The reader is here referred to my discussion of the importance of the process–content distinction for our understanding of behaviors labeled as intelligent (Zigler, 1967a).

The model represented in Fig. 10.1 is admittedly overly simplistic, arbitrary, and in many ways ambiguous. It does not go very far in resolving some of the most important general issues concerning cognitive development. Left unanswered are such questions as: Is the sequentiality in cognitive development inevitable, or does it only reflect the experiential programming of the organism? Exactly how do environmental events interact with nativistic factors in the development of any single cognitive process? Precisely what precipitates the movement from one cognitive level to the next, a movement reflected in the frequently reported striking changes in the quality of cognitive functioning? At what age does the developmentally highest level for each isolatable cognitive process occur? Is cognitive development essentially the growth of a variety of highly related cognitive processes and thus best represented by a single progression (as in Fig. 10.1), or is it better viewed as a collection of relatively independent processes developing at different rates as a function perhaps of quite different environmental and nativistic factors? Given the views of Piaget, as well as the model presented in Fig. 10.1, it is easy to see why single continuum developmental-stage theorists are more comfortable with structural views of intelligence that emphasize the g factor rather than ones that emphasize s factors. This, of course, does not mean that one cannot incorporate specific factor thinking into a developmental framework.

Despite these problems, I feel that this model has considerable value, especially in respect to work in the area of mental retardation. We certainly need not await the resolution of the issues noted previously before employing such a model. In keeping with most thought in the area of the philosophy of science, the question that must be raised is not whether a model is "true" or "untrue" but rather whether it is useful or not; that is, does the model help organize knowledge obtained up to this point in time, and, more importantly, does it generate hypotheses whose test can lead us to greater knowledge? The reader should be aware that all models and theories should be specifically constructed so that they can be proven erroneous through appropriate tests and, thus, be replaced by theoretical efforts of even greater validity. This last point becomes important in view of Milgram's insistence that I maintain this, or that I maintain that. I am not a polemicist given to the joys of speculative debate. For good or ill, I am committed to the heuristic value of theory construction; the generation from my theoretical efforts of hypotheses (i.e., statements as open to disproof as to proof); and the empirical tests of these statements as translated into predictions employing particular measures as referents of the constructs under test. (My philosophic commitments and preferred strategy as a behavioral scientist have been spelled out at some length [Zigler, 1963a], with particular reference to the general area of developmental psychology.)

Approached in this spirit, what does Fig. 10.1 tell us about mental retardation, and what specific hypotheses does it generate? The model certainly points out that all individuals, whose intellectual development is determined in large part by normal polygenic considerations, evidence over time (most strikingly from birth to approximately 16) a progression from lower to higher developmental forms, which typically results in ever-increasing cognitive effectiveness. The rate of this progression differs in individuals having different tested IQs. As a result of this differing rate, comparisons of CA-matched individuals of differing IQs must inevitably result in differences in performance on any cognitive task that is developmental in nature. This is true because such CA-matched individuals are at differing developmental-cognitive levels. In drawing conclusions from our model up to this point, I do not think there is any disagreement between developmental and difference theorists. As I have pointed out, many defect or difference theories contain an important developmental component. (However, as becomes apparent following, the argument centers on another aspect of these theories.) It should also be clear from this model why comparisons of CA-matched groups of differing IQs on cognitive tasks, although interesting and valuable in their own right, are generally irrelevant to the developmental- versus difference-theory controversy. Both developmental and difference theorists will agree that 12-year-old children having an IQ of 66 are less intelligent than 12-year-old children having an IQ of 100, and, therefore, that these two groups of children should behave differently over a wide array of cognitive tasks.

For purposes of keeping the record clear, Fig. 10.1 also highlights the fact that my developmental theory can itself be called a cognitive difference theory. Individuals of differing IQs are not alike. They differ in the rate of cognitive development and upper level of achievement. When we ask what produces such variation in rate, we are again confronted with all the uncertainties inherent in the nature–nurture controversy, a controversy that has never been very adequately resolved. My own preference here is the view that were the environment constant for every human being, there would still be differences in the rate of cognitive development due to differences in genetic composition. The biological law of variability applies to all complex traits, including intelligence, and I think that normal variation in intelligence (IQs of between approximately 50 and 150) will ultimately be related to polygenic factors interacting with a variety of processes. What must be emphasized here, however, is that the "difference" in my developmental theory of mental retardation refers *only* to a difference in the rate of development and its upper limit, a difference dictated by the normal variation inherent in the gene pool. A good analogy would be to that of another complex trait, namely height, on which people would vary, even if relevant environmental factors were held constant. The short individual, like the familial retardate, develops at a slower rate and does not reach as "high" a final level. However, in both instances, there is no very convincing evidence that the sequence of development differs, or that the general physiological functioning underlying physical growth in one instance and mental growth in the other differs in kind or form from those of more typical individuals.

This then leads us to a prediction that can be generated from the model represented in Fig. 10.1, which lies at the very heart of the developmental versus defect controversy and which forever separates my theory from those defect or difference theories that I have questioned. According to this model, the cognitive performance of individuals of differing IQs who are at the same cognitive level and, therefore, at different chronological ages, should behave *exactly* the same on cognitive tasks. Cognitive performance is thus viewed as totally a function of the cognitive level of the individual, irrespective of the amount of time it took that individual to reach that cognitive level. All the difference or defect theories that I

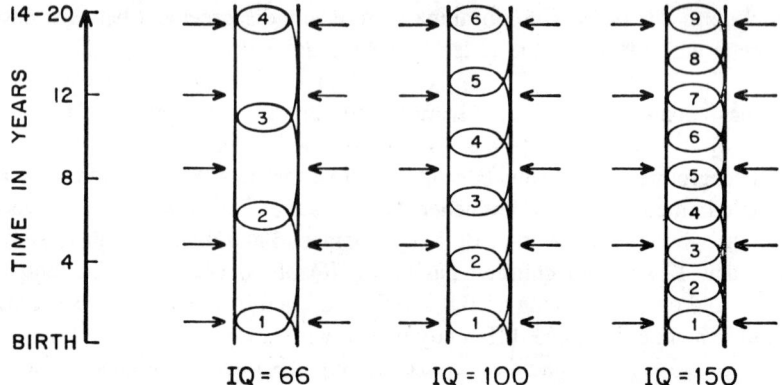

FIG. 10.1. Developmental model of cognitive growth. The single vertical arrow represents the passage of time. The horizontal arrows represent environmental events impinging on the individual who is represented as a pair of vertical lines. The individual's cognitive development appears as an internal ascending spiral, in which the numbered loops represent successive stages of cognitive growth.

have questioned will assert that the model presented in Fig. 10.1 is an erroneous one. They would assert that some of the variation on cognitive tasks is related to IQ, independent of the general level of cognition. Thus, contrary to Fig. 10.1, they would argue that the Level 2 (or any other level) of an individual with an IQ of 66 is not the same as the Level 2 of an individual having an IQ of 100.

Because IQ is nothing more than a measure of how long it took a person to attain a certain degree of cognitive proficiency, one can raise the question of why the IQ in and of itself should be related to cognitive functioning. The answer to be found in the work of the defect or difference theorists is that the IQ reflects something more about the individual than just his/her rate of cognitive development. It tells us something about the individual's neural integrity, his/her cortical satiation processes, his/her ability to use verbal mediators, or his/her information processing ability. The thinking underlying such a view has been stated most explicitly by Weir (1967), who has argued that the differential rates of cognitive development reflected in different IQs actually reflect differences in rate of learning and/or information processing. This then brings Weir to the classical difference or defect position that, at every cognitive level, the child with a low IQ will behave differently on tasks demanding learning or information processing than the child with a high IQ. This is not an untenable position, nor have I ever claimed that it was. However, as I (Zigler, 1967c) pointed out to Weir, one must be aware of the assumptions he is making when he advances such a theoretical formulation. In itself, the IQ is only a rate measure in the sense that it relates a psychological variable (level of cognition achieved as measured by the MA) to a nonpsychological one (passage of time or CA). The basic assumption in a difference approach then is that, because the IQ is a measure of one kind of rate, then it must also be a measure of another kind of rate, namely, the measure of the rate of information processing or cortical satiation, or some other determinant of cognitive functioning. One can, of course, assert that both the cognitive level and IQ (an hypothesized determinant of rate of cognitive functioning) influence the individual's performance on cognitive tasks. But, here again, we return to the heart of the developmental versus defect or difference controversy.

The theorist who holds that individuals of the same cognitive level, regardless of their IQs, will manifest exactly the same cognitive behavior is a developmental theorist (as defined by employing the model presented in Fig. 10.1). I have classified, as difference or defect theorists, all workers who assume that the IQ is a reflection of certain features of the physiological or cognitive functioning of the individual and, thus, must affect cognitive functioning over and above that predicted by the general cognitive level attained by the individual. These two positions, though different from one another, both strike me as tenable. For all their overlap, there is no problem in separating the two positions, because they clearly generate quite different predictions. The developmental position states that if you equate on cognitive level there should be no differences in cognitive functioning associated with IQ. The difference or defect position states that even when individuals are equated on general cognitive level there would be differences in cognitive performance associated with IQ. (If a theoretical position makes such a prediction, it is, by my definition, a difference or defect theory. Indeed, it is the fact that *all* defect or difference views generate this prediction that has allowed me to group a number of disparate viewpoints under a single theoretical rubric.) All that appears necessary to differentially test the two positions is a measure of general cognitive level.

COGNITIVE LEVEL AND THE ROLE OF THE MA

It is, at this point, that the MA becomes involved in our discussion. It should be clear that at the level of theoretical constructs the MA plays no role whatsoever. The theoretical construct is "cognitive level," which is admittedly a heuristic fiction. Although such constructs can enter into our hypotheses, predictions must be couched in terms of those operations that the theorist assumes constitutes a measure of the hypothetical construct, albeit a far from perfect or complete one. The MA has typically been used as a measure of cognitive level by both developmentalists and difference theorists. The paradigm is now well known. One equates groups on MA and assumes that by doing so he/she has equated groups on general cognitive level. He/she then tests these two groups to see if there is any variance upon a dependent measure attributable to IQ, independent of general cognitive level as defined by the MA. One can, of course, argue that the MA is not a very good measure. I would agree with this argument and have specifically stated that I consider the MA to be only a very rough indicator of general cognitive level. It should be clear from my writings that I would much prefer a collection of measures based on Piaget-like considerations that more clearly tap specified cognitive processes across the developmental sequence. However, no such scale is presently available. Furthermore, it would be a mistake to note only the liabilities of the MA as a measure of cognitive level without also pointing out its assets. In spite of its faults, the MA, as obtained on such standard intelligence tests as the Stanford-Binet and the Wechsler, is a wide-ranging and multifaceted measure with a great deal of its variance unquestionably reflecting a number of the individual's cognitive processes. If this were not true, all the factorial work on test scores done in order to illuminate the nature of the structure of the intellect would be meaningless.[1]

The problem, of course, is that the MA reflects factors other than cognitive ones (i.e., achievement and motivational factors that are either wholly or partly independent to the cognitive processes that the tests are thought to measure). Developmental thinkers such as myself take some solace in the fact that the MA is almost invariably found to be correlated at a respectable level with the purer Piaget-like cognitive tasks. What must be remembered is that many less than perfect measures have proven to be useful in psychology, and, until a more refined index is constructed, many of us interested in the developmental versus difference controversy will have to continue to use the MA as a measure of general cognitive level. It should be noted that it was not I who initiated the use of the MA as such a measure. I encountered this usage in the Lewin-Kounin rigidity formulation (Kounin, 1941a, b; Lewin, 1936), a difference position that captured my interest and led to my involvement in the mental retardation area over a decade ago. This formulation, which has had great influence on our

---

[1] Noting the factor analytic work calls forth a brief aside. It is not now, nor has it ever been, my contention that the simple MA-matched paradigm is the only appropriate one for the test of the developmental versus difference controversy. Another appealing methodological approach is the factor analytic one, in which the investigator equates groups of normals and retarded on MA. Then, rather than being primarily concerned with the relative performance of the two groups on a specific test or task, the investigator turns his attention to the underlying factor analytic structure across a large number of tests and/or tasks. A related aspect of such an approach is the examination of the factor-structure of the performance of the normals and retarded at differing cognitive levels, in order to assess the possibility that the two groups differ in respect to *changes* in the factor structure of their intellect with increasing maturity. The relevance of such procedures for the test of the model presented in Fig. 10.1 is clear. The factor analytic studies support the developmental model presented in Fig. 10.1 to the extent that they reveal similarities in the factor structure of normals and retarded at any particular MA level, and/or similarities in the developmental sequence of such factor structures. The model is called into question to the extent that these studies reveal differences between normals and retarded. Factor analytic studies, of course, present certain methodological and theoretical problems of their own, some of which I have noted (Zigler, 1966, 1967a). These problems notwithstanding, I do not think that I am doing an injustice to the factor analytic findings to date (Baumeister & Bartlett, 1962a, b; Butterfield, 1968; Meyers, Dingman, Attwell, & Orpet, 1961; Meyers, Dingman, Orpet, Sitkei, & Watts, 1964; Meyers, Orpet, Attwell, & Dingman, 1962), in reporting that they appear much more supportive of the developmental than of any difference formulation of mental retardation.

thinking concerning mental retardation, was instrumental in determining certain features of our care and treatment of the retarded and continues to precipitate much research. In this formulation, one can clearly see the developmental as well as the difference factors that have continued to inhere in the difference or defect theories constructed since Lewin and Kounin. It was Kounin who pointed out that over the course of development the individual's cognitive system was characterized by an increasing degree of differentiation (i.e., the system acquired more zones or regions). This concept of differentiation is a familiar one to developmentalists and has been most recently employed by Witkin, Dyk, Faterson, Goodenough, and Karp (1962), as the underlying determinant of a broad range of cognitive phenomena.

In keeping with most developmental thought, Kounin postulated that the degree of differentiation was not a function of the time since the individual's birth (i.e., age [which is essentially a nonpsychological variable]) but rather was a function of the particular cognitive level attained. Had Lewin and Kounin stopped at this point, they essentially would have been espousing the developmental theory represented by the model in Fig. 10.1. This model could very easily incorporate Kounin's view concerning differentiation. All one would have to do is to divide each of the levels in Fig. 10.1 into a certain number of regions or zones, with the number of such regions increasing as one proceeded from lower to higher levels. Consistent with this aspect of Kounin's thought and my own developmental formulation, the number of regions within a particular level would be the same for people differing in intelligence. For instance, in Fig. 10.1, Level 2 of all three individuals could be represented as consisting of four regions. Once again, however, let me emphasize that differences still exist between such individuals in even this aspect of Kounin's formulation, as they do in my own. The difference is in how long it took the individual's cognitive system to become differentiated into some assumed number of zones. Kounin recognized that it would take the retarded person longer than the person of average intellect to achieve the same degree of differentiation.

Neither Lewin nor Kounin felt, however, that the differentiation concept was adequate to the task of explaining the cognitive functioning of retarded and normal individuals. They, therefore, introduced a second factor on which they felt retardates and normals must invariably differ, given the differences in the rate at which a particular level or degree of differentiation was achieved. This factor was postulated to be cognitive rigidity. By this, they were not referring to rigid behaviors per se but rather to a formal feature of the cognitive structure itself, namely, the degree of permeability in the boundaries between regions in the cognitive structure. They felt that, at the same level of differentiation, the boundaries between regions in the cognitive structure of the retarded had to be less permeable than in the individual of normal intellect. A pictorial representation of the Lewin–Kounin model is presented in Fig. 10.2. It is this postulation of a greater "thickness" in the boundaries of retarded individuals that identifies the

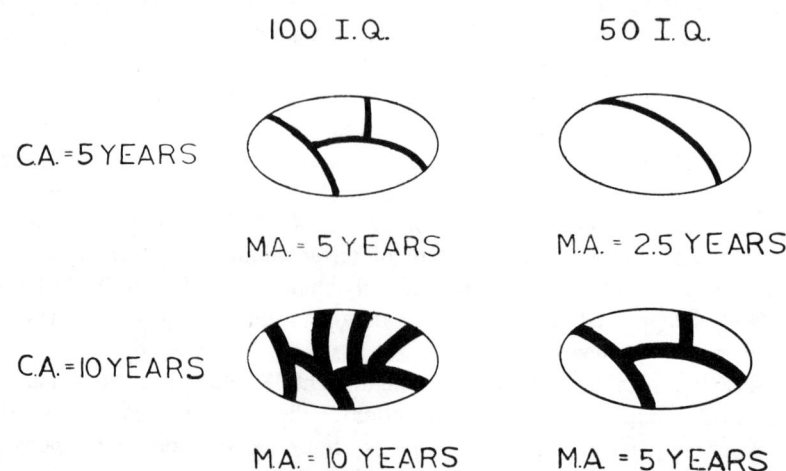

FIG. 10.2. Pictorial Representation of the Lewin-Kounin Model.

Lewin–Kounin formulation as a difference theory. Given what I have said about single-factor developmental theories also containing a difference component in respect to rate of cognitive development, those theories that I have classified as difference theories would more appropriately be called difference *plus* difference theories. The reason for this is that they postulate a difference (rigidity in the case of Lewin and Kounin) or defect over and above the difference in rate of general cognitive development. In keeping with his general formulation, Kounin criticized Lewin's earlier empirical efforts concerning rigidity in the retarded on the grounds that Lewin's research design made it impossible to attribute the discovered differences between retarded and normals to the cognitive rigidity factor, because Lewin's groups were not equated on the cognitive differentiation factor.

As can be seen in Fig. 10.2, the Lewin–Kounin formulation clearly predicts differences in performance between children who are equated on degree of differentiation, but who have differing IQs. Following his criticism of Lewin, Kounin conducted his classic series of experiments in which he employed the MA to equate normal and retarded children on degree of differentiation and did indeed find differences among his IQ groups on tasks thought to be sensitive to a postulated cognitive rigidity factor. The reader is here referred to an earlier chapter (5) for a complete discussion of the Lewin–Kounin formulation and the controversy it precipitated. I do hope that this brief overview of this position highlights the differences in thought that constitute the developmental versus difference controversy and the role in this controversy of the MA as a measure of general cognitive level.

SIGNIFICANCE OF MOTIVATIONAL FACTORS

The fact that I have now presented the basic nature of my controversy with other theorists without once alluding to motivational factors in the performance of either retarded or nonretarded individuals points out the generally misdirected nature of Milgram's criticisms. Milgram and I would certainly agree that motivational factors in the performance of either retarded or nonretarded individuals are worth investigating in their own right. Taken at this level, the issue of motivational factors is irrelevant to the controversy that I have been explicating. At another level, motivational factors are relevant to this controversy, but in a manner that seems to escape Milgram. As becomes abundantly clear in the remainder of my presentation, whereas motivational factors are essentially irrelevant to the theoretical issues inherent in the developmental versus difference controversy, they are extremely relevant at the methodological level; that is to say, either type of theorist should consider motivational factors if he/she hopes to make the interpretation of his/her findings as unambiguous as possible. In order to emphasize this point, let us turn for the moment to typical tests of the developmental versus difference controversy.

It is not uncommon to find studies in which different theorists compare groups of lower-class institutionalized familial retarded children with MA-matched groups of middle-class noninstitutionalized children on some type of learning task. As is sometimes the case, the children of normal intellect do better than the children of retarded intellect. The difference theorist who conducts such a study must then decide whether he/she has demonstrated that there is some deficit in the specific cognitive process thought to underlie learning performance that he/she can now attribute to differences in the IQs between the two groups. He/she can do so only if he/she makes an assumption that is erroneous on its face. This assumption is that the learning performance of all his/her subjects is an inexorable reflection of his/her subjects' cognitive structures and is totally uninfluenced by noncognitive factors (i.e., motivational and emotional) on which the two groups of children may differ. Tasks used to investigate the cognitive functioning of the retarded clearly vary in their susceptibility to the influence of noncognitive factors. However, as I have noted before, it is probably safe to conclude that performance on most, if not all, of our experimental tasks is most appropriately conceptualized as a multidetermined phenomenon, influenced by both cognitive or intellective factors and motivational or emotional factors. Given this, our hypothetical difference theorist has performed an experiment in which a positive finding offers the most tenuous support for his/her position. His/her results could just as easily have been interpreted in terms of differences in his/her two populations on variables other than IQs (e.g., institutionalization and social class differences, which have been found to be associated with motivational factors and which, in turn, could have affected the learning performance).

Contrary to Milgram's critique, the argument here is not between motivational theorists and cognitive theorists but between researchers who do their work well, and those who do it badly. The motivational approach, if considered independently from the developmental versus difference controversy, consists of little more than a reaffirmation of the experimental dictum: You cannot safely attribute a difference in performance on a dependent variable to a known difference in subject characteristics (e.g., IQ), if the populations also differ on other factors that could reasonably affect, or have been demonstrated to affect, performance on the dependent measure. The general mischief and downright ambiguity stemming from the failure of workers in the area of mental retardation to appreciate this dictum cannot be overemphasized. A striking example comes to mind. In a recent number of the *American Journal of Mental Deficiency,* Rohwer and Lynch (1968) compared the paired-associate learning efficiency of a group of institutionalized retardates (having a mean CA of about 25) with groups of normal children of varying economic strata (having mean CAs ranging from about 5 to 12). The finding that the institutionalized retarded group did worse than MA-matched normals (and even normals having lower MAs than the retarded) was interpreted as rather convincing evidence of the erroneousness of the developmental theory that I have been espousing. The interpretation problem posed by such a finding was made clear in another study reported by Baumeister (1968) in the same number of this journal. This investigator, employing MA-matched groups of institutionalized retardates, noninstitutionalized retardates, and children of normal intellect, found no differences in the paired-associates learning of noninstitutionalized retardates and normals. He did find that the institutionalized retarded group was inferior in their learning to both of the other two groups. Furthermore, he discovered a significant correlation between length of institutionalization and trials to criterion; that is, the longer the child was institutionalized, the worse was his/her performance. It is illuminating to note that in spite of considerable evidence (Badt, 1958; Harter, 1967; Iscoe & McCann, 1965; Kaufman, 1963; Lyle, 1959; Schlanger, 1954; Zigler & Butterfield, 1966) that institutionalization affects performance on a variety of cognitive tasks, Rohwer and Lynch not only did not correlate length of institutionalization with their performance measures but failed even to inform the reader as to how long their retarded subjects had been institutionalized. Certainly, when read together, these two articles on paired-associates learning hardly indicate that the developmental position is an untenable one.

In view of the specific predictions derived from the developmental (no differences in performance with MA-matched groups) and difference (differences in performance with MA-matched groups) positions, one could argue that the developmental theorist will champion the importance of motivational factors, and the difference theorist will not. This is simply not true. Failure to attend to motivational factors can make the developmental theorists' findings just as suspect as those of the hypothetical difference theorist noted earlier. For instance, a developmental theorist could compare a group of lower-class familial retardates and a group of middle-class normal children, equated on MA, on a learning task and employ candy or pennies as a reinforcer. Let us now assume that the mean learning performance of the two groups was equal. Does this support the developmental position? As in the case of our earlier example, we must conclude that it does so in only the most tenuous way. In view of both evidence (Cameron & Storm, 1965; Terrell, Durkin, & Wiesley, 1959) and common sense, one could conclude that the reinforcer employed was more motivating for the lower-class retardates than for the middle-class normals. As a result, the retarded children used their cognitive resources to the fullest in order to obtain the reinforcer, whereas the normal children did not. In this instance, motivational differences between the groups could act in such a way as to obscure actually existing cognitive differences.

That the good researcher, independent of theoretical affiliation, is sensitive to the importance of motivational factors in resolving the developmental versus difference controversy can clearly be seen in the efforts of at least one difference theorist, namely Kounin. Kounin explicitly stated that even after matching his groups on MA his experimental procedures would not provide an adequate test of his rigidity formulation, if his groups differed motivationally. It was for this reason that he introduced procedures that he thought would guarantee that all his subjects would perform on his experimental tasks while in psychologically comparable situations. As I have pointed out (Zigler, 1962), in introducing these procedures that were meant to equate groups on attitude and motivation, Kounin actually introduced other factors that might have produced differences in motivation among his groups. However, placing Kounin's work in its historical perspective, I view this as the normal trials and tribulations of the researcher, who must always work in the absence of complete knowledge. In principle, Kounin's position (a difference one) and mine (a developmental one) are exactly the same in respect to the importance of controlling motivational factors, if we are ever to answer the question of whether the familial retarded have a deficiency in their cognitive functioning over and above that associated with their slower rate of cognitive development.

Having made this point, that motivational factors are of equal concern to both developmental and difference theorists and are essentially neutral factors in the theoretical controversy, I would like to make an observation that may be of value to workers in the area of mental retardation. Supporters of difference or defect theories since Kounin have been surprisingly insensitive to the role of motivational factors in either confirming or disconfirming their own positions. This is only a polite way of saying that much of their work has been methodologically unsound. Of course, part of this is due to the fact that in the area of mental retardation, as in any other area, there are workers whose efforts are naive, at worst, and less than maximally sophisticated, at best. However, my reading of and personal contact with certain supporters of the difference viewpoint have convinced me that they are as sophisticated methodologically as any workers to be found in the behavioral sciences. I must, therefore, conclude that there is something inherent in the content of the mental retardation area that leads even extremely capable workers astray. I think that the problem resides in the very essence of the nature of mental retardation.

Transcending the developmental versus difference controversy, there is agreement that the essential problem of mentally retarded individuals is their intellectual or cognitive inadequacy. Because cognitive functioning lies at the core of retardation phenomena, it is easy to see why, in this particular area, workers have concentrated on cognitive functioning and have underemphasized if not almost totally excluded other factors as determinants in the behavior of the retarded. There is clearly a tendency to attribute all the atypical behaviors produced by the retarded to their cognitive deficiency. We appear to be so awed with the cognitive shortcomings of the retarded that we are led into tautologies, in which we assert that retarded individuals behave the way they do because they are retarded. Cognitive theories of retardation, be they of the developmental or difference sort, are valuable in that they force us to investigate the particular processes of the retarded that mediate performance on tasks requiring those particular processes. However, cognitive theories cannot be complete theories of the behavior of the retarded, because the behavior of the retarded like any other group of humans reflects factors other than cognitive ones. Although the analogy is far from a perfect one, it should be noted that lower-class children as a group have lower IQs than middle-class children. However, when differences are found in the behavior of lower-class children and middle-class children, the IQ difference is but one of the many factors considered in the interpretation of these differences. Workers look closely at their subjects' social milieux, the child-rearing practices to which they have been subjected, and the attitudes, motives, and goals that these children bring to the experimental situation. In contrast, when we deal with the mentally retarded, we often seem to implicitly assume that the cognitive deficiency from which our subjects suffer is such a pervasive phenomenon in their total functioning as to make them impervious to the effects of influences known to affect the behavior of the nonretarded.

For the sake of the record, I would like to demonstrate that my continual pointing out to difference theorists the importance of motivational factors stems neither from my being a motivational theorist nor from my admittedly large store of cantankerousness. Over the years, I have taken an adversarial stance toward difference theories, but I would like to convince the reader that it has been of value to all workers in this field. Let me use some of Milgram's own work to demonstrate this. As I have done in this chapter, Milgram too, in his critique, has noted the importance of controlling for nonintellective subject or task variables. Not unlike Milgram, I have been interested in whether verbal mediation ability covaries as a function of IQ, independent of MA or organicity. The evidence on this issue has proved to be equivocal (Balla & Zigler, 1964; Luria, 1961; Milgram & Furth, 1963; O'Connor & Hermelin, 1959; Reiber, 1964). In order to help resolve this issue, Milgram and Furth (1963) conducted a study in which oppositional thought was used as a referent of verbal mediation. This oppositional thought was assessed partly by having the experimenter point to an extreme object on a dimension (e.g., the largest of four wooden discs) and required the subject to spontaneously point to the object representing the opposite end of the dimension. Differences were obtained on this task in favor of normal children, and the authors concluded that the retarded children (though matched with the normals on MA) suffered a mediational deficiency.

I would conclude that the results are ambiguous, because Milgram did not follow his own dictum concerning the contaminating features of "nonintellective subject and task variables." In his critique, Milgram points to the value of the work of my colleagues and myself on outerdirectedness (Achenbach & Zigler, 1968; Green & Zigler, 1962; Sanders, Zigler, & Butterfield, 1968; Turnure & Zigler, 1964). This work has indicated that due to their many failure experiences, retarded individuals are distrustful of their own solutions to problems and, thus, tend to look for cues or solutions provided by others in their problem-solving efforts. This outerdirectedness could easily have contaminated the Milgram and Furth findings, because the retarded child would have had a greater tendency to point to the same stimulus as the adult points to than would the normal child, who has been found to show a greater innerdirectedness in his problem solving. The oppositional learning of the two groups might have been the same had the task not required the retarded child to overcome a tendency to imitate the pointing response made by the experimenter. All of this is by way of saying that a concern with motivational factors is helpful to us all, in that it tells us what we must control or at least consider before our studies allow us to assert differences in cognitive functioning between groups.

Looking back then at Fig. 10.1 and 10.2 in this chapter, a warning is in order. What is represented in these models is not the human being, but only his cognitive system. This system is but one portion of the individual's mediational armamentarium with which he processes inputs and produces outputs. So long as we confuse one determinant of behavior with all determinants of behavior, we will never construct a comprehensive theory of the behavior of the retarded. Does this mean that every worker must consider every determinant when doing his/her own research? Of course not. One can study any system or any subsystem he/she likes. However, he/she should remain sensitive to the assumptions he/she is making and to the possible effect on his/her experimental task of determinants he/she has chosen to ignore.

REPRESENTATIVE DIFFERENCE OR DEFECT POSITIONS

Let us now turn our attention to the issue of which viewpoints are and which viewpoints are not difference or defect theories. Milgram is correct in stating that I consider Luria's position and Ellis' position to be defect approaches. He might also have added that I consider the position of Lewin and Kounin as well as the formulation of Spitz (1963) as other examples of the difference or defect approach. Contrary to Milgram's statement, I have purposely remained ambiguous as to whether or not the Zeaman and House attention deficit formulation is a difference or defect position. Indeed, in my analysis (Zigler, 1967a) of the Zeaman and House work, I even questioned whether it was at all relevant to the developmental versus difference argument. It is true that, from time to time, I have alluded to this work as an example of a difference approach. But, as should be clear in my analysis (Zigler, 1967a) of this position, I have done so because the Zeaman and House formulation so easily lends itself to the support of the classical difference approach. (The reader is referred to Robinson and Robinson, 1965, for a clear example of such a translation of the Zeaman and House efforts.) As far as Zeaman and House's own statements are concerned, the etiology of the attention deficit that they have been investigating has remained too ambiguous for me to be able to classify their approach as being a difference one or not.

In order to be perfectly clear on this issue, I further explore the conditions that must be met, before I classify an approach to mental retardation as a defect or difference theory. As suggested previously, one gets an inkling that he/she is dealing with a difference theorist when a worker equates groups on some measure of cognitive level (typically MA) and then predicts differences related to IQ. Although use of such a paradigm, or some closely related one, is a necessary defining characteristic of a difference theory, it is not a sufficient one. I too, often equate groups on MA and predict differences associated with IQ on tasks usually thought to be cognitive in nature (Gruen & Zigler, 1968; Stevenson & Zigler, 1958; Turnure & Zigler, 1964; Zigler & deLabry, 1962; Zigler & Unell, 1962). This does not make me a difference theorist. The crucial factor lies in the theorist's explanation of the etiology of the process thought to be producing the differences in behavior associated with IQ. In order for a formulation to be of the difference type, the etiology of the postulated defect or difference must inhere in the low IQ itself. It is a central characteristic of the retarded and is unavoidable (which does not mean that it is irremediable), if one has a cognitive system that is characterized by the production of unintelligent behaviors. This central or inherent characteristic must then force the theorist to postulate that *every* retardate evidences this difference or defect, because it is the defining feature of the poor cognitive system. In practice, of course, one can still use group designs and satisfy himself/herself with performance differences between the means of groups differing in IQ. One does this by taking refuge in the sampling error in assigning individuals to IQ groups and in the far from perfect measuring features of the dependent performance measure.

The defining characteristics that I have used for difference or defect theories are thus very stringent ones. The position of Luria, especially as his position has been interpreted by such English and American workers as Milgram and Furth (1963), O'Connor and Hermelin (1959), Ellis (1963), Spitz (1963), Lewin

(1936), and Kounin (1941a, b), would appear to fulfill these criteria very nicely. Given these criteria, the Zeaman and House attention formulation is simply not specific enough to allow me to categorize it. I, too, believe that many institutionalized retarded individuals often do not attend to what we would like them to attend in our experimental situations. Again, this does not necessarily make me a difference theorist. What must be determined is whether the inattention is due to a central process that is thought to inherently covary with IQ, or whether it is the result of learned problem-solving strategies or motivational phenomena that are related to IQ only, because children of differing IQs have quite different learning and general experiential histories. None of this detracts in any way from the importance of Zeaman and House's fine experimental efforts. It does mean that we cannot characterize this effort as representative of the difference orientation until these investigators commit themselves to a specific view of the etiology of the attention deficit that they have been exploring.

At this point, I divide clearly the difference-defect camp into difference theories on the one hand and defect theories on the other. Throughout this presentation, as well as in earlier ones, I have grouped within one camp quite disparate theoretical viewpoints and have alternately and sometimes interchangeably referred to this orientation as a "defect" position or a "difference" position. Whereas all the positions so described appear to share the commonalities I have attributed to them, some are more correctly thought of as defect positions and some as difference positions. The distinction here rests on whether the theorist asserts that the process he/she is investigating varies continuously with IQ (a difference position), or whether the relationship is a discontinuous one (a defect position). In the former case, the theorist argues that even when equated on general cognitive level the child of superior intellect has more (or less) of something than the child of average intellect, who in turn has more (or less) of something than the child of retarded intelligence. In the latter case, the theorist argues that retarded individuals are qualitatively different than nonretarded individuals and suffer from something, typically of a physiological nature, that "normal" individuals do not have. The distinction rests completely on whether or not the theorist considers the particular shortcoming to vary across the entire range of intelligence. As stated by their progenitors, Luria's (1961) and Ellis' (1963)[2] positions would be considered defect theories, whereas Spitz' (1963) and Kounin's (1941a, b) would be considered difference theories. What must be remembered is that it is the difference between familial retardates and normals of

---

[2] Although Ellis leans toward the view that the stimulus-trace deficiency, which he postulates for the retarded, is of the defect variety, he does not preclude the view that it could be a deficiency of the difference sort. Although Ellis (1963, pp. 134-158) uses the word "differences" for both of these possibilities, his view on this point becomes clear in his statement that: "Even though differences between normal and subnormal organisms are adopted as a basis of speculation, an extension to individual intelligence differences, wherever they may occur, is not precluded [p. 134]."

the same MA that is the point of contention between the developmental theorist and both difference and defect theorists, whatever the nature of the hypothesized deficit underlying this difference may be. The gap between the developmental theorist and all the defect or difference theorists remains a wide one, because the developmental position generates the hypothesis that there are no differences in formal cognitive functioning between familial retardates and normals matched on general level of cognition (typically measured by MA). (Given the constant difference prediction across both types of theory, one could, of course, use the description *difference* orientation as the more generic term, and the *defect* orientation as the more specific one.)

On the basis of the foregoing explication of my views, I now comment briefly on certain of Milgram's specific criticisms of my approach. It is interesting that in the process of accusing me of creating false dichotomies, Milgram has erected a totally false confrontation between us. As noted earlier, there is nothing in my work that indicates that motivational theories "win," when cognitive theories "lose." The argument is between two quite identifiable cognitive viewpoints: the developmental one that I have advanced and the difference theories of other workers. By cognitive theories, Milgram is alluding only to those theories I call difference theories. He, then, attributes to me the view that these theories are antithetical to the demonstration of motivational effects on performance. He further attributes to me the totally nonsensical view that cognitive phenomena (of the deficit-type) could not independently affect performance. I, of course, believe no such thing. It is quite plausible to assume that, on a task labeled cognitive, differences discovered between groups of normals and retardates of the same MA may reflect *both* motivational differences between the groups and a deficiency of some sort in the cognitive functioning of the low IQ group. Milgram seems to think that my argument with difference theories is based on my belief that these theories are nonsensical or inherently unsound. On the contrary, I believe that each and every one of the difference theories is heuristically valuable and, without question, inherently viable. If I did not think them viable, I would not spend so much of my own time putting them to test (Balla & Zigler, 1964; Green & Zigler, 1962; Stevenson & Zigler, 1957; Zigler & Butterfield, 1966; Zigler & Unell, 1962). My questioning of the validity of these theories is not based on their viability but rather on the nature and methodological weaknesses of the findings offered in their support. Whether any of these theories, or all of them for that matter, are proven to be correct is, of course, an empirical issue. If any of them are proven to be correct, what will in turn be disproven is not any "motivational approach," but rather the cognitive developmental theory represented in Fig. 10.2. I would not consider this any great loss providing that this model, at some point in the history of our inquiry, sharpened our experimental onslaught on the nature of cognitive development. Contrary to the impression given by Milgram, I do not consider myself a champion of the motivational over the cognitive. It is true that I have spent considerable effort in the demonstration that motivational factors influence tasks typically thought to be cognitive in nature. What Milgram does not attend to is that I have also spent considerable effort in demonstrating that tasks thought to be motivational or psychodynamic in nature are highly influenced by cognitive-developmental factors (Achenbach & Zigler, 1963; Zigler, 1963b; Zigler & Kanzer, 1962; Zigler, Levine, & Gould, 1966, 1967). I believe in the importance of both motivational and cognitive factors; indeed, a single theme running throughout my work is the investigation of how each type of factor independently, or the two factors in interaction, influence performance on specific tasks.

RELEVANCE OF THE TWO-GROUP APPROACH

Milgram asserts that the nonsensical position he attributes to me is a result of my having confounded the two-group approach with the "cognitive" (i.e., difference) issue. This also is not true. The two-group approach that I have argued for is in many ways totally independent of the theoretical controversy in which I have been engaged. Where it is related to the developmental versus difference controversy, it is related in a manner that seems to have totally escaped Milgram. In many ways, the relevance of the two-group approach to the developmental-difference issue is much more methodological than theoretical.

Independent of the developmental-difference controversy, Milgram has himself presented an admirable statement of the value of the two-group approach, and I wholeheartedly agree with him. However, what is missing in Milgram's presentation is a grasp of the implications of his argument for all work in the area of mental retardation, independent of the developmental-difference controversy. Milgram and I agree that workers in the field should employ at least a two-category classificatory system when dealing with retarded individuals. What is the classificatory principle of this system? It is clearly etiology; that is, one type of retarded individual (organic) is assigned to one class (that would, of course, have a number of subclasses), because the etiology of his intellectual shortcomings can be clearly attributed to some specifiable physiological defect or other. The other type (culture–familial) is assigned to the second class by employing evidence that is both exclusive (no evidence that they suffer from the physiological defects found in group one) and inclusive (other members of the family suffering from this same type of intellectual deficiency). The etiology of the intellectual deficiency of this second group, which is by far the larger of the two, is unknown, although several causative hypotheses have been advanced.

Why group at all on the basis of etiology? We do so because we think that the correlates of class membership will increase our predictability and, thus, our understanding of retarded individuals over that which we would have discovered had we treated them as a homogeneous group. Stated somewhat differently, dichotomizing retarded individuals on the basis of etiology at least suggests that these two groups differ in respect to the course of cognitive development and the particular nature of cognitive functioning at any particular point in this course of development. Whether our two class system is blessed with such correlates is, of course, an open question, to be determined empirically. However, there is enough evidence on the effects of the lack of a physiologically intact brain to dictate that, when we perform research on retarded individuals, we should attend to etiology. Any researcher may, of course, discover that there is no difference in the functioning of the two types of retarded, but he has lost nothing by treating the two types of retarded as different groups in his research design. If, on the other hand, differences do exist between organic and familial retardates, then those differences will be obscured in designs that ignore the two-group dichotomy. Independent of any controversy, I have here only reaffirmed such basic tenets of the scientific enterprise as: (1) The classes we employ should not encompass phenomena any more heterogeneous than they have to be; and (2)- research designs should be sensitive to current knowledge and should be constructed so as to produce maximal rather than minimal information.

Given this view, I cannot understand why Milgram attributes to me the position that one should not investigate a common process (e.g., verbal mediation) across people of all IQ levels, and within mental retardation, with regard to the organic-familial dichotomy. Rather than abhoring such a practice, given the accepted metatheoretical principle of parsimony, I admire it. All that I have asked is that the investigator keep his research groups as pure as possible, so that we might optimally determine exactly what type of organism is characterized by what specific manner of cognitive functioning.

Let us now turn our attention to that aspect of the two-group approach that is germane to the developmental versus difference controversy. This relationship is not at all the one that Milgram suggests but is actually much simpler. Milgram accuses me of drawing the unwarranted conclusion that "cognitive" (i.e., difference) theories inherently obscure, ignore, or reject the two-group dichotomy. The key word here is inherent. I have never stated, nor do I presently believe, that there is anything inherent in difference theories that leads them to ignore the two-group approach. The fact is that some difference theorists have tended to ignore the two-group approach, whereas others have not. A striking case of a difference theorist who did not was Kounin, who, like myself, insisted that his theoretical model did not apply to the organic retarded and, thus, limited his experimental efforts to retarded of the familial type. It is really not difficult to establish the criteria by which we can assert that a worker of any theoretical persuasion is ignoring or not ignoring the two-group approach. By definition, the worker who identifies his/her retarded group on the basis of IQ alone (or even on the basis of IQ plus a social competence measure) and ignores the etiological characteristics of his/her retarded group has consciously determined to be noncognizant of the two-group distinction. (Indeed, some have argued that such noncognizance has considerable value [Bijou, 1966].) This is not to say that the worker who ignores the two-group approach produces efforts of no value, but only that he/she may be doing so at his/her own peril. The fact is that many difference theorists simply do not attend to this approach. This would appear to be a matter of choice rather than anything inherent in difference theories.

We come, now, to the relationship between the developmental-difference controversy and the two-group approach. So long as the two-group approach is ignored, there cannot only be no direct experimental confrontation, but evidence in support of the difference theories, as espoused, must remain unconvincing. There can be no confrontation between developmental and difference theorists when organic subjects are included in the experimental test, because the developmental theory represented in Fig. 10.2 has been clearly enunciated as applicable only to those individuals whose intellectual functioning reflects normal polygenic variation in interaction with environmental events. This includes human beings whom we have labeled as familial retardates, as well as individuals of average and superior intellect, but *not* individuals suffering from known physiological abnormalities, whatever their IQs might be. Thus, differences in cognitive performance between organic retardates and normals, even though matched on MA, are irrelevant to the developmental-difference controversy. Furthermore, as I have stated before (Zigler, 1967b), at a purely methodological level, cognitive differences obtained between a MA-matched group of normals and a retarded group comprised even partially of organic retardates do not provide clear evidence in support of the difference position. Use of organic retardates presents an almost insurmountable problem, when one attempts to evaluate the degree to which any differences in behavior support the major theoretical premise that underlies most difference approaches. This premise, clearly seen in the work of Luria, Spitz, and Ellis, is that all retardates, familials and organics alike, suffer from some specifiable deficit. However, until the etiological issue is attended to in the research design, there is no way of assessing how much of the difference between normals and retardates of the same MA is a product of the gross organic pathology known to exist in the organic retardates included in the retarded group, and how much is a product of the deficiency thought by the difference theorists to exist in all retardates.

I make this point crystal clear by giving a simple example. Let us suppose a researcher ignores the two-group approach, and he/she examines two groups matched on MA, the first composed of 20 children of average intellect and the second of 20 children having IQs below 70, which actually comprises 10 familial and 10 organic retardates. Let us suppose that the worker is a difference theorist who is testing the hypothesis that verbal mediation is related to IQ and that, therefore, all individuals having an IQ below 70 will do less well on a verbal mediation task than children of average intellect. Let us further assume that the mean performance (errors) on the experimental task of the average group is 10, that of the 10 organic retardates is 20, and that of the 10 familials is 10. The overall differences in the group means of the normals and retarded (10 versus 15, respectively) would lead the investigator to reject the null hypothesis and consider his/her findings as supportive of his/her position. All that would actually have been demonstrated is that organic brain damage leads to poorer performance and that there is no relationship, once MA is controlled for, between IQ (independent of the phenomenon of organicity) and verbal mediation. (Again, the reader should note that the two-group issue raised in this illustration has nothing to do with any motivational orientation, but only with methodological considerations that must be kept in mind before any current difference theory can receive experimental support or refutation.) However, in the illustration just given, the researcher may discover that both familial and organic retardates have means of 20, in which case he/she has provided clear support for his/her position. The one qualification here, of course, is that the researcher must also have satisfied the demand that the difference be clearly attributable to differences in cognitive functioning rather than some factor not inherently associated with IQ. But even if this were the case, the difference theorist would not know it as long as he/she obscures the etiological issue.

Milgram asserts that because I feel that the same principle of cognitive development applies throughout the educable retarded–gifted range, an extension downward to the trainable defective should be logically acceptable. Again, I try to clarify a slight confusion in this statement of Milgram's and then go on to point out why such an extension downward is illogical. For Milgram to use the classifications of educable and trainable is in essence a refutation of the two-group approach for which he argued so well in the early part of his chapter. Without stating it, he has introduced a second classification system, which, though somewhat related to the two-group classification, is also more than a little independent of it. Groups of educable and trainable retarded are classified primarily on IQ and not on the etiological considerations stressed in the two-group approach. Given the IQ range typical of familials, we would not expect to find many of these individuals in the trainable category. On the other hand, as can be seen in Fig. 10.3 (reprinted from Zigler, 1967b), a good number of organic individuals would be found in the educable group and indeed at every IQ level. Rephrasing Milgram's statement, I have asserted that the same principles of cognitive development apply throughout the normal range of intelligence with the familial retarded representing the lowest end of this distribution. I have thought it illogical to extend these principles to individuals with organic defects (whatever their IQs may be) for all of the reasons so cogently advanced by Milgram himself when discussing the value of the two-group approach. If the etiology of the phenotypic intelligence (as measured by an IQ) of two groups differ, it is, then, far from logical to assert that the course of cognitive development is the same, or that even similar contents in the behaviors of two such differing individuals are mediated by exactly the same cognitive process.

A couple more minor points are in order. As indicated previously, I have no

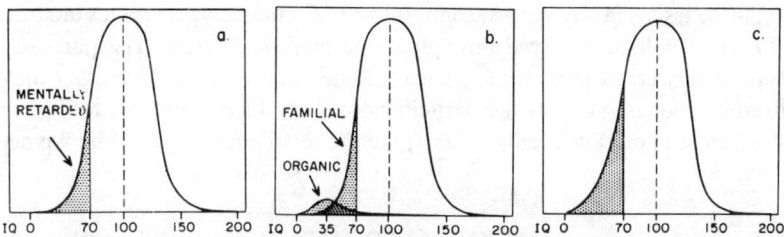

FIG. 10.3. (a) Conventional representation of the distribution of intelligence. (b) Distribution of intelligence as represented in the two-group approach. (c) Actual distribution of intelligence.

argument with the shortcomings of the MA pointed out by Milgram. I say that the developmental model in Fig. 10.1 continues to be viable, even if each of the stages or levels represented the functioning of a single cognitive process, whose general level was measured by a purer measure of that process. Finally, Milgram attributes to me the view that the motivational (i.e., developmental) viewpoint is an optimistic one, and the cognitive (i.e., difference) viewpoint is a pessimistic one. I certainly do think that theoretical positions influence how men behave. Noting the opinion of others (Sarason & Gladwin, 1958), I have concluded that the Lewin-Kounin position led us to treatment and training practices with the retarded child that were essentially pessimistic (e.g., training the retarded to do perserverative tasks in order to take advantage of their inherent rigidity). However, all things considered, I feel that the pessimism-optimism issue is irrelevant. Indeed, I have frequently argued that we have just as much to fear in the area of mental retardation from unrealistic optimism as we do from unrealistic pessimism. The important point is not the optimistic or pessimistic implications of our viewpoints, but rather their validity. As I have noted at some length (Zigler, 1963), "good" theories lead us to deal with our world in an optimal way, whereas "bad" theories lead us to deal with our world erroneously. This is true whether we are trying to navigate to the moon or to devise methods to optimize the behavior of retarded children. If our theories are right, our methods will be right, but if our theories are wrong, our methods will be wrong, at worst, or right for the wrong reasons, at best. The major issue, of course, is how does one choose between competing theoretical viewpoints so that one might know which is the better guide to action. Such choice, of course, demands the methodologically sound experimental confrontation between theoretical viewpoints for which I have argued.

In conclusion then, this chapter is more an effort to make my views as clear as possible rather than to make a point by point rebuttal of Milgram's chapter. As indicated earlier, I think that there are some real issues that separate developmental and difference or defect theorists, but I do not feel that Milgram has touched upon these issues in any very meaningful way. Fortunately, the issues are matters of fact that will be resolved through sound empirical effort. The purpose and nature of this effort is such that, whereas one point of view or another may be proved erroneous, none of the participants will be losers. Indeed, to the extent that we expand our knowledge concerning the retarded, we will all be winners.

ACKNOWLEDGMENTS

The preparation of this chapter was facilitated by Research Grant HD-03008 from the United States Public Health Service, and by the Gunnar Dybwad Award of the National Association for Retarded Children.

The author would like to acknowledge his great indebtedness to Susan Harter, not only for her cogent criticisms of an earlier version of this presentation, but, more importantly, for the significant collaborative role that she has played over the years in helping the author formulate the position presented in this chapter.

REFERENCES

Achenbach, T., & Zigler, E. Social competence and self-image disparity in psychiatric and nonpsychiatric patients. *Journal of Abnormal and Social Psychology,* 1963, *67,* 197-205.
Achenbach, T., & Zigler, E. Cue-learning and problem-learning strategies in normal and retarded children. *Child Development,* 1968, *39,* 827-848.
Badt, M. I. Levels of abstraction in vocabulary definitions of mentally retarded schoolchildren. *American Journal of Mental Deficiency,* 1958, *63,* 241-246.
Balla, D., & Zigler, E. Discrimination and switching learning in normal, familial retarded, and organic retarded children. *Journal of Abnormal and Social Psychology,* 1964, *69,* 664-669.
Baumeister, A. A. Paired-associates learning by institutionalized and noninstitutionalized retardates and normal children. *American Journal of Mental Deficiency,* 1968, *73,* 102-104.
Baumeister, A. A., & Bartlett, C. J. A comparison of the factor structure of normals and retardates on the WISC. *American Journal of Mental Deficiency,* 1962, *66,* 641-646. (a)
Baumeister, A. A., & Bartlett, C. J. Further factorial investigations on WISC performance of mental defectives. *American Journal of Mental Deficiency,* 1962, *67,* 257-261. (b)
Bijou, S. W. A functional analysis of retarded development. In N. R. Ellis (Ed.), *International review of research in mental retardation* (Vol. 1). New York: Academic Press, 1966.
Butterfield, E. C. Stimulus trace in the mentally retarded: Defect or developmental lag? *Journal of Abnormal Psychology,* 1968, *73,* 358-362.
Cameron, A., & Storm, T. Achievement motivation in Canadian Indian middle- and working-class children. *Psychological Reports,* 1965, *16,* 459-463.
Ellis, N. R. The stimulus trace and behavioral inadequacy. In N. R. Ellis (Ed.), *Handbook of mental deficiency.* New York: McGraw-Hill, 1963.
Green, C., & Zigler, E. Social deprivation and the performance of feebleminded and normal children on a satiation-type task. *Child Development,* 1962, *33,* 499-508.
Gruen, G., & Zigler, E. Expectancy of success and the probability learning of middle-class, lower-class, and retarded children. *Journal of Abnormal Psychology,* 1968, *73,* 343-352.

Harter, S. Mental age, IQ, and motivational factors in the discrimination learning set performance of normal and retarded children. *Journal of Experimental Child Psychology*, 1967, *5*, 123-141.
Hirsch, J. Behavior genetics and individuality understood. *Science*, 1963, *142*, 1436-1442.
Iscoe, I., & McCann, B. The perception of an emotional continuum by older and younger mental retardates. *Journal of Personality and Social Psychology*, 1965, *1*, 383-385.
Kaufman, M. E. The formation of a learning set in institutionalized and noninstitutionalized mental defectives. *American Journal of Mental Deficiency*, 1963, *67*, 601-605.
Kounin, J. Experimental studies of rigidity: I. The measurement of rigidity in normal and feebleminded persons. *Character and Personality*, 1941, *9*, 251-272. (a)
Kounin, J. Experimental studies of rigidity: II. The explanatory power of the concept of rigidity as applied to feeblemindedness. *Character and Personality*, 1941, *9*, 273-282. (b)
Lenneberg, E. *Biological foundations of language*. New York: Wiley, 1967.
Lewin, K. *A dynamic theory of personality*. New York: McGraw-Hill, 1936.
Luria, A. R. *The role of speech in the regulation of normal and abnormal behavior*. New York: Liveright, 1961.
Lyle, J. The effect of an institution environment upon the verbal development of imbecile children. I. Verbal intelligence. *Journal of Mental Deficiency Research*, 1959, *3*, 122-128.
Meyers, C. E., Dingman, H. F., Attwell, A. A., & Orpet, R. E. Comparative abilities of normals and retardates of MA 6 years on a factor-type test battery. *American Journal of Mental Deficiency*, 1961, 250-258.
Meyers, C. E., Dingman, H. F., Orpet, R. E., Sitkei, E. G., & Watts, C. A. Four ability-factor hypotheses at three preliterate levels in normal and retarded children. *Monographs of the Society for Research in Child Development*, 1964, *29*(5), 1-80.
Meyers, C. E., Orpet, R. E., Attwell, A. A., & Dingman, H. F. Primary abilities at mental age 6. *Monographs of the Society for Research in Child Development*, 1962, *27*(1), 1-40.
Milgram, N. A., & Furth, H. G. The influence of language on concept attainment in educable retarded children. *American Journal of Mental Deficiency*, 1963, *67*, 733-739.
O'Connor, N., & Hermelin, B. Discrimination and reversal learning in imbeciles. *Journal of Abnormal and Social Psychology*, 1959, *59*, 409-413.
Reiber, M. Verbal mediation in normal and retarded children. *American Journal of Mental Deficiency*, 1964, *68*, 634-641.
Robinson, H. B., & Robinson, N. M. *A mentally retarded child*. New York: McGraw-Hill, 1965.
Rohwer, W. D., & Lynch, S. Retardation, school strata, and learning proficiency. *American Journal of Mental Deficiency*, 1968, *73*, 91-96.
Sanders, B., Zigler, E., & Butterfield, E. C. Outerdirectedness in the discrimination learning of normal and mentally retarded children. *Journal of Abnormal Psychology*, 1968, *73*, 368-375.
Sarason, S. B., & Gladwin, T. Psychological and cultural problems in mental subnormality: A review of research. *Genetic Psychology Monographs*, 1958, *57*, 3-290.
Schlanger, B. B. Environmental influences on the verbal output of mentally retarded children. *Journal of Speech and Hearing Disorders*, 1954, *19*, 339-345.
Spitz, H. H. Field theory in mental deficiency. In N. R. Ellis (Ed.), *Handbook of mental deficiency*. New York: McGraw-Hill, 1963.
Stevenson, H. W., & Zigler, E. Discrimination learning and rigidity in normal and feebleminded individuals. *Journal of Personality*, 1957, *25*, 699-711.
Stevenson, H. W., & Zigler, E. Probability learning in children. *Journal of Experimental Psychology*, 1958, *56*, 185-192.
Terrell, G., Jr., Durkin, K., & Wiesley, M. Social class and the nature of the incentive in discrimination learning. *Journal of Abnormal and Social Psychology*, 1959, *59*, 270-272.
Turnure, J., & Zigler, E. Outerdirectedness in the problem solving of normal and retarded children. *Journal of Abnormal and Social Psychology*, 1964, *69*, 427-436.

Weir, M. Mental retardation. *Science,* 1967, *157,* 576–577.
Witkin, H. A., Dyk, R. B., Faterson, H. F., Goodenough, D. R., & Karp, S. A. *Psychological differentiation.* New York: Wiley, 1962.
Wortis, J. Mental retardation. *Science,* 1967, *155,* 1442.
Zeaman, D. Review of N. R. Ellis, *International review of research in mental retardation* (Vol. I). *Contemporary Psychology,* 1968, *13,* 142–143.
Zigler, E. Rigidity in the feebleminded. In E. Trapp, & P. Himelstein (Eds.), *Readings on the exceptional child.* New York: Appleton–Century–Crofts, 1962.
Zigler, E. Metatheoretical issues in developmental psychology. In M. Marx (Ed.), *Theories in contemporary psychology.* New York: Macmillan, 1963. (a)
Zigler, E. Social reinforcement, environment, and the child. *American Journal of Orthopsychiatry,* 1963, *33,* 614–623. (b)
Zigler, E. Discussion of Bruner's cognitive approach. In M. Garrison (Ed.), Cognitive models and development in mental retardation. *American Journal of Mental Deficiency,* 1966, *70,* 118–126.
Zigler, E. Mental retardation: Current issues and approaches. In M. L. Hoffman & L. W. Hoffman (Eds.), *Review of child development research* (Vol. II). New York: Russell Sage Foundation, 1967. (a)
Zigler, E. Familial mental retardation: A continuing dilemma. *Science,* 1967, *155,* 292–298. (b)
Zigler, E. Mental retardation. *Science,* 1967, *157,* 578–579. (c)
Zigler, E. Mental retardation. In P. London & D. Rosenhan (Eds.), *Foundations of abnormal psychology.* New York: Holt, Rinehart, & Winston, 1968. (a)
Zigler, E. Mental retardation. In *International encyclopedia of the social sciences* (Vol. X). New York: Macmillan, 1968. (b)
Zigler, E., & Butterfield, E. C. Rigidity in the retarded: A further test of the Lewin-Kounin formulation. *Journal of Abnormal Psychology,* 1966, *71,* 224–231.
Zigler, E., & deLabry, J. Concept switching in middle-class, lower-class, and retarded children. *Journal of Abnormal and Social Psychology,* 1962, *65,* 267–273.
Zigler, E., & Kanzer, P. The effectiveness of two classes of verbal reinforcers on the performance of middle- and lower-class children. *Journal of Personality,* 1962, *30,* 157–163.
Zigler, E., Levine, J., & Gould, L. Cognitive processes in the development of children's appreciation of humor. *Child Development,* 1966, *37,* 508–518.
Zigler, E., Levine, J., & Gould, L. Cognitive challenge as a factor in children's humor appreciation. *Journal of Personality and Social Psychology,* 1967, *6,* 332–336.
Zigler, E., & Unell, E. Concept switching in normal and feebleminded children as a function of reinforcement. *American Journal of Mental Deficiency,* 1962, *66,* 651–657.

11 A Behavioral Research Strategy in Mental Retardation: Defense and Critique*

Norman R. Ellis
University of Alabama

In the mid 1950s, behavioral research in mental retardation accelerated dramatically, and in the decade that followed, more studies were conducted than in all the prior years. The earlier research related to clinical problems—diagnosis, psychometric evaluation, and similar issues. The "new era" was characterized not only by quantitative increases in experimentation but by qualitative changes as well. Much of the new research was clearly not directed toward the solution of practical problems. Experiments dealt with learning, motivation, perception, memory, and other concepts from general psychology. Much normative data on the behavioral potential of the retarded resulted. They were compared with normal children and adults, occasionally with lower animals, and often with other retarded persons differing psychometrically, etiologically, or in some other way believed to be important to the behavior in question.

In the main, this plethora of data was not the product of theory testing. Researchers in mental retardation have neither articulated the long range purpose(s) of their studies nor the logic of their experimental designs. Only a few scattered articles touch on this issue. Thus, the reader has to infer purpose and the relation of experimental design to purpose. This has not always been easy, and purpose seems at times to be a gratuity provided by the reader. Much research has been of a piecemeal sort; a few investigators have been more systematic, and, as a result, some embryonic theoretical excursions have been attempted. Among this group, Cromwell (1963), Zigler (1966a, b), Zeaman and House (1963), and Spitz (1963) have published theoretical articles that have been influential. My

---

*This article is reprinted with permission from *American Journal of Mental Deficiency*, 1969, 73, 557-566.

own article in the *Handbook of Mental Deficiency* (1963) received some attention, both complimentary and pejorative.

Zigler, perhaps more than anyone else, has attempted to formulate an overview of these "theories" in mental retardation. Principally, he divides them into: (1) the psychometric approach, characteristic of the test constructors; (2) the "defect theories," reflecting a "difference orientation"; and (3) his own position, which he refers to as "cognitive," "developmental," and "motivational." In several recent, and similar, articles (1966a, b, 1967, 1968), Zigler has criticized the defect theories. He includes in this group the work of Kounin and Lewin, Luria, Siegel and Foshee, O'Conner and Hermelin, Spitz, Zeaman and House, Goldstein, and Ellis (cited by Zigler) and contrasts his own with them. In my opinion, Zigler presents a distorted view of the defect approach, making it appear pessimistic, even simpleminded, and to have emotional connotations. In one instance, he (Zigler, 1968) notes:

> the view that mental retardates, as a group, are 'different' is most vividly encountered in comparative studies where mental retardates are conceptualized as occupying a position on the phylogenetic scale somewhere between monkeys and children of average intellect [p. 226].

Also:

> the defect orientation to mental retardation originally emphasized the notion of moral defect and stemmed from the belief that the retarded were possessed by a variety of devils to the empirical evidence of their exhibiting an inordinately high incidence of socially unacceptable behaviors, such as crime and illegitimacy [p. 226].

And:

> Some of the more influential of the defect positions will be examined here, turning first to the position of the Russian investigator, A. R. Luria, whose work has influenced investigators in England and the United States. In respect to Russian efforts, it should be noted that, given the political philosophy of the U.S.S.R., workers in the area of mental retardation have no alternative but to accept a defect position [p. 235].

In another instance he says:

> Such research (his) underlines the importance of conceptualizing the familial retardate as an essentially human being, who, like the normal child [p. 000.]

Although these statements may have some validity, in this context they detract from an objective assessment, and critiques of these approaches must be couched in a more dispassionate language.

The present chapter attempts to clarify the logic of this "difference orientation," and to rebut some of Zigler's criticisms of "defect" positions. Also, a more veridical perspective of this research strategy than that offered by Zigler is attempted. Of course, the writer adopts the "difference" orientation, though he does not accept some of the premises and orienting attitudes that Zigler attributes to it. In particular, the "cognitive approach," referred to by Zigler, which attributes causative properties to "cognitive structures," is rejected. Moreover, the idea that certain cognitive defects "inhere in" or "inexorably cause" mental retardation is also rejected. Here, mental retardation is viewed as a biobehavioral syndrome and approached from the standpoint of operationalism.

The Difference Orientation

The "difference orientation" begins with the assumption that retardates exhibit retarded behavior. Perhaps more apropos, they have defective[1] behavior when compared to others of similar *chronological age* living in their culture. (This does not imply a discontinuity of normals and retardates on behavioral and psychometric measures.) Moreover, the probability that they will continue to be different, in varying amounts, from normal people in the future is quite high. Certainly, we have not witnessed any dramatic behavioral changes as a result of experimental intervention, psychological or biomedical. And, it seems evident that we are not likely to find a panacea that will normalize retarded behavior through alterations in "cognitive," "motivational," or other processes.

Given the premise that there are *behavioral* differences between normals and retarded persons of equal CA,[2] the primary task for a behavioral science is to describe these differences. This behavioral description does little more than provide clues for further research. Eventually, through experimentation, variables controlling behavioral differences may be defined. In this fashion, a series of refinements may lead to useful theory construction. Both historical and contemporary independent variables may be considered. For instance, the problem may be the dependence of differences in reaction time upon contemporary extraneous stimuli. On the other hand, the behavioral processes may relate to motivation, which, in turn, may depend on differences in early social reinforcement experiences. The latter differs from the former only in that the experimenter is able to relate a *motivational defect* to early social experience, a historical variable. This is the strategy used by Zigler and his associates, and it is a commendable one.

---

[1] In my view, according to standard dictionary definitions and common usage, the term *defectives* more accurately describes this population than does *retardates*. Nevertheless, defectives may carry some stigma, and the term retarded is used in this chapter.

[2] The equal CA methodology is my own approach and is not used by some of the other workers referred to by Zigler as "defect" positions. It will be contrasted with the equal MA comparison approach later in the chapter.

Nevertheless, he too, attempts to explain *defects* in contemporary behavior. Of course, he is not able to manipulate social experiences, except through selective sampling, and his results are correlative.

Etiology and the Physiological Defect Misconception

The difference orientation has been criticized for treating the retarded as a homogeneous group. For example, Zigler (1966a) states: "all retardates, regardless of etiology, are viewed as inherently different. Within this (difference) orientation retardates are seen as a homogeneous group of defective organisms with the specific nature of the defect varying from theoretician to theoretician [p. 78]."

Obviously, in much of the research, the retarded are treated as a homogeneous group. Usually, the researcher selects subjects according to IQ (or MA) and CA; occasionally, from one etiological category. Rarely, is the last actually accomplished. In the typical institution where most research is conducted, records are inadequate, and the validity of available diagnoses is questionable. Usually, subjects for behavioral research studies consist of retarded persons from a rather homogeneous IQ or MA and CA group. Because these subjects vary from almost no adaptive behavior to that near normal, the sensitivity range of most dependent measures requires this homogeneity.

Zigler's criticisms of the defect theorist for ignoring etiology seems to be based on the premise that the defects postulated are physiological or structural in nature. (Although Zigler states that they are "physiological or cognitive," his criticisms are based mainly on the assumption that they are physiological.) He (Zigler, 1966a) states:

> It should be noted that in respect to the familial retardate, no convincing physiological evidence has been found indicating the presence of any of the defects noted above. Rather, these defects have been postulated on the basis of differences in performance between retardates and normals on some types of experimental tasks. An implicit assumption in much of this work has been that performance on such tasks is an inexorable product of the cognitive structure or intellectual level alone [p. 78].

In another source (1966b), he suggests separating the pathological cases from the familials. Thus, his criticisms seem to be that the defect theorist has incorrectly extrapolated the defect notion to the familials. Milgram (1969) has discussed this issue thoroughly, and I do not elaborate it further here.

Most of the theories to which these comments are directed are molar behavior theories, with constructs totally defined by behavioral phenomena. Certainly, the constructs employed by Zeaman and House, Siegel and Foshee, and Ellis cited by Zigler (1966, p. 78) are based in behavior rather than physiology. Spitz does employ a quasineurological language, though it seems clear that predictions are based upon molar events. This seems true of the work of Luria and Kounin and Lewin, as well. I attempted to describe a possible physiological analogy for "stimulus trace," though it should have been clear that this concept was not indebted to physiology. It seems inappropriate to require physiological evidence for the existence of a molar behavior concept. Zigler's insistence that the defects must have a physiological basis, therefore, would appear to stem from a reductionistic bias. He (Zigler, 1966b) states:

> The evidence typically offered by the difference or defect theorists is that even when groups or normals and retardates are matched on MA, which grossly controls for differences in the stage of intellectual development, the two groups behave differently. This difference in behavior is advanced as proof of the existence of some physiological or cognitive defect which itself is responsible for the slower rate of development. Where the hypothesized defect is an explicitly physiological one, it would appear to be a simple matter to obtain direct validation for the defect's existence. Such evidence would come from biochemical and physiological analyses as well as from pathological studies of familial retardates. A number of such studies have, of course, been carried out. Although there is an occasional report of some physical anomaly, the bulk of the evidence has indicated that the familial retardate does not suffer from any gross physiological defects. Indeed, if such evidence were readily available, the defect theorist would give up his reliance on the more ambiguous data provided by studies examining molar behavior. The failure to find direct evidence for the existence of a physiological defect in the familial retarded has not deterred, and really should not deter, theorists from postulating such defects [p. 125].

There are several debatable issues raised in this paragraph. To my knowledge, none of the investigators espousing the "defect" position are attempting to use behavioral data to prove the existence of a physiological defect. Moreover, the isolation of a physiological defect in learning, memory, or attention, for example, could hardly be a "simple matter!" Zigler's reductionistic bias seems clear when he suggests that the defect theorist would give up his "ambiguous data," if the physiological defect could be found. In my opinion, the physiological answers are not necessarily better than molar behavioral ones. Indeed, they may even be more ambiguous. This is not to deny the possibility of an ultimate rapprochement between these disciplines and the value of exploring analogs. This approach may be a prime source of research clues. Nevertheless, I have faith that ultimately, with refined techniques, a physiological basis for all behavioral deviations may be found. In view of the very high brain-behavior relationship, this belief seems quite tenable. Even then, behavior may be more predictable from behaviorally based theory.

When the retarded are referred to as a heterogeneous group, the dimension along which they are heterogeneous should be defined. Otherwise, this statement is rather meaningless. Heterogeneity, in terms of etiology, should not be confused with behavioral heterogeneity. One can not be inferred from the other. It is doubtful that any degree of success is achieved, even when the experimenter attempts to select from one diagnostic category. Institutionalized "cultural–familial" retarded persons do not necessarily constitute a homogeneous group, behaviorally or physiologically. No doubt, this category includes cases of misdiagnosis, cultural retardation, genetic retardation, and those in which both genetics and environment interact. As a further case in point, it may even be hazardous to view genetically determined retardation as a single syndrome. Genetics may affect intelligent behavior on a "polygenic" or quantitative basis. In others, endocrine malfunction may be genetically determined, which, in turn, may affect brain function. In still other cases, the structure and function of sensory, motor, or associative fibers could be selectively affected. Inheritance might result in fewer fibers in the corpus callosum, for example. The effects of inheritance may be quite subtle physiologically, affecting the RNA mechanism within neurones; yet, these subtle effects could have profound implications for behavior. This is highly conjectural in view of our limited knowledge of the ways in which inheritance operates. Nevertheless, it points up the risks involved in attempting to formulate behavioral theory for a particular diagnostic category.

The Nomothetic Approach and Etiological Heterogeneity

In view of such complications, there is some merit to the approach that ignores etiology. If the retarded can be shown to have an attention deficit irrespective of etiology, for example, the construct has greater generality. Such an expectation is based on the premise that underlies all nomothetic approaches to the study of retardate behavior. Are there behavioral deficits that are common to cases of retardation resulting from different causes? Can suppurative lesions from disease, physical trauma, cultural deprivation, endocrine or metabolic errors all result in deficits in short-term memory, attention, or inhibitory mechanisms? The nomothetic approach requires faith! On the surface, it does seem more plausible that social experiences of the retardate are more likely to result in a common behavioral deficit. However, the social reinforcement history of retarded persons and their responses to this treatment are probably not as consistent or as clearly defined as the social learning theorists would have us believe.

Another serious issue facing defect theories involves the attempt to establish general laws upon group data. With the current knowledge of localization of function and brain-behavior relations, it seems likely that retarded persons with various types of c.n.s. insult may also have differing behavioral deficits. And, in a typical randomly selected group, some may show an attention deficit, a short-term memory deficit, deficits in inhibitory mechanisms, and still others may exhibit motivational deficits. A given subject might have one or a combination of deficits. Thus, a group statistic could provide evidence for a short-term memory deficit, when in fact this was true for only a part of the group, that with a certain type of c.n.s. damage. Research with normal organisms may be open to the same criticism, though it seems more crucial in this instance. In this manner, a number of deficits may be ascribed to the retarded with only some having a particular deficit. Moreover, the deficit notion implies the existence of other intact or normal behavioral processes. The logic of the deficit concept has not been explored along this line.

To summarize, it has been noted that researchers usually select subjects from a psychometrically homogeneous group that limits the generality of their findings. Further, etiology is likely to be ignored in subject selection that requires the assumption that different types of c.n.s. insult may produce common behavioral deficits. This problem cannot be avoided by selecting subjects, even from a diagnostic category such as cultural-familial retardation. Finally, the nomothetic-group data approach may provide evidence for behavioral deficits that characterize only a part of the population.

None of the preceding criticisms of the "deficit" approach seems to have been made by Zigler. Rather, his criticism involving heterogeneity is based on a false premise—that "defects" are physiological, and further that "cognitive" defects must be proven physiologically.

In spite of all the possible criticisms of ignoring etiology in behavioral research, it should be strongly emphasized that *rarely have behavioral differences characterized different etiological groups!* A few scattered studies report small differences between "brain-injured" and "familial retardates," for example. More studies can be found reporting no differences, and, in view of editors' penchant for "positive results," the significance of the few positive studies is further diminished. Moreover, subject selection in these studies must be carefully scrutinized for possible criterion contamination. It is quite unusual to find behavioral studies in which brain injury is a diagnosis based on medical history. Often, it is a behaviorally defined diagnosis.

The Single Defect Misconception

Zigler (1966a), in summarizing his position on personality structure in the retardate, states:

> It is the author's view that the psychological process underlying these hypotheses (his, concerning motivation) operate in combination more often than in isolation. This is merely to assert that the behavior of the retarded child on any task is a complex and multiply determined phenomenon. This view is congruent with the overall position of the investigator and stands in opposition to those efforts which postulate some single inherent deficiency [p. 104].

Surely, no one would argue with the concept of multiple causation. And, to postulate a single behavioral deficiency as the single cause of retardation is patently absurd, and I do not know of a single investigator who subscribes to such a position.[3] The need for a division of labor must be recognized, however!

As to the adjectives "inherent," "inexorable," and "immutable," used by Zigler to characterize the defect, it should be noted that those are his terms and reflect his conception of the "deficit." Because "defect" refers to behavioral processes, immutability is an empirical issue.

Research Design; The Equal MA Comparison

A pervasive issue in research strategies central to a difference orientation, or to any theoretical interpretation, is that of the comparison groups employed. The comparison of a 7-year-old normal child with a 16-year-old retarded child with equivalent mental age contrasts sharply with a strategy employing retarded and normal 16-year olds. Unfortunately, this distinction is usually unrecognized or else treated in a cavalier manner. Zigler recognizes these different strategies but, in his critique of the difference orientation, fails to take into account this important distinction. Obviously, the particular design used should depend on the experimental question posed.

Apparently, the rationale underlying most research using the equal MA design is that an MA match equalizes "development." Rarely is the meaning of development scrutinized. If the investigator means by "development" growth of intelligent behavior, further measures of intelligent behavior (i.e., the dependent variable in the experiment) can differ for the retarded and the normals, only if the matching instrument is incomplete or fails to measure the same intelligent behavior as the dependent variable. Zigler (1966b) states:

> if we are to understand the nature of intelligence, we must consult those workers intent on investigating the nature and development of cognitive processes, e.g., thought, memory, concept formation, and reasoning, rather than focus on the work of test constructors and psychometricians [p. 112].

If he is equating these constructs with intelligence and also insisting that current intelligence tests do not measure "nature and development of cognitive processes," then it is somewhat puzzling that he uses MA as a device for matching normals and retardates for developmental or "cognitive" level. He seems committed to view MA as a valid measure of these "cognitive processes," if he is to attribute experimental differences to motivational rather than to cognitive variables. There is the additional problem of whether MA for the retarded and

---

[3]Actually, Zigler, in making a case for the effects of motivation, has come nearer to a "single deficiency" point of view than any of the other positions with which I am familiar. However, as Douglas Detterman, a graduate student at Alabama, aptly points out, he would have to insist on at least two defects, the motivational deficit and the original defect that leads to failure experiences, etc.

normal child is based on similar test performance. For the researcher interested in "noncognitive" variables, the problem is no less knotty. Zigler's strategy in the study of motivation is to equate subjects on MA. MA is based on achievement that developmental psychologists would agree is the product of complex interactions of motivation and experience. An additional source of confounding is the motivational state of the retarded and normal child at the time the MA score is obtained. Thus, MA may well-reflect past and present motivational states as well as cognitive factors.

Zigler seems to view his approach as "developmental" because he equates retardeds and normals on MA, viewed as a measure of developmental level, in the design of his studies. He then proceeeds to find behavioral differences due to motivational variables. However, his approach would seem more "developmental," if these differences were related differently to MA levels (i.e., if MA were treated as an independent variable). As previously noted, his view that behavioral differences are relatable to early interactions between the organism and the environment does not distinguish his orientation from that of other defect theorists. From this point of view, his position is no more developmental than those he views as nondevelopmental (defect positions).

Finally, the theoretical significance of whether a 7-year-old normal child and a 16-year-old retarded child are similar or different in terms of motivation or cognition has not been formally explored. It would seem to have practical importance, and possibly theoretical significance, viewed in the context of the "child-who-never-grew-up" conception. If an intelligence test score can be viewed as a valid measure of development, then it may be useful to measure other indices of development with experimental "tests." However, I am not persuaded that a strong argument can be advanced for this approach.

Research Design; the Equal CA Comparison

The equal CA strategy is favored by the fact that it is directed to the primary characteristic of mental retardation. *It is the differences in adaptive behavior of persons of similar chronological age that define retardation.* The differences are behavioral, and the logic of analyzing the differences seems compelling.

With the equal CA design, subjects can be selected from similar environments, differing only in adaptive behavior. (Whether one uses IQ or MA in this design seems of little consequence.) They may differ as a result of some c.n.s. deficiency, as a result of genetic endowment, trauma, disease, or some combination of these factors interacting with the environment over a maturational period. If one can be sure that these *primary* causes do not exist, environmentally produced retardation may be studied in the equal CA design. In this case, behavioral differences are attributable to a complex developmental interaction between organism and environment. Bijou (1966) has aptly described this state of affairs.

There are serious methodological problems with the equal CA design. Except for the very mildly retarded, behavioral differences are usually so great as to preclude measurement on the same scale. This problem of "floor and ceiling" effects is familiar to those pursuing this research strategy. It seems likely that many statistical interactions, given theoretical significance, are merely artifacts.

No doubt many researchers have employed the equal MA design in order to avoid this measurement problem. Occasionally, the researcher resorts to the freshman chemistry students' dictum, "If a little will do it, more will do it better." Thus, he uses both types of control groups. This is hardly a solution.

Zigler, among others, seems content with "developmental level," as an explanation of behavioral differences. He (Zigler, 1968) states:

> It is no great mystery that a group of children with IQs of 70 and a group with IQs of 100 matched on chronological age differ on a variety of tasks. These children are at different developmental levels, and such differences are exactly what a developmentalist would expect. The mystery is the repeated demonstration that even when groups are matched on MA, the retardate does less well, or at least behaves differently, than the MA matched normal child [pp. 234–235].

This statement presents in bold relief the main difference between the equal MA and equal CA approaches. The great mystery to me, and to some of my colleagues, is why the children with IQs of 70 and 100 differ. The statement that they are at "different developmental levels" does not provide an explanation (even if the tenuous assumption of *developmental* differences is accepted). The explanation of behavioral differences between normal children of 3 and 12 years of age as due to differences in development leaves much unanswered. The equal CA strategy rejects IQ and/or developmental level as an explanation, and the experimental analysis is directed toward an isolation of *manipulable* variables that relate to this difference. We do not view differences between equal MA S's as the important issue. Sometimes, behavior of the retarded is like that of equal MA normals: sometimes, it is not. Such differences are usually small in comparison to equal CA differences. In another context Zigler also seems to reject tested intelligence as an explanatory construct. He (Zigler, 1966b) notes: "The plea is not that we abandon tests, for every cognitive theorist must eventually employ tests defined in the broadest sense. The plea is that workers in the field turn their attention from the superficial content of tests, i.e., the right or wrong answer, and come to grips with the problem of the cognitive structures and processes that give rise to content [p. 113]."

In spite of this statement, Zigler seems willing to explain the behavioral differences between children with IQs of 70 and 100 as due to differences in developmental level, MA! An IQ or MA score may explain why a child is failing in school. By "explain" is meant, the child's test score is based on behaviors similar to those required by the school, and, therefore, they should be highly related. Then, if it can be shown that there are no emotional or physical causes for school failure, it seems safe to conclude that school behavior is consistent with intelligence test behavior and is not associated with other adjustment problems. In this sense, IQ or MA "explains" school failure. However, it should be recognized that we merely have samples of behavior, test behavior and school behavior, and they agree. At best, we have established a low order R–R law. Both are indices of adaptive behavior, and both may measure essentially similar behavior. Thus, we ascribe low intelligence to the child, meaning that his/her behavior is consistently low and likely to remain that way. The fallacious logic in the statement, "Mickey Mantle is a great hitter because he has high athletic ability," also occurs in "children fail in school because they have low intelligence."

In the same vein, explaining behaviors as being due to "cognitive processes" or "cognitive development" is fraught with hazards. Zigler equates cognitive with memory, concept formation, attention, etc., and at the same time discusses these same phenomena as "inexorable products of the cognitive structure." Obviously, an independent definition of "cognitive structure" is required. It is appropriate to *describe* some behaviors as cognitive and others as motivational. In this case, the constructs "cognitive" or "motivational" have explanatory powers similar to those of IQ in the example of a child with school problems. Although it may not be Zigler's intent, it is difficult to read his articles without reifying cognitive structure and to feel that, in his view, it causes behavior. This complaint should not be directed to Zigler alone. Indeed, many in the behavioral sciences seem atavistic in this respect. The term cognitive seems to have multiple meaning and often is described as a cause of the same behavior from which it is inferred.

Criticisms of the Stimulus–Trace Hypothesis

Zigler and his associates have been especially critical of the stimulus–trace hypothesis and of much of the experimentation deriving from it. It is beyond the scope of this chapter to consider the detailed criticisms of the experiments, though some response to the criticisms focusing on logical properties of the theory and experimental approach seem in order here. Zigler (1966b) has charged that:

> The primary value of the same CA comparison would appear to lie in the highlighting of a specific process, i.e., short-term memory, as an important factor in the behavioral inadequacy of retardates. However, it should be noted that the demonstration that retardates are poorer on tasks requiring short-term memory than are normals of the same CA, is a somewhat circular undertaking. It is circular to the extent that a short-term memory deficit would influence the IQ score itself through its effect on certain of the intelligence subtests, e.g., digit-span. Furthermore, it should be pointed out that the discovery of a difference between normals and retardates of the same CA is just as amenable to a general developmental interpretation as to the view that all retardates suffer from c.n.s. pathology since the MA of such retardates is necessarily lower than the MA of the normals [p. 141].

Zigler's charge of circularity in this particular instance is indeed difficult to understand, in view of my statement (Ellis, 1963): "Although n_1 has been defined as an intelligence test score, the IQ is nothing more than a sampling device for selecting populations which vary in level of adaptation. Other indices could be used: success in school, institutionalization, and noninstitutionalization, or other criteria which reflect degree of adaptation [p. 140]." Obviously, if one is going to study different groups, they must be identified. In a schema showing the relationship between n_1 and the stimulus trace, some index to n_1 must be used. Because the hypothesis was based on the studies of adult retardeds, IQ was chosen. MA would have served equally well.

The fact that short-term memory behavior may have been measured by the intelligence test was of no consequence, because we did not view IQ as an *explanation* of memory. Rather, studies of memory in these S's we believe might lead to an understanding of intelligent behavior more generally. The fact that a particular IQ test happens to measure a part of these same behaviors does not amount to criterion contamination in the usual sense. It should be reemphasized that such a criticism would seem somewhat more valid, if the aim of our research were merely to demonstrate that normals and retarded persons differ in short-term memory capacity on an absolute basis.

In a recent article, Butterfield (1968) has attacked the stimulus–trace notion on several grounds. He states:

> Ellis (1963) has been particularly vague in operationally defining the n_1 construct of stimulus trace theory. While he has indicated clearly that *some* intelligence test score is the preferred, though not necessarily the only possible, measure of n_1 he has not indicated whether he means the MA or the IQ score. In some passages of his exposition of the theory, he has indicated that MA is the appropriate measure of n_1 while in other passages he has indicated that it is the IQ which should be employed. This confusion is also evident in research reports which sometimes match normal and retarded persons on MA (Girardeau & Ellis, 1964) and sometimes on neither MA nor CA (Ellis, Pryer, & Distefano, 1960).
>
> This lack of clarity concerning the relation of n_1 to MA and IQ is most unfortunate, since a psychological theory's implications for mental retardation may hinge on the relationship it posits between its chief organismic constructs and MA and IQ [p. 358].

In light of my preceding discussion concerning definitions of n_1, the reader recognizes that I attempted a *broad* definition of behavioral inadequacy, providing the occasion for a priori prediction in instances where retardates are selected on *any* commonly acceptable basis. Moreover, because the theorizing was based on results of studies with mature subjects, whether MA or IQ was used was unimportant. At that time, I (Ellis, 1963) noted: "With respect to the present theory, it is speculated that the young child has a stimulus trace deficit, and the establishment of the adult form of the short-term memory function will show a developmental trend. In view of this, it is not surprising that studies matching immature normal humans and mental defectives rarely fail to find behavioral differences [p. 140]." Thus, it may be seen that I, too, viewed this approach as "developmental" and also expected that equal MA normal and retarded subjects would exhibit similar short-term memory. Unfortunately, the word "rarely" in my quote was an error. However, this could hardly obscure the intent. Butterfield's citation of the 1960 study, which was actually conducted some 4 years prior to the formulation of the stimulus–trace idea, hardly seems fair. As for the article by Girardeau and Ellis in 1964, the purpose of this article was: "to investigate the role of 'distracting' stimuli, ability level, and interitem interval in rote learning. In addition, the influence of these variables on serial position effects was under investigation. The experiments were designed also so that comparisons between normals and retardates could be made in terms of trials to criterion on serial and paired-associate tasks [p. 525–526]."

Stimulus trace is not mentioned in this article, nor is the 1963 *Handbook* article referenced.

In this same article (1968), Butterfield, in keeping with Zigler's position, attempts to draw a sharp distinction between developmental and defect approaches, a distinction that lacks substance. Whether certain behavioral phenomena (defects or other) are developmental or not would seem to depend on whether they arise and exist during the developmental period (usually defined as birth to about 18 years of age). According to widely accepted definitions of mental retardation, all behavioral deviations exhibited by these S's are developmental. The behavioral results of a gunshot wound at the age of 25 would not be.

In a more recent article, Belmont and Butterfield (in press) present a thorough review of the literature bearing on the relation among short-term memory, development, and intelligence. Some criticism of the stimulus–trace hypothesis is included, though it is somewhat attenuated. Moreover, it is mainly directed to experimental evidence for a short-term memory deficit.

It was not the intent here to review and rebut the many criticisms of the stimulus–trace hypothesis but rather to indicate the general nature of these criticisms. Those critical comments directed toward the empirical support for the position seem to have found an easier target. Nevertheless, in light of current evidence, mental retardates, however defined, and young normal children do appear to exhibit a short-term memory deficit.[4] Advances in this area indicate that short-term memory may involve several processes—encoding, storage, and

---

[4]Belmont and Butterfield (in press) present a thorough review of this issue. They state that short-term memory "defined as how much a person recognizes, recalls, or reproduces seconds or minutes after some material is presented" does improve with age and intelligence. However, these writers go on to indicate that "short-term memory" consists of three processes: encoding, storage, and retrieval. They then equate short-term memory with *storage* only. Using this definition, they purport to show that there is no experimental evidence for a relationship among age, intelligence, and "short-term memory."

retrieval, for example—and that the deficit may reside in any one of these. The short-term memory deficit hypothesis has been reformulated by the author. This revised position along with relevant empirical results have been presented in Volume 4 of the *International Review of Research in Mental Retardation*.

ACKNOWLEDGMENTS

I wish to thank Doug Detterman, Jeanne Dugas, and Paul S. Siegel for critically reading this manuscript.

REFERENCES

Belmont, J. M., & Butterfield, E. C. The relations of short-term memory to development and intelligence. In L. P. Lipsitt & H. Reese (Eds.), *Advances in child development and behavior* (Vol. 4). New York: Academic Press, in press.

Bijou, S. W. A functional analysis of retarded development. In N. R. Ellis (Ed.), *International review of research in mental retardation* (Vol. 1). New York: Academic Press, 1966.

Butterfield, E. C. Stimulus trace in the mentally retarded: Defect or developmental lag? *Journal of Abnormal Psychology,* 1968, *73*(4), 358–362.

Cromwell, R. L. A social learning approach to mental retardation. In N. R. Ellis (Ed.), *Handbook of mental deficiency*. New York: McGraw-Hill, 1963.

Ellis, N. R. The stimulus trace and behavioral inadequacy. In N. R. Ellis (Ed.), *Handbook of mental deficiency*. New York: McGraw-Hill, 1963.

Milgram, N. A. The rationale and irrational in Zigler's motivational approach to mental retardation. *American Journal of Mental Deficiency,* 1969, *73*, 527–532.

Spitz, H. H. Field theory in mental deficiency. In N. R. Ellis (Ed.), *Handbook of mental deficiency*. New York: McGraw-Hill, 1963.

Zeaman, D., & House, B. J. The role of attention in retardate discrimination learning. In N. R. Ellis (Ed.), *Handbook of mental deficiency*. New York: McGraw-Hill, 1963.

Zigler, E. Research on personality structure in the retardate. In N. R. Ellis (Ed.), *International review of research in mental retardation*. New York: Academic Press, 1966. (a)

Zigler, E. Mental retardation: Current issues and approaches. In L. W. Hoffman & M. L. Hoffman (Eds.), *Review of child development research* (Vol. 2). New York: Russell Sage Foundation, 1966. (b)

Zigler, E. Familial mental retardation: A continuing dilemma. *Science,* 1967, *155*, 292–298.

Zigler, E. Mental retardation. In *International encyclopedia of the social sciences*. New York: Macmillan & Free Press, 1968.

12
Mental Retardation*

Morton Weir
University of Illinois, Urbana-Champaign

Although I agree with many aspects of Zigler's "developmental" theory of retardation, several points appear to merit further discussion and clarification. A key portion of his developmental theory (Zigler, 1967) is given in the following:

> the familial retardate's cognitive development differs from that of the normal individual only in respect to its rate and the upper limit achieved. Such a view generates the expectation that, when rate of development is controlled, as is grossly the case when groups of retardates and normals are matched with respect to mental age, there should be no difference in formal cognitive processes related to I.Q [p. 294].

In this statement, Zigler defines mental age (MA) as the rate of intellective development. In the same paragraph, however, he refers to MA as the "level" of intellective functioning. Zigler's apparent failure to distinguish rate of development from level of development leads to a questionable prediction from his theory—namely, that retardates and normals of the same MA will be similar with respect to their cognitive functioning.

Mental age is a transformation of the score made in an intelligence test and is a measure of the current level of intellective functioning, not of the rate of accumulation of knowledge. If an individual's chronological age (CA) is also known, then the intelligence quotient (IQ) may be calculated: $IQ = (MA/CA) \times 100$. The IQ score is a rough index of the amount of information accumulated in a given number of years of life; thus, it is a measure of rate.

---
*This material first appeared in *Science,* 1967, *157,* 576-578. Copyright 1967 by the American Association for the Advancement of Science. Reprinted by permission.

According to Zigler, if groups of retardates and normals are matched for MA, there should be no difference in formal cognitive processes related to IQ. Figure 12.1 represents the growth in mental age of a hypothetical normal child, born in 1955, and progressing at the rate of one MA unit per year (IQ = 100), and of a retarded child, born in 1950, who is progressing at the rate of one-half MA unit per year (IQ = 50).

Assume that the two children were chosen for a learning experiment in 1960, because they both had MAs of 5 years. According to Zigler, if nonintellective factors are held constant, the performance of the retarded child should equal that of the normal child. But note that the two children have different rates of intellectual growth. These differential rates should not only appear as long-term phenomena but should also be evident in short-term laboratory tasks. It therefore appears imperative that Zigler's developmental theory should predict that the two children will perform differently, providing the task they are given is sufficiently complex to be sensitive to the abilities responsible for the differential growth shown in Fig. 12.1. The fact that these two children made identical MA scores on the intelligence test may be accounted for if one assumes that the intelligence test is more a test of recall of past learning, particularly vocabulary, than it is a test of the child's ability to deal with new and unfamiliar materials. Thus, the MA score is basically a measure of achievement and may not be greatly affected by factors that determine the rate of accumulation of knowledge.

As evidence for his hypothesis of "equal-MA, equal cognitive functioning," Zigler cites research that demonstrates that the performances of normals and retardates, matched for MA, did not differ when motivational factors are controlled. However, it appears doubtful that the tasks used in the research cited are sensitive to the abilities that determine the rate of intellective growth. The tasks

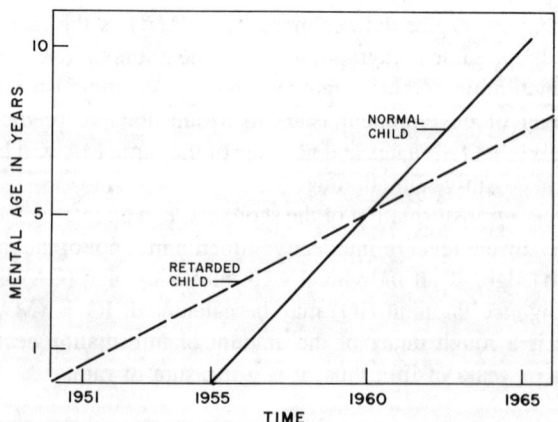

FIG. 12.1. Growth of mental age of two hypothetical chidlren, one of IQ 100 and the other of IQ 50.

appear to involve a minimum of learning and information processing, and even one that is said to be relevant to "problem solving" is, according to the authors (Green & Zigler, 1962), "an extremely simple task with successful performance depending primarily on compliance with E's instructions [p. 502]."

To summarize, I maintain that Zigler's developmental theory should predict differential performance of retardates and normals of equal MA on complex cognitive tasks, because such individuals differ drastically in the rate at which they are developing intellectually. The fact that Zigler and his associates have not found such differences is probably a function of the type of task that they have employed—one that is typically very simple and that would not be expected to be sensitive to those factors that produce differential intellective growth rates.

One final aspect of Zigler's article also deserves comment. The basic difference between his "developmental" theory of retardation and the so-called "defect" theories may be more apparent than real. There may have been theorists who separated individuals into two populations, one "retarded" and the other "normal," and claimed that the normals "had" something that the retardates did not. However, I do not think such a belief is prevalent in modern American psychology. I suggest that the term *deficit* is used in a relative sense by most modern retardation theorists; it is not that these theorists believe that normals "have" something that retardates do not, but instead that retardates may have less of something than normals do.

REFERENCES

Green, C., & Zigler, E. Social deprivation and the performance of retarded and normal children on a satiation type task. *Child Development,* 1962, *33,* 499–508.

Zigler, E. Familial mental retardation: A continuing dilemma. *Science,* 1967, *155,* 292–298.

13 MA, IQ, and the Developmental Difference Controversy*

Edward Zigler
Yale University

Weir makes a number of points in the previous chapter that merit a reply. His first criticism is based more on how I used the particular word "control" than on any substantive disagreement between us concerning the meaning of MA and IQ. As should be clear from the total context of the paragraph cited by Weir, it may well be that in the MA-matched paradigm one takes into consideration the different rates of cognitive development (IQs) of the nonretarded and retarded persons. This procedure controls for known past differences in rate, and thus guarantees that, at the point in time at which the comparison is made, the two types of subjects are at the same cognitive level. The semantic confusion possible when one attempts to distinguish between rate and level of cognitive development is demonstrated in Weir's view that the IQ score, which is a measure of rate, is "a rough index of the amount of information accumulated in a given number of years of life." This is erroneous, because the amount of information at any point is a level phenomenon. How long it took to acquire that amount of information is a rate phenomenon.

In whatever way I used the word "control" and Wier the phrase "amount of information," we are in total agreement that the IQ is in some senses a rate measure, and MA is a level measure. However, I cannot agree that it is my failure to distinguish rate of development from level of development that leads to questionable predictions from my theory. As should become apparent in the remainder of my reply, developmental theorists such as myself may be wrong, but we are certainly not confused. Weir's major point hinges on one's conception

---

*Portions of this article appeared in *Science*, 1967, *157*, 578-579. Copyright 1967 by the American Association for the Advancement of Science. Reprinted by permission.

of the cognitive characteristics of two individuals, who at the same point in time are at the same cognitive level, but who have manifested different rates in achieving that level. The crucial question is: What does this different rate imply? Weir assumes that the rate phenomenon with its IQ measurement reflects speed of learning or information processing. Given this assumption, Weir predicts that at every cognitive level the child with a low IQ will do worse than that with a high IQ on tasks demanding such learning or information processing. But is the IQ indisputably a reflection of these cognitive abilities? Of course not. As I and my colleagues have pointed out (Seitz, Abelson, Levine, & Zigler, 1975; Zigler & Butterfield, 1968), performance on an IQ test reflects a combination of three factors: (1) formal cognitive factors such as information processing ability, memory, reasoning, and abstracting ability that the test was designed to assess; (2) achievement factors involving knowledge about the specific content of the test; and (3) motivational factors, which include a wide range of personality variables. Further, IQ is only a rate measure in the sense that it relates a nonpsychological measure (passage of time) to a psychological one (level of cognition achieved). Approached in this way it is the MA (level) and not the IQ (the relationship of MA to chronological age) that determines the exact nature, including the rate, of learning any task. If one really thinks that the rate of learning or information processing is related to IQ rather than to MA, I suggest that he/she compare the learning processes of a 3-year old with an IQ of 150 and an 8-year old with an IQ of 100.

There is another sense in which the IQ cannot be taken simply as a measure of rate of mental growth. In such a position it is strongly implied that development is continuous rather than occurring in a sequence of stages. Such an implication is, to put the matter somewhat mildly, controversial. Many in the field of child development emphasize successive reconstructions of reality on the part of the child and consequently emphasize discontinuities rather than continuities in development. I, of course, refer here to workers in the Piagetian tradition, with their strong emphases on a stage approach to cognitive development in children, and on qualitative rather than simply quantitative differences in the cognitive structures of younger and older children. It is difficult to reconcile the Piagetian approach to development with Weir's position, that if IQ is a measure of rate of development, then rate differences should be observable at any level of analysis, even on the most simple learning task. Perhaps the best we can do is to acknowledge that, although the continuity–discontinuity issue has not been definitively settled, there is enough emphasis in the area of child development on the importance of qualitatively different stages in the cognitive development of children as to make a direct prediction concerning the predictability of performance on a specific cognitive task from a global IQ measure somewhat tenuous.

Weir makes much of the different slopes of the MA curves presented in his figure and argues that they tell us much about the cognitive functioning of normal and retarded children at particular points in time. Alas, understanding cognitive functioning is not so simple. If one took the trouble to extend Weir's curves for the two individuals through their adulthood, he would discover that eventually the slopes would be the same. The individual with an IQ of 50 would level off at MA 5 at the age of approximately 16-18, and therefore his MA would best be represented by a straight line. This is also true of the other individual, except that his MA curve would level off at MA 16-18. If it is the slope that allows us to make predictions concerning the quality of cognitive functioning, can we then argue that in adulthood the cognitive performances of normal and retarded individuals will be the same?

The major point is that one makes a number of theoretical assumptions when he asserts that, because the IQ is a measure of one kind of rate, then it must also be a measure of another kind of rate, namely, a measure of the rate of learning or information processing on individual tasks. One can, of course, assert that both MA (level) and IQ (an hypothesized determinant of rate of cognitive functioning) influence cognitive tasks. But, this is exactly the argument examined in my article. The person who holds that the IQ, independent of level or MA, determines rate of cognitive functioning on short-term learning tasks is a difference or defect theorist. Which general position is correct is open to investigation, but there is no doubt that the two major approaches examined in my article generate quite different predictions.

I am in sympathy with Weir's argument that the MA obtained on standard intelligence tests is a far from perfect indicator of the nature of cognitive functioning (Zigler, 1966). Indeed, if there were a consensus that the MA was a perfectly adequate measure of the formal features of cognition (for example, rate of information processing), there would be no argument between developmental and defect theorists, because by definition individuals of the same MA level would have identical cognitive structures. However, in his efforts to champion the predictive efficacy on cognitive tasks of the IQ over the MA, Weir appears to go too far. To argue that the MA is not an important determinant of the quality (including rate) of the child's learning of new and unfamiliar cognitive tasks is an error. Evidence on this point is clear, and I doubt whether anyone working in the area of cognition would take exception to it. In spite of its shortcomings, the single MA measure and its factorial components have more cognitive correlates, including performance on purer Piaget-like cognitive tasks, than any other measure in psychology.

With respect to Weir's task argument, he and I probably could agree that an investigator should use a task sensitive to the particular factor that the investigator would like to demonstrate as being operative. Thus, one interested in demonstrating the effect of motivational factors employs experimental tasks sensitive to these factors. There is no argument, therefore, that if one wishes to test the hypothesis that IQ is a measure of rate of information processing, he should use a task that makes this type of cognitive demand on his subjects. My criticism of the various difference or defect positions was not based solely on findings obtained with motivational tasks but rested also on the fact that the findings obtained by the supporters of these positions on tasks of their own choosing frequently have been equivocal. Furthermore, to imply that the holders of the developmental position have been reluctant to adequately test their views by using cognitively demanding tasks is to do them an injustice. They have frequently employed the same tasks used by the expounders of the various difference positions. These tasks include not only the concept-switching tasks referred to by Weir (Zigler & DeLabry, 1962) but a variety of discrimination learning, reversal learning, transposition (Balla & Zigler, 1964), learning of set (Harter, 1965, 1967), and opposition learning tasks (Balla, Styfco, & Zigler, 1971). Indeed, workers sympathetic to the developmental position have employed the probability-learning task used by Weir in his laboratory (Gruen & Zigler, 1968; Gruen, Ottinger, & Zigler, 1970; Ollendick, Balla, & Zigler, 1971). Although Weir does not state the criteria by which we might know if a task were truly cognitive in nature, I find it difficult to believe that none of these tasks involves information processing, and that they are therefore inadequate tests of the hypothesis of "equal MA–equal cognitive" functioning.

Weir attempts to close the gap between the developmental theory of familial mental retardation and the various "defect" positions by noting that certain "defect" theorists argue that retarded persons have less of something that nonretarded persons of the same MA have, rather than having something that nonretarded persons do not have. This is true; however, other defect theorists have argued that the retarded are qualitatively different from nonretarded persons. It is for this reason that throughout my chapter I referred to the general approach as a defect of difference orientation. It is the difference betwen familial retarded persons and normals of the same MA that is the point of contention between the developmental theorist and the difference theorist, whatever the hypothesized deficit underlying this difference may be. The gap between the developmental theorist and all the defect or difference theorists remains a wide one, because the developmental position generates the hypothesis that there are no differences in formal cognitive functioning between familial retarded persons and intellectually average individuals, matched on general level of cognition (typically measured by MA). What should be emphasized is that the developmental position at this point in time represents a tenable hypothesis. As long as the hypothesis clearly generates behavioral predictions, I certainly entertain the possibility that it is wrong. Clearly, as my chapter pointed out, most theoretical workers in the area are entertaining this possibility. The argument presented in Weir's chapter indicates that he shares their views. Fortunately, resolution of this can be achieved through thoughtful experimentation.

REFERENCES

Balla, D., Styfco, S. J., & Zigler, E. Use of the opposition concept and outerdirectedness in intellectually average, familial retarded, and organically retarded children. *American Journal of Mental Deficiency*, 1971, 75, 663-680.

Balla, D., & Zigler, E. Discrimination and switching learning in normal, familial retarded, and organic retarded children. *Journal of Abnormal Social Psychology,* 1964, *69,* 664–669.

Harter, S. Discrimination learning set in children as a function of IQ and MA. *Journal of Experimental Child Psychology,* 1965, *2,* 31–43.

Harter, S. Mental age, IQ, & motivational factors in the discrimination learning set performance of normal and retarded children. *Journal of Experimental Child Psychology,* 1967, *5,* 123–141.

Gruen, G., Ottinger, D., & Zigler, E. Level of aspiration and the probability learning of middle- and lower-class children. *Developmental Psychology,* 1970, *3,* 133–142.

Gruen, G., & Zigler, E. Expectancy of success and the probability learning of middle-class, lower-class, and retarded children. *Journal of Abnormal Psychology,* 1968, *73,* 343–352.

Ollendick, T., Balla, D., & Zigler, E. Expectancy of success and the probability learning of retarded children. *Journal of Abnormal Psychology,* 1971, *77,* 275–281.

Seitz, V., Abelson, W. D., Levine, E., & Zigler, E. Effects of place of testing on the Peabody Picture Vocabulary Test scores of disadvantaged Head Start and non-Head Start children. *Child Development,* 1975, *46,* 481–486.

Zigler, E. Bruner and the Center for Cognitive Studies: Discussion. In M. Garrison (Ed.), *Cognitive models and development in mental retardation. American Journal of Mental Deficiency,* 1966, *70,* 118–126 (Monograph Supplement).

Zigler, E., & Butterfield, E. C. Motivational aspects of changes in IQ test performance of culturally deprived nursery school children. *Child Development,* 1968, *39,* 1–14.

Zigler, E., & deLabry, J. Concept-switching in middle-class, lower-class, and retarded children. *Journal of Abnormal and Social Psychology,* 1962, *65,* 267–273.

14 Piagetian Evidence and the Developmental-Difference Controversy*

John R. Weisz
University of North Carolina

Keith O. Yeates
University of North Carolina

Edward Zigler
Yale University

For many years the study of mental retardation was a largely atheoretical enterprise heavily emphasizing a single issue: whether the grossly observable condition of low intelligence was a product of genetic inheritance or of environment. The "either-or" form that much of the nature-nurture debate took suffered from a sterility later bemoaned by a number of writers (Anastasi, 1958; Overton, 1973). A significant exception to this state of affairs in the pre-World War II period was the sweeping theoretical contribution of Kurt Lewin (1936) and Jacob Kounin (1939, 1941a, b, 1948). The Lewin-Kounin formulation used exotic constructs (e.g., "psychical systems" "cognitive regions," and it generated flamboyant, sometimes hard-to-assimilate hypotheses, as stated by Lewin (1936): "the major dynamic difference between a feeble-minded and a normal child of the same degree of differentiation [consists of] a smaller capacity for dynamic rearrangement in the psychical systems of the former [p. 210]." Yet, thanks largely to Kounin, the terms and postulates of the theory were carefully operationalized and thus testable. When tests began to cast doubt on the validity of the Lewin-Kounin position, its prominence in the field gradually declined.

---

*Portions of this article appeared in J. Weisz and E. Zigler, "Cognitive Development in Retarded and Nonretarded Persons: Piagetian Tests of the Similar Sequence Hypothesis." *Psychological Bulletin*, 1979, 86(4), 831-851.

Now, years later, the position, and the controversy and research it evoked (reviewed by Zigler & Balla, chapter 5), occasionally evoke smug sniggers from critics who have the advantages of hindsight—as indeed many of our own efforts may in years to come. Yet, the fact remains that the study of mental retardation was significantly enriched, heuristically and empirically, by its association with this major psychological theory.

Now another major theory promises to significantly influence the way we construe and investigate mental retardation. Piaget's cognitive developmental theory, or at least major parts of it, could be found in print even prior to the debates stimulated by Lewin and Kounin. Yet, few Americans showed an interest in this work until the "Piaget boom" in the 1960s and 70s. And only in the late 70s did we begin to realize that this now massive body of theory and research may have a good deal to say about the nature of mental retardation. In this chapter we survey relevant Piagetian work and discuss its implications for some of the issues that have stimulated this book.

THE DEVELOPMENTAL-DIFFERENCE CONTROVERSY: TWO ATTENDANT HYPOTHESES

To understand the relevance of Piagetian literature, we must first distinguish between two separable issues that are often linked together in the ongoing debate between "developmental" and "difference" theorists in the area of mental retardation. Zigler's (1969) *developmental position* holds that cultural-familial (now formally called "sociocultural") retarded children pass through cognitive developmental stages in the same order as nonretarded children, but that the two groups differ in two respects: Retarded children traverse the stages more slowly and attain a lower developmental ceiling than do nonretarded children. (Zigler, 1969, does not explicitly define these "stages," but he construes them in largely Piagetian terms.) Zigler also maintains that familial retarded and nonretarded children who are equated for level of cognitive development (typically operationally defined as MA) will not differ in the formal cognitive processes they employ in reasoning and solving problems.

A number of other theorists appear to differ with Zigler. Although their theories differ from one another in many respects, certain similarities have led Zigler to endow them with a common label: *difference theories*. In general, those theories maintain that mentally retarded children will differ from nonretarded children of similar MA in formal processes of reasoning or problem solving. Some of the theories also hold that the developmental stages of retarded children will differ from the stages of nonretarded children. So, there are two separable tenets of the developmental position, either or both of which a difference theorist may choose to contest. The two tenets can be stated in the form of testable hypotheses, both related in significant ways to Piagetian literature.

The Similar-Sequence Hypothesis and Piagetian Literature

Firstly, let us consider the *similar-sequence hypothesis*. It is the tenet that holds that *retarded and nonretarded persons traverse the same stages of cognitive development, differing only in the rate at which they progress and the ultimate ceiling they attain*. The developmental position actually generates this hypothesis only with respect to nonretarded and familial retarded persons (thus excluding children with identifiable organic impairment).

In Piagetian theory, however, there seems to be an even broader version of the similar-sequence hypothesis. Some Piagetians seem to regard the sequence of cognitive stages described by Piaget and expanded upon by other cognitive-developmental theorists as one of psychology's few viable candidates for universality (Weisz, 1978). A "psychological universalist" position has been taken, with qualifications, by Piaget (1956, 1966). He has argued (1956), for instance, that: "the *minimum* program for establishment of stages is the recognition of a distinct chronology, in the sense of a *constant order of succession* [p. 13]." Kohlberg (1969, 1971) has argued strongly for the invariance of what he regards as a set of cognitive–developmental stages rooted in certain invariant characteristics of the environment and of the nervous system. Kohlberg also believes that the concepts examined within the Piagetian tradition generally partake of certain "inherent orderings," which are logically essential and independent of individual differences among people—when one must understand certain aspects of a concept before it is possible to understand other aspects, the order in which those aspects are understood *must* be invariant. According to Kohlberg (1969), "The invariance of sequence in the development of a concept or category is not dependent upon a prepatterned unfolding of neural patterns; it must depend upon a logical analysis of the concept itself [p. 355]." Given this rationale, it seems that the similar sequence hypothesis as advanced by Piagetian theorists must predict a truly universal ordering of developmental stages for all persons, regardless of cultural, intellectual, or neurological characteristics.

Of course, we can never *know* whether any given developmental phenomenon is truly universal, because we can never test all possible exceptions (Popper, 1959); however, if we are not to let the claims of cognitive developmental theorists go unchallenged, it is important to gauge the extent to which "transcontextual validity" (Weisz, 1978) has been demonstrated for the Piagetian account of development. One approach to assessing such validity-across-experimental-contexts is to examine developmental sequences across various cultures (Buck–Morss, 1975; Simpson, 1974). Another approach, of most importance to the present chapter, is to compare groups of children who differ markedly in their measured intelligence (i.e., mentally retarded and nonretarded children). If children at very different IQ levels were to show identical Piagetian developmental sequences, then the transcontextual validity of the Piagetian account of development would be substantially supported. If retarded and nonretarded children were to differ in their sequence of developmental stages, then universality could hardly be claimed for the Piagetian account, and its strong form of the similar-sequence hypothesis would not be supported. If in such tests differences were found between nonretarded and retarded children who had been carefully screened for organicity, then the more conservative form of the similar-sequence hypothesis advanced by Zigler (1969) would not be supported. Such findings, showing retarded-nonretarded differences, would support those difference theorists who hold something that might by called the *dissimilar sequence hypothesis*.

One difference theorist who has specifically addressed Piagetian research is Milgram (1973). He has reviewed a number of relevant studies in the Piagetian domain and given particular attention to a book by Piaget's colleague, Barbel Inhelder, in which she reports on her own use of Piagetian tasks with retarded persons (we discuss the Inhelder book later). "A critical reading of her study," Milgram (1973) reports, "is no source of comfort to Zigler's developmental theory [p. 206]." Following Inhelder, Milgram (1973) maintains that the stages or levels of the retarded person's cognitive development are different from those of the nonretarded person: "When a retardate moves from one cognitive level to the next, traces of the previous level persist much longer, and the retardate is more likely to regress to earlier long-practiced modes of thought [p. 206]." This position appears to differ from the similar-sequence hypothesis in two respects: (1) It implies that certain formal characteristics of the retarded individual's reasoning at a given stage of cognitive development will differ from characteristics of the nonretarded individual's reasoning at a similar stage—and thus that the cognitive stages of the two groups may be qualitatively different; (2) It implies that, in contrast to the progressive, monotonic developmental sequence that Piaget depicts for nonretarded persons, the retarded may under some circumstances move (i.e., "regress") from more mature to less-mature levels of reasoning.

The Similar-Structure Hypothesis and Piagetian Literature

The second testable proposition growing out of the developmental-difference controversy is the *similar-structure hypothesis*.[1] This is the view that *as long as familial retarded persons are matched for general level of intellectual development with nonretarded persons, the two groups should be similar with respect to the formal cognitive processes they employ in reasoning and problem solving*. The label, similar-structure hypothesis, seems appropriate because this hypothesis is based on the view that such carefully matched retarded and non-

---

[1]The review of evidence on the *similar-sequence hypothesis*, which makes up roughly the first half of this chapter, is drawn largely from Weisz and Zigler (1979). This material was published in *Psychological Bulletin*, 1979, 86, 831–851.

retarded children will be similar with respect to the kinds of cognitive structures described by Piaget (see Zigler, 1969, esp. pp. 537–541). It follows that one of the best ways to get at these structures is to employ the kinds of measures Piagetians use to assess children's concepts of their world. These concepts, according to the similar-structure hypothesis, should be the same in two children who are matched for general level of development, even if one of the children is familial retarded and the other is nonretarded. In sharp contrast, Milgram (1973) argued that retarded children are inferior to their nonretarded MA peers in the conceptual processes required to perform Piagetian tasks. He maintained that generally: "given tasks without a ceiling or floor effect for the general MA of the subjects being used, the retarded will dependably demonstrate an equal-MA deficit [p. 209]." In arguing that retarded subjects will be inferior, Milgram took what might be called the *conventional* difference position.

A more unconventional difference position has been taken by Kohlberg (1968). He believes that the kind of conceptual development described by Piaget requires massive doses of "general experience"; consequently, Kohlberg has argued that retarded children should be *more* advanced with respect to Piagetian concepts than their nonretarded MA peers, because the retarded children have lived longer and thus taken on a richer base of experience.

Evidence from the Piagetian tradition seems nicely suited to a test of the similar-structure hypothesis, for two reasons. Firstly, the hypothesis itself grew, in part, out of a focus on precisely the kinds of underlying processes Piagetian measures of conceptual development are designed to tap. Secondly, it is specifically within the realm of Piagetian research that an unusual triangular theoretical conflict has taken shape. In a carefully designed and well-controlled experiment, one in which retarded and nonretarded children are matched for MA, then administered a Piagetian test of some aspect of conceptual development, extant theoretical perspectives generate three conflicting predictions: The developmental position (Zigler, 1969) predicts no difference between the groups, the conventional difference position (Milgram, 1973) predicts inferiority in the retarded group, and the unconventional difference position (Kohlberg, 1968) predicts superiority for the retarded group. This three-way conflict provides an opportunity for an unusual form of strong inference.

In what follows, we survey evidence bearing on both the similar-sequence and similar-structure hypotheses. In our review we have excluded studies of reading and of language development. Both areas can be viewed from a Piagetian perspective, but neither is an integral component of Piaget's theory. We also omitted studies in which children were *trained* to perform on Piagetian conceptual tasks, because this chapter was not intended to deal with the question of amenability to training. In other respects, however, we have tried to sample as comprehensively as possible those studies that promise to shed some light on either of the central hypotheses.

EVIDENCE ON THE SIMILAR-SEQUENCE HYPOTHESIS

Evidence from Cross-Sectional and Order-of-Difficulty Studies

One means of testing the similar-sequence hypothesis is cross-sectional. Groups of mentally retarded children at more than one developmental level are tested with multiple Piagetian tasks. If the *direction* of the difference in performance between one developmental level and the next is the same for the mentally retarded population as for nonretarded persons, then the similar sequence hypothesis is supported. A second general approach to testing the similar-sequence hypothesis is to rely less upon the developmental levels of the groups sampled than upon the relative difficulty levels of the various tasks or behavioral items being employed.

The simplest but also the least informative variant of this approach is to rank-order the items with respect to the number of subjects passing each. This procedure operates under the assumption that the item passed by the largest number of subjects represents the simplest, and developmentally earliest process, and that the item passed by the fewest subjects represents the process that develops latest. If the rank-ordering of difficulty levels among a nonretarded population matches the rank-ordering among the nonretarded, then the similar-sequence hypothesis is supported, albeit modestly. A more informative type of order-of-difficulty evidence is the type associated with scaling procedures. With this evidence, developmental sequence is inferred from the pattern of passes and failures across multiple items, calculated for each individual subject. For example, suppose that three test items, 1, 2, and 3, are said to represent a developmental sequence involving stage 1, stage 2, and then stage 3. If this hypothesis is valid, we would expect to see a high proportion of children who show one of the following pass–fail patterns: (1) fail all three items; (2) pass #1, fail #2 and #3; (3) pass #1 and #2, fail #3; (4) pass all three items. If the hypothesized stage sequence does occur, then pass–fail patterns other than (1) through (4) should be very rare and should only occur as measurement error. When both retarded and nonretarded groups show pass–fail patterns consistent with the same hypothesized sequence of stages, then relatively strong support has been generated for the similar-sequence hypothesis. The studies reviewed in this section have all employed some type of cross-sectional evidence, order-of-difficulty evidence, or combination of the two.

Research on Development in the Sensorimotor Period. Interesting evidence bearing on the similar-sequence hypothesis in the sensorimotor stage of development was provided by Mary Woodward (1959, 1961, 1962, 1963). The first of these studies (Woodward, 1959) was focused primarily on a group of 65 institutionalized children and adolescents (CA range: 7–16 years) who were so severely retarded that they failed to attain a basal age of 2 years on the Terman–Merrill scale. Although Woodward maintained that this sample excluded cases involving "motor or sensory disability," the cases involved diverse medical problems (e.g., 19 were epileptic), and 38 of the children were "emotionally unstable." Woodward used three means of assessing the sensorimotor stages of this heterogeneous group. Firstly, she observed their spontaneous mannerisms and manipulation of toys presented individually in a standardized order. Secondly, each subject was presented with six "problems" to solve; in one, for example, an object was shown to the subject, then withdrawn and attached to a piece of string, with the other end of the string near the subject's hand. The six problems included three pairs of tasks, with each pair designed to tap one of Piaget's last three sensorimotor stages (there are six stages in all). Thirdly, Woodward presented each child with a series of object concept tasks, in which a piece of candy or a toy were first used to attract the subject's attention, then withdrawn and concealed to varying degrees. The object concept task data were not analyzed in a way that would shed light directly upon the similar-sequence hypothesis, but data from the other tasks were. Each task was classified with respect to the Piagetian sensorimotor stage that it was designed to represent; then the tasks were rank-ordered with respect to the percentage of subjects passing each. The difficulty-level rankings of these 11 items were identical to the stage-level order reported by Piaget with one exception. A task involving coordination of vision and hearing (sensorimotor stage II) proved to be slightly more difficult than a task involving manipulation of objects (sensorimotor stage III), with 53 subjects passing manipulation and only 49 passing coordination. Furthermore, when the possibly insensitive coordination task was removed from the analyses, 59 of the 65 children passed all the items at stages below their highest stage-level response. Given the extreme diversity of the sample, the high incidence of emotional instability, and the apparent tendency of many not to show responses of which they were actually capable (e.g., some delayed for a half-hour before grasping an object placed before them), these data are surprisingly strong in their support of the similar-sequence hypothesis. Woodward's (1959) own conclusion seems to agree with this assessment:

> It has been found in this inquiry that sensori-motor responses ranked in the order in which mental defectives show them, in decreasing order of frequency, agree closely with those observed by Piaget to appear in normal infants at successive ages. Furthermore, most of the idiots showing the responses of Piaget's later stages also exhibited those of earlier stages. This suggests that the sensori-motor development of severe mental defectives follows the sequence described by Piaget [p. 70].

Recently, Rogers (1977) conducted a study similar to that of Woodward in several respects. Forty profoundly retarded children ranging in age from 8–14 years and all having IQs below 20 were given a series of Piagetian tasks. Each child's performance on the tasks was classified into sensorimotor stage III, IV, V, or VI, in each of four conceptual domains: Object Permanence (tasks involving searching for a hidden object), Causality (tasks involving the use of physical prompts, removal of obstacles, use of tools, and inference as to the cause of a jingling sound inside a box), Imitation (tasks involving the reproduction of both self-initiated and experimenter-initiated movements and sounds), and Spatiality (tasks involving movement in space). Performance within each of the four domains was analyzed via scaling procedures, with Guttman's (1950) coefficient of reproducibility and Green's (1956) index of scalability calculated for each scale. The object permanence and imitation tasks formed highly reproducible scales in the orders described by Piaget. Causality tasks also formed a highly reproducible scale, although the item order differed from the predicted sequence in one respect: one stage-VI item preceded one stage-V item. The author (Rogers, 1977) attributes this irregularity to a poor choice of stage-VI task (i.e., opening a box to obtain a bell, when box opening has just been demonstrated for the subject), because: "the task used might have been accomplished using imitation rather than problem-solving skills [pp. 841–842]." Finally, the individual spatiality tasks did not all form highly reproducible scales, but when the tasks within each stage were combined (and subjects credited with a stage level for passing one or more of the tasks from that level), the stages formed a highly reproducible scale. On these four scales just described, the index of scalability statistics (Green, 1956) ranged from .57 to .79, and the coefficients of reproducibility (Guttman, 1950) ranged from .94 to .98. Rogers concluded that her findings support "the invariant sequentiality of sensori-motor stages."

The Preoperational Concrete–Operational Transition—the Inhelder Studies of Conservation. One of the earliest studies bearing on the similar-sequence hypothesis was, appropriately enough, carried out by Piaget's associate, Barbel Inhelder, in the early 1940s. This study, now published in English (Inhelder, 1968), involved the assessment of conservation of substance, weight, and volume among persons who had been labeled mentally retarded by the Department of Public Instruction of the canton of St. Gallen in Switzerland. The sample was extremely heterogeneous (Jordan, 1976). Ages ranged from 7½ to 52 years, IQs ranged from 35 to 104, institutionalized and noninstitutional persons were included, and the range of etiologies and physical maladies included "defective environment," rickets, lordosis, epilepsy, visual defect, alcoholism, microcephaly, Little's disease, hearing defect, "abandoned," tuberculosis, psychopathy, and schizophrenia. Inhelder's procedure involved semistructured, "clinical method" interviews conducted individually with each subject. The procedure was not perfectly standardized, and little in the way of formal data analysis is presented; so the author's conclusions are difficult to evaluate. Inhelder concluded, in part, that the cognitive stages observed in the development of nonretarded children are traversed in the same order by retarded persons, but that retarded persons pass through the stages more slowly and stop their development at an earlier stage. In Piaget's (1968) description of the Inhelder study, he explained that in the entire sample: "not one (individual) understood the conservation of weight without having the conservation of substance, nor the conservation of volume without both weight and substance, while the conservation of substance *was* found without the other two, and the conservation of weight was found without the conservation of volume [p. 11]." This evidence seems to support the similar-sequence hypothesis. However, Inhelder went on to advance clinical judgments about various characteristics of the reasoning of her "retarded" subjects. She used such terms as *false equilibrium, oscillation,* and *viscosity* to describe the way that some of her subjects reasoned. She suggested that such characteristics are partly reflections of social-environmental and motivational factors. She (Inhelder, 1968) argued, for example, that: "the retardate who has reached the elementary forms of operatory organization is capable of remaining at this level for years. It is as though he lacked the interest, the curiosity, and the general activity which, in the normal child lead the subject to ask new questions and to find the solutions, both of which lead him to superior levels. There is therefore in the retardate a sort of 'false equilibrium' [p. 291]." Elsewhere in her report, Inhelder maintained that: "The disequilibrium of thought in suggestible retardates is conditioned by difficulties in interpersonal relations [p. 266]." Because of their intense "need for approval," and the experimenter's consistent failure to agree or disagree with the answers given, she reported, a number of subjects vacillated so markedly that they could not decide on any solution to some of the problems presented. In several other ways, the behavior of these "retarded" subjects during the interviews differed from that seen among nonretarded children; yet, despite these differences, Inhelder (1968) seemed convinced that retarded persons pass through the same sequence of developmental stages as nonretarded children. As she put it:

> It goes without saying that the manner of approaching the problems, the interest, the use of information, and the satisfaction drawn from the experimental confrontation are very different from the intellectual dynamics met in younger, normal children. Nonetheless, it is striking to see how closely the structures of reasoning and the modes of justification correspond to those present in young children when they start the transition from preoperational thought to the most elementary manifestations of operativity. These indications support the hypothesis that operational construction, while certainly not independent of the behavior on which it is built, is elaborated, nevertheless, according to its own laws [p. 324].

Other Studies of Conservation and Related Concepts Using Retarded Samples Only. Since the Inhelder report there have been several other studies of conservation and related concepts that have a bearing on the similar-sequence hypothesis, despite the fact that only retarded subjects were sampled. Klauss and Green (1972) assessed conservation of number and of volume among 27 "trainable" mentally retarded subjects ranging in age from 13 to 19 years, and in IQ from 29 to 57. These investigators found that volume conservation presented greater difficulty than did number conservation. This finding is consistent with the view that number conservation precedes volume conservation in the trainable retarded as it evidently does among the nonretarded. Marchi (1971) tested conservation of mass, weight, and volume among 106 educable mentally retarded children. Difficulty-level evidence suggested that, contrary to Marchi's (1971) prediction, the retarded: "follow a similar sequence in the acquisition of mass, weight, and volume as postulated for normals [p. 6442-A]." Roodin, Sullivan, and Rybash (1976) assessed qualitative identity, quantitative identity, and equivalence conservation among 60 institutionalized retarded children averaging 13 years of age and about 47 in IQ. Dyed water was poured from a standard 100 ml beaker; to test qualitative identity, subjects were asked, "Is the water in this glass (comparison) the same water that was in that glass (empty standard)?" To assess quantitative identity, subjects were asked, "Is there as much water in this glass (comparison) as there was in that glass (empty standard)?" To assess equivalence conservation, two standard beakers were filled with equal levels of water, and the contents of one was then poured into a comparison beaker; the experimenter then asked, "Is there as much water in this glass (standard) as there is in this glass (comparison)?" Previous research (Papalia & Hooper, 1971) among nonretarded children had suggested that these three concepts are attained in the following order: qualitative identity, quantitative identity, then equivalence conservation. In the Roodin et al. study, analyses of the number of conservers on each task revealed a parallel order of difficulty. In a similar study also employing 60 institutionalized retarded children (age range approximately 10-16 years, average IQ approximately 57), McManis (1969d) investigated identity and equivalence conservation with three types of material (styrofoam balls, clay, and water). Like Roodin et al. (1976), McManis found that the developmental sequence among his retarded subjects replicated that of nonretarded children. The notion that identity conservation must precede equivalence conservation was supported by the finding that no subject who failed to achieve identity conservation showed equivalence conservation, whereas 13-18% of the subjects (precise percentage depending on particular task used) displayed identity conservation without equivalence conservation.

At least three studies have examined conservation of number, and number concepts generally, among mentally retarded groups. The findings are quite similar, despite differences among the studies in methodology employed. Woodward (1961) investigated numerical concepts among 94 institutionalized individuals (50 adults, averaging 19 years of age; 44 children and adolescents, averaging 12 years of age) ranging in IQ from 25 to 73. Tests given to the subjects included assessments of their understanding of: (1) one-to-one correspondence and equivalence of corresponding sets; (2) ways of equalizing unequal groups; (3) seriation; and (4) conservation of continuous quantity (water and sand). Children's performance on these measures was scored as indicative of one of two preoperational stages or of concrete operational thinking. Stage-level assignments were plotted as a function of the IQs (and thus roughly the MAs) of the adult subjects sampled. The resulting table reflected what one would expect if Piaget's stage scheme applied to retarded individuals as well as to the nonretarded. In a related study, Mannix (1960) administered eight of Piaget's number-concept tasks to 48 "educationally subnormal" individuals ranging in mental age from 5 to 9 years. The tasks included two tests of additive composition, one test of coordination of equivalence relations, two tests of judgment of correspondence between sets of items, and two conservation tasks (continuous and discontinuous quantities). Responses to these tests were classified into Piagetian stage levels, a scalogram was constructed, and its coefficient of reproducibility was .94. The brief published report of this masters thesis (Mannix, 1960) actually gives little information as to the precise nature of the scale types; but apparently the scalogram was consistent with Piaget's stage theory, because the author concludes that: "test behavior suggests that they ("educationally subnormal" children) pass through the three stages of development described by Piaget [p. 181]." One writer (Lunzer, 1961) who evidently had access to the complete thesis by Mannix reported the following, indicating that Piaget's stages as applied to nonretarded children were also applicable to the performance of Mannix's subjects:

> An important feature of Mannix's work was the use of scalogramme analysis.... The evidence suggests that the understanding of number is indeed a single progression. The first step in that progression is the mastery of 'provoked correspondence' (e.g., the numerical equivalence of eggs and egg-cups). The conservation of continuous quantities (e.g., the equivalence of equal quantities of liquids transferred to containers of different shapes) is appreciably more difficult. The additive composition of groups (e.g., the equivalence of a set of 7 + 1 with a set of 4 + 4) proved to be the hardest item in Mannix's series [p. 15].

The third in this series of number-concept studies was conducted with institutionalized mentally retarded persons in New Zealand. The 20 individuals tested ranged in age from 8 to 17 years and in IQ from 29 to 65. Singh and Stott (1975) presented these subjects with a series of number conservation tasks designed to classify them with respect to three Piagetian number stages: Stage 1—child fails to attend to relevant cues and fails to conserve; Stage 2—child selectively attends to only certain relevant cues, can match perceptually, but cannot conserve; Stage 3—child conserves, showing understanding of invariance of properties despite transformation in appearance. From their report it is difficult to determine what analyses these two investigators used other than item and response-difficulty level rankings and calculations of the MAs at which the stages tended to be reached, but their conclusion is quite clearly stated (Singh &

Stott, 1975): "Retarded children apparently develop sequentially in the same order as normals but at a slower rate and at a later CA [p. 220]."

One other study that used only a retarded sample deserves attention, both because of its scope and because it raises an important issue. In this study, Lister (1972) assessed six types of conservation among 115 "educationally subnormal" pupils in Great Britain. The subjects were 8- to 16-years old, and their IQs ranged from 47 to 81. Both difficulty-level rankings and a scaling procedure strongly suggested the following developmental sequence in the emergence of various types of conservation: number, substance, length, weight, volume, and area. No scalogram statistics were calculated, but only 6 of the 115 subjects showed a scalogram response pattern inconsistent with the preceding order. Lister notes that the order with respect to substance, weight, and volume is consistent with previous Piagetian research, whereas the suggested order of the remaining attributes differs from at least some previous findings with nonretarded subjects. Her own interpretation of the discrepancies is that they result from variations across experiments in the specifics of the problems used to assess the various types of conservation. This is a very real possibility, and it is one reason why tests of the similar-sequence hypothesis that expose retarded and nonretarded subjects to the *same* experimental procedures must be regarded as stronger evidence than experiments that sample only retarded children and then compare their findings with those of different experiments. We now turn to six studies of the first type.

Studies of Conservation and Related Concepts Employing Both Retarded and Nonretarded Subjects. Four experiments in which the performance of retarded and nonretarded subjects was directly compared were conducted by McManis (1969b, c, e). In McManis (1969e), 90 institutionalized retarded subjects (IQ range: 47–73) and 90 nonretarded elementary school children (IQ range: 85–115) were tested for conservation of mass, weight, and volume of clay, using Piaget's "sausage" technique. About half the retarded sample were organically impaired. In the experiment, prior to the usual question about constancy of quantity in the face of transformations, the subjects were asked to make a prediction regarding conservation. One such question was, "Suppose I roll one of the balls out into a hotdog; will there be as much clay in the hotdog as in the ball; will they both have the same amount of clay?". Analyses of mean scores indicated that conservation of mass was easiest and conservation of volume most difficult for both the retarded and nonretarded groups. This supported the notion that the order of emergence of these types of conservation is mass, weight, and volume, in groups of both average and below-average IQ. Elsewhere, McManis (1969c) reported an assessment of conservation and transitivity of weight (clay) and length (sticks) among what appears (given the sample data reported) to be the same sample used in McManis (1969e). The study was designed to test an hypothesis derived from Kooistra (1963); it was that for any given property (e.g., weight) conservation will appear developmentally earlier than transitivity. The results supported this hypothesis for both weight and length among both retarded and nonretarded subjects. For weight and length separately and for the two properties combined, among retarded and nonretarded subjects showing discrepant performance on conservation and transitivity, significantly greater than chance proportions showed conservation without transitivity, whereas few subjects at either IQ level showed evidence of transitivity without conservation. In a third investigation, McManis (1970) explored relations among conservation, seriation, and transitivity (of length) within groups of 80 institutionalized mentally retarded persons (IQ range: 46–72) and 80 nonretarded elementary school children (IQ range: 85–116). Among both retarded and nonretarded children who showed discrepant performance on the conservation and seriation tasks, nearly all showed conservation without seriation. Among both retarded and nonretarded children who showed discrepant performance on the seriation and transitivity tasks, nearly all showed seriation without transitivity. These findings indicated that seriation falls developmentally between conservation and transitivity (at least with respect to the property of length as measured in this experiment) for both retarded and nonretarded persons. In a fourth article based on the same sample used in two of the preceding studies (McManis, 1969c, e), McManis (1969a) tested Piaget's view that there are three hierarchically ordered stages in the development of quantitative comparison processes. In the first stage, children are said to focus on only uncoordinated perceptual relations of gross qualitative equality or difference; in the second stage, intensive quantity, children are said to compare quantities by seriating them along more than one dimension (e.g., width and height) simultaneously; in the third stage, extensive quantities, children are said to be capable not only of comparing things along more than one dimension simultaneously but also to be capable of overruling apparent differences between two equal quantities by imposing equal units of measurement upon them. McManis tested his young subjects' performance at these three types of comparison, using sticks, colored water, and beads. The analysis of scores on these tasks indicated that for both the retarded and the nonretarded group gross comparisons were the simplest (they were passed by nearly all subjects in both groups), and extensive comparisons were the most difficult. This finding, McManis notes, supports the view that, for both retarded and nonretarded children, the developmental order is: gross, intensive, then extensive quantity, the order posited by Piaget. One other study by McManis should be mentioned in this connection. In this study (McManis, 1969b) McManis' (1969a) tests of gross, intensive, and extensive quantity comparison were given to groups of institutionalized mentally retarded persons at two different IQ levels (IQ range: 30–49, $N = 70$; IQ range: 50–69, $N = 70$). The procedure and analyses were similar to those employed in the preceding study (McManis, 1969a). As in that experiment, comparison of gross quantities was easiest, and comparison of extensive quantities was most difficult, regardless of the IQ level of the subjects.

To our knowledge, there have been three other comparative studies of conservation attainment designed to address the problem of order of events across types of conservation. In one, Gruen and Vore (1972) assessed conservation of number (poker chips), continuous quantity (water), and weight (clay rolled into various shapes) among familially retarded (IQs: 55-80) and nonretarded (IQs: 90-120) public school pupils. Both retarded and nonretarded groups were divided into three subgroups: MA 5 yr., MA 7 yr., and MA 9 yr. Evidence on the order of developmental events came in the form of mean scores for the three types of conservation, analyzed within each MA level. In one set of analyses, conservation judgments alone (i.e., disregarding the subjects' verbal explanations) constituted the dependent variable. With this dependent variable, performance of nearly all subjects at MA 9 was correct; however, for the other two MA levels, both retarded and nonretarded subjects tended to score significantly better on the number task than on the quantity or weight tasks. For nonretarded children at MA 7, however, the differences were not significant. For both retarded and nonretarded children the quantity and weight tasks did not differ significantly in difficulty. In a second set of analyses by Gruen and Vore, the dependent measure was conservation judgment in combination with the subject's explanation for that judgment. Using this judgment-plus-explanation criterion, there was no significant task effect at the MA-5 level. At the MA-7 level, both retarded and nonretarded subjects did somewhat better at the number task than at the quantity and weight tasks, but the differences were only significant for the retarded subjects. At the MA-9 level, both retarded and nonretarded subjects scored significantly higher on the number than the weight task, and significantly higher on the quantity task than on the weight task. Thus, whereas order of difficulty patterns were similar for retarded and nonretarded subjects, using judgments alone and judgments plus explanations, task differences tended to be statistically significant among the retarded more often than among the nonretarded. In attempting to account for this trend, Gruen and Vore (1972) made a useful point:

> McManis [1969] has suggested that there is a transitional period (MAs of 7-10) in which the various concrete operations are obtained and that retarded children pass through this period more slowly than do normal children. If this is true, it would be expected that the performance of normal children on various conservation tasks would vary less from task to task than that of retarded children. This also suggests that retarded children may be ideal subjects for investigating the transition process from preoperational to concrete-operational thinking.

We conclude this section of the review by discussing two conservation studies by Achenbach (1969, 1973). Because the earlier study raises an issue that bears discussion at the end of this section, we consider the more recent investigation first. In it, Achenbach (1973), building upon the work of Charlesworth (1969) and Mermelstein and Shulman (1967), inferred children's identity concepts with respect to color, number, length, and continuous quantity, from their surprise reactions to contrived changes in those properties. Among nonretarded subjects (mean IQ: 116) there were significantly more frequent reactions of surprise to a change in color than to changes in the three quantitative properties, a finding consistent with Piaget's view that children develop identity concepts for qualitative properties such as color prior to the emergence of such concepts with respect to quantitative properties, such as number, length, and continuous quantity. Among the 45 familial and 16 Down Syndrome retarded subjects (mean IQ: 47) surprise reactions to changes in color also outnumbered such reactions to changes in quantity (significantly) and length (nonsignificantly); but the frequencies of surprise reactions to changes in color and number were virtually identical in the retarded group. For both retarded and nonretarded subjects, frequencies of surprise reactions to changes of the three different quantitative properties were consistent with the findings of others (including Gruen & Vore, 1972), indicating that successful performance on conventional length and number conservation tasks is simpler than, and thus presumably developmentally prior to, success on conventional continuous quantity tasks. Thus, once again we find fairly strong support for the view that the sequence of developmental events for the retarded child is similar to that for the nonretarded child.

A different type of similarity was illustrated by the other Achenbach study. In it, Achenbach (1969) used nonretarded public school children (IQ range: 94–168) and nonorganically impaired retarded children (IQ range: 31–78) from public schools and institutions. Optical illusions were employed to create discrepancies between the actual and apparent sizes of various stimuli. The procedure made it possible to assess children's conservation concepts with respect to length, area, and volume, using four tasks for each of the three properties. To test conservation of length, for example, the experimenter presented each child with a barbell illusion: A small metal rod that had fit into a groove that just touched the inner edges of two circles was placed into another groove that passed through two circles, touching their outer edges. This made the rod appear longer in the second position than in the first. Subjects were then asked whether the rod would actually fit into the original groove. An important feature of the study was that the 12 tasks were designed to be relatively free of intellectual demands in the areas of additivity, numeration, conservation of equivalence, or complex verbal expression—dimensions along which more traditional conservation tasks often vary. This made it possible to test the contention of Braine and Shanks (1965a, b) that the attainment of conservation with respect to the various properties would be parallel if the performance criteria used were standard across the types of conservation. Consistent with the Braine–Shanks hypothesis, Achenbach (1969) found a: "total absence of evidence for a horizontal *decalage* [p. 677]" among the three types of conservation. This was true for both the retarded and nonretarded groups. In both groups there were neither consistent nor significant differences in success rates among length, area, and volume tasks. This finding, together with the reasoning of Braine and Shanks, suggests that some of the order-of-difficulty and scalogram-type evidence reviewed in the preceding paragraphs may be more indicative of differences in the specific requirements of the contrived tasks employed than of differences in the actual order of emergence of the various types of conservation.

Concepts of time. Several studies have addressed the similar-sequence hypothesis in content areas other than conservation. To the best of our knowledge, only one has dealt specifically with the concept of time. In this study Lovell and Slater (1960) interviewed 50 "educationally subnormal" children (IQs not reported) aged 8, 9, 11, and 15 years, and 50 "average to above average" children aged 5 to 9 years. The interview included tasks (some borrowed from Piaget's experiments) designed to measure concepts of *simultaneity and equality of synchronous intervals* (e.g., asking the child to judge whether two dolls traveling at different rates but starting and stopping at the same time had actually traveled for the same amount of time). There were also tasks involving *ordering of events* (e.g., arranging into proper chronological order some pictures of various stages in the process of pouring water from a beaker to a cylinder). Similar tasks (e.g., arranging pictures of an apple tree in order from youngest to oldest) were designed to reveal the children's concepts of age. Finally, some questions concerned the concept of interior time; for example, children were asked to compare time spent sitting motionless with eyes closed (1 minute) to an equal period of time spent looking at pictures in a book. Responses of both groups of children to the various tasks were examined as a function of age, but little in the way of statistical analysis was reported. Nonetheless, Lovell and Slater (1960) concluded the following: "Summing up, we may say that the understanding of simultaneity, equality of synchronous intervals, order of events, age, and estimation of interior time follows roughly the same sequence in E.S.N. children as in normal infant and junior school children [i.e., the "average to above average" group], but the stages in understanding are reached some years later [p. 188]."

Concepts of Space. Two studies that we have located that included a retarded sample were specifically concerned with spatial concepts. In one of these, conducted by Houssiadas and Brown (1967), only retarded children were sampled. Forty institutionalized, mentally retarded Southern Australians (mean IQ: 55), showing no evidence of "Mongolism or other specific defects," were selected to represent an age range of 8 to 15 years. The subjects were administered two perspective-taking tasks (one pictorial, one using manipulation of actual objects), in which they were asked to identify their own perspective on a perceptual array as well as the perspective of another person seated at a different position. No statistical analyses were reported; however, the pattern of passes and failures on the different items, displayed as a function of subjects' age levels, was consistent with the view that retarded individuals pass through the stages identified by Piaget; that is, firstly, children experience difficulty identifying their own perspective and that of another; later, they only have difficulty in identifying how a perceptual array might look from another position; and, finally, they are able to "coordinate perspectives," identifying not only their own perspective but that of another person as well. Summing up, Houssiadas and Brown (1967) concluded: "it is clear that the pattern of predominant responses follows the same sequence suggested by Piaget, whose data were derived from normal children [p. 213]."

In a more fine-grained analysis of spatial concepts, Woodward (1962) tested the same group of 50 institutionalized retarded adults and 44 institutionalized retarded children used in the study of number concepts described previously (Woodward, 1961). In her sample, 20% of the adults and 43% of the children were Downs syndrome, whereas 30% of the adults and 18% of the children "showed clinical signs of structural or metabolic abnormality of the brain." Her spatial tasks included measures of the ability to reproduce a spatial order under varying degrees of transformation (e.g., reproducing a circular array of beads on a horizontal rod). Using a similar procedure with nonretarded children, Piaget and Inhelder (1956) had identified seven stages through which their children passed as they improved on the tasks. With her retarded sample, Woodward constructed a table of scale types to assess the comparability of her results to those of Piaget and Inhelder. No scalogram statistics were calculated, but the great majority of Woodward's subjects fit scale types consistent with the developmental sequence posited by Piaget and Inhelder. A second task employed by Woodward involved drawing 21 geometric figures used by Piaget and Inhelder. Her subjects' scores on these tasks were reportedly quite consistent with a four-stage sequence advanced by Piaget and Inhelder (1956); Woodward (1962) reported that: "subjects classified by the features of a given stage showed the features of the lower stages in most cases [p. 31]." However, once again, no scalogram statistics were reported, and five of the 14 performance criteria by which stage assignments were made were outside the appropriate difficulty level for at least some of the subjects. Woodward's third task was a "reference points" problem, in which adult subjects were presented with drawings of a bottle tilted at various angles and said to be about ¼ full of water. The subjects' task was to pencil in the portion of the bottle occupied by the water. The performance data presented for this task were extremely sketchy, but Woodward indicated that the order of difficulty of the tasks was the same as that found by Piaget and Inhelder. In her overview of the findings, Woodward (1962) describes the rationale for, and results of, her scaling procedures:

> The second hypothesis (of the study) concerned the sequence of Piaget's stages. . . .
> It is possible . . . to examine this hypothesis by determining whether subjects who show a response ranked at a certain point in the sequence also show all the re-

sponses placed earlier in the sequence by Piaget.... The sequence suggested by Piaget and Inhelder was confirmed for all three spatial concepts that were investigated. For the spatial order tasks, the order of difficulty for subnormal subjects was found to be the same as that claimed by Piaget and Inhelder to develop at successive ages in normal children [1962, p. 35].

Relative Thinking. In investigating "the logic of relations" in children, Piaget (1928) used a "brothers and sisters" problem and a "right and left" problem. In the former, children's understanding of the relation between being and having a sibling was explored via such questions as, "George has three brothers, Paul, Henry, and Charles. How many brothers has Paul? How many brothers are there in this family?" In the "right and left" problem, children's understanding of the relative nature of the concepts of "right" and "left" was explored via instructions such as, "Show me your right hand, your left. Show me my right hand, my left." Lane and Kinder (1939) used the two Piagetian problems with 50 institutionalized retarded individuals of unspecified etiology who were divided, for data analysis, into four different IQ groups with means of 38, 51, 64, and 77. Difficulty levels of the questions were reported in the form of percentages of the subjects in each IQ group who correctly answered each. Although no scalogram or other statistics are reported, the table of percentages presented indicates that the rank-ordering of difficulty for the 11 questions employed by Lane and Kinder is similar across the different IQ levels. This parallelism is, of course, consistent with the similar-sequence hypothesis.

Moral Judgment. Abel (1941) investigated *moral judgment* among 74 institutionalized "subnormal adolescent white girls" (age range 15 to 21 years, IQs unspecified). She questioned her subjects about seven stories that raised specific moral issues. These concerned concepts of *imminent punishment* (the inevitability of punishment following a misdeed), *retributive justice* (punishment orientation, particularly of the "eye for an eye" variety), and *judging the gravity of a misdeed* (particularly with regard to the relative importance of the magnitude of the consequences relative to the intent of the transgressor). Consistent with previous research using nonretarded subjects (Lerner, 1937, 1938), Abel found that with increasing maturity (defined in terms of MA level) her subjects gave nonsignificantly greater weight to intent and less weight to consequences, in judging the gravity of a misdeed. With increasing maturity, they were also significantly less likely to consistently advocate retributive punishment. In findings inconsistent with at least some research on nonretarded persons, Abel reported that her more mature subjects (MAs 9–11 years) did not show a less-pronounced belief in imminent punishment than did her less-mature subjects (MAs 6–8 years). In fact, about 82% of both groups showed such a belief. Abel (1941) attributes this puzzling outcome to the "constraining" institutional environment "that controls the girls with threats of immanent punishment [p. 386]." Except for this one anomaly, which the author attributes to specific situational influences, the Abel data appear to be consistent with the similar-sequence hypothesis.

Studies of Multiple Concepts. We conclude the section on nonlongitudinal research with a discussion of broad-based studies that have assessed concepts in more than one conceptual domain. In one such investigation, DeVries (1970, 1973a, b, 1974) assessed a variety of Piagetian concepts among bright (mean IQ about 130), average (105), and retarded (72) children, all enrolled in public schools. The etiology of children in the retarded group was not reported. The tasks given to the children included the "brothers and sisters" and "right and left" problems described earlier; tests of generic and sex identity and of conservation of mass, number, length, and liquid; interviews on magic and dream concepts; object sorting and class inclusion problems; and a guessing game ("Which hand has the penny?") designed to reveal the level of children's role-taking skills. Of all the tasks used, data from the guessing-game task are presented in the most complete manner with respect to their bearing on the similar-sequence hypothesis (DeVries, 1970). Using an independent sample of 64 bright children, DeVries (1970) classified behavior on the guessing game with respect to 10 characteristics (e.g., does not always hide penny in the same hand). These 10 characteristics formed a highly reproducible Guttman-type scale with a reproducibility of .95 and an index of consistency of .66. The scale was then used with the bright, average, and retarded samples and checked against Kohlberg's (1969) criteria for developmental sequentiality: (1) mean scale scores should increase with age; (2) success on each individual scale item should increase with age; and (3) the sequence of items should be justifiable with a logical rationale based on Piagetian theory. DeVries (1973b) maintains that her scale meets criterion number 3, and her data (DeVries, 1970) indicate that the first two criteria were met within the bright, average, and retarded groups separately. Similar analyses were carried out with respect to the other 14 Piagetian tasks, with a Guttman scale constructed for each, then retained for each task whose scale met Green's (1956) criterion of an index of consistence greater than .50. It is unclear from DeVries' report (Note 2) whether all 15 scales met this criterion, but DeVries (1973b) does indicate (without presenting supporting data) that all the Kohlberg criteria for sequentiality: "were applied to each ability group (i.e., bright, average, and retarded subjects) separately, and the order of scale items was the same for each ability group on all tasks [p. 3]."

Stearns and Borkowski (1969) investigated conservation of continuous quantity (water) and discontinuous quantity (blocks and marbles) as well as horizontal-vertical space perception among institutionalized retarded individuals (IQs unspecified) ranging in age from 7 years, 6 months, to 27 years, 1 month. Their findings were consistent with Piaget's view (and supporting evidence from Elkind, 1961) that conservation of continuous quantity is more difficult and emerges developmentally later, than conservation of discontinuous quantity. The investigators found performance on their test of the former concept to be significantly poorer than performance on their two tests of the latter concept. The two tests of discontinuous quantity yielded quite similar scores. Scores were also very similar for the tests of horizontal and vertical frames of reference. This finding was consistent with Piaget's view (Piaget & Inhelder, 1956) that the concept of vertical and the concept of the horizontal are acquired at the same time.

Finally, we examine two studies by Lovell and his colleagues (Lovell, Healey, & Rowalnd, 1962; Lovell, Mitchell, & Everett, 1962), in which statistical analyses bearing on the similar-sequence hypothesis were minimal but in which the diversity of concepts examined makes the data worthy of some attention. In the Lovell, Mitchell, and Everett study, the subjects were groups of nonretarded and "educationally subnormal" individuals (no IQs reported), divided into separate age groups. The skills investigated included *additive classification* (of objects differing in shape, color, material, and letter of the alphabet), *multiplicative classification* (using pictures of black rabbits and white rabbits, sitting and running), *seriation,* and *multiplication of asymmetrical transitive relations* (constructing a two-dimensional array in which size and color seriation were coordinated), and *class inclusion* (e.g., after being shown 18 brown plastic beads and two white plastic beads, children were asked whether a necklace using all the brown beads or one using all the plastic beads would be longer). For each task, children's responses were classified into stage levels. Both "subnormal" and nonretarded subjects showed a general increase in stage levels attained with increases in age level, but the statistical significance of these age group differences was not assessed. Several other tasks were presented to the children and scored for quality of response or number of correct answers, without any classification of children into stage levels. These tasks involved *heirarchical classification and class inclusion* involving animals, and visual and *tactile classification* involving the ability to change the attributes on which the classification is based. For these tasks, tabled data indicated a general improvement in performance with increasing age level, for both normal and subnormal groups (no significance tests reported).

Lovell, Healey, and Rowland (1962) studied geometric concepts among groups of nonretarded and "educationally subnormal" persons from "Special Schools" (IQs unreported). The subjects, divided into separate age groups, were presented with 12 of the tasks used by Piaget, Inhelder, and Szeminska (1960) to study the child's emerging concepts of geometry. The tasks included four that involved different aspects of the measurement and conservation of length and distance. Other tasks involved reproducing the experimenter's subdivisions of a straight line, locating a point in two dimensional space, measuring angles and triangles, locating points equidistant from two stimuli, subtracting smaller from larger areas, and measuring and subdividing areas. For each task, responses were classified into Piagetian stages (with intermediate stages added by Lovell et al. in a few instances). Within normal and subnormal groups separately, correlation coefficients were calculated relating stage levels to age levels. Of the 24 coefficients, 23 were significant at the .01 level; the one nonsignificant relationship involved the subnormal group's performance on the task involving locating points equidistant from two stimuli. In this study, and in the Lovell, Mitchell, and Everett (1962) study, the patterns described must be regarded as only suggestive. The statistical analyses reported are minimal and are not the type that would be most revealing with respect to the similar-sequence hypothesis. Furthermore, the data on subject characteristics are so skimpy that it is not even clear that the successive age levels within the two ability groups would show progressive increments in actual cognitive maturity (as measured by MA, for example). Nonetheless, although they do not constitute strong evidence, the data of these two studies by Lovell and his colleagues appear to be in harmony with the similar-sequence hypothesis.

Summary of the Cross-sectional and Order-of-Difficulty Evidence on the Similar-Sequence Hypothesis

Thus far, we have reviewed 28 studies in which cross-sectional and order-of-difficulty evidence are reported in ways that have some bearing on the *similar-sequence* hypothesis. The degree of retardation involved in the samples has ranged from profound to mild; the retarded persons sampled have been both institutionalized and noninstitutionalized and have included both familial cases and individuals with Down syndrome, brain trauma, microcephaly, epilepsy, emotional disturbance, alcoholism, and histories involving diverse organic disorders; the retarded persons sampled have ranged in age from childhood through adulthood. The nonretarded contrast groups, when employed, have ranged from slightly below average to extremely high in IQ. The studies reported have varied widely in their methodology and in the level of appropriateness of their analyses with respect to the hypothesis being addressed in this section of the review. Despite this diversity of methodologies and sample characteristics, the data show rather consistent support for the similar-sequence hypothesis. This is true with respect to both the conservative form of the hypothesis, which applies only to nonretarded and familial retarded persons (Zigler, 1969), and to the strong form, in which universality of developmental sequence is seen as independent of individual subject characteristics such as organic impairment (see Kohlberg, 1969).

There were a few exceptions to this generalization: (1) Woodward (1959) did find that among her profoundly retarded subjects one sensorimotor task out of a set of 11 proved to be more difficult than another task that Piaget had designated as being one sensorimotor stage higher; (2) among Rogers' (1977) profoundly retarded subjects, a causality task designed to be at stage VI proved to be easier than one of the tasks at stage V, whereas individual spatiality tasks within each stage had to be combined to yield a highly reproducible scale; (3) among Achenbach's (1973) familial and Down syndrome retarded sample, surprise reactions indicative of color and number identity occurred with equal frequency, whereas among his nonretarded sample color surprise was significantly more frequent than number surprise; (4) Abel (1941) found no significant decline with increasing MA in belief in imminent punishment among her institutionalized female retarded sample, a finding differing from some earlier research with nonretarded children; (5) when Lovell, Healey, and Rowland (1962) calculated age x stage level correlations for 12 tests of geometric concepts, the correlations were highly significant for 11 of the tests between both "normal" and "educationally subnormal" groups, but for the test involving locating points equidistant from two stimuli the correlation was only significant for the normal group. These five instances of no support for the similar-sequence hypothesis are rather minor; they could, as the authors of these studies occasionally suggest, result from idiosyncratic (or misinterpreted) properties of the tasks selected, or from other measurement errors, and in some cases (Abel, 1941) they might reflect the suppressive influence of an idiosyncratic environment, which delays the shift from one level of reasoning to another.

In each of the five studies cited previously, negative findings were outnumbered by findings supporting the similar-sequence hypothesis. Such support has now been reported in studies of sensorimotor stages (including object permanence, spatiality, causality, and imitation), many types of conservation, seriation, transitivity, moral reasoning, comparison processes (gross, intensive and extensive quantity), time, space, relative thinking, role-taking, classification and class inclusion, and geometry.

Although noting the support that this evidence has yielded for the similar-sequence hypothesis, we must also note that such cross-sectional and level-of-difficulty evidence, even at its best, can support only indirect inference regarding the actual process of development. More direct inference is possible when an investigator observes the same individuals at more than one point during the course of development (i.e., in the form of longitudinal research). Such research is often expensive and complex, and consequently it is relatively rare, particularly among samples of mentally retarded persons. However, there have been three longitudinal studies that have some relevance to the similar-sequence hypothesis. We now examine them.

Longitudinal Evidence

Development in the Sensorimotor Period. Wohlhueter and Sindberg (1975) conducted an experiment designed as an extension of Woodward's (1959) cross-sectional study of sensorimotor development among profoundly retarded persons (described earlier). The investigators conducted monthly assessments of institutionalized 1- to 6-year-old profoundly, severely, and moderately retarded children (no IQs reported). Piagetian object concept tasks used by Decarie (1965) were employed for 1 to 1½ years or until a child performed at the highest of the 10 substage levels for two consecutive monthly sessions. Of the principal sample of 49 children, 20 had progressed to the highest substage level by the end of the study; of the 29 remaining subjects, 10 showed a generally monotonic increase (i.e., with nearly every session's substage level equal to or higher than that of the preceding session, and 9 seemed to be at a plateau, with object concept levels the same for most of the 12 or more sessions). Thus, 39 of the 49 subjects showed patterns that were apparently consistent with the pattern of object concept stages posited by Piaget and found by subsequent investigators using nonretarded samples. The remaining 10 subjects, however, showed a "variable" developmental pattern in which substage levels rose and fell from session to session, ranging over as many as three or four stages during the 12 or more sessions. The pattern shown by these individuals was clearly inconsistent with expectations based on Piaget's theory and on findings with nonretarded children. In an effort to determine what characteristics might distinguish this group of 10 atypical subjects, Wohlhueter and Sindberg (1975) examined medical histories and clinical findings for their sample; a distinguishing feature of the "variable" group was that the majority: "were found to have EEG abnormalities, especially dysrhythmias or a history of seizures [p. 516]." This finding raises at least two possible interpretations with respect to the variable developmental pattern: (1) that individuals with brain anomalies associated with EEG abnormalities often show atypical sequences of development with respect to the object concept; and (2) that behavioral and attentional abnormalities in individuals with anomalous EEG patterns make accurate *assessment* of object concept substages difficult.

One other unusual pattern was noted by the investigators—some children seemed to bypass or skip over some of the substages. Although this is an interesting phenomenon, it is difficult to know how often "skipped" substages might have actually been traversed by children in the intervals between experimental sessions. Furthermore, the apparent skipping phenomenon is not unique to studies of retarded children. It has been noted in research with nonretarded children as well (see Uzgiris, 1968), although not as frequently as in the Wohlhueter-Sindberg study. Both the "skipping" and the "variability" phenomena might be better understood if it were possible to rule out specific method effects; this could have been done if a nonretarded sample had been included in the study for comparative purposes. Nonetheless, the Wohlhueter-Sindberg investigation does raise significant questions about the validity of the similar-sequence hypothesis with respect to substages in development of the object concept.

A longitudinal study reported by Cicchetti and Sroufe (1976), however, appears to yield strong support for the similar-sequence hypothesis within the sensorimotor period. The study addressed the relationship between cognitive and affective development among home-reared Down syndrome infants during the period from 4 to 18 months of age. Sroufe and his colleagues (Sroufe & Wunsch,

1972) have demonstrated that among normal infants there is a developmental progression from mirth responses to auditory and tactile stimulation that is physically intense or vigorous (e.g., tickling the baby's chin or saying "BOOM!" at 1-second intervals) to mirth responses to social and visual stimulation that is progressively more subtle and complex (e.g., the sight of mother sucking on baby's bottle). At monthly intervals the Down infants sampled by Cicchetti and Sroufe were presented with 15 auditory and tactile items of the intense or vigorous type and 15 social and visual items of the more subtle and complex type. As had been found in earlier research with normal infants, the Down infants laughed earliest in response to auditory and tactile items, and later in response to "more cognitively complicated social and visual items." The responses of the Down infants, of course, came months later (in CA) than the corresponding responses of normal infants. Smile responses, a more sensitive index of positive affect in the Down sample, showed the same pattern and revealed even more clearly than laughter responses the developmental decline in positive affect aroused by simpler auditory and tactile items, as the Down infants matured beyond 13 months. This inverted U-shaped developmental pattern also resembled earlier findings with normal infants. In stressing the similarity of their findings with Down infants and those with normal infants, Cicchetti and Stroufe (1976) point out that: "the laughter items are ordered as they were for normal infants, category by category and, in the main, *item by item* [p. 923]."

An interesting feature of the item by item similarity in pattern was that, among both normal and Down infants, there was a clearly emerging preference for items involving the infant's own participation (e.g., an item requiring the infant to tug at a piece of yarn) over items involving mere passive stimulation. To assess the merits of their claim that the affective responses they were measuring were closely related to cognitive development, Cicchetti and Sroufe calculated correlations of "indices of affective expression" (e.g., earliest laugh, total amount of smiling to all items, etc.) with the Bayley mental and motors scales and the Uzgiris-Hunt object permanence and operational causality scales. All 44 correlations were statistically significant.

Research on the Preoperational-to Concrete-Operational Transition—the Temple Longitudinal Study. The third longitudinal study we review is by far the broadest in scope. In this ongoing investigation, the Temple longitudinal study, Stephens and her colleagues (Stephens, 1972; Stephens, Mahaney, & McLaughlin, 1972; Stephens, McLaughlin, Hunt, Mahaney, Kohlberg, Moore, & Aronfreed, 1974) are conducting biennial assessments of the performance of retarded and nonretarded persons on a variety of Piagetian tasks. The sample included 75 retarded persons (IQs: 50–75) from special education classes and 75 nonretarded persons (IQs: 90–110) from the same Philadelphia schools. In the first wave of testing, the age range in both subject groups was 6 to 18 years. Results from the first two waves of testing have now been reported in several places (see references listed earlier) and are discussed here under two content headings.

Moral Judgment in the Temple Study. The test battery included 11 measures designed to assess three aspects of moral judgment: (1) the relative importance assigned to intent versus consequences in judging the seriousness of a misdeed; (2) awareness of the injustice of punishing an entire group for the acts of only one or a few members; and (3) ability to judge the relative fairness of various types of punishment, including retributive and reciprocal justice. To determine whether judgment along these three dimensions follows the same developmental course in the retarded as in the nonretarded, Mahaney and Stephens (1974) examined changes in scores on the 11 component measures over the 2-year period from the first to the second wave of testing. On one of the intent versus consequences measures, they found that the retarded group showed a nonsignificant decline in score (i.e., they made slightly less-mature moral judgments according to the scoring criteria adopted by the authors). On one of the group punishment items, nonretarded subjects showed a nonsignificant decline. However, on the nine remaining items the direction of change was the same for both the retarded and nonretarded subjects; this similarity extended to two items on which both groups showed significant declines in score, raising questions about validity of the scoring scheme for these particular items.

In our earlier discussion of Inhelder's (1968) study, we noted her mention of "oscillations" in the reasoning of the retarded. Mahaney and Stephens (1974) (who was the translator of the Inhelder book) also report oscillations as instances when: "the improvement which occurred in one area of moral judgment was not maintained when opinions were solicited on another, but similar, situation [p. 137]." These oscillations occurred among both retarded and nonretarded subjects. There is some indication that such oscillations, although occurring in both groups, were somewhat more frequent among the retarded. One line of evidence suggesting this possibility came from Mahaney and Stephens' analysis of change scores for three separate age groups within both the retarded and nonretarded samples. Of the 29 change scores reported for the nonretarded groups, 20 were increases (11 significant), 7 were decreases (3 significant), and 2 showed no change. Among the retarded subjects, 17 change scores were increases (7 significant), 11 were decreases (4 significant), and 1 involved no change. In a supplementary analysis, retarded comparison groups were staggered in order to broaden the age difference (e.g., by comparing Phase I 6–10-year olds with Phase II 12–16-year olds). In this analysis, 26 difference scores were involved. The *only* ones showing a decrease with age were the two items that had shown a decrease among nonretarded subjects as well. Overall, the report by Mahaney and Stephens (1974) seems to show that, whereas growth in moral judgment concepts among the retarded may be "torporific and sporadic [p. 141]," the direction of development is the same for both retarded and nonretarded persons.

Whether this apparent similarity in the direction of development is actually a function of an invariant, stage-like progression is, thus far, an open question because of the questionable nature of the measures themselves. In a critique of this portion of the Temple study, Kohlberg (1974) maintained that the Piagetian moral judgment measures used in the Temple study do not warrant detailed longitudinal analysis because: "Piaget himself does not consider that his moral judgment measures yield genuine stages, nor do they pair up with his logical stages in ways compatible with his current thinking about cognitive stages. . . . Empirical research confirms the fact that Piaget's moral stage measures do not meet the criteria of structural stages which his logical stages do meet [p. 142]." Given this critique, perhaps the most appropriately cautious conclusion that can be drawn with respect to the moral judgment portion of the Temple investigation is: *To the extent that the measures employed tap a truly stage-like developmental sequence,* the findings are generally consistent with the similar-sequence hypothesis.

Conservation, Classification, Symbolic Imagery, and Formal Operations in the Temple Study. In addition to its moral judgment measures, the Temple investigation included 29 measures of cognitive development across four conceptual domains: (1) *conservation* (of substance, length, weight, continuous quantity, and volume, as well as term–to–term correspondence); (2) *logic— classification* (class inclusion and class intersection, relative thinking measured by the brothers and sisters and right and left tests); (3) *operativity and symbolic imagery* (tests involving imagined rotations of objects through space, transferring from two to three dimensions, and changing one's perspective on a stimulus); and (4) *combinatory logic* (Piaget and Inhelder's combination of liquids task). Explanations given by subjects on each of the 29 items were scored on a 9-point scale. The scale took into account, among other things, the degree to which the subject wavered between a correct and an incorrect answer, and the degree to which reversibility was shown. Stephens and McLaughlin (1974) reported changes in scores on the 29 measures over the 2-year period separating the two waves of testing. The nonretarded group, they found, showed improvement on all 29 measures, with 25 statistically significant; the retarded group also improved on all 29 measures, with 26 statistically significant. This finding indicates that the direction of development on these Piagetian reasoning tasks was similar among the retarded and nonretarded groups. In another report following the second wave of the Temple study, Stephens, Mahaney, and McLaughlin (1972), the Piagetian reasoning tasks were rank-ordered with respect to the MAs, at which 50% of the subjects (in the retarded and nonretarded groups, considered separately) made correct responses. As Stephens et al. indicate, the order of difficulty for both subject groups is generally consistent with previous findings that conservation of substance precedes weight, and weight precedes volume. In addition, our own calculations yield a Spearman rho of .634 between the rank order given for the retarded group and that of the nonretarded group.

The preceding data are consistent with the similar-sequence hypothesis, as far as they have been taken. However, they could have been taken considerably further. With the one exception listed in the preceding paragraph, we are unaware of any effort by the Temple investigators to check their findings against specific developmental stage sequences reported elsewhere. Such "horizontal decalages" have been reported for nonretarded subjects in previous Piagetian research by Kohlberg and DeVries (1971), Nassafat (1963), Siegelman and Block (1969), Smedslund (1964), and Uzgiris (1968). Moreover, data from the Temple study have generally been reported in the form of group means, rather than in terms of *the number of individuals* (retarded and nonretarded) who show specific developmental patterns. This latter form of analysis is the unique province of longitudinal research and can only be approximated indirectly by scaling procedures in research of the nonlongitudinal variety. There is some indication (Stephens, 1974) that efforts to profile individual's performance changes over time, and to cross-validate specific vertical and horizontal decalages, will be forthcoming from the Temple investigators. Such efforts are needed if the investigators are to fully capitalize on the power of their longitudinal design.

STATUS OF EVIDENCE ON THE SIMILAR-SEQUENCE HYPOTHESIS

Evidence bearing on the similar-sequence hypothesis has now been drawn from three longitudinal and 28 nonlongitudinal studies. Of the longitudinal studies, only one—the Wohlhueter and Sindberg (1975) investigation of object concept substages—produced findings clearly inconsistent with the similar-sequence hypothesis. In that investigation, it was only a distinct subgroup of 10 (out of 49) children who showed apparent atypical developmental sequences, and most of these children, according to Wohlhueter and Sindberg (1975), showed: "EEG abnormalities, especially dysrhythmias or a history of seizures [p. 516]." This finding may indicate that brain-wave anomalies can be associated with atypical developmental patterns. Alternatively, the EEG abnormalities may simply have been associated with attentional and other deficits that interfered with accurate assessment of substage levels in children, whose actual development was consistent with the similar-sequence hypothesis. The latter interpretation has special credence in the area of object concept assessment, in which procedures demand that the subject sustain attention to an object long enough to seek after it, once it has been removed from the perceptual field.

Of the 28 nonlongitudinal studies reviewed, only four contained a finding inconsistent with the similar-sequence hypothesis, and in each of these studies the inconsistent finding was relatively minor and was alone among a number of findings supporting the hypothesis. Furthermore, the questions raised generally concerned rather fine-grained steps or substages within horizontal decalages, on which even studies of nonretarded subjects alone have not always agreed.

These facts, plus the measurement problems inherent in these experimental procedures, make the degree of consistency in the findings of these 31 studies rather surprising. Positive findings have now been reported in conceptual areas that include sensorimotor spatial concepts, object permanence, causality, imitation, affective responding, identity and equivalence conservation (of many properties), seriation, transitivity, moral reasoning, comparison processes (or gross, intensive, and extensive quantities), time, space, relative thinking, role taking, mental imagery, geometric concepts, and classification and class inclusion. For the 31 studies spanning this list of conceptual areas, the bulk of the evidence is consistent with the hypothesis that retarded and nonretarded persons traverse the same stages of development in the same order, differing only in the rate at which they progress and in the ultimate ceiling they attain. The hypothesis seems to be generally supported in studies of retarded individuals, regardless of etiology, with the possible exception of individuals suffering from pronounced EEG abnormalities. With that exception, then, the findings seem to support not only the conservative version of the similar-sequence hypothesis allied with the developmental position on retardation (Zigler, 1969) but the strong form of the hypothesis generated by Piagetian theory.

CRITIQUE OF THE EVIDENCE

Having said this, however, we believe it is important to qualify our conclusion by commenting on the quality of the available evidence. Cross-sectional data relevant to the similar-sequence hypothesis have most often been presented in ways that provide only the weakest inferential power. A table displaying the percentage of subjects at each age level who pass each Piagetian item can yield only faint glimmers of developmental sequence, compared with the information generated when *each child* is classified with respect to specific pass–fail patterns—that is, with respect to response scale types. When such a scaling analysis is combined with calculation of scalogram summary statistics (Green, 1956; Guttman, 1950), the potential power of the nonlogitudinal design is more fully exploited.

Similarly, the bulk of the *longitudinal* data we found was presented only in terms of mean difference among experimental groups, or changes in group means, or percentages over time. Such procedures represent a waste of the potential power of longitudinal data. As Hunt (1974) has noted, reporting only group summary statistics at Time 1 and Time 2 can mask the fact that some individuals progressed, whereas others regressed over time. So, although it is useful to know that the Time 1 and Time 2 means differed in the same direction for retarded and nonretarded groups, such information is no substitute for an analysis of the number of individuals in each group showing specific developmental patterns over time. In both longitudinal and nonlongitudinal research aimed at testing the similar-sequence hypothesis, it makes little sense to invest the time and energy necessary to gather relevant data and then analyze the data in ways that fail to capitalize on their full potential.

TOWARD IMPROVED RESEARCH

These problems, and others to which we referred earlier in the text, suggest three principles that if widely adopted would substantially improve the quality of evidence on the similar-sequence hypothesis.

Structuring Direct Comparisons

A problem with many of the studies reviewed in earlier sections is that their samples included only mentally retarded subjects. In those few instances in which findings of these studies disagree with findings of other studies that involved only nonretarded subjects, the discrepancies are difficult to interpret. This is because of uncertainty over whether the discrepancies reflect actual process differences between the retarded and the nonretarded, or whether differences in experimental methodology across studies are responsible for differences in results. An obvious way to prevent such difficulties is to expose retarded and nonretarded children within a similar cognitive-developmental range to precisely the same procedure by including both groups in the same study. To fail to do so is to risk uninterpretable findings.

Attending to Etiology

The marked heterogeneity of many of the mentally retarded samples described earlier suggests a somewhat opportunistic approach to subject selection, or perhaps an approach in which the etiology of retardation is simply not regarded as an important factor. Yet, theoretical considerations discussed early in this chapter (Weisz, 1976; Zigler, 1969, 1971) point to the need to distinguish between retarded children who do and those who do not suffer from organic impairment or genetic disorder. Furthermore, Wohlhueter and Sindberg's (1975) report of atypical development in a group of children with high incidence of EEG anomalies suggests the possible importance of efforts to identify distinct subgroups within the organically impaired population. Their findings illustrate that subgroup analyses can be useful, even when they are post hoc.

Promoting Uniformity

Finally, there is a clear need for increased uniformity across studies in the kinds of statistical analyses carried out and in the way statistics are reported. Toward this end, we suggest that every cross-sectional study addressing the similar-sequence hypothesis should yield data bearing on the following threefold question:

1. Within the retarded and nonretarded groups, do the task items form the same scale, and does this scale show high reproducibility (á la Guttman, 1950) and a high index of consistency (á la Green, 1956)?

2. Do mean scale scores increase with level of cognitive maturity in each separate subject group (Kohlberg, 1969)?

3. Do mean levels of success on each individual item increase with levels of cognitive maturity in each separate subject group (Kohlberg, 1969)?

In longitudinal research, Questions 2 and 3 should also be asked in a way that only longitudinal investigation permits: Over the period spanned by the longitudinal study, in what percentage of individual subjects (from retarded and nonretarded groups) do scale scores and individual item scores: (a) increase either smoothly or monotonically; (b) remain stable throughout; and (c) show at least some declines.

If these recommended questions were consistently answered, the result would be greater uniformity and thus enhanced comparability, among studies addressing the similar-sequence hypothesis. In opposition to such uniformity, one might argue that the degree of consistency in the findings of the numerous studies reviewed here is impressive precisely because of the methodological diversity of the studies. There is some truth to this argument, at least for those cases in which findings support the similar-sequence hypothesis. Yet, even in those cases apparent group similarities in developmental sequence may result from a failure to ask the most probing questions of one's data. It seems clear from our review that evidence from the 31 studies currently available offers fairly consistent support for the similar-sequence hypothesis; however, it also seems likely that the best evidence has yet to be gathered.

EVIDENCE ON THE SIMILAR-STRUCTURE HYPOTHESIS

Next, we turn our attention to the second major tenet of the developmental position, the similar-structure hypothesis. In tests of this hypothesis, four methodological issues assume particular importance. Each issue needs to be addressed here before we examine the Piagetian studies relevant to the hypothesis.

METHODOLOGICAL ISSUES INVOLVED IN STRUCTURING A FAIR TEST

Matching Groups for Level of Development

The similar-structure hypothesis predicts similar reasoning in retarded and nonretarded children who are equated for developmental level. The most widely accepted operational definition of developmental level is the psychometric MA. Yet, MA is at best a rough index, and it could quite possibly be improved on by a collection of measures derived from current theory and evidence in developmental psychology. On the other hand, the MA, as derived from such standardized tests as the Stanford–Binet, is a broad-based measure that taps a variety of cognitive activities. Moreover, evidence has shown that nonorganically impaired mentally retarded and nonretarded children matched for total Stanford–Binet MA (either short form or standard) are also similar in the *patterns* of Binet items they pass (Achenbach, 1970, 1971). So, although the MA may be a less than ideal measure of developmental level, it appears to be an adequate matching device for tests of the similar-sequence hypothesis.

The Problem of Etiology

The developmental position generally, and the similar-structure hypothesis in particular, apply only to persons who are not suffering from specific genetic or other physiological defects. Critics of the developmental position (Ellis, 1969; Milgram, 1969; 1973) have denied the importance of organicity in this context. Ellis (1969), for example, insists that only: "rarely have behavioral differences characterized different etiological groups [p. 561]." And Milgram (1973) asserts: "I am not convinced that etiology in and of itself relates to behavioral differences [p. 171]." At least one review that touches on this question reveals rather mixed evidence (Blount, 1968), but some studies employing the specific kinds of reasoning and problem-solving tasks most often used in research on the developmental-difference ontroversy have demonstrated apparent effects of organicity among both retarded and nonretarded populations (Balla, Styfco, & Zigler, 1971; Balla & Zigler, 1964; Elkind, Koegler, Go, & Van Doorninck, 1965; Harter, Brown, & Zigler, 1971). (Later in the chapter, we discuss a difficulty faced in this research and in studies to be reviewed later—that of keeping organicity and IQ level unconfounded. This problem makes it difficult to interpret apparent effects of organicity in several of these studies with complete confidence.)

Given that some rather carefully designed studies point to performance differences between organically impaired and nonimpaired persons, and given that difference theorists (with the possible exception of Luria, 1963) do not *require* the inclusion of organically impaired subjects for fair tests of their theories, it seems accurate to say that the clearest tests of the similar-structure hypothesis will be those experiments that include efforts to eliminate cases involving organicity from the sample. This does not mean that experiments not including such efforts are excluded from the present review; but it does mean that such studies are evaluated at the end of our review in the light of the basic scientific standard, that the classes we employ in experimentation should be no more heterogeneous than those that afford the most precise test of the proposition in question.

The Influence of Noncognitive Factors

The behavior of retarded persons reflects more than their formal cognitive processes alone. Although there is general agreement that a deficiency in cognitive functioning is the essential defining feature of mental retardation, it is possible that the operation of noncognitive factors in comparative studies has obscured the precise nature of this deficiency. Over the past 2 decades, the work of the Peabody group (see Cromwell, 1963), Gordon and O'Connor (reviewed by Heber, 1964), Stevenson and his colleagues (Stevenson, 1965), and the Yale group (Zigler, 1971) has brought to light a number of factors that distinguish the motivational makeup of the retarded from that of the nonretarded, and that appear particularly detrimental to experimental task performance. For example, numerous studies by the Yale group (Zigler, 1971) have exposed the impact of such factors as heightened motivation for social reinforcement, wariness of adults, idiosyncratic reinforcer heirarchies differing from those of nonretarded children, a tendency to anticipate failure, and a willingness to settle for relatively low levels of success. There is also evidence from the Yale group and others that institutionalization can influence motivation, self-confidence, and task performance. In addition, incipient evidence on "learned helplessness" indicates that retarded persons, particularly those of relatively high MA, are less likely than nonretarded persons of similar MA to ascribe failure to controllable factors, and less likely to persist in applying their abilities in the face of failure and negative feedback (Gibson, 1980; Weisz, 1979, in press-b). Findings on motivation and on helplessness have suggested that the better tests of the similar-structure hypothesis will be those that involve a reasonable effort to insure that retarded and nonretarded subjects are equally motivated to perform at their best, and equally confident that success is possible.

This standard simply reflects the experimental principle that one cannot conclusively attribute a group difference on a dependent variable to one known difference in subject characteristics (e.g., IQ), when the respective groups also differ on other factors that could reasonably be expected to affect performance on the dependent variable. The importance of this principle is underscored in the writings of Cole and Bruner (1971), Labov (1970), and Tulkin and Konner (1973), concerning the dangers that inhere in attempts to infer competence directly from performance. On the other hand, one must sympathize with the conscientious investigator who undertakes a comparative study and finds that there are myriad possible motivational and expectancy factors that may distinguish retarded from nonretarded children. To achieve anything approaching control over this broad network of factors may seem an impossible dream. Perhaps the only workable approach for the careful investigator is to remain well-informed about the evidence on noncognitive factors, and to control for those that seem likely to influence performance on the particular tasks that are to be used. This of course means that decisions will be matters of judgment to a certain extent, because no a priori set of rules can anticipate the diversity of experimental specifics that may arise in the future. It is not our purpose here to second guess the judgments made by authors of the Piagetian studies. But we attempt to describe experimental procedures in enough detail to permit readers to form judgments of their own; then, at the conclusion of this section, we return to the question of noncognitive factors, with an overall evaluative comment.

On the Reliability of "No Difference" Findings

The reader should be sensitive to one other aspect of the studies to be reviewed following. The similar-structure hypothesis is, in essence, a null hypothesis. Findings supporting the hypothesis are findings of no significant difference between MA-matched groups differing in IQ. In such cases it is useful to determine whether the no-difference finding in any given study might have resulted from excessive variability in the data. Such an interpretation of a no-difference finding loses some credibility, when other group comparisons using the same data result in statistically significant differences. For this reason, we indicate, with each no-difference finding reported, whether other group differences in the study being considered attained significance. After describing all the relevant studies, we combine and evaluate their findings. This necessitates some more general comments on null hypothesis testing in the kinds of comparative research discussed here.

These four methodological issues are central to the developmental-difference controversy. The views one takes with respect to each will figure significantly in one's interpretation of results bearing on the similar-structure hypothesis. Let us now turn to a study-by-study survey of those results.[2]

SURVEYING THE STUDIES

Moral Judgment

Given the frequency with which retarded persons have been labeled immoral by the nonretarded in our society (see accounts in Zigler & Harter, 1969; Kamin,

---

[2]The evidence to be reviewed with regard to the similar-structure hypothesis unfortunately does not include any of the data from the Temple longitudinal study (Stephens, McLaughlin, Hunt, Mahaney, Kohlberg, Moore, & Aronfreed, 1974), described in our section surveying evidence on the similar-sequence hypothesis. Although the Temple data are potentially applicable to the similar-structure hypothesis, the published analyses of the data (Mahaney & Stevens, 1974; Stephens, 1972; Stephens et al., 1974) are not. Retarded and nonretarded groups in the study were not matched for MA, and when analysis of covariance was employed (Stephens & McLaughlin, 1974) in contrasting the performance of retarded and nonretarded subjects, it was used to control for both MA *and CA*. This analysis, which in principle also controls for group differences in IQ, is not appropriate for a test of the similar-structure hypothesis (Weisz, 1976) and poses other statistical problems as well (Kappauf, 1976).

1975; Sarason & Doris, 1969), research comparing the moral judgment of retarded and nonretarded persons should be of particular interest. Our literature search has yielded two relevant experiments, both rather carefully designed. In the first, Taylor and Achenbach (1975) compared responses of MA-matched retarded (mean IQ: 75) and nonretarded (mean IQ: 111) subjects at three MA levels (6½, 8, and 9½ years) on two pairs of stories calling for moral judgment; the stories concerned promises, stealing, punishment, and the value of life. Responses were scored according to Kohlberg's system. All retarded subjects were from public schools, and school records were used to select only children showing no indication of organicity. The retarded and nonretarded children thus selected did not differ significantly in their level of moral judgment. That this finding of no-difference did not result from excessive variability in the data is suggested by the fact that there was a significant effect of MA level on moral judgment.

In a study designed partly as a sequel to the Taylor–Achenbach experiment, Kahn (1976) administered a five-story moral judgment interview based on Kohlberg's procedures to three MA-matched groups: (1) public school nonretarded subjects averaging 101 in IQ; (2) public school mildly retarded subjects, screened to eliminate cases of organicity and averaging 66 in IQ; and (3) public school moderately retarded subjects with etiologies involving Down syndrome, rubella, congenital syphilis, and other organic patterns, and averaging 45 in IQ. Consistent with the similar-structure hypothesis, groups (1) and (2) did not differ in level of moral judgment. Furthermore, the group suffering from organic impairment was significantly inferior to the nonretarded group in moral judgment. Kahn (1976) noted that this pattern of findings is consistent with the view that: "similarity of performance by [MA-matched] retarded and nonretarded children does not extend to retarded children with etiologies other than cultural–familial retardation [p. 213]."

Role-Taking

One conceptual skill that many consider related to moral judgment is role-taking. The Taylor–Achenbach (1975) investigation just described included among its measures two role-taking tasks. In the first, the subject's level of awareness of the experimenter's thought processes was inferred from behavior on successive games of tic-tac-toe. The second was a guessing game adapted from Flavell, Botkin, Fry, Wright, and Jarvis (1968) to tap higher levels of role-taking skill; in the game the child tried to fool an observer who attempted to guess which of two boxes the child had taken pennies from. When responses to both tasks were scored according to Kuhn's (1972) role-taking criteria, it was found that the retarded and nonretarded groups did not differ. There was a significant MA effect on the simpler role-taking task and a significant sex effect (boys superior) on the more advanced task.

The study by DeVries (1970, 1973a, b), described earlier, included a task in which the child tried to fool an experimenter who guessed which hand the child had hidden a penny in; at other times the child did the guessing. Intellectually average (mean IQ: 105) and retarded children (mean IQ: 72—apparently not screened for organicity) from public schools were similar in MA. In contrast to the findings of Taylor and Achenbach (1975), DeVries found retarded children significantly inferior to the nonretarded in role-taking performance.

Perspective-Taking and Perceptual–Spatial Concepts

Perspective-Taking (Spatial Egocentrism). A number of problems outside the social real per se involve reasoning that bears a conceptual similarity to social role-taking. One is the problem of identifying how a perceptual array would look from a perspective other than one's own. Rubin and Orr (1974) compared MA-matched retarded and nonretarded children on such a task. Both groups were from public elementary schools; their IQs averaged 73 and 105, respectively. There is no indication that cases of organicity were screened out. Nonetheless, on both measures—one involving identification, the other construction of the perspective of another person on a stimulus array—the MA matched groups did not differ reliably; however, the retarded group was significantly inferior to a CA-matched group on both tasks.

Perceptual Decentering. Smith (1977a) assessed a related skill using a slightly modified version of Elkind, Koegler, and Go's (1964) Picture Integration Test. The test consisted of several complex pictures (e.g., a face composed of a bat, balls, acorns, and a drum). To assess the child's ability to decenter, the experimenter first asked what the picture looked like, then whether the child saw anything else. Responses were scored for the number of responses involving parts, the number involving whole "gestalts," and the number of part–whole integrations (the most advanced response developmentally). Public school retarded (mean IQ: 69—apparently unscreened with respect to organicity) and nonretarded (mean IQ: 115) subjects, matched for MA, did not differ significantly on this task, but both groups had significantly more part–whole integrations than did a retarded group matched to the nonretarded group for CA.

Logical Contradiction. At the beginning of a child's movement into the concrete operational stage of cognitive development, a transition takes place from the predominance of perceptually dominated thought to logically guided thought. Cognition begins to be less "stimulus bound." Smith (1977b), in order to investigate the relative progress of retarded and nonretarded subjects into concrete operational thought, compared the performance of 30 nonretarded and 30 retarded school children (IQ data not reported) matched for MA, on a task involving logical contradiction. There is no indication that children were screened for organicity. The task used was a modification of the Jastrow ("ring segment") Illusion. In this illusion, the child is asked to pick the "big" ring segment, the position of the two ring segments is reversed, and the subject is asked to pick the "little" ring segment; changing the position results in what was first identified as big by the child now appearing to be little. Smith and an independent observer rated reaction to the illusion and found that, whereas a group of retarded children matched for chronological age with the nonretarded group gave significantly fewer reactions, the MA-matched retarded and nonretarded children showed no significant difference in their number of reactions to contradiction.

Relative Thinking. Related to the problem of decentering is the problem of relative thinking as measured by Piaget's "brother-sister" and "right-left" tests. The first test taps children's grasp of the relation between being and having a sibling. A sample item: George has three brothers, Paul, Henry, and Charles. How many brothers does Paul have? How many brothers are there in the family? On the right-left test, children point to their own right and left hands, then to the experimenter's. McManis (1969f) gave both tests to 15 retarded and 15 nonretarded subjects at each yearly MA level from 5 to 10 years. IQs for the two groups averaged about 58 and 100, respectively, and the source of subjects (public schools versus residential institutions) was not specified. McManis reports no significance tests but does indicate that on both tasks retarded subjects showed increasing MA deficits (i.e., correctly answering questions at later MA levels than nonretarded subjects) as the level of abstractness in the test questions increased. Given the well-established linkage between brain damage and difficulty with abstraction, it is important to note that McManis' retarded sample included significant percentages suffering from organic impairment: At MA 5, the percentage of organically impaired was 62%, at MA 6, 43%, at MA 7, 43%, at MA 8, 23%, at MA 9, 8%, and at MA 10, 46%.

Lane and Kinder (1939), in a study described earlier, used the same two Piagetian tasks with five groups of institutionalized retarded subjects of unspecified etiology. Two of the groups differed in IQ (means: 51 and 64, respectively) but were matched for MA. Although no significance tests were reported anywhere in the study, the two MA-matched groups were quite similar, not only in the gross percentage of questions answered correctly, but also in the percentage of subjects answering each individual question correctly; other groups in the Lane-Kinder sample differed markedly in both respects. Summing up, Lane and Kinder (1939) noted that: "The records of the two groups with the same mental age are thus found to be strikingly similar, whereas comparisons on the basis of chronological age or IQ show marked differences in performance [p. 113]."

In a third study of relativism, Prothro (1943) administered the right-left test to MA-matched institutionalized retarded (mean IQ: 39) and public nursery and elementary school nonretarded (mean IQ: 113) subjects. The retarded sample included only individuals diagnosed "familial" or "undifferentiated," with cases involving "motor defect" or epilepsy excluded. It is unclear what etiologies may have characterized the undifferentiated group; however, it is possible that some of these were organically impaired, because an IQ of 50 is the approximate lower limit for the familial retarded (Zigler, 1967), and Prothro's retarded group mean was 39. Performance of the nonretarded children on the right–left test, though at a very low level, was nonetheless significantly superior to that of the retarded.

The DeVries (1970, 1973a, b) and Taylor and Achenbach (1975) studies also assessed relative thinking in their subjects. DeVries found no significant difference between MA-matched retarded and nonretarded subjects on either the brother–sister or right–left test, whereas the brother–sister test did differentiate significantly between high-IQ and average -IQ children of the same CA. Taylor and Achenbach (1975) found, similarly, that whereas performance on the two tests improved significantly with MA there were no significant differences between retarded and nonretarded persons matched for MA.

Conceptions of the World and Physical Causality

Animism. One of Piaget's earliest interests concerned children's interpretations of naturalistic phenomena. Of the many that Piaget investigated, one of the first subjected to American comparative research was the child's concept of life. Russell, Dennis, and Ash (1940) administered a standardized interview in which subjects were asked to classify a series of objects as living or nonliving and to justify each classification. The retarded subjects were 430 inmates in two institutions for the "feebleminded" but are not described with respect to etiology or IQ. A nonretarded contrast group (no IQ or institutional status reported) was matched to the retarded group for MA range at two MA levels—6-7 years and 8-9 years. At the lower MA level, there was a close similarity between the patterns of dispersion of Piaget's animism stage levels for the two groups, and the groups did not differ significantly in stage level. At the higher MA level, however, the retarded subjects (who were, of course, also older than the nonretarded group) had significantly *more* advanced life concepts than their nonretarded MA peers. Following up on this finding, Russell et al. compared that portion of the retarded sample who were under 21 years of age with their older retarded MA peers; the group that had been at their presumably terminal MA for more years showed significantly more advanced life concepts. Russell et al. concluded that, although MA imposes restrictive limits on the effects of CA, experience does seem to enhance the development of the life concept, over and above the effects of MA alone. This conclusion and the finding upon which it is based represent our first support for Kohlberg's (1968) unconventional difference position on retardation.

Prothro (1943), however, in the study previously described, used the same interview procedure used by Russell et al. with his sample that included retarded individuals ranging in CA from 17 to 45 years and found no significant difference in life concepts between this group and much younger MA-matched normal subjects.

Granich (1940) used an interview similar to, but more diversified than, that used by Russell et al. and by Prothro. Granich's sample included public school boys of average (mean IQ: 102) and retarded (mean IQ: 56) intelligence who were matched for MA range (7 yr., 2 mo.-8 yr., 5 mo.). The etiologies represented in the retarded sample are not reported. Granich found that, in frequency of attribution of life (or attributes of living things) to animate and inanimate objects, these two subject groups were very similar, and that both were markedly inferior to a high-MA group of normal children. However, no significance tests were reported.

More recently, Smeets (1973, 1974) studied children's attributions of both life and specific life traits (e.g., dying, growing, feeling) to both animate and inanimate objects. In his first study, children's attributions were followed by the question, "What makes you think so?" Included in the sample were retarded subjects (IQs: 50-65; etiologies and setting unspecified) and nonretarded children (IQs: 90-110) matched for MA range (5 yr., 10 mo.-7 yr., 2 mo.). A third group of older nonretarded children (IQs: 90-110) were matched to the retarded group for CA range (11 yr., 0 mo.-12 yr., 0 mo.). Errors were most frequent among the young normal subjects and least frequent among the older normal subjects, but no tests of the significance of these differences were reported. However, a probability analysis of the distribution of types of errors indicated that the errors made by the retarded and younger normal group were largely due to guessing, whereas the errors made by the older normal group were not only less frequent but less capricious as well. In a second report, apparently based on the same experiment, Smeets (1974) presents significance tests for differences among the groups just described. In the attribution of life to animate objects the three groups differed significantly overall, but the retarded and MA-matched nonretarded did not. In the attribution of life to *inanimate* objects, and in the attribution of life *traits* to animate objects, the three groups did not differ significantly. Finally, attribution of life traits to *inanimate* objects was significantly less frequent among the older normal than the younger normal group, but neither group differed significantly from the retarded.

Artificialism. In Piaget's, *The Child's Conception of the World* (1929), he includes among the child's "prelogical" beliefs not only animism but artificialism—(i.e., the tendency to explain natural phenomena as resulting from deliberate activity of man or anthropomorphic beings). In the study by Granich, discussed earlier, there were a number of questions about the origin of natural phenomena (e.g., flower seeds). Granich found that responses indicative of artificialism were virtually nonexistent among the 13- and 14-year-old nonretarded boys in his sample, and slightly *less* frequent among his retarded sample than among their normal MA peers. The difference between these latter two groups was not tested for significance, but it is very small and would almost certainly have been nonsignificant.

Realism and the Dream Concept. A third "prelogical" belief attributed by Piaget (1929) to the young child is *realism*, one reflection of which is the inability to distinguish between external objects and one's thoughts and dreams. Granich's (1940) interviews also included questions designed to tap realism (e.g., the belief that dreams actually appear during the night on the ceiling of the bedroom). Again, Granich found that the 13- and 14-year-old boys he had sampled showed virtually no realism, whereas the retarded group showed slightly (but almost certainly nonsignificantly) fewer such responses than their nonretarded MA peers.

The DeVries (1970, 1973a, b) investigation, described previously, also included an assessment of children's dream concepts. In this portion of the study, whereas average-IQ children differed significantly from their CA peers of high IQ, the MA-matched average- and high-IQ children did not differ significantly.

Magic. In a related feature of the DeVries study, children's notions with regard to magic (Piaget, 1930) were assessed. Here again, whereas the CA-matched average- and high-IQ children did differ significantly, the MA-matched average- and low-IQ subjects did not.

Causality. In *Judgment and Reasoning in the Child,* Piaget (1928) discussed the child's developing ability to understand causal relations, partly reflected in a growing capacity to use the word "because" correctly. In Prothro's (1943) comparative study, described earlier, the subjects were all asked to complete five sentence beginnings ending in the word, "because" (e.g., "The boy hurt his leg because . . ."). Responses were scored on the basis of whether they actually described a causal relationship. Prothro's retarded sample was significantly less adept at this task than the MA-matched group of nonretarded children.

Quantitative Concepts (Other than Conservation)

Classification and Class Inclusion. Turning now to concepts in the quantitative domain, we begin with a discussion of research on one of the simplest quantitative behaviors—grouping objects into classes. Apparently, the earliest comparative study of classification bearing on the similar-structure hypothesis was the Prothro (1943) investigation described earlier. Prothro presented subjects with three tasks (beads, pencils, and pasteboard shapes), each of which called for the child to sort objects twice into groups of things "that are just alike" or "that go together." Classification on the basis of color and of form were both possible in each task. With scores summed across the three tasks, Prothro's institutionalized retarded subjects were significantly inferior to nonretarded children of similar MA.

Because this task involves abstraction there is some question as to whether Prothro's findings may have been influenced by the possible inclusion of organic cases among his "undifferentiated" group of retarded subjects. At first glance, the Taylor-Achenbach (1975) study described earlier would appear to provide a helpful contrast to the Prothro experiment, because Taylor and Achenbach excluded all cases with signs of organicity and because their procedure included a classification task quite similar to those used by Prothro. However, Taylor and Achenbach's finding of no difference between MA-matched retarded and nonretarded subjects must be interpreted with caution; the fact that *all* their subjects succeeded at the task suggests that it may have been too simple to reveal group differences.

Finally, the DeVries (1970, 1973a, b) investigation described earlier included a classification ("sorting") and a class inclusion problem (neither problem described in detail). On neither problem did DeVries' retarded and average-IQ children of similar MA differ significantly. This may have reflected a floor effect on the sorting task, which did not show a CA effect either; but the no-difference finding with the class inclusion task appears to be more meaningful, because this task did show a highly significant ($p < .0001$) effect of CA.

Additive Composition. A concept closely related to classification is additive composition. Piaget (1952) described a three-stage, age-related process in the development of the ability to additively compose classes. Children in the first stage cannot compare subclasses with whole classes but can compare separate subclasses; during the second stage, children identify subclasses with the whole; finally, at the third stage, children have an abstract conception of subclasses within wholes. McManis (1968) tested this hypothesis using 90 elementary school nonretarded children (IQs: 85-115) and 90 institutionalized retarded children (IQs: 47-73; evidently not screened for organicity), matched at 6 MA levels. Presenting 22 round wooden beads, 20 yellow and 2 red, he asked children whether there were more wooden or more yellow beads. McManis found a significant increase in the proportion of stage-three responses and decrease in the proportion of stage-one responses (no stage-two responses were obtained) across MA levels for both retarded and nonretarded children. However, he found no significant difference between the retarded and nonretarded groups in their distributions of responses at the three stage levels.

Concept of Probability. The concept of probability was one of nine foci of a comparative study conducted by Stevenson, Hale, Klein, and Miller (1968). The concept was assessed by means of films and a test booklet employed with intact school classes, each seen as a group. The first task involved faces. Subjects were asked to notice that in a group of boys pictured in the test booklet some had dark hair and some light, whereas some wore glasses and some did not. There followed a series of questions asking the subjects to infer which of two characteristics was more probable, given certain information about characteristics and their frequency in the target population. Stevenson et al. (1968) gives an example: "I am thinking of a certain boy in the group who wears glasses. What color do you think his hair is, light or dark [p. 19]?" In the second task, information was presented concerning how many pegs of various colors were inside a certain box. Subjects were asked to use this frequency information to predict the outcome of blind drawings in which different numbers of pegs were taken from the box. The original sample used by Stevenson et al. included high-IQ (mean: about 119) children from a university laboratory school, average-IQ (mean: about 102) children from a public junior high school, and low-IQ (mean: about 72) children from public school classes for the educable retarded. Retarded subjects were reported to be "primarily" of the familial type, with cases of "gross motor or sensory impairment" excluded. In selecting this original sample, Stevenson et al. (1968) did not attempt to achieve MA matching, but they did compare the performance of retarded subjects with a fourth-grade, average-IQ group, whose MA was said to be: "comparable with that of the retarded S's [p. 29]." Mean MAs of the two groups are not reported, nor is any test reported to indicate whether the two groups differed significantly in MA. On both tests of the probability concept the retarded subjects were significantly inferior to the nonretarded fourth-grade contrast group.

Comparison of Gross, Intensive, and Extensive Quantities. In his analyses of the development of quantitative thinking, Piaget (1952) described three kinds of perceived quantity by which things are compared without actual measurement. The first and developmentally earliest is *gross quantity;* it is in evidence when children consider only uncoordinated perceptual relations of gross qualitative equality or difference. In the second, *intensive quantity,* children are said to compare quantities by seriating them along more than one dimension (e.g., width and height) concurrently. The third, and developmentally most advanced, was labeled *extensive quantity;* in this type of perceived quantity, children are capable of overruling apparent differences between two equal quantities by imposing equal units of measurement upon them. Using this typology, McManis (1969a) scored retarded and nonretarded children on their use of comparison processes with sticks, colored water, and beads. There was apparently no effort to systematically exclude retarded children suffering from organic impairment. The retarded children (IQ range: 47–73) were institutionalized, and the MA-matched nonretarded comparison subjects (IQ range: 85–115) were from public schools. Analyses indicated that across all three types of comparison combined nonretarded subjects significantly outperformed their retarded MA peers. Separate task-by-task analyses revealed that the two groups performed similarly in comparing gross quantities, but that the retarded individuals were significantly inferior in comparing intensive and extensive quantities. McManis' analysis of the cognitive operations required for comparison of intensive and extensive quantities led him to hypothesize that retarded persons may show deficits in seriation relative to their nonretarded MA peers.

Seriation. In a subsequent study McManis (1970) tested this hypothesis. The sample included institutionalized retarded persons (IQ range: 46-72) and nonretarded elementary school children (IQ range: 85-116), matched for MA at several MA levels (5 years-11 years). There is no indication that retarded subjects were screened for organicity. Subjects were asked first to arrange five sticks in order of increasing length, and second to insert four additional sticks of differing lengths into the arrangement in their appropriate position. As predicted (in McManis, 1969a), a significantly greater proportion of nonretarded than retarded subjects succeeded at the seriation task. When the analysis was broken into MA levels, McManis found that the retarded-nonretarded difference was only significant for subjects in the 5 to 7-year MA range.

Unlike the McManis (1970) study, the investigation by Taylor and Achenbach (1975) discussed earlier did systematically rule out retarded children suffering from organic impairment, and the Taylor-Achenbach study also included a measure of logical seriation. Subjects were presented with the following problem: "There are three brothers—Bob, Joe, and Dick. Bob is taller than Joe and Joe is shorter than Dick. Who is the shortest brother [p. 47]?" On this problem—which requires the ability to coordinate quantitative relations into a triadic series— Taylor and Achenbach found no significant difference between their MA-matched retarded and nonretarded subjects. They also found, however, that there was no significant effect of MA ($p = .13$) on this measure; for the purposes of our review, this raises a question as to whether the task employed may have been too simple to reveal group differences.

Transitivity. In the thinking of most Piagetians, the capacity to make transitive inference (e.g., "If $A > B$, and $B > C$, than $A > C$.") is closely related to the capacity to seriate. There are five studies of transitivity that have some bearing on the similar-structure hypothesis. One is the DeVries (1970, 1973a, b) investigation described previously. Her battery of tasks is described as including a "length transitivity" task (no other task details given in the available reports). Although the task did differentiate significantly between CA-matched high- and average-IQ subjects, low- and average-IQ subjects of similar MA did not differ in transitivity performance.

Gruen (1973) assessed transitivity of length among MA-matched familial retarded (mean IQ: 64) and nonretarded (mean IQ: 102) children, both from public schools. Three sticks of differing length were used, with stick A longer than B, and B longer than C. Subjects made comparisons between A and B, and between B and C, then were asked to infer the relative sizes of A and C. To prevent solutions based on perceptual acuity alone, sticks A and C were placed inside the arms of a Mueller–Lyer illusion so that the shorter stick appeared longer and vice versa. For half the subjects in each group a memory aid was provided to remind subjects of the results of the A versus B and the B versus C comparisons. In the memory-aid condition the retarded subjects made significantly fewer correct transitive judgments than the nonretarded subjects; in the no-memory-aid condition, the two groups did not differ significantly. Another way of describing the results is to note that for nonretarded subjects performance was significantly better in the memory-aid than in the no-memory-aid condition, whereas among retarded subjects the introduction of a memory aid made no significant difference. Gruen's interpretation was that these results reveal superior logical inference by nonretarded subjects (i.e., when all the information ordinarily stored in memory was concretely available, the retarded children did not use this information in the same logical, sequential manner as their nonretarded MA peers).

The Mueller–Lyer illusion procedure was also used by McManis (1970) to assess transitivity of length among the retarded and nonretarded samples described earlier. Although no concrete memory aid was employed, subjects were asked to recall the results of the original A versus B and B versus C transitive judgment. McManis found that nonretarded subjects made significantly more correct transitive inferences than did the MA-matched retarded subjects.

In another comparative investigation, McManis (1969a) assessed transitivity of length using the Mueller–Lyer procedure of McManis (1970), and transitivity of weight using a roughly parallel procedure, in which the weight of clay balls of different sizes was varied by imbedding differing amounts of metal within them. A substantial proportion of the institutionalized persons who made up the retarded sample were organically impaired. McManis does not report significance tests for the retarded versus MA-matched nonretarded contrast in his sample, but our own chi-square analyses of his data indicate that the retarded group made significantly fewer correct transitive inferences than the nonretarded, on both the length ($p < .01$) and the weight ($p < .01$) task.

Whereas the magnitude of Gruen's and McManis' findings on transitivity is certainly strong enough to make the findings convincing, the methodology they used has come under fire. In a study designed to assess the validity of the McManis findings in particular, Lutkus and Trabasso (1974) assessed length transitivity among institutionalized retarded adolescents at two MA levels, 5 years (mean IQ: 45) and 6 years (mean IQ: 51). The two MA groups were selected in an effort to match comparison groups of nonretarded children who had been administered the same transitivity procedure in a previous study (Bryant & Trabasso, 1971). Lutkus and Trabasso report no effort to screen the retarded sample for organicity. They express several concerns about the procedure used by McManis (key parts of which were also used by Gruen, 1973). One concern is the potentially distracting or conflict-inducing property of the inaccurate perceptual impression that the Mueller-Lyer illusion creates. A second concern is that requiring correct verbal explanations for transitive judgments can lead to misclassification of children who can actually reason transitively but cannot give lucid explanations of their reasoning processes; thus, requiring explanations can bias the results in favor of children with greater verbal facility. Using a procedure designed to deal with these concerns and to insure that children had learned the necessary preinference information (e.g., that $A > B$), Lutkus and Trabasso obtained results that differed substantially from those of both McManis (1969a, 1970) and Gruen (1973). Compared to the nonretarded, retarded subjects did require more trials to demonstrate learning of and memory for the necessary preinference information. However, once retention of this information was insured, the transitivity performance of the retarded and nonretarded groups did not differ significantly at either MA level.

Number-Concept Development. Finally, we located one study that compared nonretarded children on multiple number concepts (Cohn-Jones & Seim, 1978). There was apparently no screening for organicity in this study. The investigators compared the performance of 24 retarded (IQs: 61-85) and 24 nonretarded (IQs: 87-115) school children, matched for MA, on the Dodwell Number Concept Test (Dodwell, 1960). This test examines children's abilities in several areas, including the Piagetian domains of conservation of discontinuous quantity, seriation, and serial correspondence, then yields an overall number-concept score and an overall explanation score. The results indicated that no significant difference existed between the two groups on either score. The investigators concluded that MA, not IQ or chronological age per se, is most closely related to Piaget's stages of number concept development.

Studies of Conservation, with Etiology Uncontrolled

We now review studies in the most frequently studied Piagetian conceptual domain—conservation. Because the studies are so numerous it is useful to divide them into subgroups, and because of the concerns we expressed earlier about the importance of controlling etiology, we have chosen to group the studies according to whether they included systematic efforts to exclude organically impaired children from the retarded sample. Because cultural-familial retardation accounts for only about 75% of all cases of mental retardation (Zigler, 1967), experimenters who do not systematically exclude organic cases can reasonably be expected to have included a substantial proportion of them in any sizeable retarded sample. In our division of studies into two groups we have assigned to the "Etiology Uncontrolled" group, not only those that report no effort to eliminate organic cases, but also those whose authors somewhat ambiguously declare that cases involving "*gross* sensory or motor defect" were eliminated or that the retarded sample was "primarily" familial, because both declarations seem to imply the inclusion of at least some organically impaired children.

The study by DeVries (1970, 1973a, b), described earlier, included measures of conservation of *mass* (two tasks), *number, length,* and *continuous quantity* (liquid). In addition, two related concepts were assessed—the notions of constancy of *generic identity* and *sex identity*. On all these measures except one conservation of mass task, DeVries' high-IQ group was significantly superior to her CA-matched average-IQ group. Yet the MA-matched average- and low-IQ groups did not differ significantly on any of the seven tasks, save the sex-identity task. And on sex identity, the retarded group performed significantly *better* than the nonretarded group.

Kahn's (1976) investigation of moral and cognitive development, described earlier, included measures of conservation of *mass* and *weight.* Scores on the two measures were combined to form a composite "cognitive functioning" measure. When Kahn's sample of nonretarded children was compared to an MA-matched sample of moderately retarded children suffering from a variety of organic syndromes, the retarded group proved to be significantly inferior on the composite measure.

We have already described three studies by McManis that included assessments of conservation among MA-matched retarded and nonretarded groups. In one of these (McManis, 1969e), tests of conservation of *mass, weight,* and *volume* were employed. For each, children were asked to make a conservation *prediction* (e.g., "... *will* there be as much clay in the hotdog as in the ball...?"), a conversation *judgment* (e.g., "... *do* they both have the same amount of clay?"), and an *explanation* of their judgment. These three responses were summed to obtain a score for each type of conservation. Weight conservation scores showed significant effects of MA but did not differentiate MA-matched retarded and nonretarded subjects. There were significant retarded–nonretarded group differences on mass and volume conservation scores, with the nonretarded group superior on mass and the retarded group superior on volume.

In a second study, McManis (1969c) assessed conservation of *weight* (clay—using a procedure like that of McManis, 1969e) and of *length* (sticks) among MA-matched retarded and nonretarded groups. McManis' report does not include tests of the significance of MA effects or of retarded–nonretarded group differences; however, both MA effects are clearly very strong, whereas our own calculations (chi-square) using McManis' frequency data indicate that the negligible retarded–nonretarded group differences did not approach significance with respect to either type of conservation.

In the third study by McManis' (1970) MA-matched retarded and nonretarded subjects were given a two-part *length* conservation task. Whereas part one was a relatively standard-length conservation procedure, the second part, patterned after Smedslund (1961), was designed to assess subjects' susceptibility to inducement and extinction of conservation responses, and their ability to retain the conservation thus induced for a 1-week period. Success at this rather elaborate procedure was strongly MA related (though the MA effect was not tested); however, there was no reliable difference between retarded subjects and their nonretarded MA peers.

We have already described the study by Stevenson et al. (1968) in which children were group administered a variety of Piagetian and learning tasks by means of films and test booklets. The procedure included a conservation of *volume* task, in which subjects were asked to estimate the relative amounts of liquid displaced by two balls of clay with equal mass but dissimilar shapes. On this task, retarded subjects (both boys and girls, calculated separately) were significantly inferior to nonretarded fourth graders of "comparable" MA.

In an investigation by Goodnow and Bethon (1966), several subject groups were included, but for our purposes the only two of interest were a group of "dull" public school children (median IQ: 81) and an "average" public school group (median IQ: 110), matched person-for-person on MA. The Goodnow-Bethon procedure included measures of conservation of *mass* (clay), *weight* (clay), and *area* (of two fields, one with houses clustered at the side, the other with houses scattered about). In addition, there were two measures of conservation of *volume* (clay balls displacing water). Summing across all conservation measures except mass, the investigators found significant differences favoring 11-year olds of high IQ over 11-year olds of average IQ. Yet, summing over all conservation measures, Goodnow and Bethon found that the *MA-matched* groups of average and low IQ did not differ significantly. They did find some differences, however, when the measures were analyzed separately. On the weight measure and the two volume measures, the nonretarded group was significantly superior; on conservation of mass and area, differences were negligible and nonsignificant.

Brown (1973) studied conservation of *number* (two tasks, using colored blocks and colored M&Ms) and *continuous quantity* (colored water) among MA-matched children at three IQ levels. The bright (CA 4 yr., MA 6 yr.), average (CA and MA 6 yr.), and retarded (CA 8, MA 6) subject groups were all selected from public- and university-supported nursery and primary schools in England. On both conservation of number (two tasks combined) and of continuous quantity, Brown found the bright group significantly *inferior* to both average and retarded children of similar MA. But on both types of conservation the MA-matched retarded and average groups failed to differ significantly. Brown (1973) interpreted this overall pattern of findings as evidence that: "the young child with a high IQ is held back by sheer lack of experience that the additional CA provides [p. 378]." This interpretation is, of course, reminiscent of the unconventional difference theory advanced by Kohlberg (1968) and discussed earlier in this chapter.

Brekke and Williams (1974) administered three conservation of *weight* measures to nonretarded children (IQ range: 81-160) from public schools, and retarded children (IQ range: 24-86—note overlap with the "nonretarded" group), about half from public school special-education classes and half from residential institutions. The experimental procedure was patterned after Furth's (1964) 13-step sequence in which equal-sized balls of clay are taken through various transformations, and subjects' judgments as to their weight equivalence are obtained, along with explanations for those judgments. Combining subjects' responses to all conservation questions yielded one overall conservation of weight measure. Scores on this measure were higher for nonretarded subjects than for either institutional or public school retarded children. However, this difference was not meaningful, because the three groups had not been matched for MA, and the nonretarded group had much higher MAs than the other groups. In an effort to correct for this problem, Brekke and Williams carried out an analysis of covariance, with MA as covariate. The result was that the group difference continued to be significant, with nonretarded subjects superior and the two retarded groups very similar to one another. It should be noted, however, that the application of analysis of covariance to Piagetian data may pose both conceptual and statistical problems (Kappauf, 1976; Weisz, 1976), in part because the assumption of a linear relationship between variate and covariate (Winer, 1971) may be violated when the dependent variable is a stage-like phenomenon.

In a study that compared institutionalized retarded children (mean IQ: 63) to nonretarded public and private school children (mean IQ: 107) of similar MA, Cardozo and Allen (1975) used the Goldschmid-Bentler (1968) Concept Assessment Conservation Test. The test is designed to measure conservation concepts in six different areas: mass, number, weight, continuous and discontinuous quantity, and two-dimensional space. The investigators summed scores across all six types of conservation and found that retarded subjects were significantly inferior to the nonretarded contrast group having similar MA.

We have already described Achenbach's (1973) experiment in which children's surprise reactions to contrived changes in color, number, length, and continuous quantity were assessed. Nonretarded nursery and elementary school children (mean IQ: 116) were compared to a mixture of institutional and public school retarded subjects (mean IQ: 47). The retarded sample included 45 familial cases and 16 Down syndrome children. Initial analyses revealed no significant differences in frequency of surprise reactions between the Down and familial subgroups, so their data were analyzed together in the comparison of retarded with MA-matched nonretarded subjects. To effect this comparison, Achenbach formed 49 subject pairs in which retarded and nonretarded child were matched for MA, sex, race, and order of presentation of the tasks. Although there were significant differences among the four tasks in the frequency of surprise reactions they evoked, only one task revealed retarded-nonretarded differences. On the continuous quantity task retarded subjects showed marginally *more* frequent surprise reactions than the nonretarded ($p = .058$).[3]

Studies of Conservation, with Etiology Controlled

In another conservation study, Achenbach (1969) screened out all cases showing any indication of organicity. In this experiment, which we described earlier, conservation of length, area, and "volume" (actually, "continuous" and "discontinuous" quantity, in Piagetian terms) were assessed using four different tasks for each property. Each task involved an optical illusion that created a discrepancy between the actual and apparent size of a stimulus. Retarded subjects in the study averaged 58 in IQ; the nonretarded children averaged 128. From these two samples 48 retarded–nonretarded subject pairs were formed, with pair members matched for MA, sex, race, and task order. Of the 12 tasks, the majority showed no significant effects of MA or CA, and only one (discontinuous quantity—beads) revealed significant IQ-group differences, in conservation judgments, with nine retarded and one nonretarded subject failing to show a conservation response. Achenbach also scored subjects' explanations for their responses to the 12 illusion items. For all 12 items, these conservation explanations differentiated significantly ($p < .10$ for one item) between nonretarded subjects of low CA and MA and nonretarded subjects of higher CA and MA; yet, there were no significant differences on any item between the MA-matched retarded and nonretarded groups.

Keasey and Charles (1967) assessed conservation of *mass* (plasticine balls) among institutionalized retarded and public school nonretarded subjects matched, person-for-person, on MA. Subjects' simple conservation judgments (i.e., answers to the question of whether both balls have the same amount of clay even after a transformation in shape) and their explanations were recorded and scored. Both responses and explanations were significantly related to MA, but neither differentiated significantly between retarded and nonretarded subjects,

---

[3]The Achenbach study provides two examples of means by which problems resulting from motivational characteristics of retarded children may be circumvented. The use of brief, minimally verbal techniques for assessing conservation concepts could reasonably be expected to minimize the influence of group differences in motivation to persist (and group differences in verbal facility as well). In addition, Achenbach assessed subjects' IQ and MA scores by means of an "optimizing" procedure. The Stanford-Binet was administered in a manner calculated to encourage motivation to succeed, with each series of failures followed by simpler problems aimed at producing a success experience, before the examiner proceeded to the next items. Evidence (Zigler, Abelson, & Seitz, 1973; Zigler & Butterfield, 1968) suggests that such a procedure may correct mean underestimates of IQ as high as 10 points in children of lower socioeconomic status. Because the organically intact retarded are almost always from the lower SES, the maximizing procedure may contribute importantly to precision in the formation of experimental groups in any study having a bearing on the similar-structure hypothesis.

even when explanations were scored along four different dimensions according to content.

Earlier, we described Gruen and Vore's (1972) study of number (poker chips), weight (clay in various shapes), and continuous quantity (water) conservation, in retarded IQs: 55–80) and nonretarded (IQs: 90–120) public school pupils. The retarded and nonretarded groups were divided into three subgroups, at MAs of 5, 7, and 9 years. Using both conservation-judgment-alone and judgment-plus-explanation as dependent variables, Gruen and Vore found significant differences between MA levels within their sample and between CA-matched retarded and nonretarded subjects; yet, neither dependent variable differentiated significantly between retarded subjects and their MA peers, on any of the three conservation tasks, at any of the three MA levels.

Taylor and Achenbach's (1975) study of moral and cognitive development in public school retarded (mean IQ: 75) and nonretarded (mean IQ: 111) youngsters (described earlier) included two conservation tasks. One was a surprise task (from Achenbach, 1973) designed to gauge subjects' *color–identity* concepts; the second was an illusion task (from Achenbach, 1969) designed to gauge conservation of *continuous quantity*. The continuous-quantity task differentiated significantly between MA levels, but the color-identity task did not. On neither task were there significant differences between MA-matched retarded and nonretarded groups.

In Kahn's (1976) sequel to the Taylor–Achenbach (1975) study, more traditional measures were used to assess conservation of mass (clay) and weight (clay), and scores on both measures were combined to form a "cognitive score." As was described earlier, Kahn's sample included three MA-matched groups: nonretarded (mean IQ: 101), mildly retarded (mean IQ: 66), and moderately retarded (mean IQ: 45). The second group was screened for organicity, whereas the third group included organically impaired individuals. Composite scores of the nonretarded group were significantly superior to both the moderately and mildly retarded group.[4]

STATUS OF EVIDENCE ON THE SIMILAR-STRUCTURE HYPOTHESIS

Evidence having a direct bearing on the similar-structure hypothesis has now been drawn from 29 published experiments, involving a total of 104 comparisons between retarded and nonretarded groups with MA controlled. The Piagetian conceptual domains involved included moral judgment, role-taking, perspective

---

[4]This information was provided by Dr. Kahn in correspondence with Dr. Herman Spitz and with us. We are grateful for this supplement to data reported in Kahn (1976).

taking (spacial egocentrism), perceptual decentering, relative thinking, animism, artificialism, realism, magic, causality, logical contradiction, classification and class inclusion, additive composition, probability, seriation, number-concept development, transitivity, and numerous types of conservation. An uncritical overview of the box-score totals reveals the following: (1) of the 104 group comparisons, only 4 (4%) supported Kohlberg's (1968) *unconventional difference position* by revealing significantly superior performance among the retarded group; (2) some 25 comparisons (24%) supported the more *conventional difference position* (Milgram, 1973) by revealing significantly superior performance among the nonretarded group; and (3) 75 (72%) supported the similar-structure hypothesis generated by the *developmental position* (Zigler, 1969) by revealing no reliable difference between retarded and nonretarded groups.

Support for the developmental position seems even stronger if one critically examines the methodology employed in these studies. Throughout this review, we have stressed the importance of sampling homogeneous groups of retarded subjects by excluding the organically impaired. If we limit ourselves to those comparisons that meet this standard in their sampling procedures, we find that of the 33 comparisons satisfying the condition only three comparisons (10%) are inconsistent with the similar-structure hypothesis. So, the simple box-score evidence, to the extent that it can shed light on the developmental versus difference debate, seems to provide the greatest support for the developmental position and the allied similar-structure hypothesis.

The Similar-Structure Prediction and the Null Hypothesis

However, this body of evidence deserves more intense analysis than these simple tallies provide. Firstly, let us consider how the nature and direction of the evidence may have been influenced by the nature of the similar-structure hypothesis: It is essentially a null hypothesis—it predicts no difference between target groups. Within our discipline there has been a tradition of prejudice against the null hypothesis, a prejudice that may work against the similar-structure hypothesis in reviews like the present one. We are taught early in our statistics courses that the null hypothesis may be disconfirmed but never confirmed, we learn to regard findings of "no difference" as failure, and we discover that such findings do not often make it into print. For some time there has been a lively debate between statisticians of the Fisher and Yule school, who regard acceptance of a null hypothesis as inappropriate, and statisticians of the Neyman and Pearson school, who argue that if the null hypothesis can be tested it can also be accepted as valid (for discussion of the issues involved see Binder, 1963 and Grant, 1962). In defense of the latter position, Greenwald (1975) has argued that the tradition of discrimination against the null hypothesis may impede scientific progress; there may be inappropriately few publications on problems for which the null hypothesis is at least to a reasonable approximation true, and of these, a substantial proportion will incorrectly reject the hypothesis of no difference. According to this reasoning, findings supporting the similar-structure hypothesis may be underrepresented in the published reports reviewed here; this may have been particularly true in the years prior to a clear articulation of the developmental position and its "no-difference" prediction (Zigler, 1967, 1969), because the absence of a theoretical explanation for findings of no difference would, no doubt, undermine the publishability of such findings. We can neither gauge nor correct for the kind of bias discussed by Greenwald (1975); but we should note that if he is correct, then whatever support the present review identifies for the similar-structure hypothesis should probably be regarded as a conservative estimate.

Combining the Evidence

There remains the task of combining the results of the several studies reviewed previously, to provide for a statistically sound overall test of the similar-structure hypothesis. A variety of methods exists (Rosenthal, 1978). The most precise methods involve the pooling of exact significance levels and their corresponding Z scores, but these methods cannot be used in the absence of very complete statistical data. Such data (e.g., exact significance levels) were not reported in many of the published studies we reviewed and in many cases were not available through the authors. So, we selected an alternate approach that allowed us to use all the studies reviewed, while maintaining statistical rigor.[5] Our approach was a counting method that relies on the fact that, if a null hypothesis is true, differences between any two groups across independent studies should approximate a normal distribution. One consequence of this fact is that the proportion of significant differences in either direction found by chance should equal whatever alpha level is selected. As a result, an analysis can be performed using a chi-square statistic to determine whether the distribution of differences approximates a normal distribution, as it should if the null hypothesis is true. All that is required is knowledge concerning the number of significant differences and their respective directions.

All 104 comparisons summarized here satisfied this requirement. For our

---

[5]In an effort to obtain the information needed for pooling of exact significance levels, we mailed requests to the authors, then used follow up letters and phone calls where necessary. We reached nearly all the authors, but many had discarded or misplaced the data we needed. We also requested information on the *direction* of all nonsignificant differences between MA-matched retarded and nonretarded groups. Such information would have permitted a four-cell chi-square analysis (i.e., significant and nonsignificant differences favoring retarded and nonretarded groups) that would have allowed us to check for trends in directionality of differences. Even this information was unavailable for almost 20% of the total comparisons reviewed previously. We have satisfied ourselves that the analysis we have selected is the most precise one that allows us to include all relevant comparisons.

TABLE 14.1
Directional Comparisons of MA-Matched Retarded and Nonretarded Persons on Various Piagetian Tasks

Study	Direction of Difference		
	MR > NMR	MR ≅ NMR	MR < NMR
		Etiology Controlled	
Achenbach (1969)		C. of length × 4 C. of area × 4 C. of continuous quantity × 2 C. of discontinuous quantity	C. of discontinuous quantity[a]
Gruen (1973)		Transitivity (no memory aid)	Transitivity (memory aid)
Gruen & Vore (1972)		C. of number × 3 C. of weight × 3 C. of continuous quantity × 3	
Kahn (1976)		Moral judgment	
Keasey & Charles (1967)		C. of mass	C. of mass and weight (combined)
Taylor & Achenbach (1975)		C. of continuous quantity Color identity Relative thinking Role taking × 2 Seriation Moral judgment	
		Etiology Uncontrolled	
Achenbach (1973)	C. of continuous quantity	C. of number C. of color C. of length	
Brekke & Williams (1974)			C. of weight
Brown (1973)		C. of number C. of continuous quantity	

(continued)

TABLE 14.1 (*Continued*)

Study	Direction of Difference		
	MR > NMR	MR ≅ NMR	MR < NMR
		Etiology Controlled	
Cardozo & Allen (1975)		C. of mass, weight, two-dimensional space, continuous and discontinuous quantity (combined)	
Cohn-Jones & Seim (1978)		Multiple number concepts Number concept judgments	
DeVries (1970, 1973a,b)	Sex identity	C. of mass × 2 C. of number C. of length C. of continuous quantity Generic identity Classification Class inclusion Transitivity Relative thinking × 2 Dream concepts Magic	Role taking
Goodnow & Bethon (1966)		C. of mass C. of area	C. of weight C. of volume × 2
Granich (1940)[b]		Animism Artificialism Realism	
Kahn (1976)			Moral judgment C. of mass and weight (combined)
Lane & Kinder (1939)[c]		Relative thinking × 2	
Lutkus & Trabasso (1974)		Transitivity × 2	
McManis (1968)		Additive composition	
McManis (1969a)		C. of weight C. of length	Transitivity × 2
McManis (1969b)		Gross qualities	Intensive qualities Extensive qualities

(*continued*)

TABLE 14.1 (*Continued*)

Study	Direction of Difference		
	MR > NMR	MR ≅ NMR	MR < NMR
		Etiology Controlled	
McManis (1969c)	C. of volume	C. of weight	C. of mass
McManis (1969d)[b]			Relative thinking × 2
McManis (1970)		C. of length	Transitivity
			Seriation
Prothro (1943)		Animism	Relative thinking
			Classification
			Causality
Rubin & Orr (1974)		Perspective taking × 2	
Russell, Dennis, & Ash (1940)	Animism		
Smeets (1973, 1974)		Life attributions × 2	
		Life trait attributions × 2	
Smith (1977a)		Logical contradiction	
Smith (1977b)		Perceptual decentering	
Stevenson, Hale, Klein, & Miller (1968)[d]			Probability × ?
			C. of volume

Note: The abbreviation *MR* stands for mentally retarded subjects; *NMR* stands for nonretarded subjects; the symbol ≅ indicates that there was no reliable group difference; C. stands for Conservation.

[a] This result was only true for the initial conservation *response*. Conservation *explanation* scores on this task did not differentiate significantly between retarded and nonretarded groups.

[b] The directional designation of each comparison from this study in this table relies on the respective judgments of the authors, because no significance tests were reported.

[c] Lane and Kinder actually compared two groups of retarded persons, matched for MA but differing significantly in IQ.

[d] In this study, MA matching is only approximate and MA differences between retarded and nonretarded groups were not actually tested for significance.

purposes, we chose an alpha level of .05 for both tails of the distribution; thus, the expectation would be for 10% of the findings to be significant (5% on each tail) and 90% of the findings not to be significant. In other words, if the developmental hypothesis is true, then the comparisons should be distributed as follows: 5% should show the retarded significantly superior to the nonretarded; 90% should show no significant difference between retarded and nonretarded; and 5% should show the retarded significantly inferior to the nonretarded. Chi-square statistics were computed comparing the actual to the expected proportions, separately for etiology controlled and uncontrolled comparisons. A breakdown of each comparison into its appropriate category, with etiological groups separated, can be seen in Table 14.1. We classified studies as "etiology controlled" if their authors explicitly state that organically impaired persons were excluded from the retarded sample. The remainder of the studies were labeled "etiology uncontrolled." A tabulation of actual and expected frequencies for both etiology-controlled and -uncontrolled comparisons can be seen in Table 14.2.

The analyses indicated that the distribution of the etiology-uncontrolled comparisons was significantly different from that expected by chance, $X^2(2) = 101.53$, $p < .001$; the difference is attributable to a greater number of comparisons than expected showing differences favoring nonretarded subjects (see Table 14.1). The distribution of the etiology-controlled comparisons, on the other hand, was not significantly different from that expected by chance, $X^2(2) = 2.76$, $p > .25$; that is, the distribution of comparisons excluding the organically impaired retarded is not significantly different from that expected if the similar-structure hypothesis is true.[6,7]

Evidence on the Similar-Structure Hypothesis: Current Status and Future Prospects

Our analysis of the evidence indicates that research in which etiology has been systematically controlled (with cases of organicity screened out of the mentally retarded sample) has supported the similar-structure hypothesis, whereas research in which etiology has not been systematically controlled has supported the conventional difference position. The similar-structure hypothesis has been

---

[6]Spitz (in press), in a critique of the developmental position, has argued that four of the studies included in this table are questionable as regards the diagnostic categories in which we have placed them (i.e., whether or not they include organically impaired retarded persons). Whereas we agree with Spitz that the sample descriptions given in some of the studies do not permit complete certainty, we have adopted what seems to us a reasonable policy of classifying studies as having excluded organically impaired persons if their authors state explicitly that this procedure was followed. Nonetheless, as a check on whether the experiments questioned by Spitz might have distorted the pattern of results, we recalculated the chi-square analyses depicted in Table 14.2, excluding the four studies regarded by Spitz as doubtful (Achenbach, 1969; Cardozo & Allen, 1975; Goodnow & Bethon, 1966; Stevenson et al., 1968). The pattern of results was similar to that shown in Table 14.2. The table for comparisons in which organic subjects were not systematically excluded was again significant, $X^2 (2) = 25.28$, $p < .001$; the table for comparisons in which organic subjects were excluded was again nonsignificant, $X^2 (2) = 1.00$, $p > .5$. Spitz (in press) has also questioned eight of the studies cited in the table on the grounds that ceiling or floor effects on some of the measures used made findings of "no difference" mere artifacts. Once again, we recalculated the chi-square analyses, dropping those comparisons questioned by Spitz on these grounds. Once again, the etiology-uncontrolled table was significant, and the etiology-controlled table was not.

[7]The chi-square analyses reported in Table 14.2 involve some Ns and some expected frequencies that are lower than traditional standards permit. However, recent work by Camilli and Hopkins (1976) and by Roscoe and Byers (1971) indicates that the chi-square test is quite robust, even with expected values as low as 1 or 2 and Ns as low as 20.

TABLE 14.2
Directional Comparisons of MA-Matched Retarded and
Nonretarded Persons Summed Across Various Piagetian Tasks

Group	Direction of Difference		
	MR > NMR	MR ≅ NMR	MR < NMR
Etiology Controlled[a]			
Actual Total	0	30	3
Expected Total	1.65	29.7	1.65
Etiology Uncontrolled[b]			
Actual Total	4	45	22
Expected Total	3.55	63.9	3.55

Note: The abbreviation *MR* stands for mentally retarded subjects; *NMR* stands for nonretarded subjects; the symbol ≅ indicates that there was no reliable group difference.
[a] $X^2 (2) = 2.76, p > .25$.
[b] $X^2 (2) = 101.53, p < .001$.

clearly articulated as applicable *only* to nonorganically impaired children (Weisz & Zigler, 1979; Zigler, 1967; 1969). Thus, we must conclude that evidence drawn from populations actually addressed by the similar-structure hypothesis has supported that hypothesis.

On the other hand, the evidence is not without its flaws. Research bearing on the similar-structure hypothesis reflects a widespread inattention to the kinds of personality characteristics that may undermine performance in retarded children (Weisz, in press-a; Zigler, 1971). In few of the studies reviewed here was there an explicit effort to maximize motivation or self-confidence in the children sampled, prior to assessment of performance on the Piagetian tasks. Moreover, a substantial number of the retarded persons sampled in this research resided in institutions, and a number of these were adults, some middle aged. Previous research has demonstrated significant depressing effects of institutional living on quality of language behavior (Lyle, 1959; Schlanger, 1954), level of abstraction in vocabulary (Badt, 1958), and diverse types of learning activity (Denny, 1964; Harter, 1967). If we add to such potential environmental effects the motivational impact of asking a mentally retarded adult to work with modeling clay or otherwise engage in Piagetian tasks designed for preschool and elementary children, we must at least ponder the meaning of many of the retarded–nonretarded comparisons available in the data bank currently available.

Much of the evidence can also be faulted for imprecise MA matching, and of course for a failure to control for organicity. It is tempting to conclude that the differential pattern of results found here for studies that evidenced such control, versus those that did not, supports the "two-group" approach advocated by Zigler (1967)—the view that organically impaired retarded persons are cognitively different from those not suffering from specific organic deficits. This could mean that much of the support found for the conventional difference position is an artifact of organic impairment in the retarded samples. However, the data reviewed here do not yet warrant such a conclusion. This is because mean IQs in the samples that included organically impaired subjects were generally lower than mean IQs of the screened samples. Thus, IQ level and organicity are confounded across the studies reviewed. To generate more definitive evidence on the two-group approach in the future, investigators will need to accomplish the difficult task of disentangling organicity and IQ level by structuring designs in which the two factors are orthogonal.

OVERVIEW AND CONCLUDING COMMENTS

We have now examined a sizeable fund of Piagetian evidence, all of it relevant to the similar-sequence hypothesis, the similar-structure hypothesis, or both. Our review has revealed rather consistent support for the similar-sequence hypothesis, and somewhat equivocal support for the similar-structure hypothesis. As we noted earlier, many studies relevant to both hypotheses can be faulted on methodological grounds. Yet, pulling this evidence together and evaluating it can be a useful means of distilling what is known and retargeting our pursuit of knowledge in the future. A similar service is needed in domains of research other than Piagetian. Because of its vigorous cognitive-developmental emphasis, evidence from the Genevan tradition is certainly an appropriate focus for a review on the status of the developmental-difference controversy. But, as other chapters in this book illustrate, the controversy addresses numerous processes of learning and reasoning that fall outside the range of Piagetian theory. Some of these processes have stimulated sufficient research by now that they too warrant critical analysis of the sort undertaken here. It is through such analysis, critical in its perspective and ever broadening in its purview, that we may best consolidate the gains in knowledge stimulated by this important theoretical debate.

REFERENCES

Abel, T. M. Moral judgments among subnormals. *Journal of Abnormal and Social Psychology,* 1941, *36,* 378–392.

Achenbach, T. M. Conservation of illusion-distorted identity: Its relation to MA and CA in normals and retardates. *Child Development,* 1969, *40,* 663–679.

Achenbach, T. M. Comparison of Stanford–Binet performance of nonretarded and retarded persons matched for MA and sex. *American Journal of Mental Deficiency,* 1970, *74,* 488–494.

Achenbach, T. M. Stanford–Binet Short-Form performance of retarded and nonretarded persons matched for MA. *American Journal of Mental Deficiency,* 1971, *76,* 30–32.

Achenbach, T. M. Surprise and memory as indices of concrete operational development. *Psychological Reports,* 1973, *33,* 47–57.

Anastasi, A. Heredity, environment, and the question "How?" *Psychological Review*, 1958, *65*, 197-208.
Badt, M. I. Levels of abstraction in vocabulary definitions of mentally retarded school children. *American Journal of Mental Deficiency*, 1958, *63*, 241-246.
Balla, D., Styfco, S. J., & Zigler, E. Use of the opposition concept and outerdirectedness in intellectually average, familial retarded, and organically retarded children. *American Journal of Mental Deficiency*, 1971, *75*, 663-680.
Balla, D., & Zigler, E. Discrimination and switching learning in normal, familial retarded, and organic retarded children. *Journal of Abnormal and Social Psychology*, 1964, *61*, 664-669.
Binder, A. Further considerations on testing the null hypothesis and the strategy and tactics of investigating theoretical models. *Psychological Review*, 1963, *70*, 107-115.
Blount, W. R. Concept usage research with the mentally retarded. *Psychological Bulletin*, 1968, *69*, 218-294.
Braine, M. D. S., & Shanks, B. The conservation of a shape property and a proposal about the origins of the conservations. *Canadian Journal of Psychology*, 1965, *19*, 197-207. (a)
Braine, M. D. S., & Shanks, B. The development of conservation of size. *Journal of Verbal Learning and Verbal Behavior*, 1965, *4*, 227-242. (b)
Brekke, B., & Williams, J. D. Conservation of weight with the mentally retarded. *Journal of Genetic Psychology*, 1974, *125*, 225-231.
Brown, A. L. Conservation of number and continuous quantity in normal, bright, and retarded children. *Child Development*, 1973, *44*, 376-379.
Bryant, P. E., & Trabasso, T. Transitive inferences and memory in young children. *Nature*, 1971, *232*, 456-458.
Buck-Morss, S. Socioeconomic bias in Piaget's theory and its implications for cross-culture studies. *Human Development*, 1975, *18*, 35-49.
Camilli, G., & Hopkins, K. D. Applicability of chi-square to 2 × 2 contingency tables with small expected cell frequencies. *Psychological Bulletin*, 1976, *85*, 163-167.
Cardozo, C. W., & Allen, R. M. Contribution of visual perceptual maturation to the ability to conserve. *American Journal of Mental Deficiency*, 1975, *79*, 701-704.
Charlesworth, W. R. The role of surprise in cognitive development. In D. Elkind & J. H. Flavell (Eds.), *Studies in cognitive development: Essays in honor of Jean Piaget*. New York: Oxford University Press, 1969.
Cicchetti, D., & Sroufe, L. A. The relationship between affective and cognitive development in Down syndrome infants. *Child Development*, 1976, *47*, 920-929.
Cohn-Jones, L., & Seim, R. Perceptual and intellectual factors affecting number concept development in retarded and nonretarded children. *American Journal of Mental Deficiency*, 1978, *83*, 9-15.
Cole, M., & Bruner, J. Cultural differences and inferences about psychological processes. *American Psychologist*, 1971, *26*, 867-876.
Cromwell, R. L. A social learning approach to mental retardation. In N. R. Ellis (Ed.), *Handbook of mental deficiency*. New York: McGraw-Hill, 1963.
Decarie, T. G. *Intelligence and affectivity in early childhood*. New York: International Universities Press, 1965.
Denny, M. R. Research in learning and performance. In H. A. Stevens & R. Heber (Eds.), *Mental retardation: A review of research*. Chicago: University of Chicago Press, 1964.
DeVries, R. The development of role-taking as reflected by behavior of bright, average, and retarded children in a social guessing game. *Child Development*, 1970, *41*, 759-770.
DeVries, R. *Performance on Piaget-type tasks of high-IQ, average-IQ, and low-IQ children*. Paper presented at the meeting of the Society for Research in Child Development, Philadelphia, Pa., 1973. (ERIC Document Reproduction Service No. ED086 374/PS007 129). (a)
DeVries, R. *The two intelligences of bright, average, and retarded children*. Paper presented at the

meeting of the Society for Research in Child Development, Philadelphia, Pa., 1973 (ERIC Document Reproduction Service No. ED 079/102/SE 016 419). (b)

DeVries, R. Relationships among Piagetian, IQ, and achievement assessments. *Child Development,* 1974, *45,* 746-756.

Dodwell, P. Children's understanding of number and related concepts. *Canadian Journal of Psychology,* 1960, *14,* 191-205.

Elkind, D. The development of quantitative thinking. *Journal of Genetic Psychology,* 1961, *98,* 36-46.

Elkind, D., Koegler, R., & Go, E. Studies in perceptual development: II. Part-whole perception. *Child Development,* 1964, *35,* 81-90.

Elkind, D., Koegler, R. R., Go, E., & Van Doorninck, W. Effects of perceptual training on unmatched samples of brain-injured and familial retarded children. *Journal of Abnormal Psychology,* 1965, *70,* 107-110.

Ellis, N. R. A behavioral research strategy in mental retardation: Defense and critique. *American Journal of Mental Deficiency,* 1969, *73,* 557-566.

Flavell, J. H., Botkin, P. T., Fry, C. L., Wright, J. W., & Jarvis, P. E. *The development of role-taking and communication skills in children.* New York: Wiley, 1968.

Furth, H. G. Conservation of weight in deaf and hearing children. *Child Development,* 1964, *35,* 143-150.

Gibson, B. J. *An attributional analysis of performance outcomes and alleviation of learned helplessness on motor performance tasks: A comparative study of educable mentally retarded and nonretarded boys.* Unpublished doctoral dissertation, University of Alberta, 1980.

Goldschmid, M., & Bentler, P. M. The dimension and measurement of conservation. *Child Development,* 1968, *39,* 787-802.

Goodnow, J. J., & Bethon, G. Piaget's tasks: The effects of schooling and intelligence. *Child Development,* 1966, *37,* 573-582.

Granich, L. A qualitative analysis of concepts in mentally deficient schoolboys. *Archives of Psychology,* 1940, *251,* 1-47.

Grant, D. A. Testing the null hypothesis and the strategy and tactics of investigating theoretical models. *Psychological Review,* 1962, *69,* 54-61.

Green, B. F. A method for scalogram analysis using summary statistics. *Psychometrika,* 1956, *21,* 79-88.

Greenwald, A. G. Consequences of prejudice against the null hypothesis. *Psychological Bulletin,* 1975, *82,* 1-20.

Gruen, G. E. Memory, IQ, and transitive inference in normals and retardates. *Developmental Psychology,* 1973, *9,* 436.

Gruen, G. E., & Vore, D. A. Development of conservation in normal and retarded children. *Developmental Psychology,* 1972, *6,* 146-157.

Guttman, L. The basis of scalogram analysis. In S. A. Stouffer et al. (Eds.), *Measurement and prediction* (Vol. 4). Princeton, N. J.: Princeton University Press, 1950.

Harter, S. Mental age, IQ, and motivational factors in the discrimination learning set performance of normal and retarded children. *Journal of Experimental Child Psychology,* 1967, *5,* 123-141.

Harter, S., Brown, L., & Zigler, E. The discrimination learning of normal and retarded children as a function of penalty conditions and etiology of the retarded. *Child Development,* 1971, *42,* 517-536.

Heber, R. T. Personality. In H. A. Stevens & R. T. Heber (Eds.), *Mental retardation: A review of research.* Chicago: University of Chicago Press, 1964.

Houssiadas, L., & Brown, L. B. The coordination of perspectives by mentally retarded children. *Journal of Genetic Psychology,* 1967, *110,* 211-215.

Hunt, J. McV. Discussion: Developmental gains in reasoning. *American Journal of Mental Deficiency,* 1974, *79,* 127-133.

Inhelder, B. *The diagnosis of reasoning in the mentally retarded.* New York: Day, 1968 (Originally published, 1943).
Jordan, V. B. *Cognitive development among retardates: Reanalysis of Inhelder's data.* Paper presented at the meeting of the Society for Research in Child Development, Denver, Colo., 1976 (ERIC Document Reproduction Service No. EB 121 035/EC 082 713).
Kahn, J. V. Moral and cognitive development in moderately retarded, mildly retarded, and nonretarded individuals. *American Journal of Mental Deficiency,* 1976, *81,* 209-214.
Kamin, L. J. *The science and politics of IQ.* Potomac, Md.: Lawrence Erlbaum Associates, 1975.
Kappauf, W. E. Critique of the use of covariance adjustments for CA and MA in comparative studies of retarded and nonretarded persons. *American Journal of Mental Deficiency,* 1976, *81,* 240-247.
Keasey, C. T., & Charles, D. C. Conservation of substance in normal and retarded children. *Journal of Genetic Psychology,* 1967, *111,* 271-279.
Klauss, S. D., & Green, M. B. Conservation in trainable mentally retarded children. *Training School Bulletin,* 1972, *69,* 108-114.
Kohlberg, L. Early education: A cognitive-developmental view. *Child Development,* 1968, *39,* 1013-1062.
Kohlberg, L. Stage and sequence: The cognitive-developmental approach to socialization. In D. Goslin (Ed.), *Handbook of socialization theory and research.* Chicago: Rand McNally, 1969.
Kohlberg, L. From is to ought: How to commit the naturalistic fallacy and get away with it in the study of moral development. In T. Mischel (Ed.), *Cognitive development and epistemology.* New York: Academic Press, 1971.
Kohlberg, L. Discussion: Developmental gains in moral judgment. *American Journal of Mental Deficiency,* 1974, *79,* 142-146.
Kohlberg, L., & DeVries, R. Relations between Piagetian and psychometric assessments of intelligence. In C. Lavatelli (Ed.), *The natural curriculum.* Urbana: University of Illinois Press, 1971.
Kooistra, W. H. Developmental trends in the attainment of conservation, transitivity, and the relativism in the thinking of children: A replication and extension of Piaget's ontogenetic formulations. (Doctoral dissertation, Wayne State University, 1963). *Dissertation Abstracts,* 1964, *25,* 2032 (University Microfilms No. 64-9538).
Kounin, J. *Experimental studies of rigidity as a function of age and feeblemindedness.* Unpublished doctoral dissertation. State University of Iowa, 1939.
Kounin, J. Experimental studies of rigidity: I. The measurement of rigidity in normal and feebleminded persons. *Character and Personality,* 1941, *9,* 251-272. (a)
Kounin, J. S. Experimental studies of rigidity: II. The explanatory power of the concept of rigidity as applied to feeblemindedness. *Character and Personality,* 1941, *9,* 273-282. (b)
Kounin, J. S. The meaning of rigidity: A reply to Heinz Werner. *Psychological review,* 1948, *55,* 157-166.
Kuhn, D. *The development of role-taking ability.* Unpublished manuscript, Columbia University, 1972.
Labov, W. The logical nonstandard English. In F. Williams (Ed.), *Language and poverty.* Chicago: Markham Press, 1970.
Lane, E. B., & Kinder, E. F. Relativism in the thinking of subnormal subjects as measured by certain of Piaget's tests. *Journal of Genetic Psychology,* 1939, *54,* 107-118.
Lerner, E. *Constraint areas and the moral judgment of children.* Memasha, Wis.: Banta, 1937.
Lerner, E. Observations sur le raisonnement moral de l'enfant. *Cahiers pedagogiques experimentaux et psychologiques de l'enfant* (Vol. No. 11). Geneva: Palais-Wilson, 1938.
Lewin, K. *A dynamic theory of personality.* New York: McGraw-Hill, 1936.
Lister, C. The development of ESN children's understanding of conservation in a range of attribute situations. *British Journal of Educational Psychology,* 1972, *42,* 14-22.

Lovell, K., Healey, D., & Rowland, A. D. Growth of some geometric concepts. *Child Development,* 1962, *33,* 751-767.
Lovell, K., Mitchell, B., & Everett, I. R. An experimental study of the growth of some logical structures. *British Journal of Psychology,* 1962, *53,* 175-188.
Lovell, K., & Slater, A. The growth of the concept of time: A comparative study. *Child Psychology and Psychiatry,* 160, 1, 179-190.
Lunzer, E. A. *Recent studies in Britain based on the work of Jean Piaget.* Occasional Publication No. 4. The National Foundation for Educational Research in England and Wales, 1961.
Luria, A. R. Psychological studies of mental deficiency in the Soviet Union. In N. R. Ellis (Ed.), *Handbook of mental deficiency.* New York: McGraw-Hill, 1963.
Lutkus, A., & Trabasso, T. Transitive inferences by preoperational retarded adolescents. *American Journal of Mental Deficiency,* 1974, *78,* 599-606.
Lyle, L. The effect of an institutional environment upon the verbal development of imbecile children: I. Verbal intelligence. *Journal of Mental Deficiency Research,* 1959, *3,* 122-128.
Mahaney, E. J., & Stephens, B. Two-year gains in moral judgment by retarded and nonretarded persons. *American Journal of Mental Deficiency,* 1974, *79,* 134-141.
Mannix, J. B. The number concepts of a group of E. S. N. children. *British Journal of Educational Psychology,* 1960, *30,* 180-181.
Marchi, J. U. Comparison of selected Piagetian tasks with the Wechsler Intelligence Scale for Children as measures of mental retardation. (Doctoral dissertation, University of California, Berkeley, 1970). *Dissertation Abstracts International,* 1971, *31,* 6442A (University Microfilms No. 71-51, 833).
McManis, D. L. Additive composition by normal and retarded children of matched MA. *Psychonomic Science,* 1968, *11,* 207.
McManis, D. L. Comparisons of gross, intensive, and extensive quantities by normals and retardates. *Child Development,* 1969, *40,* 237-244. (a)
McManis, D. L. Comparison of gross, intensive, and extensive quantities by retardates. *Journal of Genetic Psychology,* 1969, *115,* 229-236. (b)
McManis, D. L. Conservation and transitivity of weight and length by normals and retardates. *Developmental Psychology,* 1969, *1,* 373-382. (c)
McManis, D. L. Conservation of identity and equivalence of quantity by retardates. *Journal of Genetic Psychology,* 1969, *115,* 63-69. (d)
McManis, D. L. Conservation of mass, weight, and volume by normal and retarded children. *American Journal of Mental Deficiency,* 1969, *73,* 762-787. (e)
McManis, D. L. Relative thinking by normals and retardates. *Developmental Psychology,* 1969, *1,* 69. (f)
McManis, D. Conservation, seriation, and transitivity performance by retarded and average individuals. *American Journal of Mental Deficiency,* 1970, *74,* 784-791.
Mermelstein, E., & Shulman, L. S. Lack of formal schooling and the acquisition of conservation. *Child Development,* 1967, *38,* 39-52.
Milgram, D. A. The rationale and irrational in Zigler's motivational approach to mental retardation. *American Journal of Mental Deficiency,* 1969, *73,* 527-532.
Milgram, N. A. Cognition and language in mental retardation: Distinctions and implications. In D. K. Routh (Ed.), *The experimental psychology of mental retardation.* Chicago: Aldine, 1973.
Nassafat, M. *Etude quantitative sur l'evolution de operations intellectuelles: Le passage des operations concretes aux operations formelle.* Neuchatel, Switzerland: Delachaux et Niestle, 1963.
Overton, W. F. On the assumptive base of the nature-nurture controversy: Additive versus interactive conceptions. *Human Development,* 1973, *16,* 74-89.
Papalia, D., & Hooper, F. A developmental comparison of identity and equivalence. *Journal of Experimental Child Psychology,* 1971, *12,* 347-361.
Piaget, J. *Judgment and reasoning in the child.* New York: Harcourt Brace, 1928.

Piaget, J. *The child's conception of the world*. New York: Harcourt Brace, 1929.
Piaget, J. *The child's conception of physical causality*. London: Kegan Paul, 1930.
Piaget, J. *The child's conception of number*. New York: Humanities Press, 1952.
Piaget, J. The general problem of the psychobiological development of the child. *Discussions on Child Development*, 1956, *4*, 3-27.
Piaget, J. Necessité et signification des récherches comparatives en psychologie genetique. *International Journal of Psychology*, 1966, *1*, 3-13.
Piaget, J. Preface. In B. Inhelder, *The diagnosis of reasoning in the mentally retarded*. New York: Chandler, 1968.
Piaget, J., & Inhelder, B. *The child's conception of space*. New York: Humanities Press, 1956.
Piaget, J., Inhelder, B., & Szeminska, A. *The child's conception of geometry*. New York: Routledge & Kegan Paul, 1960.
Popper, K. R. *The logic of scientific discovery*. New York: Basic Books, 1959.
Prothro, E. T. Egocentricity and abstraction in children and in adult aments. *American Journal of Psychology*, 1943, *56*, 66-77.
Rogers, S. J. Characteristics of the cognitive development of profoundly retarded children. *Child Development*, 1977, *48*, 837-843.
Roodin, P. A., Sullivan, L., & Rybash, J. M. Effects of a memory aid on three types of conservation in institutionalized retarded children. *Journal of Genetic Psychology*, 1976, *129*, 253-259.
Roscoe, J. T., & Byars, J. A. An investigation of the restraints with respect to sample size commonly imposed on the use of the chi-square statistic. *Journal of the American Statistical Association*, 1971, *66*, 755-759.
Rosenthal, R. Combining results of independent studies. *Psychological Bulletin*, 1978, *85*, 185-193.
Rubin, K. H., & Orr, P. R. Spatial egocentrism in nonretarded and retarded children. *American Journal of Mental Deficiency*, 1974, *79*, 95-97.
Russell, R. W., Dennis, W., & Ash, F. E. Studies in animism: III. Animism in feebleminded subjects. *Journal of Genetic Psychology*, 1940, *57*, 57-63.
Sarason, S. B., & Doris, J. *Psychological problems in mental deficiency*. New York: Harper & Row, 1969.
Schlanger, B. B. Environmental influences on the verbal output of mentally retarded children. *Journal of Speech and Hearing Disorders*, 1954, *19*, 339-345.
Siegelman, E., & Block, J. Two scalable sets of Piagetian tasks. *Child Development*, 1969, *40*, 951-956.
Simpson, E. L. Moral development research: A case study of scientific culture bias. *Human Development*, 1974, *17*, 81-106.
Singh, N. N., & Stott, G. The conservation of number in mental retardates. *Australian Journal of Mental Retardation*, 1975, *3*, 215-221.
Smedslund, J. The acquisition of conservation of substance and weight in children: VI. Practice on continuous versus discontinuous material in conflict situations without external reinforcement. *Scandinavian Journal of Psychology*, 1961, *2*, 203-210.
Smedslund, J. Concrete reasoning: A study of intellectual development. *Monographs of the Society for Research in Child Development*, 1964, *29* (2, Serial No. 93).
Smeets, P. M. The animism controversy: A probability analysis. *Journal of Genetic Psychology*, 1973, *124*, 17-27.
Smeets, P. M. The influence of MA and CA on the attribution of life and life traits to animate and inanimate objects. *Journal of Genetic Psychology*, 1974, *124*, 17-27.
Smith, J. D. EMR and nonretarded children's reactions to contradiction. *American Journal of Mental Deficiency*, 1977, *82*, 94-97. (a)
Smith, J. D. Perceptual decentering in EMR and nonretarded children. *American Journal of Mental Deficiency*, 1977, *81*, 499-501. (b)

Sroufe, L. A., & Wunsch, J. P. The development of laughter in the first year of life. *Child Development*, 1972, *43*, 1326-1344.

Stearns, K., & Borkowski, J. G. The development of conservation and horizontal-vertical space perception in mental retardation. *American Journal of Mental Deficiency*, 1969, *73*, 785-790.

Stephens, B. *The development of reasoning, moral judgment, and moral conduct in retardates and normals: Phase II.* Philadelphia: Temple University, 1972.

Stephens, B. Symposium: Developmental gains in the reasoning, moral judgment, and moral conduct of retarded and nonretarded persons. *American Journal of Mental Deficiency*, 1974, *79*, 113-115.

Stephens, B., Mahaney, E. J., & McLaughlin, J. A. Mental ages for achievement of Piagetian reasoning assessments. *Education and Training of the Mentally Retarded*, 1972, *7*, 124-128.

Stephens, B., & McLaughlin, J. A. Two-year gains in reasoning by retarded and nonretarded persons. *American Journal of Mental Deficiency*, 1974, *79*, 116-126.

Stephens, B., McLaughlin, J. A., Hunt, J. McV., Mahaney, E. J., Kohlberg, L., Moore, G., & Aronfreed, J. Symposium: Developmental gains in the reasoning, moral judgment, and moral conduct of retarded and nonretarded persons. *American Journal of Mental Deficiency*, 1974, *79*, 113-161.

Stevenson, H. W. Social reinforcement of children's behavior. In L. P. Lipsitt & C. Spiker (Eds.), *Advances in child development* (Vol. II). New York: Academic Press, 1965.

Stevenson, J. W., Hale, G. A., Klein, R., & Miller, L. Interrelations and correlations in children's learning and problem solving. *Monographs of the Society for Research in Child Development*, 1968, *33* (7, Serial No. 123).

Taylor, J. J., & Achenbach, T. M. Moral and cognitive development in retarded and nonretarded children. *American Journal of Mental Deficiency*, 1975, *80*, 43-50.

Tulkin, S. R., & Konner, M. J. Alternative conceptions of intellectual functioning. *Human Development*, 1973, *16*, 33-52.

Uzgiris, I. Situational generality of conservation. In I. Sigel & F. Hooper (Eds.), *Logical thinking in children: Research based on Piaget's theory*. New York: Holt, Rinehart, & Winston, 1968.

Weisz, J. R. Studying cognitive development in retarded and nonretarded groups: The role of theory. *American Journal of Mental Deficiency*, 1976, *81*, 235-239.

Weisz, J. R. Transcontextual validity in developmental research. *Child Development*, 1978, *49*, 1-12.

Weisz, J. R. Perceived control and learned helplessness among mentally retarded and nonretarded children: A developmental analysis. *Developmental Psychology*, 1979, *15*, 311-319.

Weisz, J. R. Learned helplessness and the retarded child. In E. Zigler & D. Balla (Eds.), *Mental retardation: The developmental-difference controversy*. Hillsdale, N. J.: Lawrence Erlbaum Associates, in press. (a)

Weisz, J. R. Learned helplessness in black and white children identified as retarded and nonretarded: Performance deterioration in response to failure. *Developmental Psychology*, in press. (b)

Weisz, J. R., & Zigler, E. Cognitive development in retarded and nonretarded persons: Piagetian tests of the similar-sequence hypothesis. *Psychological Bulletin*, 1979, *86*, 831-851.

Winer, B. J. *Statistical principles in experimental design* (2nd ed.). New York: McGraw-Hill, 1971.

Wohlhueter, M. J., & Sindberg, R. M. Longitudinal development of object permanence in mentally retarded children: An exploratory study. *American Journal of Mental Deficiency*, 1975, *79*, 513-518.

Woodward, M. The behavior of idiots interpreted by Piaget's theory of sensorimotor development. *British Journal of Educational Psychology*, 1959, *29*, 60-71.

Woodward, M. Concepts of number of the mentally subnormal studied by Piaget's method. *Journal of Child Psychology and Psychiatry*, 1961, *2*, 249-259.

Woodward, M. Concepts of space in the mentally subnormal studied by Piaget's method. *British*

Journal of Social and Clinical Psychology, 1962, *1,* 25-37.

Woodward, M. The application of Piaget's theory to research in mental deficiency. In N. R. Ellis (Ed.), *Handbook of mental deficiency.* New York: McGraw-Hill, 1963.

Zigler, E. Familial mental retardation: A continuing dilemma. *Science,* 1967, *155,* 292-298.

Zigler, E. Developmental versus difference theories of mental retardation and the problem of motivation. *American Journal of Mental Deficiency,* 1969, *73,* 536-556.

Zigler, E. The retarded child as a whole person. In H. E. Adams & W. K. Boardman (Eds.), *Advances in experimental clinical psychology.* New York: Pergamon Press, 1971.

Zigler, E., Abelson, W., & Seitz, V. Motivational factors in the performance of economically disadvantaged children on the Peabody Picture Vocabulary Test. *Child Development,* 1973, *44,* 294-303.

Zigler, E., & Butterfield, E. C. Motivational aspects of changes in IQ test performance of culturally deprived nursery school children. *Child Development,* 1968, *39,* 1-14.

Zigler, E., & Harter, S. Socialization of the mentally retarded. In D. A. Goslin (Ed.), *Handbook of socialization theory and research.* Chicago: Rand-McNally, 1969.

15 Possible Contributions of the Study of Organically Retarded Persons to Developmental Theory

Dante Cicchetti
Petra Pogge-Hesse
Harvard University

INTRODUCTION

The perspective within which development is viewed greatly influences the interpretation of data on child behavior and growth. Research questions, of course, follow directly from an investigator's conceptualizations. Even analysis and interpretation of the same set of data can be seen as validation of a construct from one conception or as disconfirmation of that construct from another viewpoint.

Personality development, for example, may be viewed in terms of static traits or in terms of organizational constructs (Block, 1971, 1977; Block & Block, 1979). From the static trait view isomorphic stability (what Kagan, 1969, 1971, has called homotypic continuity) is predicted; that is, "dependent" infants are expected to be dependent children, and so forth. Moreover, various indices of the trait (for example, crying, clinging, proximity seeking) are expected to intercorrelate highly and to be manifested similarly across situations and across time. A number of reviews of personality research have underscored the failures of personologists to show stability of frequency, amount, and duration of discrete behaviors over time (Fiske, 1974; Kagan & Moss, 1962; Mischel, 1968). In addition, whereas variance in behavior attributable to situational factors or to the interactions of individuals and situations has frequently been demonstrated, variance attributable to individual differences in person variables has been difficult to establish (Endler & Magnusson, 1976; Mischel, 1968, 1969). When behavioral indices do not intercorrelate or fail to demonstrate stability, as has been amply shown in the case of attachment *behaviors,* the veridicality of the construct (especially with respect to individual differences) is called into question (Masters & Wellman, 1974).

On the other hand, Carlson (1971), in an article of basic importance in the field of personality, noted that among the large body of research that she reviewed: "*not a single published study attempted even minimal inquiry into the organization of personality variables within the individual* [p. 209, emphasis added]." Recently, however, a number of investigators have approached this problem from an organizational perspective (Block & Block, 1979; Sroufe, 1979a). According to this point of view, stability *in the way the behaviors are organized* with respect to context and other behavioral systems is predicted. Within the organizational perspective, the specific pattern of behavior manifested in one situation at a particular developmental level *cannot* be expected to recur in the exact form in either the same or other contexts at later developmental periods. Rather, with development, behaviors are expected to undergo transformation, hierarchical integration, and reorganization (Emde, Gaensbauer, & Harmon, 1976; Santostefano, 1979; Serafica, 1978; Sroufe, 1979a). Instead of seeking stability of behavioral expression across time, the organizational viewpoint requires *coherence of patterns* of behavioral organization or adaptation, such that early adaptation is related to later adaptation in a lawful fashion (Block & Block, 1979; Lewis, 1967; Sroufe, 1979b). Within this framework, continuity refers to the prediction that competence in dealing with one developmental issue (for example, the formation of a secure attachment relationship) will be related to competence with respect to subsequent issues (for example, successful integration into and mastery of the peer world). The salient methodological issues are to utilize broad-band, age-appropriate measures of competence and to select age-appropriate situations, each of which elicit a variety of behavioral patterns that are more or less adaptive for that developmental period (Matas, Arend, & Sroufe, 1978; Sroufe, 1979b). From the organizational framework, continuity in the organization of attachment behavior (Connell, 1976; Waters, 1978) and even relationships to later individual differences in adaptation (Ainsworth, Blehar, Waters, & Wall, 1978; Arend, Gove, & Sroufe, 1979; Matas et al., 1978; Waters, Wippman, & Sroufe, 1979) have been clearly demonstrated. Thus, one research perspective leads to disillusionment with individual differences in attachment, whereas the other reveals their utility.

Similarly, development may be viewed in terms of milestones—tasks that are to be accomplished by a certain age—or it may be viewed in terms of issues around which development is organized. The milestone view led to numerous critiques of the concept of stranger fear (Rheingold & Eckerman, 1973). Critics argued that because stranger fear varied in its age of onset and never was completely dominant in the repertoire (affiliative tendencies always being prominent), the concept should be abandoned. From the organizational view, however, negative reactions are important in terms of what they reflect about the complex organization of social behavior in the second half-year of life (Bronson & Pankey, 1977; Cicchetti & Mans, 1976, Cicchetti, Mans, & Breitenbuecher, 1977; Emde et al., 1976; Sroufe, 1979a) and in terms of the extent to which the attachment relationship modulates reactions to strangers for *individual* babies (Bischof, 1975; Bretherton, 1978; Bretherton & Ainsworth, 1974; Cicchetti & Serafica, 1981). The literature is quite coherent from within this perspective, whereas it appears inconsistent when viewed in terms of milestones (Sroufe, 1977).

Issues of perspective are especially crucial in the study of retarded children. Retarded children can be seen as qualitatively different from or as similar to normal children in essential ways. They can be seen as a homogeneous group or as unique individuals, who are affective and social beings as well as cognitive beings. From the static-trait view, retardation is something the child *has* as it goes from being a retarded infant to a retarded child to a retarded adult. Such a view can obscure the fact that retarded children are individuals with vastly different personalities, just like other children, and that their personality unfolds through a series of developmental reorganizations. Moreover, when development is viewed in terms of milestones, the emphasis is on the *difference* between retarded and nonretarded children. Over and over again, it is confirmed that the retarded child is deficient. Such a view completely overlooks the possibility that the behavior and development of retarded children is organized, adaptive, and integrated—just as is the case for nonretarded infants and children. *We know that they are retarded; the important and challenging research questions concern the developmental process.*

In the literature on mental retardation the issue has been cast in terms of "developmental" models versus "difference" models. According to the "developmental" position, spelled out most lucidly by Zigler (1969, 1973) and intended to apply only to retarded individuals free from organic impairment (that is, "familial" retarded individuals), the retarded child progresses through the cognitive-developmental stages *in the same sequence* as the normal child, albeit at a slower pace and with a lower upper limit. Thus, according to developmental theorists, the performance of individuals of differing levels of intelligence who are functioning at the same developmental stage (and therefore at different chronological ages) should be *exactly the same on cognitive tasks*. The differences in rate and ultimate level of developmental attainment are thought to be dictated by the normal variability inherent in the gene pool.

According to the "difference" position (Milgram, 1969, 1973), the development of cultural-familial retardates differs from that of nonretarded children in ways that transcend mere differences in the rate and ceiling of development. Difference theorists argue that the retarded child's cognitive stages differ from those of the nonretarded child. Impaired neurophysiological functioning is hypothesized to disrupt cognitive processing in all retardates, even those without *demonstrable* organic involvement, so that, even when individuals are equated on general level of cognition, differences would be found in their cognitive performances associated with their level of intellectual functioning (the IQ). Difference theorists maintain that the IQ reflects other factors about an individual than merely his/her rate of cognitive development. For example, Weir (1967) has stated that the differential rates of progression through the cognitive developmental stages manifested as different IQs reflects inherent differences in rate of learning and/or information processing in these individuals (see Odom–Brooks & Arnold, 1976, for a summary of information-processing perspectives on mental retardation). There are several difference theories of mental retardation with the hypothesized defect ranging from underdeveloped verbal systems to inadequate neural satiation.

In summary, the developmental position generates the testable hypothesis that the formal cognitive functioning of familially mentally retardated persons and nonretarded individuals matched on general level of cognition (most often the person's mental age) should be identical, whereas the difference position asserts that qualitative differences (for example, *abnormal developmental patterns*) would still be found. The experimental evidence for these two positions has been reviewed by contributors to the volume and as such are not the focus of this chapter. Rather, we attempt to illustrate the potential usefulness of a broader developmental approach to the study of behavior for elucidating the process of development in organically mentally retarded persons as well.

PROCESSES INVOLVED IN SKILL ACQUISITION

Questions focusing on elucidating the process of development in organically retarded persons have become interesting for various reasons. They may be divided into several categories. Those that follow are meant to serve as prototypical illustrations of the problems faced by process-oriented theorists and should neither be construed as exhaustive in scope nor as necessarily mutually exclusive.

Sequencing of Stages. One major focus includes inquiries into the *sequence* of developmental stages (Flavell, 1971, 1972; Pinard & Laurendeau, 1969; Woodward, 1963): Do organically retarded persons show the same developmental progression from recognizable sensorimotor stage-one behaviors to sensorimotor stage-two, and so on, up through the attainment of formal operations, or do they skip some stages and never attain others? Inhelder's research (1968), for example, has produced evidence that retarded children never obtain the highest or formal operational stage of development. Once a problem becomes too difficult, the mentally retarded child gives up trying to organize the situation and repeats the same actions, expecting that an accumulation of repetitions will have the desired effect (Inhelder, 1967a).

Hierarchy of Stages. Furthermore, it would be interesting to ascertain whether retarded individuals show the same hierarchical organization of their structures of thinking as do nonretarded children. This question has been motivated by Inhelder's findings that retarded children display difficulties of integration from one developmental level to the next; that is, their reasoning often shows traces of previous levels of thinking, a phenomenon Inhelder calls "viscosity." Inhelder observed this viscosity in retarded children who remained in a state of transition between two stages for a much longer duration than nonretarded children, oscillating between different levels of construction not only on different tasks but also at different times on the same task. It would be worthwhile to consider what the coexistence of Piaget's hierarchy of stages would imply with respect to the organization of retarded children's thinking.

Consolidation of Stages. Related to the issue of whether or not retarded children's thinking is hierarchically organized is the question of the consolidation, or internal organization of stages. Inhelder found that mentally retarded children frequently show a false equilibrium, a phenomenon she calls "closure" or "passive stability" of thought. Due to the fact that retarded children do not obtain the two highest stages of development that are genuinely equilibrated,— because the operations of thought are completely reversible—Inhelder claims that these children look as if they had obtained a stage of equilibrium of thought, only because they do not develop beyond a certain stage level. However, she postulates that this stagnation of development reflects mentally retarded children's lack of development of fixation at a certain stage level rather than their complete equilibration. The fragility of this "false equilibrium," in conjunction with other psychological factors, contributes to the susceptibility of the retarded child to influence by emotional and social factors. In some children, Inhelder noted a high degree of susceptibility; in others, she found that emotional tension and lack of self-confidence interfered with their task performance. These factors, however, play a small, unelaborated role in Inhelder's (and Piaget's) theoretical formulations—but constitute a major role in Zigler's conceptualization (1969, 1973).

According to Inhelder (1976a), the following laws govern normal and atypical development: completion of structural levels in normals and closure of structural levels in mentally retarded children. "A system is said to be completed once it has attained a level of structuration such that each of its elements has become consolidated with the others. It is thus capable of becoming integrated into larger systems. That is, a completed system at the same time constitutes an opening—it has the germ for further development. In the mentally retarded child access to certain structures seems to be an end in itself, without hope of subsequent evolution [p. 223]." Thus, further research on mentally retarded children will have to show whether the internal structure of the respective stages of development is the same as in nonretarded children.

Transitions between Stages. Another aspect of development closely related to the lack of hierarchization and consolidation of stage structures in mentally retarded children is the explanation of stage transitions. Inhelder discovered so-called "oscillations," that is, fluctuations between various stage levels in retarded children. In other words, retarded children's stage transitions do not reflect a clear trend toward increasing integration or organization as postulated by Piaget. Therefore, the further investigation of stage transitions in retarded children may either reveal that the processes accounting for their development are different than in the normal children studied by Piaget, or if the oscillations are a universal phenomenon but become visible only in retardates due to the slower nature of their development. The study of these transitions may enable us to come up with a more microscopic account for developmental changes.

Processes of Development. Inhelder's results with respect to retarded children's viscosity, rigidity, and oscillations of thinking imply that their processes or strategies of development may differ from those of normal children at least to some extent. Thus, one might ask whether organically retarded persons encode, store, and retrieve information in the same way as do nonretarded individuals, in order to address this issue more carefully.

The Organization of Developmental Domains. Finally, one may leave the cognitive realm and inquire whether the other domains of development, like language, emotions, and motivation, are similarly integrated in organically retarded children as in nonretarded individuals. For example, Anthony (1956) refers in this context to the often impoverished emotional life of psychotic children who do not seem to be capable of expressing distress or joy, emotional expressions normally coming in at a very early stage of development (Bridges, 1932). Thus, an analysis of the relationship between various domains of development could reveal whether cognitive and emotional problems tend to be correlated, or whether cognitive retardations can occur without emotional ones and vice versa. Furthermore, retarded children with different types of etiologies could have different types of such emotional problems, either correlated or uncorrelated with cognitive or other problems. The answer to these questions is important with respect to the ultimate goal of formulating an integrated theory of human development that can account for all aspects or domains of development in both nonretarded and retarded children.

WAYS IN WHICH THE INVESTIGATION OF ABNORMAL DEVELOPMENT CONTRIBUTES TO THE FORMULATION OF THEORIES OF NORMAL DEVELOPMENT

It is hoped that at least some of the focal issues we have delineated indicate why the study of the process of development in organically retarded individuals should be a legitimate concern for developmental theorists. There are many controversies in developmental theory to which the study of organically retarded persons *is* relevant. We believe that the psychology of atypical mental processes can make many significant contributions to our theory of normal development—primarily through contributing precision to developmental theory, affirming it, challenging it, and forcing us to examine our theory of development more critically in relation to our knowledge about psychopathology.

Universality of Developmental Patterns. Just as is the case with cross-cultural research, another approach to validating the claim of universality of a developmental sequence is to study samples where one might expect on a priori grounds to find differing patterns. As such, the study of atypical populations can illustrate rather conclusively which developmental processes and contents are necessary, sufficient, or necessary and sufficient for the emergence of new behaviors and their underlying organizations. The results of such empirical and theoretical investigations may be the description of alternative developmental pathways leading to the same or different outcomes of the developmental sequence, and a weighting of the respective roles of, for example, biological, social, and linguistic factors in mental growth.

This universality of developmental patterns has to be investigated with respect to all the aspects of development discussed previously. Thus, at a descriptive level, the universality of the observed phenomenon has to be considered. At a more abstract level, the universal existence of stage structuring, the sequencing of stages, stage transitions, the hierarchical organization, and the consolidation of stages will have to be addressed. Finally, we will have to elaborate on the universality of the processes or strategies of development and the organization of various developmental domains with respect to one another.

Whereas the issue of universality is of a theoretical nature, our further discussion addresses methodological concerns.

Rate of Development. Because the development of nonretarded children is more rapid than is the case with children with developmental deviations, the study of pathological populations can permit us to dissociate homogeneous factors from heterogeneous ones, thereby enabling us to ascertain purer convergences and discontinuities in developmental processes.

If, for example, organically retarded children manifest developmental arrestations at certain stages—within or across developmental domains—then this provides a much clearer portrait of the groupings of these stages than would be possible to derive from the transitions characteristic of normal development. Because his/her speed of development is slower, a retarded child is more likely to remain at a given stage or level longer; thus, diagnosis of this child's development will most probably reveal arrested structures rather than periods of transition (Cicchetti & Sroufe, 1976b, 1978; Inhelder, 1943, 1966). Inhelder (1976b) reported that psychotic children's symbolic functions tend to be fixated at an early stage of development during which the distinction among symbol, sign, and reality cannot be made yet. Anthony (1956) claimed that some psychotic children, whose etiology is not further specified, never advance beyond the stage of sensorimotor functions.

Homogeneous and Heterogeneous Subgroups of Retarded Children. Another potentially fruitful strategy for broadening our understanding of normal developmental processes lies in studying etiologically homogeneous subgroups of retarded children. Because the cause of cultural–familial retardation is as yet unknown to us, groups of organically retarded individuals loom as more appropriate targets upon which to focus our inquiries. As Wing, Gould, Yeates, and Brierly (1977) have noted after finding that Down syndrome children were especially likely to develop the capacity for symbolic representation, whereas children with other identifiable organic anomalies associated with mental retardation (such as childhood psychosis, encephalitis, rubella, and so on) were not:

> It would be of great interest to know what pathological processes can produce on the one hand, general retardation with a pattern of behavior that is reasonably similar to a normal child of the same mental age, *as in most cases of Down's syndrome,* or on the other hand, marked discrepancies between different aspects of cognitive function, leading to behavior that cannot be predicted from the child's mental age [p. 176, emphasis added]).

Whereas it seems necessary to study the sequencing of development in populations of different etiologies or heterogeneous groups in order to discover logically necessary processes and structures in the course of normal development, it is necessary to study homogeneous groups with the same etiologies to come up with adequate explanations for the logic inherent in those alternative pathways of development.

In essence, we are advocating that an elaboration and extension of Zigler's model—that is, a more liberal developmental position—can provide us with many important answers to the enigma of human development.

THE ORGANISMIC/DEVELOPMENTAL ("LIBERAL") POSITION

Perhaps the core issue of research with handicapped children is the problem of predicting later maladaptation, or, more broadly, the problem of demonstrating continuity in the quality of adaptation across the life span. What seems to be of paramount importance in the field at the present time is the need to formulate a developmental model that is adequate and broad enough to guide prospective, long-term studies of the process of adaptation in handicapped as well as nonhandicapped children, and the factors that shape its course. An all-encompassing, yet theoretically meaningful model of development must yield a formulation of developmental continuity that can embrace both change and stability. Additionally, it must be sufficiently complex to reflect the multifaceted ways in which constitutional, organismic, and environmental factors affect development. This notion is similar to the gene-environment interaction model prevalent in current research in behavior genetics.

Zigler's theoretical viewpoint is in the developmental tradition of Jean Piaget and Heinz Werner, a perspective that holds that growth is due to an *active* structuring by the individual of the environment. From such a structural-developmental position, retarded children, psychotic persons, members of "primitive" cultures, in short *all* human beings are depicted as individuals who actively construct their own experience.

Zigler's primary emphasis has been on the retarded child's cognition as it reveals itself in performance on cognitive tasks. He is interested in other behavioral systems, such as affect, primarily for the ways in which they change performance on cognitive tasks (Zigler & Balla, 1977). Organismic developmental theorists construe development in a wider sense. They are interested in the *organization* of cognition and in the organization and interrelation of all the behavioral systems, both during development in general, and in terms of their interactions at a given point in time. In this more inclusive sense of developmental theory, development is conceptualized as a uniform process found throughout nature, governed by a body of universal laws and principles. Development is viewed as an orderly, cumulative ("epigenetic"), unidirectional process, involving an invariant sequence of qualitative changes in organization. Quantitative changes occur along with and sometimes as part of these qualitative changes.

The basic nature of these changes is elucidated in the "orthogenetic principle" adhered to by the vast majority of "liberal" developmental theorists. The orthogenetic principle states that wherever development occurs, it proceeds in a directed manner, from a state of relative globality and lack of differentiation, to a state of increasing differentiation, complexity, integration, and hierarchic organization (Werner, 1948, 1957; Werner & Kaplan, 1963); that is, development involves the successive progression of control from more diffuse, automatic, lower-level stages of organization to more specific, differentiated, voluntary, and higher-level stages. Thus, we see that with development the organism becomes increasingly less stimulus bound, less impelled by his/her own affective states, and more adroit at actively manipulating the environment. The developmental approach that we have delineated has also provided tremendous heuristic value in systematizing many aspects of biological phenomena in diverse fields of the life sciences, such as neurophysiology (Jackson, 1884; Sherrington, 1906), neurology (Milner, 1967), embryology (Waddington, 1957, 1966), neurobiology (Jacobson, 1978), and comparative and physiological psychology (Teitelbaum, 1971, 1977).

The qualitative aspect of development is assessed through detecting change in structure–function relationships across time (Reese & Overton, 1970), and in tracing the relation of earlier forms to later forms of behavior. Researchers might attempt to ascertain how earlier and later forms of behavior are related, focusing on the *nature* of the transition from earlier to later forms. For example, *all* atypical children may have difficulties in hierarchical integration. As suggested by Inhelder (1966, 1968, 1976a), their reasoning oftentimes shows traces of previous levels, and the states of equilibrium they achieve do not seem to be as stable as those of normal children—that is, oscillation between stages is characteristic of retarded children.

Other rather quantitative aspects of development involve such issues as whether there is a gradual or abrupt increase with time, of magnitude, of efficiency, or of frequency of occurrences of a newly acquired operation in an individual or in a group. Quantitative and qualitative aspects of a developmental change need not be in concordance.

Both quantitative and qualitative aspects of change affect, and are affected by, hierarchic integration. In hierarchic integration, several activities of a lower level are integrated and represented differently at a higher level. The preceding structures are not lost, rather on the one hand they become part of later structures, whereas on the other these lower levels of functioning may come to the fore in their original shape under special internal or external circumstances, such as when an organism is confronted with especially difficult or novel tasks.

In this context, Flavell (1972) has suggested five types of relationships between earlier and later stages of development: Addition, Substitution, Modification, Inclusion, and Mediation. This classification of the relationship between stages may be relevant for the investigation of retarded populations in that retarded individuals in general might show different developmental sequences than nonretarded individuals; furthermore, there could be differences within the retarded group as far as the transition between stages is concerned—that is, Mediation-type sequences could be characteristic of one, Addition-type sequences, however, of another subgroup of the retarded.

The concept of hierarchical integration and organization in development is a specific solution to the problem of an individual's continuous adaptation to its environment on the one hand, and of how integrity of function is maintained in the face of this change on the other. Because an organism's early structures are not lost in development via hierarchic integration, the organism can maintain feelings of integrity and continuity in the face of change so rapid that it might otherwise cause problems for the sense of internal continuity. Simultaneously, hierarchic organization is the most likely way for rapid developmental change to occur. Complex systems are hierarchically organized, *because* they are then more likely to adapt to biological and environmental processes and to evolve more rapidly than if they were not so organized. Within the organismic-developmental perspective, one studies how behaviors become hierarchically organized into more complex patterns within developmental systems, how later modes and functions evolve from earlier prototypes, and how part functions become integrated into wholes (Cicchetti & Sroufe, 1978; Emde et al., 1976; Serafica, 1978; Spitz, 1959). This organismic-developmental approach also refers to relationships among systems—cognitive, social, emotional, and neurophysiological—as well as to consequences of advances[1] and lags[1] within one system for other systems (Cicchetti & Serafica, 1981; Cicchetti & Sroufe, 1976b, 1978; Sroufe & Waters, 1976; Zigler, 1973). It also refers to the consequences of earlier experience and adaptations for later adaptation (Block & Block, 1979; Erikson, 1950; Arend et al., 1979; Mahler, Pine, & Bergman, 1975; Matas et al., 1978; Waters et al., 1979). Because early structures are incorporated into later structures, an early disturbance in functioning can ultimately cause much larger disturbances to appear. It is assumed that there are certain regularities present in organized systems (Weiss, 1969). Accordingly, development occurring in separate but similarly organized systems will have common properties (see Teitelbaum, 1977, for a similar position). One implication of this is that a thorough understanding of one system (for example, cognition) may greatly facilitate our quest for understanding a second, more unfamiliar system that is somehow similar to the first in an important way. This aspect of current developmental theory is foreshadowed by Herbert Spencer's (1870) conception of development as a uniform process governed by laws and principles, leading to the proposition that the discovery of an *organizing principle* in one system may have direct bearing upon our understanding of other systems (Fishbein, 1976).

Characteristics of systems are *integrity* (parts of systems work together to control or regulate interaction with other systems and with the environment), *interreference* (systems have feedback mechanisms; one part can "know" what another part is doing or where it stands), *structure* (systems are made up of components and can be analyzed into their parts), *adaptation* (systems are adapted to the environment in which they operate), *access to environmental input* (systems need environmental support in order to become properly organized and optimally adapted), and *specificity of stimuli* to which they will respond.[2] Systems epitomize developmental phenomena in that they need not be present at birth and rarely are present in fully organized form early in life,

---

[1] Advances and lags may be defined with respect to different systems of reference: (a) the timing of "normal" development (that is, most children's development); or (b) the timing of the relationship between developmental domains. In the first case, "advance" and "lag" refer to the early or late emergence, compared to nonretarded children, of certain behaviors; in the second case, "advance" and "lag" imply that the quantitatively or qualitatively new behaviors of one developmental domain emerge earlier or later than the ones in a different domain.

[2] Whereas systems are responsive only to those inputs that are relevant to the system performing its functions, this is not to say that a system cannot be affected by other factors such as traumas of various sorts.

because they require environmental support during development in order to become properly organized and optimally adapted (von Bertalanffy, 1968).

A basic axiom of organismic-developmental theory is that a given behavior can have multiple meanings and serve multiple functions, whereas the same function can also be served by multiple behaviors. Because of this, multiple systems can be activated simultaneously or sequentially in the same external situation. Meaning is inferred from patterns or constellations of behavior *in context*. The role of physiological maturation in changing patterns of behavior is likewise considered. Because systems are interrelated, a change in the phenomena of one system is evidence for changes in several systems. For example, changes in affect provide evidence for cognitive development. There is a change across time in the relationship between structure and function in any given system. The systems approach organizes behavior into units that can be followed across the lifespan, demonstrating coherence of adaptation across situations, contexts, and time, providing explanations for what might otherwise appear to be discontinuity. The organismic-developmental perspective, with its emphasis on understanding evolving systems, is an invaluable approach for the study of the person—normal, retarded, or otherwise pathological—as a whole being.

Sequences. Developmental changes within and across systems often follow in easily recognized *sequences*. Each stage in a sequence is based on the preceding stage, and this new stage in turn prepares the ground for the stage to follow (see Flavell, 1971; 1972 for two thought provoking articles on the role stages and sequences play within a structural developmental framework). Kohlberg (1969) predicts a truly universal ordering of cognitive stages, based on a logical analysis of orderings inherent in given concepts and on assumed invariance in certain features of the environment and nervous system. Because this invariance depends on a logical analysis of the concept itself, a truly universal ordering of stages is predicted.

Within the organismic-developmental perspective, continuity of adaptation and alternate pathways to competence are important issues for both nonretarded and retarded children. What is sought is an understanding of the organization of various capacities of the child, rather than a mere cataloguing of these capacities. The stress on the organization of behavior not only allows but also *requires* the study of individual as well as group differences. Because this approach attempts to analyze pathways to competence, whatever those pathways may be, it is a broad enough approach to include all persons. Indeed, in the case of cognitive development, organismic-developmental theorists predict a truly universal ordering of stages for all children, normal and retarded, regardless of the etiology of the retardation (for example, cultural–familial, brain damage, genetic anomaly, neurophysiological defect, and so on), whether or not they would predict differences in manner or rates of solving particular tasks.

ZIGLER'S DEVELOPMENTAL ("CONSERVATIVE") POSITION

Perhaps the best example of the conservative developmental position is Zigler's developmental theory (1969, 1973). Zigler is interested in cognitive development, especially as revealed in performance on particular *tasks* (for example, number of trials to criterion). He believes that all nonretarded persons at a given developmental level (as usually assessed by the child's mental age on a standardized IQ instrument) will show equivalent cognitive functioning. Zigler believes that the cultural-familial retarded are "normal" persons whose intelligence is at the low end of the polygenic distribution. Because he sees them as essentially normal, he believes that their cognitive functioning should be exactly like that of MA-matched normals in every way. He notes, however, that the cognitive development of the familially retarded is characterized by a slower progression *through the same sequence* of cognitive stages and a *more limited upper stage* of cognition. Zigler believes that, because organically retarded persons have identifiable physiological or anatomical deficits contributing to their retardation, they may show a different course of cognitive development, and a different nature of cognitive functioning at a given point in time, than nonretarded persons or the cultural-familial retarded.

Zigler wishes to uncover those processes that are common to all retarded persons without evidence of central nervous system pathology. He believes that the uncertain effects of gross organic pathology make organic retardates poor subjects for such investigations. Zigler (1969) asserts that investigators should keep their research groups as pure as possible to optimally determine *what* etiology is characterized by *what* specific manner of cognitive functioning. He notes:

> *differences in cognitive performance between organic retardates and normals, even though matched on MA, are irrelevant to the developmental-difference controversy.* . . . If the etiology of the phenotypic intelligence . . . of two groups differ, it is, then, far from logical to assert that the course of cognitive development is the same, or that even similar contents in the behaviors of two such differing individuals are mediated by exactly the same cognitive process [pp. 352-353, emphasis added]

(For example, whether the process being investigated is asserted to vary with IQ, to be some defect, or some qualitative difference that all retardates have.)

Although much of Zigler's work has primarily dealt with motivational/personality factors in the retarded child's performance on specific cognitive tasks, as noted, he is a theorist clearly within the developmental tradition of Piaget and Werner. For instance, within Zigler's model a cognitive level or stage is the totality of formal cognitive processes; it is not the specific contents of behavior or phenotypic achievements of the individual. Likewise, Zigler believes that cognitive development takes place through an interaction between experience and a variety of nativistic or autochthonous factors, some of which are probably influenced almost exclusively by biological rather than environmental events.

Zigler (1969) himself notes that his developmental model leaves many questions unanswered, such as:

> Is the sequentiality in cognitive development inevitable, or does it only reflect the experiential programming of the organism? Exactly how do environmental events interact with nativistic factors in the development of any single cognitive process?... What precipitates the movement from one cognitive level to the next, a movement reflected in the frequently reported striking changes in the quality of cognitive functioning? At what age does the developmentally highest level for such isolatable cognitive process occur? Is cognitive development essentially the growth of a variety of highly related cognitive processes and thus best represented by a single progression... or is it better viewed as a collection of relatively independent processes developing at different rates as a function perhaps of quite different environmental and nativistic factors [p. 538]?

EXPANSION OF ZIGLER'S POSITION IN TERMS OF THE LIBERAL DEVELOPMENTAL MODEL

We believe that the study of organically retarded persons—that is, the testing of hypotheses asked from within the framework of liberal (organismic-developmental) developmental theory—can provide or help to provide answers to many of these questions.

For instance, in regard to the sequentiality of cognitive processes, Weisz and Zigler (1979) cite data showing that for all pathological groups studied, with the possible exception of children with pronounced electroencephalographic abnormality, there is an invariant sequence through the sensorimotor stages and through the preoperational stages of conservation. This finding is particularly important, because Zigler is interested in those processes that are common to all retarded children without central nervous system pathology. It might be argued that demonstrating this process or any process across different etiological groups is a better test for universality in retardates than demonstrating said process only in familially retarded children.

The study of how environmental events interact with nativistic factors in the development of any single cognitive process can perhaps best be answered by studying organically retarded individuals, the nature of whose handicap is identified from early life, so that the development of the cognitive process can be charted across different sets of nativistic factors. For example, children with a broad-band impairment that particularly affects language development, such as in Down syndrome, may be contrasted with children whose primary impairment is of language alone to see how each group develops a particular skill such as conservation. The study of organically retarded persons can help answer the question, important for the study of individuals of average intellect and for intervention and public policy, of what precipitates the movement from one cognitive stage to the next. Persons of different degrees of brain damage, the extent and nature of which are known, can be compared as to whether and how they manage to achieve skills that are not highly canalized. The study of which specific skills emerge in invariant sequences—that is, contemporaneously or subsequently—in the brain-damaged retarded, will strengthen any assertion on the logical necessity of such emergences for specific skills.

The Process–Achievement Distinction. The distinction between process and achievement is relevant to another interest of Zigler's, the controversy within the conservative developmental camp between difference/defect theorists and developmentalists. As Werner (1937) noted, similar levels of achievement do not necessarily reflect the differing processes by which they are reached (for example, a given achievement can be attained by *multiple sequences*). Although we have undoubtedly enhanced our knowledge about the laws governing mental growth by measuring development through assessing levels of accomplishment, such a focus has left a large hiatus in our body of knowledge. As organismic-developmental theorists have underscored, researchers must pay attention to uncovering the processes that underlie these formal achievements (Werner, 1937; Werner & Kaplan, 1963). For instance, what level of functioning does a child use in solving a given problem? Sometimes a more concretely oriented child may perform better than a more intellectually oriented child who attempts to employ functions of a higher order. Such a decline in accomplishment occurs as well during the transition from a more primitive to a more refined, differentiated stage. These two cases may even be reconcilable in that a more intellectually oriented child may be conceived of as having advanced to or being in a transitory phase to a more complex stage of development. Moreover, if we are intent upon finding out the extent to which a child is capable of generalizing new achievements, we must search for the underlying processes of development and not merely its products in order to extract the principle characteristic of all those achievements. Thus, noting that MA-matched retarded and nonretarded individuals have similar achievements does not tell us whether or not they employ the same processes to manage these achievements; conversely, even if their levels of achievement differ, they may be using similar processes, albeit less efficiently. *More studies are needed both of processes and strategies in problem solving or other task performance in nonretarded and in retarded children.* If the organic and cultural-familial retarded should be consistently similar to each other and different from nonretarded individuals on some dimension, that dimension will have been shown to be common to all retarded persons, regardless of diagnostic subgrouping.

AN ORGANIZATIONAL VIEW OF DEVELOPMENT: ILLUSTRATION FROM THE STUDY OF DOWN SYNDROME INFANTS AND TODDLERS

The study of handicapped children has an urgency characteristic of all research that touches upon great problems of social concern. Developmental psychology has held out the hope that it could generate the substantive base for elucidating the normal development of psychological processes against which, in time, deviant development could be appraised. Whereas the importance of undertaking such a research enterprise is obvious, to date most investigations of handicapped children have paid perfunctory attention to developmental *processes*. It is evident that the paucity of sound developmental research with these children hinders the implementation of effective intervention. For handicapped children in particular, growth and development are related to a number of factors, particularly the severity of the handicap and the quality of care the handicapped child receives (Sameroff & Chandler, 1975). A developmental scheme is necessary for tracing the roots, etiology, and nature of maladaptation so that interventions may be timed and guided.

Investigators writing about and working with retarded infants and children typically have focused on their intellectual development. Similarly, research with nonretarded children has also emphasized the cognitive domain. Such a strong emphasis on mental development may suggest firstly that affective or emotional development is not as important as intellectual development, and, secondly, that it is possible to dissect the child in this way—that intellectual development can be understood without also comprehending the child's development as a socioemotional being. Those seeking to understand behavioral organization in retarded children certainly have not intended such implications. Their focus on cognition is simply the unfortunate by-product of a concern about the intellectual retardation of these children. As Zigler (1969) has stated: "Since cognitive functioning lies at the core of retardation phenomena, it is easy to see why . . . workers have concentrated on cognitive functioning and have underemphasized . . . other factors as determinants in the behavior of the retarded [p. 546]."

Of course, the socioemotional development of any child is of utmost importance. Following Piaget and others (Piaget, 1952, 1954; Piaget & Inhelder, 1969; Sroufe, 1979a), researchers are beginning to view affect and cognition as mutually influential (reciprocally interacting developmental processes). As is true for cognition, so, too, does affect organize the child's behavior. Affect is the meaning and motivational system that cognition serves (Sroufe, 1979a; Stechler & Carpenter, 1967). As such, it has a central role in the assessment of the retarded child's general functioning. As Zigler (1969, 1973) has suggested, a comprehensive understanding of retarded children requires an integration of social and emotional factors with cognitive factors. Zigler (1969) states: "So long as we confuse one determinant of behavior with all determinants of behavior, we will never construct a comprehensive theory of the behavior of the retarded [p. 548]." As the organization of development refers to the nature of the developmental process, understanding the ontogenesis and function of socioemotional processes would greatly enhance our comprehension of the principles inherent in developmental organization. It is clear that, with retarded children, attention to emotional growth must accompany the previous concern for cognitive factors. *For all children, development is an integrated process* (Cicchetti & Sroufe, 1976b; Inhelder, 1943, 1966; Piaget, 1952; Werner, 1948, 1957). Although the unfolding of perceptual, cognitive, socioemotional, and neurophysiological systems may be examined separately, increasingly what is being sought is an integrated conceptualization of development.

Special Advantages Inherent in the Study of Down Syndrome Infants. Despite the appeal of these theoretical propositions, there has been little systematic investigation of the interaction between developing affective, cognitive, and physiological systems. Our research, with infants certain to be cognitively retarded to varying degrees, was undertaken with this task specifically in mind. We felt that the study of Down syndrome would offer important opportunities for formulating a more precise organizational perspective.

Children with Down syndrome are, indeed, a particularly interesting population to study from a developmental view. For example, an examination of the postnatal development of individuals with an extra autosomal chromosome may provide a clear test of the hypothesis that abnormal chromosomal material may be used as an independent variable to study behavioral differences. Whereas very few autosomal trisomies are viable, nor do they occur frequently enough to be tested for behavioral phenotypes, Down syndrome is a notable exception. For example, Down syndrome is etiologically homogeneous and is detectable at birth so that it can be charted developmentally. It possesses a suitable complexity and intactness of phenotypic expression and occurs with sufficient frequency to allow for meaningful developmental analysis. It results in diverse outcomes varying from severe retardation to near normal development.

The slower cognitive development of infants with Down syndrome allows a separation of the early prototypes of what will later be affective expression from genuine emotional reactions that are dependent on psychological processes (Cicchetti & Mans, 1976; Cicchetti & Sroufe, 1978). Their developmental heterogeneity allows specification of the interdependence between affect and cognition. In fact, these retarded infants provide an important test of the relationship between emotional and cognitive development. Unlike the case with the rapidly developing normal infant, in whom the simultaneous emergence of behaviors may be viewed as coincidental, the slower advance of retarded infants through the same stages enables us to demonstrate true convergences and discontinuities in development. In addition, the obvious autonomic deficiencies, especially of some Down syndrome infants (Penrose & Smith, 1966; Serafica &

Cicchetti, 1976) suggest first formulations of the role of tension and affect in promoting development.

Summary of Work Completed. Over the past 7 years, we have been conducting a large-scale study of the early development of Down syndrome infants and toddlers. More than 200 children have participated in the studies; 40 have been intensively studied from 2 months through the first 5 years of life. Others have participated in shorter longitudinal studies. To be sure, the handicap of Down syndrome infants is apparent, though varying widely from individual to individual. In fact, our research is among the most extensive documentations of their retardation to date. However, we are more impressed with the similarities between these babies and nonretarded babies in developmental process and organization.

The studies have been broad in scope, with assessment of social and emotional development as well as cognitive growth. Whereas we have investigated mechanisms underlying the Down syndrome baby's handicap (Butterworth & Cicchetti, 1978; Cicchetti et al., 1977; Hoffman, Salapatek, Kuskowski, & Cicchetti, 1979), the major emphasis has been on the organization of development of these babies—the developmental process. Like others, we have obtained evidence suggesting a difficulty with arousal modulation (Cicchetti & Mans, 1976; Cicchetti & Sroufe, 1978; Serafica & Cicchetti, 1976). Like others, we have found Down syndrome infants slow to achieve various developmental milestones and generally to show retarded cognitive development (Cicchetti & Sroufe, 1976a, b, 1978; Mans, Cicchetti, & Sroufe, 1978). However, we have also illustrated the striking similarity of the developmental process in Down syndrome and nonretarded infants.

The Ontogenesis of Smiling and Laughter in Down Syndrome Infants. After approximately a 40-year hiatus (Bridges, 1932, 1936), developmental psychologists have rekindled their interest in studying affective processes in infancy (Cicchetti & Pogge-Hesse, 1981; in press; Lewis & Rosenblum, 1978; Sroufe, 1979a; Sroufe & Waters, 1976). The notion that underlying cognitive structures are reflected in affective development has been strongly corroborated by an impressive array of empirical research (Charlesworth, 1969; Decarie, 1965; Lewis & Rosenblum, 1978; Shultz & Zigler, 1970; Sroufe & Wunsch, 1972). In addition, affective expression has been shown to serve an important function for cognitive development (Izard, 1977, 1978; Sroufe, 1979a).

When the study of affect or emotions is the starting point, the integrated, organized nature of development very quickly becomes apparent. In attempting to unravel the complexities and nuances of emotional development, one must try to understand the growth of the whole child. In studying the unfolding of joy, fear, and the other emotions, we encounter such processes as memory, expectation, relational abilities, intentionality, the ability to distinguish persons, and other major themes in cognitive development. In our view, then, the topic of emotional development involves an understanding of the growing child as an integrated, organized, and dynamic system (see Cicchetti & Pogge-Hesse, 1981; in press, for an elaboration of our viewpoint).

In previous research with several samples of nonretarded infants between 4 and 12 months of age, changes in laughter were found that were *associated* with cognitive development (Sroufe & Wunsch, 1972). Infants in the first half year of life laughed primarily in situations that were physically intense or vigorous (auditory and tactile stimulation). Increasingly during the second half year, however, infants laughed at progressively more subtle and complex social and visual stimulation, whereas laughter at simple stimuli abated. For example, young babies laughed at being kissed on the stomach, popping sounds of the lips, and bouncing on the knee, whereas only older infants laughed consistently at mother sucking on the baby's bottle, crawling on the floor, or covering her face with a human mask. These findings suggested that later laughter is related to developmental changes in available schemata.

The question thus arises: Would infants who show atypical cognitive development also show a corresponding lag in their affective development? Organismic-developmental theory would *predict* such an affective and cognitive interdependence. Accordingly, a study of infants with Down syndrome was conducted to extend and elaborate the reported association between affect and cognition. If affective development is a function of cognitive development and not merely a coincidental co-occurrence of chronological age, then the sequence of affective stages should occur in the same order as that reported by Sroufe and Wunsch (1972), but at a rate corresponding to the degree of cognitive retardation of the child. Because items such as mother hiding behind a human mask elicit laughter when the nonretarded infant has achieved the appropriate cognitive-developmental level (for example, when the infant is capable of finding an object that is completely covered—stage-4 object permanence), such affective and cognitive occurrences should also appear concurrently in the retarded child, although they would be delayed until a later age.

We studied 25 Down syndrome infants between 4 and 24 months of age. All babies were presented with our standard series of 30 laughter items each month in their homes, using their mothers as the stimulus agent (see Table 15.1). Each infant received the items in a different random order, usually across two 45-minute administrations.

In addition, each infant was administered a series of cognitive and motor assessments by persons who were neither cognizant of any experimental hypotheses nor aware of how the infants had performed on the laughter items. The Uzgiris-Hunt ordinal scales (1975) of cognitive development were administered at 13, 16, 19, 21, and 24 months, and the Bayley Mental and Motor scales were given at 16, 19, and 24 months. Muscle tone (that is, degree of neuromuscular hypotonia) was assessed by culling together observations of resistance to passive

TABLE 15.1
Instructions for Individual Laughter Items

Specific Instructions: See note.

Auditory

1. Four pops in a row, then pause. Starts with lips pursed, cheeks full.
2. Say "Aah," starting low, then crescendoing to a loud voice, with an abrupt cut-off. Six-second pause.
3. Using a loud, deep voice, pronounce BOOM, BOOM, BOOM, at 1-second intervals.
4. With a mechanical type of sound, varying voice pitch from low to high and back down again, say Boo-Boo-Boo-Baa-Baa-Baa-Boo-Boo-Boo.
5. With mouth one foot from baby's ear, whisper "Hi, baby, how are you?" Avoid blowing in ear.
6. Falsetto voice (like Mickey Mouse), say, "Hi, baby, how are you?"
7. With lips relaxed, blow through them as a horse does when he is tired.

Tactile

8. Blow gently at hair for 3 seconds. Blow from the side, across the top of the baby's head.
9. Four quick pecks, on bare stomach.
10. Gently stroke cheek three times with soft object.
11. Place baby on knees facing away. Five vigorous bounces.
12. Hold baby waist high, horizontal, face toward floor and jiggle vigorously 3 seconds.
13. Using finger, gently tickle under baby's chin for 3 seconds.
14. Open mouth wide, press lips on back of neck and create a suction for 2 seconds.

Social

15. Allow baby to grasp yarn, then tug three times trying not to pull it away from the infant. Pause to repeat.
16. Put cloth in mouth and lean close enough for baby to grasp. Allow baby to pull cloth out and replace it if this is its tendency. Place the end of the cloth in baby's hand if this is necessary.
17. Say lyrically, "I'm gonna get you" ("I'm" quite protracted), while leaning toward baby with hands poised to grab. Then grab baby around stomach. If laughter is achieved, do another trial not followed by grabbing.
18. Stand at baby's side. Cover baby's face with cloth. If baby does not uncover his face immediately, uncover for him/her. Do not drag cloth across baby's face. Emphasis is on baby getting out from underneath.
19. Stick out tongue until baby touches it. (Make the infant's hand touch it if necessary.) Quickly pull tongue back in as soon as baby touches it.
20. Using blank cardboard, get baby's attention with face uncovered, cover face for 2 seconds, uncover quickly and pause 3 seconds. Do *not* say, "peek-a-boo."

Visual

21. Focus baby's attention on your fingers. Walk fingers toward baby, then give baby a poke in the ribs. If laughter is achieved, do another trial *not* followed by poking.
22. Using a white cloth, proceed as in #28 below.

(*continued*)

TABLE 15.1 (*Continued*)

Specific Instructions: See note.

Visual

23. Use one of baby's favorite toys. Focus baby's attention on it (out of reach). Cover it 2 seconds, uncover quickly.
24. First make sure that the baby is not hungry, then take bottle, bring toward lips, take three pretend sucks, lower bottle. Minimize noise of sucks.
25. Place baby in high chair or infant seat. Crawl *across* his/her field of vision, *not* toward baby. *Stand,* return to starting point.
26. Stand with arms extended to sides, walk in an exaggerated waddle, across baby's field of vision. Return to starting point walking normally.
27. Shake head vigorously at a distance of 1 foot from baby's face three times. Do not allow hair to touch baby.
28. Obtain baby's attention. Hold human mask up so baby can see it. Place mask in front of your face, lean slowly to within 1 foot of baby's face, pause 2 seconds. Lean back slowly, remove mask slowly.
29. Lift baby slowly to position overhead, looking down back. Minimize tactile and kinesthetic aspects.
30. To reduce peek-a-boo effects move baby slowly in front of full-length mirror. Hold 3 seconds, remove slowly, then pause 4 seconds.

Note: Pauses between trials are 4 seconds unless otherwise noted. All items are presented to the infant by the mother, up to six times.

movements of the arms and legs, of palpation of the muscle mass, and of posture, based on monthly assessments. Moreover, four independent raters, blind to any experimental hypotheses, assessed degree of hypotonia through clinical observation. All these assessments occurred in the infant's home.

We found that, even though Down syndrome infants show a later onset of laughter, they laughed at these incongruous stimulus items *in the same order* as normal infants—first to intrusive auditory and tactile items, later to the more complex social and visual items (see Table 15.1). Such an ordering suggests a tie between cognitive development and laughter at the more sophisticated items. Moreover, as is the case with the nonretarded infant, with development it is the Down syndrome infant's *effort* in processing the stimulus content or participation in the event that produces the tension necessary for smiling and laughter, rather than stimulation *per se* (Kagan, 1971; Sroufe & Waters, 1976); that is, as schema formation becomes increasingly important in the elicitation of positive affect, it is no longer stimulation per se that produces the affective response, but the infant's "effort" in processing of stimulus content. Down syndrome and nonretarded infants progress from smiling and laughing to intrusive stimulation, to stimulation mediated by active attention, to smiling and laughing in response to stimulus content, and, finally, toward an ever *more active participation* in producing affectively effective stimulation.

In other words, the tendency is for Down syndrome infants to smile or laugh in situations in which they are the *agent* rather than the recipient as development takes place. The infant's active participation in its development is supported by the social world. The developmental changes signified by this active involvement promotes care-giving responses; reciprocally, cognitive changes promote exploration, social development, and affective growth (Cicchetti & Sroufe, 1976a, b; 1978; Sroufe & Waters, 1976; Stern, 1977). This progressively more active involvement has parallels in various realms of development during infancy, such as persistence in the pursuit of an object or other goal (Bühler, 1930). Our data clearly indicate that this general developmental principle also applies to Down syndrome infants.

Perhaps the most persuasive data on the affect-cognition interchange were found in the cognitive test results. It was found that the level of cognitive development as measured by performance on the Uzgiris-Hunt and Bayley scales parallelled the level of affective development as measured by our 30 laughter items. Thus, the earlier suggested *association* between affective and cognitive development appears to be a valid *relationship*. It seems clear to us that cognitive and socioemotional aspects of development are inextricably intertwined (Cicchetti & Pogge-Hesse, 1981; in press). Within the organizational perspective, affect and cognition are viewed as inseparable—as two aspects of the same developmental process. Our research offered clear support for the premise that affective and cognitive development proceed in an integrated, interlocking manner. Studying the development of infant affective expression is clearly integral for understanding emerging cognitive capacities.

The Ontogenesis of Negative Reactions. From an organizational perspective, questions about *whether* infants show negative or positive reactions to novel events become subsumed by questions concerning contextual and developmental factors mediating those reactions. As Sroufe (1977) has noted, in some circumstances infants react positively to strangers, whereas in others they respond negatively. More broadly, empirical research has shown that incongruous events can produce the range of affective reactions from laughter and smiling to wariness and distress, depending on agent, setting, sequence of events, familiarization time, and other aspects of context (Sroufe, Waters, & Matas, 1974). A close-relationship between strong positive and strong negative affect is assumed within the organismic-developmental perspective, as they are linked by degree of cognitively produced arousal. However, because the same event can produce the range of affective reactions, factors beyond information inherent in the event are seen as influencing the direction of and thresholds for affective reactions (Cicchetti & Sroufe, 1976b, 1978; Sroufe & Waters, 1976).

Looming and Visual Cliff Studies. Two of the classic paradigms utilized to assess the development of depth perception employed by researchers in perceptual development have been the study of infants' reactions to "looming" objects and the study of infants' (both prelocomotor and locomotor) responses to the "visual cliff" (Bower, Broughton, & Moore, 1970; Cicchetti & Mans, 1976; Gibson & Walk, 1960; Schwartz, Campos, & Baisel, 1973; Yonas, Bechtold, Frankel, Gordon, McRoberts, Norcia, & Sternfels, 1977). In our own research, we have found that these experimental procedures have provided valuable information about the Down syndrome infant's socioemotional and cognitive development as well. Again, these results are not at all surprising; rather, they are *predictable* from within an organizational perspective. Because development is viewed as an integrated process, perceptual, cognitive, and learning processes clearly contribute to determining which particular socioemotional response will be elicited in a given stimulus context; conversely, social and emotional factors influence perceptual and cognitive development.

We have compared Down syndrome and nonretarded infants' responses to looming objects at 4, 8, and 12 months and studied Down syndrome infants' responses at 16 months (Cicchetti & Sroufe, 1978). Focusing on the defensive reactions manifested by each group of infants, we found very few differences between Down syndrome and nonretarded babies. Down syndrome and nonretarded babies "defended" themselves from looming objects primarily by blinking, raising their arms in front of their faces, withdrawing, turning away, and crying when approached by objects on a collision course. Only three differences were found in the behavior of these two groups of babies. Eight- and 12-month-old Down syndrome babies blinked significantly more often than did nonretarded infants of these same ages. Across all age groups, more Down syndrome infants emitted multiple blinks to the collision trials than did nonretarded controls. Finally, although there were no differences in the amount of crying displayed at 4 months, significantly more nonretarded than Down syndrome babies cried at 8 and 12 months. In fact, it was not until 16 months that Down syndrome babies showed any substantial crying. Just as we found in our studies of positive affect, there was a close relationship between negative reactions and cognitive development. Those Down syndrome babies who cried had significantly higher scores on the Bayley scales of mental and motor development than those who did not. Thus, those Down syndrome children who have high Bayley scores and show fear and distress reactions early are more differentiated in their cognitive and emotional development.

We conducted two studies examining Down syndrome infants' responses to being placed atop the visual cliff. One group of babies was tested after they had approximately had 1 month of crawling experience. A second sample of infants was studied as soon as they began to crawl. The average age of both groups of infants was approximately 16 months. In those babies with crawling experience, we found that the vast majority (91% of 70 infants) did not traverse the apparent chasm from the "shallow" to the "deep" side of the visual cliff. These data are consistent with findings reported by Gibson and Walk (1960) in their research examining the development of depth perception in nonretarded infants who were capable of locomotion. However, we found that far fewer Down syndrome than normal infants exhibited fear reactions (for example, crying, heart rate acceleration, behavioral freezing), when placed directly atop the deep side. Just as we found for the looming data, the Down syndrome infants who manifested negative reactions were more cognitively sophisticated, having significantly higher scores on the Bayley scales of development than those Down syndrome babies who did not show fear.

In the group of Down syndrome infants who had recently begun crawling, the majority crossed from the shallow to the deep side of the visual cliff. However, after these same infants had been crawling for 3 to 4 weeks, they refused to crawl across the deep gradient. These results are consistent with recent work reported by Campos, Hiatt, Ramsay, Henderson, and Svedja (1978) on nonretarded babies. The results from these two laboratories suggest that "fear" of heights is not innate, as suggested by Gibson and Walk's (1960) early studies, but must be learned by both Down syndrome and nonretarded babies.

Cognitive and Physiological Components of Affect. The organizational perspective of development refers to relationships between systems—physiological and psychological—and to consequences of advances and lags in one system for other systems. Down syndrome infants provide an important entree into the study of these relationships.

Arousal and Assimilation. A number of arousal models of affective expression have been proposed (Berlyne, 1969; Rothbart, 1973; Sroufe & Waters, 1976; Sroufe & Wunsch, 1972). All these models propose that the level of initial tension must exceed a basic threshold for an affective response to occur; similarly, they predict that either positive or negative affect will be greater, the higher the initial tension aroused by the stimulus.

In Sroufe's model of affective expression, both tension and cognitive factors play basic roles. When the infant confronts an incongruous event, there is first an affect-free orienting reaction, leading to a period of appraisal process (Arnold, 1960; Sroufe & Waters, 1976). During orienting and appraisal, tension develops. *Tension refers to cognitively produced arousal in contrast to physiological excitation, its prototype.* This tension may be expressed as positive *or* negative affect, depending on the infant's evaluation. The *magnitude,* but not the direction, of the positive or negative affect will vary with degree of incongruity ("discrepancy," Kagan, 1971) and level of prestimulus arousal. Prestimulus-arousal level is more important the younger or less cognitively developed the infant. Experiential factors and level of cognitive functioning would influence the appraisal process and thereby tension production (Arnold, 1960; Kagan, 1971; Sroufe & Waters, 1976), as would setting familiarization time, and other aspects of context (Sroufe et al., 1974).

Our studies with Down syndrome infants suggest that cognitive factors alone are not sufficient to account for the affective behavior of these babies. Although the results point to a close association between cognitive and affective development, inspection of the data illustrates that the slower cognitive development of the Down syndrome infants only partially explains the reduced incidence of extreme forms of affect (for example, laughter and crying). In the laughter studies, for example, even after comparing the Down syndrome infants with their equivalent developmental-age normal counterparts, a diminution in laughter was observed. This occurred even when the Down syndrome infants were attending carefully and smiling differentially to the items and was especially salient when examining the amount of laughter exhibited to the more complex social and visual presentations. Moreover, there were very few instances of *active* smiles (that is, smiles accompanied by vigorous motor movements) in these babies. Emde, Katz, and Thorpe (1978) report an analogous result in their finding that Down syndrome babies *rarely* exhibit the characteristic pumping arms or "bicycling" pattern displayed by normal infants in interaction with caregivers or strangers. Taken in tandem, these results provide strong corroborative evidence for Sroufe's "tension" model of affective expression.

Down syndrome infants, as a group, are generally *hypo*tonic (McIntire & Dutch, 1964). Accordingly, a lag in affect expression would be predicted by Sroufe's model, especially with intense affect as in laughter and crying. For example, the five most hypotonic babies in our longitudinal sample lagged most, laughing quite late and only to the most vigorous physical stimulation. Our view is that the Down syndrome infant could not process the incongruous stimulus presentations with sufficient speed to generate the tension ("arousal jag," Berlyne, 1969) required for laughter (see also in this regard, Hoffman et al., 1979). This notion is supported by the long latencies to smile and laugh with these babies (a clear delay versus immediate or anticipatory response with nonretarded babies). For these babies the smiles observed seemed to be low-level laughs. Unlike the case with normal infants (who smile to virtually any item presented by the mother in a game-like context), smiling and laughter data ordered the items in the same way.

Likewise, even when cognitive-developmental level was comparable between Down syndrome and nonretarded infants, normal babies showed more negative reactions to the loom and visual cliff. For example, on the visual cliff, the group of Down syndrome infants who had had approximately 1 month of crawling experience rarely ventured out over the deep gradient. There was no relationship found between those who crossed the apparent chasm and cognitive development, as both high-functioning and low-functioning Down syndrome infants did so. These results are in agreement with Campos et al. (1978), who state that locomotor experience, rather than cognitive developmental level, appears to be sufficient to account for infants not traversing the deep side. However, fewer Down syndrome infants were fearful of being placed directly upon the deep side than their cognitive-developmental level would have led us to predict. Far fewer Down syndrome than normal infants cried, even taking developmental level into account. They would not cross the chasm, but they did not show heart-rate acceleration and they did not cry. The Down syndrome infants perhaps had a general arousal modulation problem. They were not readily highly aroused and when highly aroused did not readily recover. Those infants that did cry on the loom, for example, had great difficulty settling again.

Attachment and the Organization of Behavioral Systems. The organizational point of view emphasizes the way in which part functions are integrated into wholes (Werner, 1948; Werner & Kaplan, 1963). The assumption is that any specific means–end relationship or behavioral system can be adequately understood only if its goal and its interrelatedness to other behaviors with the same goal are taken into consideration (Serafica, 1978).

By the end of the first year of life, social behavior can be viewed as organized into major systems that interact in predictable ways. Bowlby (1969) thinks of the attachment behavior system as interacting with other behavior systems, such as exploration and affiliation or social responsiveness to people in general. Once a certain level of development is reached, the infant is not only genetically predisposed to exhibit proximity-maintaining behavior toward a specific object but also to approach and examine the properties of novel animate and inanimate objects. The infant is also able to behave in ways that elicit positive social responses from conspecifics other than the primary caretaker. Bowlby's (1969) ethological/systems-theory perspective of attachment stresses the fundamental nature of the child's tie to its mother. Bowlby states that this attachment relationship is a product of the activity of a number of behavioral systems that have proximity to the mother as a predictable outcome or "set goal." Attachment represents a superordinate construct integrating systems of clinging, sucking, following, crying, and smiling. With development, these systems become more fully differentiated and articulated, making for both flexibility and efficiency in the attainment of the "set goal" of attachment. Bowlby postulates that between 9 and 18 months these become incorporated into more sophisticated goal-corrected systems. He believes that, in the usual course of events, distance between mother and child will seldom exceed a certain maximum. When it does, one or the other will initiate proximity; as the child becomes more mobile, the mother will leave maintenance of proximity increasingly up to the child. Smiling and crying are examples of behavioral systems that have proximity to the mother as a predictable outcome but are not goal corrected, in the sense of varying according to whether the mother is far or near. Following, in contrast, is a goal-corrected activity. When a child is tired, hungry, or otherwise unhappy, it is more likely than at other times to seek proximity to the mother.

One hallmark of Bowlby's attachment theory is its evolutionary perspective. In drawing heavily upon the work of the ethologists, Bowlby has sought to delineate the biological function of attachment behavior within the context of human evolution. According to Bowlby, man's environment of evolutionary adaptedness is the hunting and gathering existence in the preagricultural savannah. Bowlby argues that, in this environment, the biological function of attachment behavior was protection of the organism from attacking predators, and attachment behavior achieved this end by assuring the predictable outcome of close proximity between infant and mother.

Ainsworth, in an interpretation closely related to Bowlby's, stresses that attachment mediates an infant's ability to use the mother as a "secure base" from which to explore the environment. Ainsworth (1973) has generated the most popularly accepted definition of attachment in the developmental literature: "An attachment is an affectional tie that one person forms to another specific person, binding them together in space and enduring over time [p. 1]."

Concomitant with the growing interest in the reciprocal effects that emotion and cognition have upon one another has been a mounting concern over the generalization of the concept of attachment to the understanding of interpersonal relations throughout the human life cycle. For example, it is obvious that Ainsworth's conceptualization of attachment is not confined to the period of infancy. Rather, she speaks of special relationships between people that are both affectional and long lasting. Despite this emphasis, few researchers have studied attachment outside the mother–infant (or toddler) age span.

Ainsworth has been especially interested in studying individual differences in the quality of an infant's attachment relationship with its mother. Insofar as there are differences in the degree to which mothers provide adequate stimulation, and differences in the constitution of infants, there are individual differences in the outcome of the interaction, and therefore in the opportunity for infants to prosper within the mother–child relationship. Ainsworth and Barbara Wittig (1969) developed a laboratory procedure known as the "strange situation" precisely to enable them to categorize infant's according to the security of their attachment to the caregiver. Infants between the ages of 12 and 24 months are classified into securely attached ("B" babies) and insecurely attached ("A" and "C" babies) categories on the basis of their behaviors in the "strange-situation" procedure, comprised of a fixed series of eight increasingly stressful play, separation, and reunion episodes (see Table 15.2 for a description of the strange-situation procedure). The infant's behavior upon reunion with the mother is especially important in assessing the quality of the attachment relationship. This procedure was developed to capture individual differences in the quality of attachment that had been determined through and validated by extensive home observations (Ainsworth et al., 1978).

According to Ainsworth's theoretical position, an infant is viewed as securely attached to the extent that it is able to utilize the mother as a secure base from which to explore the environment; that is, in a nonstressful situation (for example, in a playroom with the mother present as is the case in episode 2 of the

TABLE 15.2
The Strange Situation

Episode	Time	Entrances and Exits
1. Mother, child, experimenter	1 minute	Experimenter leaves room
2. Mother, child	3 minutes	
3. Mother, child, stranger	3 minutes	Stranger enters room
3a. Stranger enters room and sits quietly in her chair.	1 minute	
3b. Stranger converses with mother and remains seated in stranger's chair.	1 minute	
3c. Stranger gradually approaches child and attempts to initiate interaction.	1 minute	
4. Child, stranger	3 minutes	Mother leaves room
5. Mother, child	3 minutes	Mother enters room Stranger leaves room
6. Child alone	3 minutes[a]	Mother leaves room
7. Child, stranger	3 minutes	Stranger enters room
8. Mother, child	3 minutes	Mother enters room Stranger leaves room

[a] Curtailed if the child is unduly distressed.

"strange situation"), a securely attached infant would be expected to be curious, actively engaged in exploration and play, and, although interested in sharing its experiences with the caregiver, not preoccupied with the mother, nor excessively clingy or demanding of her attention. The securely attached infant can thus expend time and energy developing competencies in the object world but is still able to derive satisfaction and security from affective sharing with the mother.

Both in the home and in the strange-situation procedure, securely attached infants tend to be attracted by available toys and to be curious, though somewhat reticent when a stranger comes into the room. When left with the stranger, the securely attached infant may or may not be distressed. The infant generally engages in searching behavior, particularly if distressed, and may be very reluctant to accept comfort from the stranger. Upon reunion, these securely attached infants seek contact with the mother if distressed and maintain contact until comforted, when they return to play. If not distressed, they actively greet the caregiver (for example, by smiling, vocalizing, or showing a toy) and are active in seeking interaction across a distance. A secure attachment appears to be founded on the infant's belief, based on early experience, that the caregiver is a reliable source of comfort. Individual differences are best conceptualized in terms of the quality of attachment; that is, infants are viewed as varying not in the quantity or strength of attachment, but in the quality or security of their attachment relationship.

One inappropriate characterization of Down syndrome infants suggests a failure to form attachment relationships. According to the "Prince Charming" stereotype, these babies generally have cheerful dispositions, are amusing mimics, and show indiscriminate affection. The latter quality would imply a failure to establish a special bond with caregivers. But each aspect of this stereotype is fallacious. Infants with Down syndrome, like nonretarded babies, form attachment relationships. Evidence for this proposition is clear upon careful study.

We studied 3-year-old-Down syndrome children in Ainsworth and Wittig's (1969) strange situation. Down syndrome infants showed specific attachment late, but attachment was still characterized by attachment-exploration balance and use of the caregiver as a secure base (Serafica & Cicchetti, 1976). The only significant difference between Down syndrome and normal infants was that fewer Down syndrome babies cried when their mothers left them alone in the novel environment, a finding that corroborates the work we reported on the ontogenesis of the emotions in these children.

Bretherton and Ainsworth (1974) have proposed that the outcome of an infant's encounter with a stranger in an unfamiliar environment represents the complex inter relationships among behavioral systems: Affiliation, fear-wariness, attachment, and exploration-curiosity. Within this ethological framework, a single behavior may serve one or more systems. This axiom is consistent with a proposition of organismic-developmental theory that a particular behavior may be used as a means to attain one or more goals (Werner & Kaplan, 1963). For example, the behaviors used to maintain proximity to the mother may also be employed for the same purpose via à vis a stranger. Hence, some behavioral indices of attachment may overlap with those of affiliation, and a response indicative of attachment may also reflect fear-wariness (Bretherton, 1978; Tracy, Lamb, & Ainsworth, 1976).

We studied Down syndrome children in the strange situation in order to explore the interplay of the attachment, affiliation, exploratory-curiosity, and fear-wariness systems in these children (Cicchetti & Serafica, 1981). Although there were differences found in *degree* of responsiveness, the *patterns* of response were similar. Down syndrome children showed the same range of behavior as did normal children when they encountered a stranger. Their patterns of interacting with the mother in a reunion situation were quite like those of their nonretarded counterparts. Like the nonretarded controls, Down syndrome children may have initially favored the stranger over the mother as a target of visual regard and smiling, but they were also more likely to have averted gaze from a stranger than from the mother, and their "big" smiles were reserved for the mother. Moreover, behavioral systems appeared to be similarly organized in Down syndrome and nonretarded infants. As was the case with normal infants (Bischof, 1975; Bretherton & Ainsworth, 1974), we demonstrated that a stranger evoked affiliative behaviors in Down syndrome children but also elicited wariness, exploratory, and attachment behaviors. The emergence of these different behavioral systems, the sequence, and their intensity varied with the context and the behaviors of both stranger and mother, just as was found in normal infants. The finding that more than one behavioral system was activated suggests that an adequate description and explanation of social responsiveness must be sufficiently broad and integrative to encompass different but interrelated behavioral systems with their respective functions and determinants.

The behavioral organization manifested by these retarded children may be construed as a reaffirmation of Zigler's (1973) contention that it is more parsimonious to view the development of the personality of the retarded as no different in nature than the development of personality in individuals of normal intelligence. Lower intelligence per se does not necessarily imply a lag in social development nor a different developmental sequence (Bridges & Cicchetti, in press). The relationship between intelligence and social development is far more complex, and the prediction of social responding must take into account, not only the individual's level of cognitive development, but also the environmental context and the diversity of socialization experiences (Serafica & Cicchetti, 1976).

Developmental Reorganization. Perhaps most significant for developmental theory are our data concerning the way development of these Down syndrome babies was organized and reorganized around certain developmental issues. Within the theoretical perspective guiding this research, development is not viewed as a linear acquisition of skills. Rather, development proceeds within one "modus operandus" (Spitz, 1965) until the press of development forces a reorganization—a qualitative turning point after which development proceeds at a new pace and even in a new manner (Emde et al., 1976). In Spitz' theory, the first reorganization is marked by the social smile and generally an increased responsivity to the surround. This increased awareness of external events—the distinction between the "in-here" and the "out-there"—paves the way for response to the particular content of events and recognition memory. Ultimately, such differentiated experience promotes the emergence of recall memory, object permanence, and attachment. This is another qualitative turn in development, with the infant now able to respond to events no longer present, and in anticipation of events. The infant now has a past and a future as well as a present. According to Spitz, stranger anxiety marks this second organization. In his system, the third reorganization, marked by negativism, occurs in the second year when the infant becomes aware of its will in distinction to that of the caregiver. It is aware of itself as actor. Sroufe (1979b) has extended this scheme through the preschool years and has related it to a series of developmental issues pointed to by a number of theorists. An early issue is the regulation of arousal or tension. In the second half year, the formation of an effective attachment relationship is the salient issue. Separation from the caregiver, mastery of the inanimate environment, and the emergence of the autonomous self are subsequent developmental issues (Mahler et al., 1975).

We have found these issues to be as fruitful for viewing the development of Down syndrome infants as they are for viewing normal development. Attachment–exploration balance, wariness of strangers, stage-IV object permanence, categorical fear reactions, and joy in mastery were as characteristic of the "phase of attachment" for Down syndrome infants as they were for normal babies. Likewise, self-recognition, negativism, and increased autonomous functioning occur together (Mans et al., 1978). In normal infants, at about 18 months, visual self-recognition and the development of shame have been found to coincide with the emergence of the autonomous self and positive valuation of the self. Human infants show a changing pattern of mirror behavior over the first 2 years of life (Amsterdam, 1972; Lewis & Brooks-Gunn, 1979). In the very first months, an infant responds to its mirror image with sober staring and little sustained attention. Soon, however, the infant begins to respond socially to its reflection by smiling (or even laughing), vocalizing, touching, and "playing", in much the same manner as it behaves toward other human beings. Between 6 and 12 months, the infant also shows repetitive and deliberate actions, as though it were attempting to relate the mirror image to itself. By the time the infant is a year old, "coy" and avoidant behavior occurs to the mirror. The emergence of self-directed behaviors is first observed at 18 months. Amsterdam (1972) observed the mirror behavior of children before and after a mark of rouge had been placed on their face. Self-directed rather than mirror-directed responses were seen occasionally by 18 months and became common by 20 months. Using the same procedure, Lewis and Brooks (1978) found very similar results. None of their 9- to 12-month olds, one-quarter of the 15- to 18-month group, and three-quarters of the 21- to 24-month olds touched their noses when shown their rouge-marked images in a mirror. Thus, these studies consistently show the emergence of self-directed behavior at 18 months.

We reasoned that, if this index of self-recognition reflected a cognitively based change in self-awareness, then, it would have an explicit relationship with assessments of developmental level. We found that indeed it did. When Down syndrome infants achieved the appropriate developmental level, they, too, showed the emergence of self-recognition. Thus, self-recognition was not the coincidental result of a particular chronological age but, rather, was closely tied to and emerged with other aspects of development. For example, self-recognition begins to appear in normal children by 15 months and is well established by 22 months. However, in these retarded children only those with a nearly normal level of cognitive functioning showed evidence of self-recognition by touching their noses before 23 months. It was not until the age of 34 months and beyond that nearly all Down syndrome children showed self-recognition. Clearly, the emergence of self-directed mirror behavior in these retarded children was delayed, as is their cognitive development. The predominant affective response of younger Down syndrome children was a change from positive affect before rouge smearing to being sober or puzzled afterwards. Older Down syndrome children tended to show surprise or an increase in positive affect following the rouge application. Thus, these reactions, like nose touching, reflected the differential understanding of this event with development in both Down syndrome and normal infants. Given the striking heterogeneity of Down syndrome infants, there are great individual differences in onset, duration, and quality of adaptation within each phase of development, but the stage description fits across the sample.

FUTURE PERSPECTIVE

We have tried to show that the organizational perspective extends the applicability of Zigler's "developmental" position to include individuals suffering from organic impairment. Because Down syndrome infants displayed a similar sequence of development to nonretarded infants on the Uzgiris–Hunt scales (Cicchetti & Mans, in press) and showed similar patterns of organization of cognitive and emotional development as the nonretarded babies, there is some evidence that at least the developmental sequencing and organization are not necessarily different in organically retarded individuals. Furthermore, we have argued that the investigation of the organically retarded in general, from within a developmental perspective, may be more fruitful than the study of the familially retarded. We do not know the true etiology of cultural-familial retardation in any given case. Polygenes for low intelligence may be a necessary factor, but perhaps malnutrition, disease, exposure to environmental toxins, and so on also play a role. When different polygenes are involved in different children's handicaps, they may be interacting with some other factors (that is, they may be *linked* to other genes that will differ depending on which polygenes are involved). If we are to keep etiological groups as homogeneous as possible, Down syndrome may well be the best form of mental retardation to study. Until we can be sure of the etiology of cultural-familial retardation, and that there is no organic pathology in these children, we may be better off studying children whose handicap's nature is known. We have better clues in the latter group of children as to *how* the impairment of the processes underlying performance actually affects their behavior.

As successful as our research strategy has been, much of the important work lies ahead. Further research is needed in order to solve the following questions:

1. Will Down syndrome children show the same stage sequence as normal children throughout their development? So far, we have been able to demonstrate a similar developmental pattern only with respect to infancy and early childhood. Because sensorimotor intelligence has such a long evolutionary history, it is conceivable that it is buffered against even dramatic biologic insults due to its being more highly genetically determined (that is, canalized) (Fishbein, 1976).

Thus, it may very well be possible that the early development is very similar in normal and retarded children, but that, as soon as less-canalized behaviors emerge, differences will be found in the sequencing of development in retarded and nonretarded children.

2. Will other groups of organically retarded children with identifiable syndromes also display the same developmental sequencing as Down syndrome and nonretarded children? We need to study the organization of development in other organically retarded individuals. For example, there is no reason to assume that the cognitive performance of a Down syndrome child will be any more similar to that of a child who has experienced brain damage from anoxia at birth than to that of a child with cultural–familial mental retardation. Demonstrating that developmental predictions are met in only some cognitive domains and not others is still useful for isolating those aspects of the functioning of the organically retarded that are especially affected by any physiological defects. If such similarity in developmental organization could be demonstrated, then our claim that the investigation of organically retarded persons may make useful contributions to a theory of development would be even more strongly supported.

3. What are the *processes* and *strategies* utilized by the familial retarded? For example, it is relevant to Zigler's position on the similarity of mental functioning in MA-matched nonretarded and retarded groups to ask whether a task is solved by the same or different strategies, with or without equal efficiency to that of MA-matched nonretarded groups or perhaps lower-MA nonretarded groups; that is, is or is not the sequence of tool using strategies the same, and is or is not there a delay over and above the delay in mental age? Because familial retardation is thought to reflect the lower-normal distribution of intelligence in the gene pool, it is understandable that researchers have assumed that, a fortiori, its underlying processes must be the same. However, this assertion has yet to be empirically demonstrated across all developmental domains. Thus, the present focus on *achievements* in this population is unwarranted and needs to be supplemented by more process-oriented work. The organizational perspective offers many exciting possibilities upon which a more developmentally sound edifice can be erected.

When studying the familial retarded, we could find, for example, one of the following two types of outcomes: (a) The familial retarded could display *the same* processes and strategies as nonretarded children, just at a slower pace, as suggested by Zigler; or (b) they could show *different* processes and strategies than nonretarded children. In case (a), the familial retarded would have to be considered as much more similar to the nonretarded than Down syndrome children. This case would support Zigler's contention that it may be more fruitful to study the familial rather than the organic retarded in order to contribute to a theory of normal development. If possibility (b) were the case, Zigler's preference for studying the familial retarded would have to be considered as unfounded. Of course, it is highly possible that the experiences of the organic and familial retarded could be different enough to promote motivational differences between them.

It is process-oriented testing that will provide the ultimate empirical solution to the developmental-difference debate. As Weisz and Achenbach (1977) have stated: "for at the heart of this controversy is the question of whether retarded-normal differences exist in the underlying cognitive *processes* [p. 304, emphasis added]."

4. The differences in degree of emotional expression found in Down syndrome infants and toddlers do not seem to impair their coexisting cognitive functions. We were able to conclude that the *qualitative* organization of the emotional and cognitive systems is very similar in Down syndrome and nonretarded infants. Ongoing research in our laboratory is attempting to demonstrate: (a) Which *processes* lead to the differences in *degree* of emotional expression in these children; (b) whether emotions are only the epiphenomena of cognition, as is suggested by the fact that the quantitative differences in emotional expression do not seem to impair cognitive functioning; and (c) whether the cognitive and emotional systems are independent to such an extent that the impairment of one of the systems does not necessarily affect the other one. If these questions can be answered in more detail in the course of our present and future research, we shall be able to explicate more precisely which achievements of the cognitive system are necessary for the emergence of emotional behaviors and vice versa.

5. In order to elucidate the relationship between other behavioral domains, we are studying the linguistic and symbolic development of these children. Language retardation, for example, is an outstanding feature of Down syndrome children. In development after the sensorimotor period, will the developmental process continue to parallel that of nonretarded children, or will the language deficit lead to different patterns of organization? Will the impact of language retardation be primarily cognitive? Will there be handicaps of social and emotional development, over and above problems due to handicaps in reasoning? Does language itself develop along the same path as in nonretarded individuals (for example, in regard to mean length of utterance, morpheme acquisition, case-grammar usage, and type-function of language)? Is their prelinguistic behavior the same? Or, because of the language handicaps, does it become more elaborate than that of nonretarded persons? Is the ontogenesis of symbolic, fantasy, and rule-bound play the same in retarded as in nonretarded individuals? What are the interdependences between higher-order play and cognitive structures? What is the effect of extreme psycholinguistic retardation on the development of symbolic thought?

We shall have to relate the findings on language and symbolization to our results with respect to these children's cognitive and emotional functions. Several outcomes of this research are possible:

a. We could find that all behavioral domains show the same stage sequences in normal and retarded children throughout their development. Perhaps the retarded children would not display the later stages of development at all; that is, retardation would be defined in terms of the lack of development of the later stages of the normal sequence (Inhelder, 1968).

b. Another outcome could be that the retarded children will show lags of development only in one or more, but not all, of the behavioral domains. For example, they could display normal stages and sequences of development for their mental age in cognition and language, whereas behaving emotionally and socially at a level normally characteristic of earlier stages of cognitive and language development. In this case, retardation would be defined as the lag in the emergence of behaviors in one or more behavioral domains compared to the other areas of development.

c. Similar to the results found in Down syndrome children, retarded children in general could be quantitatively different in some domains of development, but not in others. For example, they could display less or more intense emotional and social behaviors without developing qualitative impairments. Retardation would be defined in this case in terms of the quantitative deficiencies of these children.

Outcomes a, b, and c could have the following consequences for a theory of development: Findings of type a would reveal that the later stages of development are not logically necessary, and in that sense not universal for all human beings. Results of type b could provide evidence for the independence of some or all of the assumed behavioral domains, if, for example, the lags in social development did *not* affect the cognitive functions. Furthermore, an outcome of this type could give us some clues as to which achievements in one domain are necessary for the emergence of new behaviors in another domain, if, for example, we were able to show that certain emotional expressions develop only if certain cognitive functions emerge as well. Findings of type c could also provide some evidence with respect to the independence of the behavioral domains, if differences in the degree of behavioral expression in one domain were shown not to affect the behavioral expressions in other domains. Moreover, one would be able to get some idea as to the differences in quantity of behavioral expression that are necessary in order to bring about qualitative changes, and thus different types of developmental stages and sequences. The answers to these questions may have practical as well as theoretical significance for the field of mental retardation. To the extent that we can demonstrate the nature of the relationship between the various developmental domains across the life span (for example, the relationship between cognitive and socioemotional development), we may gain new insights into the best ways to operationalize the definition of mental retardation.

6. The possible experimental results discussed previously may provide fruitful hypotheses as to the linkage between the known organic impairment of Down

syndrome children and its behavioral manifestations. Qualitative lags, missing stages, and/or differences in the degree of behavioral expression in one or more of the domains of development (for example, cognition, emotion, or language) are indicators as to how the known underlying impairment expresses itself or is translated into behavior. With respect to a theory of development, these results can provide us with indirect evidence as to which organic functions underlie certain behavioral manifestations—that is, are necessary for the occurrence of normal behavior.

7. Because we want to learn more about the transitions from one developmental stage to the next, we intend to present Inhelder, Sinclair, and Bovet's (1974) cognitive conflict paradigms to nonretarded and retarded children in order to come up with a more microscopic or microgenetic analysis of the stage transitions that are possible (see Flavell, 1972, for the analysis of possible developmental sequences). Several outcomes may eventuate:

a. Nonretarded children could display the same types of transition from one stage to the next. This case, however, would not be very informative with respect to the definition of retardation, because the investigation of the transitions as such would not allow for a distinction between nonretarded and retarded children. It would, however, provide us with support for the claim that a certain type of stage transition is universal and thus necessary and sufficient for the course of development.

b. Nonretarded and retarded children could both show different types of transitions from stage to stage that nonetheless lead to the same structures; that is, different transitions could be sufficient for the same outcome in both nonretarded and retarded children. As in case a, nonretarded and retarded children could not be distinguished on the basis of their stage transitions.

c. Non-retarded and retarded children could use different strategies to make the transition from one stage to the next, and, within the retarded population, there could be further subgroups distinguishable in terms of different stage transitions. Depending on whether differing strategies could be detected as leading to the same or different outcomes, conclusions could be derived as to which transitions are necessary, sufficient, or necessary and sufficient for the emergence of a particular new stage structure. The information about the necessity of certain types of transition for the emergence of particular stage structures is not likely to be obtained by exclusively studying normal populations. It is conceivable that normal children would use the same or similar types of strategies when making the transition from one stage to the next.

In conclusion, the study of the mentally retarded, organic and cultural–familial, is necessary for the same reasons that cross-cultural research is necessary. Both kinds of studies can tell us what developmental sequences are logically necessary, what alternate pathways of development are possible, and provide evidence on which factors accounting for mental growth are most important (biological, social, emotional, cognitive, or linguistic). We should study not "does x have y," but rather, "in what ways does x use y," and "does a particular mental structure interact with other mental structures in the same way in one culture or etiological group as in another?". Organically retarded persons are not only "different" from nonretarded persons; they are organized in their own right, and the study of that organization will tell us what developmental processes are common to all retarded persons. Thus, a contribution will be made to a general and integrated structural–organismic theory of development that tries to account for development in *all* human beings across *all* behavioral domains.

ACKNOWLEDGMENTS

The authors would like to thank David Balla, Andrea Celenza, Linda Mans, Michael Pakaluk, Hazel Rovno, and Edward Zigler for their careful reading and helpful comments throughout the writing of this chapter. In addition, we want to express our gratitude to the parents of the children who participated in our research. Without their enthusiasm and cooperation, none of this research would have been possible. Most of all, we would like to thank the children themselves who have not only provided us with exciting information but also have made our research enjoyable to carry out. This research was supported in part by grants from the Milton Fund of the Harvard University Medical School and from the Spencer Foundation to author Cicchetti.

REFERENCES

Ainsworth, M. D. S. The development of infant–mother attachment. In B. Caldwell & H. Ricciutti (Eds.), *Review of child development research* (Vol. 3). Chicago: University of Chicago Press, 1973.

Ainsworth, M. D. S., Blehar, M., Waters, E., & Wall, S. *Patterns of attachment*. Hillsdale, N. J.: Lawrence Erlbaum Associates, 1978.

Ainsworth, M. D. S., & Wittig, B. Attachment and exploratory behavior of 1-year olds in a strange situation. In B. M. Foss (Ed.), *Determinants of infant behavior* (Vol. 4). London: Methuen, 1969.

Amsterdam, B. Mirror self-image reactions before age 2. *Developmental Psychobiology*, 1972, *5*, 297–305.

Anthony, E. J. Six applications de la théorie génétique de Piaget à la théorie et à la pratique psychodynamique. *Schweizerische Zeitschrift für Psychologie und ihre Anwendungen*, 1956, *15*, 269–277.

Arend, R., Gove, F., & Sroufe, L. A. Continuity of individual adaptation from infancy to kindergarten: A predictive study of ego resiliency and curiosity in preschoolers. *Child Development*, 1979, *50*, 950–959.

Arnold, M. *Emotion and personality* (2 vols.). New York: Columbia University Press, 1960.

Berlyne, D. E. Laughter, humor, and play. In G. Lindzey & E. Aronson (Eds.), *Handbook of social psychology* (2nd ed, Vol. 3). Boston: Addison–Wesley, 1969.

Bertalanffy, L. von. *General system theory*. New York: Braziller, 1968.

Bischof, N. A systems approach toward the functional connections of attachment and fear. *Child Development*, 1975, *46*, 801–817.

Block, J. *Lives through time*. Berkeley, Calif.: Bancroft Books, 1971.

Block, J. Advancing the science of personality: Paradigmatic shift or improving the quality of research? In D. Magnusson & N. Endler (Eds.), *Psychology at the crossroads*. N. J.: Lawrence Erlbaum Associates, 1977.

Block J. H., & Block, J. The role of ego control and ego resiliency in the organization of behavior. In W. A. Collins (Ed.), *Minnesota Symposium on Child Psychology* (Vol. 13). N. J.: Lawrence Erlbaum Associates, 1979.

Bower, T. G. R., Broughton, J., & Moore, M. K. Infant responses to approaching objects. *Perception and Psychophysics*, 1970, *9*, 193–196.

Bowlby, J. *Attachment and loss* (Vol. 1). New York: Basic Books, 1969.

Bretherton, I. Making friends with 1-year olds: An experimental study of infant–stranger interaction. *Merrill-Palmer Quarterly*, 1978, *24*, 29–51.

Bretherton, I., & Ainsworth, M. Response of 1-year olds to a stranger in a strange situation. In M. Lewis & L. Rosenblum (Eds.), *The origins of fear*. New York: Wiley, 1974.

Bridges, F. A., & Cicchetti, D. Mothers' ratings of the temperament characteristics of Down syndrome infants. *Developmental Psychology*, in press.

Bridges, K. M. B. Emotional development in early infancy. *Child Development*, 1932, *3*, 324–341.

Bridges, K. M. B. The development of the primary drives in infancy. *Child Development*, 1936, *7*, 40–56.

Bronson, G., & Pankey, W. On the distinction between wariness and fear. *Child Development*, 1977, *48*, 1167–1183.

Bühler, C. *The first year of life*. New York: Day, 1930.

Butterworth, G., & Cicchetti, D. Visual calibration of posture in normal and Down syndrome infants. *Perception*, 1978, *7*, 513–525.

Campos, J., Hiatt, S., Ramsay, D., Henderson, C., & Svejda, M. The emergence of fear on the visual cliff. In M. Lewis & L. Rosenblum (Eds.), *The development of affect*. New York: Plenum, 1978.

Carlson, R. Where is the person in personality research? *Psychological Bulletin*, 1971, *75*, 203–219.

Charlesworth, W. R. The role of surprise in cognitive development. In D. Elkind & J. Flavell (Eds.), *Studies in cognitive development: Essays in honor of Jean Piaget*. New York: Oxford University Press, 1969.

Cicchetti, D., & Mans, L. *Down syndrome and normal infants' responses to impending collision*. Paper presented at the annual meetings of the American Psychological Association, Washington, D.C., September 1976.

Cicchetti, D., & Mans, L. Stages, sequences, and structures in the organization of cognitive development in Down syndrome infants. In I. C. Uzgiris & J. McV. Hunt (Eds.), *Research with scales of psychological development in infancy*. Urbana-Champaign: University of Illinois Press, in press.

Cicchetti, D., Mans, L., & Breitenbuecher, M. *The ontogenesis of fear in Down syndrome infants: Implications for the study of brain development*. Paper presented at the biennial meetings of the Society for Research in Child Development, New Orleans, March 1977.

Cicchetti, D., & Pogge-Hesse, P. The relation between emotion and cognition in infant development: Past, present, and future perspectives. In M. Lamb & L. Sherrod (Eds.), *Infant social cognition*. Hillsdale, N.J.: Lawrence Erlbaum Associates, 1981.

Cicchetti, D., & Hesse, P. Affect and intellect: Piagetian contributions to the study of emotional development. In R. Plutchik & H. Kellerman (Eds.), *Emotion: Research and theory*, Vol. 2. N.Y.: Academic Press, in press.

Cicchetti, D., & Serafica, F. The interplay among behavioral systems: Illustration from the study of attachment, affiliation, and wariness in young Down syndrome children. *Developmental Psychology,* 1981, *17,* 326-339.

Cicchetti, D., & Sroufe, L. A. The emotional development of the infant with Down syndrome. In J. L. Poor (Ed.), *Aim to fight low expectations of Down syndrome children.* Forest Lake, Minn.: Forest Lake Printing, 1976. (a)

Cicchetti, D., & Sroufe, L. A. The relationship between affective and cognitive development in Down syndrome infants. *Child Development,* 1976, *47,* 920-929. (b)

Cicchetti, D., & Sroufe, L. A. An organizational view of affect: Illustration from the study of Down syndrome infants. In M. Lewis & L. Rosenblum (Eds.), *The development of affect.* New York: Plenum, 1978.

Connell, D. *Individual differences in attachment: An investigation into stability, implications, and relationships to structure of early language development.* Unpublished doctoral dissertation, Syracuse University, 1976.

Decarie, T. *Intelligence and affectivity in early childhood.* New York: International Universities Press, 1965.

Emde, R., Gaensbauer, T., & Harmon, R. *Emotional expression in infancy: A biobehavioral study.* New York: International Universities Press, 1976.

Emde, R., Katz, E., & Thorpe, J. Emotional expression in infancy: II. Early deviations in Down syndrome. In M. Lewis & L. Rosenblum (Eds.), *The development of affect.* New York: Plenum, 1978.

Endler, N., & Magnusson, D. *Interactional psychology and personality.* New York: Wiley, 1976.

Erikson, E. *Childhood and society.* New York: Norton, 1950.

Fishbein, H. *Evolution, development, and children's learning.* Pacific Palisades: Goodyear, 1976.

Fiske, D. *Strategies for personality research.* San Francisco: Jossey-Bass, 1974.

Flavell, J. Stage-related properties of cognitive development. *Cognitive Psychology,* 1971, *2,* 421-453.

Flavell, J. An analysis of cognitive-developmental sequences. *Genetic Psychology Monographs,* 1972, *86,* 279-350.

Gibson, E. J., & Walk, R. The "visual cliff." *Scientific American,* 1960, *202,* 2-9.

Hoffman, M., Salapatek, P., Kuskowski, M., & Cicchetti, D. *Evidence for visual memory in the evoked potential of human infants.* Presented at the Society for Research in Child Development Meeting, San Francisco, April 1979.

Inhelder, B. Cognitive development and its contribution to the diagnosis of some phenomena of mental deficiency. *Merrill-Palmer Quarterly,* 1966, *11,* 299-319.

Inhelder, B. *The diagnosis of reasoning in the mentally retarded.* New York: Day, 1968 (Originally published, 1943).

Inhelder, B. Some pathologic phenomena analyzed in the perspective of developmental psychology. In B. Inhelder & H. Chipman (Eds.), *Piaget and his school.* New York: Springer Verlag, 1976. (a)

Inhelder, B. Operatory thought process in psychotic children. In B. Inhelder & H. Chipman (Eds.), *Piaget and his school.* New York: Springer Verlag, 1976. (b)

Inhelder, B., Sinclair, H., & Bovet, M. *Learning and the development of cognition.* Cambridge: Harvard University Press, 1974.

Izard, C. *Human emotions.* New York: Plenum, 1977.

Izard, C. On the ontogenesis of emotions and emotion-cognition relationships in infancy. In M. Lewis & L. Rosenblum (Eds.), *The development of affect.* New York: Plenum, 1978.

Jackson, J. H. Evolution and dissolution of the nervous system. In J. Taylor (Ed.), *The selected writings of John Hughlings Jackson* (Vol. 2). New York: Basic Books, 1958 (Originally published, 1884).

Jacobson, M. *Developmental neurobiology.* New York: Plenum, 1978.
Kagan, J. The three faces of continuity. In D. Goslin (Ed.), *Handbook of socialization theory and research.* Chicago: Rand McNally, 1969.
Kagan, J. *Change and continuity in infancy.* New York: Wiley, 1971.
Kagan, J., & Moss, H. *Birth to maturity.* New York: Wiley, 1962.
Kohlberg, L. Stage and sequence: The cognitive-developmental approach to socialization. In D. Goslin (Ed.), *Handbook of socialization theory and research.* Chicago: Rand McNally, 1969.
Lewis, M. The meaning of a response or why researchers in infant behavior should be Oriental metaphysicians. *Merrill Palmer Quarterly,* 1967, *13,* 7-18.
Lewis, M., & Brooks, J. Self-knowledge and emotional development. In M. Lewis & L. Rosenblum (Eds.), *The development of affect.* New York: Plenum, 1978.
Lewis, M., & Brooks-Gunn, J. *Social cognition and the acquisition of self.* New York: Plenum, 1979.
Lewis, M., & Rosenblum, L. (Eds.), *The development of affect.* New York: Plenum, 1978.
Mahler, M., Pine, F., & Bergman, N. *The psychological birth of the infant.* New York: Basic Books, 1975.
Mans, L., Cicchetti, D., & Sroufe, L. A. Mirror reactions of Down syndrome infants and toddlers: Cognitive underpinnings of self-recognition. *Child Development,* 1978, *49,* 1247-1250.
Masters, J., & Wellman, H. The study of human infant attachment: A procedural critique. *Psychological Bulletin,* 1974, *81,* 218-237.
Matas, L., Arend, R., & Sroufe, L. A. Continuity of adaptation in the second year: The relationship between quality of attachment and later competence. *Child Development,* 1978, *49,* 547-556.
McIntire, M. D., & Dutch, S. J. Mongolism and generalized hypotonia. *American Journal of Mental Deficiency,* 1964, *68,* 669-670.
Milgram, N. The rationale and irrational in Zigler's motivational approach to mental retardation. *American Journal of Mental Deficiency,* 1969, *73,* 527-535.
Milgram, N. A. Cognition and language in mental retardation: Distinctions and implications. In D. K. Routh (Ed.), *The experimental psychology of mental retardation.* Chicago: Aldine, 1973.
Milner, E. *Human neural and behavioral development.* Springfield, Ill.: Thomas, 1967.
Mischel, W. *Personality and assessment.* New York: Wiley, 1968.
Mischel, W. Continuity and change in personality. *American Psychologist,* 1969, *24,* 1012-1018.
Odom-Brooks, P., & Arnold, D. Cognitive development in mental subnormality. In V. Hamilton and M. Vernon (Eds.), *The development of cognitive processes.* New York: Academic Press, 1976.
Penrose, L., & Smith, G. *Down's anomaly.* Boston: Little, Brown, 1966.
Piaget, J. *The origins of intelligence in children.* New York: International Universities Press, 1952.
Piaget, J. Les relations entre l'intelligence et l'affectivité dans le developpement de l'enfant. *Bulletin de Psychologie,* 1954, *7.*
Piaget, J., & Inhelder, B. *The psychology of the child.* New York: Basic Books, 1969.
Pinard, A., & Laurendeau, M. "Stage" in Piaget's cognitive-developmental theory: Exegesis of a concept. In D. Elkind & J. Flavell (Eds.), *Studies in cognitive development: Essays in honor of Jean Piaget.* New York: Oxford University Press, 1969.
Reese, H., & Overton, W. Models of development and theories of development. In L. R. Goulet & P. Baltes (Eds.), *Life span developmental psychology: Research and theory.* New York: Academic Press, 1970.
Rheingold, H., & Eckerman, C. Fear of the stranger: A critical examination. In H. Reese (Ed.), *Advances in child development and behavior.* New York: Academic Press, 1973.
Rothbart, M. Laughter in young children. *Psychological Bulletin,* 1973, *80,* 247-256.
Sameroff, A., & Chandler, M. Reproductive risk and the continuum of care-taking casualty. In F. Horowitz (Ed.), *Review of child development research* (Vol. 4). Chicago: University of Chicago Press, 1975.

Santostefano, S. *A bio-developmental approach to clincial child psychology.* New York: Wiley, 1979.
Schwartz, A., Campos, J., & Baisel, E. The visual cliff: Cardiac and behavioral correlates on the deep and shallow sides at five and nine months of age. *Journal of Experimental Child Psychology,* 1973, *15,* 85-99.
Serafica, F. C. The development of attachment behaviors: An organismic-developmental perspective. *Human Development,* 1978, *21,* 119-140.
Serafica, F., & Cicchetti, D. Down's syndrome children in a strange situation: Attachment and exploratory behaviors. *Merrill-Palmer Quarterly,* 1976, *22,* 137-150.
Sherrington, C. *The integrative action of the nervous system.* New York: Scribner's, 1906.
Shultz, T., & Zigler, E. Emotional concomitants of visual mastery in infants. *Journal of Experimental Child Psychology,* 1970, *10,* 390-402.
Spencer, H. *The principles of psychology* (Vol. II). New York: Appleton, 1896 (Originally published, 1870).
Spitz, R. *A genetic field theory of ego formation.* New York: International Universities Press, 1959.
Sroufe, L. A. The developmental significance of the construct of wariness. *Child Development,* 1977, *48,* 731-746.
Sroufe, L. A. Socioemotional development. In J. Osofsky (Ed.), *Handbook of infant development.* New York: Wiley, 1979. (a)
Sroufe, L. A. The coherence of individual development. *American Psychologist,* 1979, *34,* 834-831. (b)
Sroufe, L. A., & Waters, E. The ontogenesis of smiling and laughter: A perspective on the organization of development in infancy. *Psychological Review,* 1976, *83,* 173-189.
Sroufe, L. A., Waters, E., & Matas, L. Contextual determinants of infant affective response. In M. Lewis & L. Rosenblum (Eds.), *The origins of behavior* (Vol. 2), *Fear.* New York: Wiley, 1974.
Sroufe, L. S., & Wunsch, J. The development of laughter in the first year of life. *Child Development,* 1972, *43,* 1326-1344.
Stechler, G., & Carpenter, G. A viewpoint on early affective development. In J. Hellmuth (Ed.), *Exceptional infant.* Seattle: Special Child Publications, 1967.
Stern, D. *The first relationship.* Cambridge: Harvard University Press, 1977.
Teitelbaum, P. The encephalization of hunger. In E. Stellar & J. Sprague (Eds.), *Progress in physiological psychology* (Vol. 4). New York: Academic Press, 1971.
Teitelbaum, P. Levels of integration of the operant. In W. K. Honig & J. Staddon (Eds.), *Handbook of operant behavior.* Englewood Cliffs, N. J.: Prentice-Hall, 1977.
Tracy, R., Lamb, M., & Ainsworth, M. D. S. Infant approach behavior as related to attachment. *Child Development,* 1976, *47,* 571-578.
Uzgiris, I., & Hunt, J. *Assessment in infancy.* Urbana: University of Illinois Press, 1975.
Waddington, C. H. *The strategy of genes.* London: Allen & Unwin, 1957.
Waddington, C. H. *Principles of development and differentiation.* New York: Macmillan, 1966.
Waters, E. The reliability and stability of individual differences in infant-mother attachment. *Child Development,* 1978, *49,* 483-494.
Waters, E., Wippman, J., & Sroufe, L. A. Attachment, positive affect, and competence in the peer group: Two studies in construct validation. *Child Development,* 1979, *50,* 821-829.
Weir, M. Mental retardation. *Science,* 1967, *157,* 576-577.
Weiss, P. *Principles of development.* New York: Hafner, 1969.
Weisz, J., & Achenbach, T. Effects of IQ and mental age on hypothesis behavior in normal and retarded children. *Developmental Psychology,* 1977, *11,* 304-310.
Weisz, J., & Zigler, E. Cognitive development in retarded and nonretarded persons: Piagetian tests of the similar sequence hypothesis. *Psychological Bulletin,* 1979, *86,* 831-851.

Werner, H. Process and achievement: A basic problem of education and developmental psychology. *Harvard Educational Review,* 1937, *7,* 353-368.
Werner, H. *Comparative psychology of mental development.* Chicago: Follett, 1948.
Werner, H. The concept of development from a comparative and organismic point of view. In D. Harris (Ed.), *The concept of development.* Minneapolis: University of Minnesota Press, 1957.
Werner, H., & Kaplan, B. *Symbol formation.* New York: Wiley, 1963.
Wing, J., Gould, G., Yeates, S., & Brierly, L. Symbolic play in severely mentally retarded and in autistic children. *Journal of Child Psychology and Psychiatry,* 1977, *18,* 167-178.
Woodward, M. Application of Piaget's Theory to Research in Mental Deficiency. In N. R. Ellis (Ed.), *Handbook of Mental Deficiency: Psychological theory and research.* New York: McGraw-Hill, 1963.
Yonas, A., Bechtold, A. G., Frankel, D., Gordon, F. R., McRoberts, G., Norcia, A., & Sternfels, S. Development of sensitivity to information for impending collision. *Perception and Psychophysics,* 1977, *21,* 97-104.
Zigler, E. Developmental versus difference theories of mental retardation and the problem of motivation. *American Journal of Mental Deficiency,* 1969, *73,* 536-556.
Zigler, E. The retarded child as a whole person. In D. Routh (Ed.), *The experimental study of mental retardation.* Chicago: Aldine, 1973.
Zigler, E., & Balla, D. Personality factors in the performance of the retarded: Implications for clinical assessment. *Journal of the American Academy of Child Psychiatry,* 1977, *16,* 19-37.

Author Index

Italics denote pages with bibliographic information.

A

Aaronson, D., 146, *149*
Abel, T. M., 230, 234, *269*
Abelson, W. D., 9, 19, *24, 25*, 208, *211*, 260, *276*
Abramson, L. Y., 28, 33, 37, *38*
Achenbach, R., 19, 20, 21, 22
Achenbach, T. M., 32, *38*, 70, *80*, 177, 181, *186*, 226, 227, 233, 234, 243, 246, 247, 249, 252, 254, 259, 260, 261, 264, 267, *269, 275*, 290, 310, *317*
Ainsworth, M. D. S., 278, 279, 303, 305, *314, 317*
Allen, G., 73, *81*
Allen, R. M., 259, 265, 267, *270*
Allik, J. P., 146, *152*
Amsterdam, B., 307, *313*
Anastasi, A., 213, *270*
Andrews, D. R., 38, *38*
Anthony, E. J., 282, 284, *313*
Arend, R., 278, 287, *313, 316*
Arnold, D., 280, *316*
Arnold, M., 300, *313*
Ash, F. E., 249, 266, *274*
Atkinson, R. C., 128, *149*
Attwell, A. A., 170, *187*

B

Backer, M. H., 74, *80*
Baddeley, A. D., 147, *149*
Badt, M. I., 174, *186*, 268, *270*
Baisel, E., 299, *316, 317*
Balla, D., 11, 12, 13, 14, 15, 16, 19, 20, 21, 22, 23, 24, 25, 42, 45, 46, 48, 49, *50*, 52, 53, 54, 55, 56, *57, 58*, 72, 77, *80*, 82, 115, 116, 117, *119, 120*, 131, 132, *149*, 176, 180, *186*, 210, *210, 211*, 243, *270*, 285, *318*
Bartlett, C. J., 170, *186*
Baumeister, A. A., 41, *56*, 123, 126, 127, 137, 141, *149*, 170, 174, *186*
Bell, R., 48, *56*
Bechtold, A. G., 299, *318*
Belmont, J. M., 124, 126, 138, 142, 143, 144, 145, 149, *149*, 201, *202*
Bentler, P. M., 259, *271*
Berch, D. B., 146, *150*
Bergman, N., 287, 306, *316*
Berlyne, D. E., 300, *313*
Bertalanffy, L. von., 288, *313*
Bethon, G., 258, 265, 267, *271*
Bialer, I., 29, *39*
Bigelow, G., 33, *39*

AUTHOR INDEX

Bijou, S. W., 182, *186*, 197, *202*
Bilsky, L. H., 125, *150*
Binder, A., 262, *270*
Bischof, N., 379, 305, *314*
Bjaanes, A. T., 50, *56*
Bjork, R. A., 147, *152*
Blackwell, J., 35, *39*
Blehar, M., 378, 303, *313*
Block, J., 239, *274*, 277, 278, 287, *314*
Block, J. H., 277, 278, 287, *314*
Blount, W. R., 243, *270*
Bolles, R. C., 139, *150*
Borkowski, J. G., 125, *150*, 231, 236, 245, *275*
Botkin, P. T., 246, *271*
Bovet, M., 312, *315*
Bower, T. G. R., 299, *314*
Bowlby, J., 52, *56*, 302, *313*
Braine, M. D. S., 227, *270*
Bransford, J. D., 147, *151*, *152*
Brekke, B., 259, 264, *270*
Breitenbuecher, M., 278, 293, 294, 299, *314*
Bretherton, I., 279, 305, *314*
Bridges, F. A., 306, *314*
Bridges, K. M. B., 282, 294, *314*
Brierly, L., 284, *318*
Bronson, G., 278, *314*
Brooks, J., 307, *316*
Brooks-Gunn, J., 307, *316*
Broughton, J., 299, *314*
Brown, A. L., 78, *80*, 125, 128, 129, 145, *150*, 258, 264, *270*
Brown, L. B., 228, 229, 243, *271*
Brownlee, L., 54, *57*
Bruner, J., 244, *270*
Bryant, P. E., 255, *270*
Buck-Morss, S., 215, *270*
Budoff, M., 79, *80*
Bühler, C., 298, *314*
Burke, D., 146, *151*
Burlingham, D., 14, *23*
Burt, C., 89, *98*
Bush, E. S., 30, 33, *39*
Butler, E. W., 50, *56*
Butterfield, E. C., 9, 11, 12, 19, *22*, 24, *25*, 44, 45, 46, 52, 53, 54, *56*, *58*, 74, 77, *82*, 124, 132, 138, 142, 143, 144, 145, 149, *149*, 170, 174, 177, 180, *186*, *187*, *188*, 200, 201, *202*, 208, *211*, 260, *276*
Butterworth, G., 294, *314*

Byars, J. A., 267, *274*
Byck, M., 18, *22*

C

Cameron, A., 175, *186*
Camilli, G., 267, *270*
Campione, J. C., 78, *80*, 125, 128, 129, *150*
Campos, J., 299, 300, 301, *314*, *316*, *317*
Caparulo, B. K., 17, *22*
Capobianco, F., 44, 45, *58*
Cardozo, C. W., 259, 265, 267, *270*
Carkhuff, R. R., 73, *80*
Carlson, R., 278, *314*
Carpenter, G., 292, *317*
Cavalier, A. R., Jr., 145, *150*
Cavanaugh, J. C., 125, *150*
Chandler, M., 292, *316*
Chapin, M., 38, *39*
Charles, D. C., 260, 264, *272*
Charlesworth, W. R., 226, *270*, 294, *314*
Child, I., 21, *25*
Cicchetti, D., 235, 236, *270*, 278, 279, 293, 294, 295, 298, 299, 301, 306, 307, *314*, *315*, *316*, 317
Clark, A. D. B., 11, *22*, 44, *56*
Clarke, A. M., 11, *22*, 44, *56*
Cohen, H., 55, *56*
Cohen, R. L., 142, 143, 146, *150*
Cohn-Jones, L., 256, 265, *270*
Cole, M., 146, *150*, 244, *270*
Connell, D., 278, *315*
Conroy, J. W., 55, *56*
Corter, H. M., 73, *80*
Cox, F., 14, *22*
Craig, E. M., 10, *24*
Craik, F. I. M., 146, 147, *150*
Crome, L., 126, *150*
Cromwell, R. L., 15, *22*, 33, *39*, 189, *202*, 244, *270*
Croskery, J., 73, *81*

D

Dark, V. J., 147, *150*
Davidson, W., 33, 35, 37, *39*
Davis, K. E., 35, *39*
Debus, R. L., 38, *38*

Decarie, T. G., 234, *270*, 294, *315*
de Labry, J., 17, *25*, 178, *188*, 210, *211*
Demaine, G., 54, *57*
Dennis, W., 249, 266, *274*
Denny, M. R., 268, *270*
DeVries, R., 231, 247, 249, 251, 252, 254, 257, 265, *270*, *271*
Diener, C. I., 30, 31, 32, *39*
Dingman, H. F., 170, *187*
Dodwell, P., 256, *271*
Doris, J., 246, *274*
Durkin, K., 175, *187*
Dutch, S. J., 301, *316*
Dweck, C. S., 30, 31, 32, 33, 35, 37, 38, *39*
Dyck, D. G., 38, *39*
Dyk, R., 21, *25*, 171, *188*

E

Eckerman, C., 278, *316*
Edgerton, R. B., 49, *57*
Elkind, D., 231, 243, 247, *271*
Ellis, N. R., 122, 124, 125, 132, 138, 142, 143, 144, 145, *150*, 156, *161*, 178, 179, *186*, 200, *202*, 243, *271*
Emde, R., 278, 287, 301, 306, *315*
Endler, N., 277, *315*
Enna, B., 33, 35, 37, *39*
Everett, I. R., 232, 233, *273*
Eyman, R. K., 54, *57*

F

Fahel, L. S., 78, *81*
Faterson, H. F., 21, *25*, 171, *188*
Ferretti, R. P., 139, 145, *150*
Field, D., 79, *80*, *81*, 118, *119*
Fishbein, H., 287, 308, *315*
Fiske, D., 277, *315*
Flavell, J. H., 129, *150*, 246, *271*, 280, 286, 288, 312, *315*
Floor, L., 29, 30, *39*
Foshee, J. G., 73, *81*
Frank, H. S., 146, *151*
Frankel, D., 299, *318*
Frankel, F., 146, *150*
Franks, J. J., 147, *151*
Frazer, D. W., 55, *56*
Freud, A., 14, *23*

Fry, C. L., 246, *271*
Furth, H. G., 115, 116, *119*, *120*, 159, *162*, 176, 177, 178, *187*, 259, *271*

G

Gaensbauer, T., 278, 287, 306, *315*
Gardener, D. H., 21, *23*
Gasstrom, L. L., 35, *39*
Gergen, K. J., 35, *39*
Gibbons, B. N., 35, *39*
Gibbons, F. X., 35, *39*
Gibson, B. J., 32, 37, *39*, 244, *271*
Gibson, E. J., 299, 300, *315*
Gladwin, T., 61, *81*, 185, *187*
Glaser, R., 129, 141, *152*
Glenn, L., 54, *57*
Glidden, L. M., 125, *151*
Go, E., 243, 247, *271*
Goetz, T. E., 37, *39*
Goff, G., 12, *25*
Goldfarb, W., 14, *23*
Goldschmid, M., 259, *271*
Goldstein, K., 66, 67, *81*
Goodenough, D. R., 21, *25*, 171, *188*
Goodnow, J. J., 16, *23*, 258, 265, 267, *271*
Gordon, D. A., 19, *23*
Gordon, F. R., 299, *318*
Gould, G., 284, *318*
Gould, L., 18, *26*, 181, *188*
Gove, F., 278, 287, *313*
Gowen, A., 142, *150*
Granich, L., 250, 251, 265, *271*
Grant, D. A., 262, *271*
Grant, G. W. B., 50, *57*
Gray, W. D., 147, *151*
Green, B. F., 220, 231, 240, *271*
Green, C., 16, 18, *23*, 77, *81*, 177, 180, *186*, 205, *205*
Green, M. B., 221, *272*
Greenwald, A. G., 262, 263, *271*
Grossman, H., 123, *151*
Gruen, G., 16, *23*, *24*, 178, *187*, 210, *211*, 226, 227, 256, 261, 264, *271*
Gruneberg, M. M., 147, *151*

H

Hagen, J. W., 41, *57*
Hale, G. A., 252, 253, 258, 266, 267, *275*

Hall, J. F., 146, *151*
Harcum, E. R., 146, *151*
Harmon, R., 278, 287, 306, *315*
Harter, S., 13, 15, 18, *23*, 25, 26, 159, *161*, 174, *187*, 210, *211*, 243, 245, 268, *271*, 276
Havighurst, F. J., 17, *23*
Healey, D., 232, 234, *273*
Hebb, D. O., 126, *151*
Heber, R. T., 244, *271*
Henderson, C., 300, 301, *314*
Herman, J. F., 146, *152*
Hermelin, B., 72, *81*, 114, *120*, 176, 178, *187*
Hiatt, S., 300, 301, *314*
Hiroto, D. S., 33, *39*
Hirsch, J., 164, *187*
Hodgden, L., 19, *26*, 75, *82*
Hoffman, M., 294, 301, *315*
Hooper, F., 222, *273*
Hopkins, K. D., 267, *270*
House, B. J., 124, *152*, 156, *162*, 189, *202*
Houssiadas, L., 228, 229, *271*
Howell, H. H., 49, *57*
Hubbell, M., 54, *57*
Hunt, J. McV., 236, 240, 245, *271*, 275, 295, *317*
Huntsman, N. J., 41, *57*
Huttenlocher, J., 146, *151*

I

Inhelder, B., 220, 221, 229, 232, 237, *272*, 274, 280, 281, 283, 286, 292, 293, 311, 312, *315*, *316*
Irons, N. M., 12, *23*
Irvine, E., 14, *23*
Iscoe, I., 174, *187*
Izard, C., 294, *315*

J

Jackson, J., 54, *57*, 285, *315*
Jacobson, M., 285, *315*
Jarvis, P. E., 246, *271*
Jellinger, J., 126, *151*
Jones, E. E., 35, *39*
Jongeward, R. H., 147, *152*

Jordan, C., 35, *39*
Jordan, V. B., 220, *272*

K

Kagan, J., 277, 297, 300, *315*, *316*
Kahn, J. V., 245, 246, 257, 261, 264, 265, *272*
Kantowitz, B. H., 145, *152*
Kanzer, P., 181, *188*
Kaplan, B., 285, 290, 302, 305, *318*
Kaplun, D., 11, *23*
Kappauf, W. E., 245, 259, *272*
Karp, S. A., 21, *25*, 171, *188*
Katz, E., 301, *315*
Katz, P., 20, 21, *23*, 41, *57*
Kaufman, M. E., 73, *81*, 174, *187*
Keasey, C. T., 260, 264, *272*
Kelley, H. H., 35, *39*
Keogh, B. K., 16, *23*
Kern, W. H., 73, *81*
Kessler, S., 29, *39*
Kier, R. J., 16, *23*
Kinder, E. F., 230, 248, 265, *272*
King, R. D., 47, 48, 49, 50, *57*
Klauss, S. D., 221, *272*
Klein, M., 55, *56*
Klein, R., 252, 253, 258, 266, 267, *275*
Kleinman, J. S., 50, *57*
Klem, L., 146, *152*
Knight, J. L., Jr., 145, *152*
Knopf, E. D., 16, *24*
Koegler, R., 243, 247, *271*
Kohlberg, L., 215, 217, 231, 233, 237, 242, 258, 262, *272*, 288, *316*
Konner, M. J., 244, *275*
Kooistra, W. H., 224, *272*
Kossan, N., 12, 15, 19, 20, 22, 50, *56*
Kounin, J., 14, 17, *23*, 43, *57*, 61, 64, 66, 69, *81*, 121, *151*, 170, 179, *187*, 213, *272*
Kuhn, D., 246, *272*
Kurlander, H. M., 30, *39*
Kuskowski, M., 294, 301, *315*

L

Labov, W., 244, *272*
Lamb, M., 305, *317*

Landesman-Dwyer, S., 50, *57*
Lane, E. B., 230, 248, 265, *272*
Laurendeau, M., 280, *316*
Leahy, R., 21, *23*
Lehtinen, M. A., 121, *152*
Lei, T., 54, *57*
Lenneberg, E., 165, *187*
Lerner, E., 230, *272*
Levine, E., 9, *24*, 208, *211*
Levine, J., 18, *26*, 181, *188*
Levine, M., 31, *39*
Lewin, K., 43, *57*, 61, 62, *81*, 121, *151*, 170, 179, *187*, 213, 272
Lewis, M., 278, 294, 307, *316*
Light, C. S., 21, *23*
Lister, C., 224, *272*
Lobb, H., 138, *151*
Loftus, G. R., 147, *150*
Lovell, K., 228, 232, 233, 234, *273*
Lunzer, E. A., 223, *273*
Luria, A. R., 72, *81*, 93, 96, *98*, 99, 100, 101, 102, 103, 105, 106, 107, 108, 109, 110, 111, 112, 113, *119*, *120*, 156, *161*, 176, 179, *187*, 243, *273*
Lustman, N. M., 20, *23*, 53, *57*
Lutkus, A., 255, 265, *273*
Lyle, J., 174, *187*
Lyle, L., 268, *273*
Lynch, S., 174, *187*
Lyon, D. R., 146, *151*

M

MacIntyre, A., 11, *22*
MacLean, W. E., Jr., 19, *23*, 123, 126, 127, 141, *149*
MacMillan, D. L., 16, 19, *23*, *24*, 33, *39*
Magaret, A., 70, *81*
Magnusson, D., 277, *315*
Mahaney, E. J., 236, 237, 238, 245, *273*, *275*
Mahler, M., 287, 306, *316*
Maier, S. F., 33, *39*
Malamud, N., 126, *151*
Mannix, J. B., 223, *273*
Mans, L., 294, *314*, 278, 293, 299, 307, *316*
Marchi, J. V., 221, *273*
Masland, R. L., 127, *151*
Masters, J., 277, *316*
Matas, L., 278, 287, 298, 300, *316*, *317*

May, A. E., 49, *57*
McCann, B., 174, *187*
McCarthy, E., 15, *22*
McCarver, R. B., 10, *24*
McCormick, M., 21, *24*, 48, 49, 50, *57*
McIntire, M. D., 301, *316*
McKinney, J. D., 73, *80*
McLain, R., 54, *57*
McLaughlin, J. A., 236, 238, *275*
McManis, D., 222, 224, 225, 226, 252, 253, 254, 255, 256, 257, 265, 266, *273*
McPherson, M. W., 121, *151*
McRoberts, G., 299, *318*
Melmelstein, E., 226, *273*
Melton, A. W., 144, 147, *151*
Milgram, N. A., 114, 115, 116, 117, 119, *120*, 122, *151*, 159, *162*, 176, 177, 178, *187*, 192, *202*, 216, 217, 243, 262, *273*, 279, *316*
Miller, C., 54, *57*
Miller, W. R., 30, *39*
Milner, E., 285, *316*
Mischel, W., 277, *316*
Mitchell, B., 232, 233, *273*
Moore, M. K., 299, *314*
Moores, B., 50, *57*
Morris, C. D., 147, *151*, *152*
Moss, H., 277, *316*
Myers, B., 14, *25*
Myers, C. E., 170, *187*

N

Nakamura, C., 19, *24*, 53, *57*
Nassafat, M., 239, *273*
Nealon, J., 143, 146, *150*
Nelson, S., 33, 35, 37, *39*
Nelson, T. O., 147, *151*
Netley, C., 143, *150*
Norcia, A., 299, *318*
Norman, D. A., *152*
Nugent, C. M., 138, *151*

O

O'Connor, N., 72, *81*, 114, *120*, 176, 178, *187*
Odom-Brooks, P., 280, *316*

Ollendick, R., 16, 23, 24, 210, 211
Orpet, R. E., 170, 187
Orr, P. R., 247, 266, 274
Ottinger, E., 16, 23, 210, 211
Overton, W. F., 213, 273, 286, 316

P

Pagell, W., 79, 80
Pankey, W., 278, 314
Papalia, D., 222, 273
Penney, R. H., 73, 81
Penrose, L. S., 10, 24, 293, 316
Peterson, W. M., 73, 81
Phillips, D., 21, 24
Phillips, L., 21, 24
Piaget, J., 119, 120, 215, 221, 229, 230, 232, 250, 251, 252, 253, 273, 274, 292, 293, 316
Pinard, A., 280, 316
Pine, F., 287, 306, 316
Plenderleith, M., 17, 24, 71, 72, 81
Pogge-Hesse, P., 294, 295, 298, 314
Popper, K. R., 215, 274
Postman, L., 147, 151
Prothro, E. T., 248, 249, 251, 266, 274

R

Raber, S., 33, 37, 39
Rabinovitch, M. S., 21, 24, 146, 151
Rakover, S. S., 147, 152
Ramsay, D., 300, 301, 314
Raynes, N. V., 47, 48, 49, 50, 57
Reese, H., 286, 316
Reiber, M., 176, 187
Reitman, J. S., 139, 152
Resnick, L. B., 129, 141, 152
Rheingold, H., 278, 316
Rholes, W. S., 35, 39
Robinson, H. B., 178, 187
Robinson, N. M., 178, 187
Roediger, H. L., III, 145, 152
Rogers, S. J., 219, 220, 233, 274
Rohwer, W. D., 174, 187
Roodin, P. A., 222, 274
Roscoe, J. T., 267, 274
Rosen, M., 29, 30, 39
Rosenberg, S., 41, 57

Rosenblum, L., 294, 316
Rosenthal, R., 263, 274
Ross, L. E., 138, 152
Ross, S. M., 138, 152
Rothbart, M., 300, 316
Rowland, A. D., 232, 234, 273
Ruble, D. M., 19, 24, 53, 57
Rubin, K. H., 247, 266, 274
Rundus, D., 147, 152
Russell, R. W., 249, 266, 274
Rybash, J. M., 222, 274

S

Sackett, G. P., 50, 57
Salapatek, P., 294, 301, 315
Sameroff, A., 292, 316
Sandberg, T., 142, 150
Sanders, B., 19, 24, 177, 187
Santostefano, S., 278, 316
Sarason, S. B., 10, 24, 61, 81, 185, 187, 246, 274
Sawin, L. G., 35, 39
Schlanger, B. B., 174, 187, 268, 274
Schonebaum, R. M., 137, 152
Schwartz, A., 299, 316, 317
Scott, P., 48, 58
Seim, R., 256, 265, 270
Seitz, V., 9, 24, 208, 211, 260, 276
Seligman, M. E. P., 28, 30, 33, 37, 38, 39
Serafica, F. C., 279, 287, 293, 294, 302, 306, 314, 317
Severance, L. J., 35, 39
Shallenberger, P., 14, 24
Shanks, B., 227, 270
Sharpe, D., 146, 150
Sherrington, C., 285, 317
Shif, Z. I., 79, 81
Shiffrin, R. M., 128, 149
Shulman, L. S., 226, 273
Shultz, T., 18, 24, 294, 317
Siegel, A. W., 146, 152
Siegel, P. S., 73, 81
Siegelman, E., 239, 274
Silverstein, A., 54, 57
Simpson, E. L., 215, 274
Sinclair, H., 312, 315
Sindberg, R. M., 234, 235, 239, 241, 275
Singh, N. N., 223, 224, 274
Sitkei, E. G., 170, 187

Slater, A., 228, *273*
Smedslund, J., 239, 257, *274*
Smeets, P. M., 250, 266, *274*
Smith, G., 293, *316*
Smith, J. D., 247, 266, *274*
Snelbecker, G., 55, *56*
Spencer, H., 287, *317*
Spitz, R. A., 14, *24,* 33, *39,* 52, *57,* 178, 179, *187,* 189, *202,* 287, 306, *317*
Spreat, S., 55, *56*
Sroufe, L. A., 235, 236, 270, *275,* 278, 283, 287, 292, 293, 294, 295, 297, 298, 299, 300, 306, 307, *313, 314, 315, 316, 317*
Stearns, K., 231, *275*
Stechler, G., 292, *317*
Stein, B. S., 147, *152*
Stephens, B., 236, 237, 238, 245, *273*
Stern, D., 298, *317*
Sternberg, R. J., 78, *81*
Sternfels, S., 299, *318*
Stevenson, H. W., 16, 17, 19, *24, 26,* 71, 72, 75, 78, *81, 82,* 178, 180, *187,* 244, *275*
Stevenson, J. W., 252, 253, 258, 266, 267, *275*
Storm, T., 175, *186*
Stott, G., 223, 224, *274*
Strauss, A. A., 121, *152*
Styfco, S. J., 19, *22,* 53, *56,* 116, *119,* 210, *210,* 243, *270*
Sullivan, L., 222, *274*
Svejda, M., 300, 301, *314*
Szeminska, A., 232, *274*

T

Taylor, J. J., 246, 247, 249, 252, 254, 261, 264, *275*
Teasdale, J. D., 28, 33, 37, *38*
Teitelbaum, P., 285, 287, *317*
Terdal, L. G., 73, *81*
Terrell, G., Jr., 175, *187*
Thompkins, B. A., 147, *151*
Thompson, C., 70, *81*
Thorpe, J., 301, *315*
Tizard, J., 10, *24,* 47, 48, 49, 50, *57*
Tolman, E. C., 127, *152*
Trabasso, T., 255, 265, *270, 273*
Tracy, R., 305, *317*
Tulkin, S. R., 244, *275*
Tulving, E., 146, *150*
Turnure, J. E., 19, *24,* 178, *187*

U

Unell, E., 17, *26,* 178, 180, *188*
Uzgiris, I., 295, *317*

V

Van Doorninck, W., 243, *271*
Vining, S. K., 147, *151*
Vore, D. A., 226, 227, 261, 264, *271*

W

Waddington, C. H., 285, *317*
Walk, R., 299, 300, *315*
Wall, S., 278, 303, *313*
Walters, E., 36, *39*
Waters, E., 278, 287, 294, 297, 298, 300, 303, *313, 317*
Watkins, M. J., 147, *150*
Watts, C. A., 170, *187*
Waugh, N. C., *152*
Waxler, C., 48, *58*
Weaver, S. J., 10, 15, *24, 25*
Weir, M., 164, 168, *188,* 280, *317*
Weiss, P., 287, *317*
Weisz, J. R., 19, *22,* 30, 31, 32, 33, 35, 36, 37, *39, 40,* 213, 215, 216, 241, 244, 245, 259, 268, *275,* 310, *317*
Wellman, H., 277, *316*
Werner, H., 21, *25,* 69, *81,* 285, 290, 293, 302, 305, *317, 318*
White, R. W., 18, *25*
Whittenborn, J., 14, *25*
Wickelgren, W. A., 147, *152*
Wiesley, M., 175, *187*
Williams, J., 44, 45, *58*
Williams, J. D., 259, 264, *270*
Windle, C., 10, *25*
Wing, J., 284, *318*
Wippman, J., 278, 287, *317*
Wittig, B., 303, 305, *313*
Winer, B. J., 259, *275*
Witkin, H. A., 21, *25,* 171, *188*
Wohlhueter, M. J., 234, 235, 239, 241, *275*
Wolf, K. M., 14, *24,* 52, *57*
Wolfensberger, W., 54, *57*
Wolff, J. L., 72, *81*
Woodward, A. E., Jr., 147, *152*

Woodward, M., 218, 219, 222, 229, 233, 234, *275, 276,* 280, *318*
Wortis, J., 164, *188*
Wozencraft, F., 146, *152*
Wright, D. L., 19, *24*
Wright, J. W., 246, *271*
Wunsch, J. P., 235, 236, *275*, 294, 295, 300, *317*

Y

Yando, R., 19, 20, *25, 26,* 53, 57, *58*
Yarrow, M., 48, *58*
Yeates, S., 284, *318*
Yntema, D., 146, *152*
Yonas, A., 299, *318*

Z

Zalk, S., 21, *23*
Zax, M., 21, *23*
Zeaman, D., 124, *152,* 156, *162,* 164, *188,* 189, *202*
Zinober, J. W., 137, *152*
Zigler, E., 9, 10, 11, 12, 13, 14, 15, 16, 17, 18, 19, 20, 21, *22, 23, 24, 25, 26,* 33, 34, *40,* 43, 45, 46, 48, 49, 50, 52, 53, 54, *56, 57, 58,* 61, 71, 72, 74, 75, 76, 77, *80, 81, 82,* 111, 115, 116, 117, *119, 120,* 125, 127, 130, 131, 132, 133, 134, *149, 152,* 156, 160, 161, *162,* 164, 165, 166, 168, 170, 174, 176, 177, 178, 181, 183, 184, 185, *186, 188,* 189, 190, 192, 193, 195, 196, 198, 199, *202,* 203, *205,* 208, 209, 210, *210, 211,* 213, 214, 216, 217, 222, 240, 241, 243, 244, 245, 249, 256, 260, 262, 263, 268, *270, 271, 275, 276,* 279, 281, 285, 287, 289, 290, 292, 294, 306, *317, 318*

Subject Index

A

Adaptive Behavior Scale, 54
Affect, 235-236
  interaction with cognition, 293-295, 298, 299, 303, 306, 310, 311;
  and tension model, 300-301
Age,
  and concept of life, 249, 250, 268;
  and rigidity, 63, 69, 171
Agrammatism, 90
Animism, 249-250
Aphasia, 93
Artificialism, 250-251
Attachment, 19, 20, 277, 278-279,
  definition, 303;
  and study of Down's syndrome infants, 305-308;
  theory, 302-304
Attention, 124
Attention theory, 122, 134, 137, 156, 178, 179
Attribution, 16,
  and learned helplessness syndrome, 31, 32-33, 35-36

B

Behavior,
  and central nervous system dysfunction, 126-128;
  difference/defect position and, 191, 192-199;
  mediated by verbal ability, 114-118, in motor/verbal dissociation, 108-111, 114, 117, speech, and, 102-103;
  organizational perspective of study of, 277-279, 282, 288;
  research and theory, studies, 121-125, 176-177, prediction from, 124;
  self-directed, 307;
  socialization and, 100
Brain damage, *see* central nervous system dysfunction

C

CA,
  and difference position, 191;
  matching on cognitive tasks, 166, 167;
  in rigidity formulation, 62, 64, 66, 69;
  and stimulus trace theory, 133, 136, 199;
  used in research, 124-125, 131
Causality, 251
Central nervous system dysfunction, *see also* mental retardation, 84, 88, 89, 91, 93-96, 122, 123, 179, 181, 182, 184, 243, 246, 252, 256, 283, 284, 289, 308, 313;
  and abnormal chromosomes, 293;
  "defect" position and, 193, 194-195, 197;
  and deficits in relative thinking, 248;

Central nervous system dysfunction (*cont.*)
and development/difference controversy, 112–113, 155, 157–158;
and EEG abnormalities, 235, 239, 241, 290;
as "feebleminded", 107;
mental retardation and evidence of, 126–128;
and organization of development, 309;
in speech, 108;
in stimulus trace theory, 136–137, 147, 148, 199
Cerebro-asthenic defects, 106–108, 110
Characteristics of the Treatment Environment measure, 54
Child's Conception of the World (Piaget), 250
Chronological age, *see* CA
Classification, 251–252
Cognition,
and affect, 293–295, 298, 299, 303, 306, 310, 311; content/process issues, 159–160;
continuity/discontinuity issue, 208;
developmental, 85–88, 89, 96, 119, 125, 159, 242–243; stages, 164, 165, 208, 215, 216, 220, 229, 235, 237, 239, 252, 256, of language acquisition, 104–106, 110–111, 119, sensimotor, 218–220;
developmental theory, Piagetian, 214; similar sequence hypothesis, 215–216; and affective development, 236; studies of, 218–242, improvement of studies, 240–241, no support for, 233–234, 239, variabilities in, 235, 239; similar structure hypothesis, 216–217, 242–269, developmental position and, 262, difference position and, 267, studies of, 245–261, and two-group approach, 268–269;
differentiation, 171, 172;
measurement of rate and level, 203–205, 207–209, 280, MA as measure of level, 169–170, 172;
Piagetian tasks, 79, 118, 170, 234–236, 248, 264–266, and conflicting predictions, 217;
and research strategies, 158–159, 160;
rigidity explanation of, in mental retardation, 62–68, 170–172, 175;
and stimulus trace theory, 133;
structural vs. control process, 128–130;

and universality of development patterns, 283;
Zigler's model of development, 165–169, 177, 180–181, 183, 185, 284–285, 289–291
Cognitive development, and developmental/difference controversy, 113; and outer-directedness, 19; and self-image, 21
Cognitive strategy, and learned helplessness, 31–32
Concept attainment, *see also* number, quantity, 115–118, 240; of life, 249–250; of magic, 251; of probability, 252–253; of time, 228
Conservation, 79, 118, 220–225, 231–232, 238, 257–261;
and analysis of covariance, 259;
and subjects' explanations of, 260;
and subjects' predictions of, 224, 257;
and surprise reactions, 259–260;
Cortical satiation theory, 134, 169
Cosatiation of tasks, 66, 75, 76
Crying, 299, 302
Cultural-familial retardation, 118, 123, 179, 210, 246, 279, 284, 289, 308;
and defect position, 112–113, 125, 148, 194;
definition of, 126, 156;
and developmental position, 131, 156, 164, 181–184, 192, 193, 214, 216;
and future research, 309–310;
incidence in mental retardation population, 256;
and rigidity theory, 69;
social histories of, 10

D

Deficit theories, 205; *see also* difference/defect position
Dependency, 12–14;
and institutionalization, 43;
and "passive-dependency" scale, 29
Developmental position, 112–114, 122, 134, 148, 163–164, 210;
criticisms of, 155–161, 190, 202–205, 207;
definition of, 169, 180–181, 279;
etiology and, 125–127, 156–157, 279, 308;
and MA as measure of cognitive skills, 130–133, 196–197;

SUBJECT INDEX   329

motivational factors in, 175, 180, 204, 208;
and predicting performance, 207–210, 242–243, 262–263, 266;
and rate/level differences, 214;
two-group approach, 125–127, 268–269, 289;
Zigler's model, 284–285, 289–291, 308
Developmental theory, *see also* cognition
and abnormal development patterns, 282–284;
adequate model of, 284–285;
and affect/cognition interaction, 295, 298, 299;
attachment theory and, 302–308;
consequences of future research to, 311, 312;
history of, 287;
organizational view of, 292–295, 297–308;
and "orthogenetic principle", 285;
personality development and, 277–280, milestone view of, 278–279;
stages, 280–282, 291; consolidation, 281, 283; domains, 282; heirarchy, 280, 283, 286–287; relationships between, 286–287, 310–311; processing, 282; sequences, 280, 283, 284, 288, 289, 308; transitions, 281, 283, 312;
systems of, 287–288, 305–306;
and Zigler's theory, 289–291
Developmental-difference controversy, 137, 147, 164, 201, 279;
cognitive theories, characterization of, 156–161, 214;
definition, 179–181, 210, 214;
and developmental levels of cognition, 167–169, 172;
equal CA/MA research strategy and, 198;
etiology and, 243, 282–283;
hypotheses of, 215–216;
levels of analysis, 113, 135;
MA and IQ as measurements and, 207–210;
motivational factors in, 173–177;
pessimism/optimism issue in, 185–186;
summarized, 280, 310;
two-group issues in, 133, 181–186, 193–194;
and verbal mediation of behavior, 114–119
Difference/defect position,
CA used in research design, 197–199;
cognitive theories, 122–125, 135, 137, 148, 156, 159, 160, 167, 170–171,

190–194, 279–280; and dissimilar sequence hypothesis, 216; "unconventional" position, 217, 249, 258;
cognitive continuity and, 114;
conceptualizing and, 117;
criticisms of, 209–210;
cultural familial retardation and,113,156, 279;
definition of "defect", 179–180, 186, 205, 210;
definition of "difference", 124, 164, 172, 177–179, 191, 214;
definition of mental retardation and, 111;
definition of theorists, 133–134;
etiology and, 127–128, 134, 182, 194–195, 243, 267;
role of IQ in, 168–169, 173, 178, 182, 279–280;
and MA as measure of cognitive skills, 131–132, 168, 196–197, 198;
milestone theory of development, 279;
motivational factors in, 174–175;
process/achievement issue in, 291;
structure/control issue in, 128–130;
verbal ability and, 110–112
Dodwell Number Concept Test, 256
Down's syndrome children, 126, 259, 284, 305–308,
and affective development, 235–236;
interaction of developing systems in, 293–308, 311–312;
reinforcement studies, 19
Dreams, 251
Dysgraphia, 85, 92–96
Dyslexia, 85, 92, 96

E

EEG abnormalities, 235, 239, 241
Effectance motivation, 18
Etiology, 213, 241, 246, 260, 279, 282, 284;
cerebro-asthenic children, 106–108, 110;
continuum position, 11, 113–114, 127;
controversy over, in research design, 127–128, 192–194, 243, 290, 308;
"ignoring", 194–195;
personality and, 10;
in similar structure studies, 256;
stimulus trace trace theory and, 133–134;
"symptomatic" approach, 84–96; and secondary symptoms, 87, 91–97;

Etiology (*cont.*)
  two-group approach, 111–112, 125–127, 148, 157–158, 160, 178, 181, 182, 183, 184, 192, 267–269
Encoding strategies, 140–141, 145

F

Failure, *see also* success, 63, 244;
  as agent in learned helplessness syndrome, 33–34;
  expectation of, and performance, 11, 15–17, 19–20, 35–36

G

Generalization, *see also* transfer, 80, 129–130

H

Handbook of Mental Deficiency, The, 122, 190
Hearing, defective, 88–92, 97,
  and auditory analyzer, 93–94
Helpless Behavior Checklist, 32

I

Identity concepts, 227, 257
Imitation, *see also* outerdirectedness,
  and institutionalization, 53
Intelligence, *see also* IQ, 165, 179
  measures of, 132;
  and polygenic model of inheritance, 125–126, 164, 167, 289, 308;
  training and, 129
Institutionalization, 41–56, 179
  and behavioral characteristics of inmates, 43, 51–53;
  care practices, 47–50;
  Characteristics of the Treatment Environment measure, 54;
  central nervous system dysfunction evidence and, 126;
  cross-institutional studies of, 46–51; and Resident Management Practices Inventory, 47, 48, 49, 50, 52, 54;
  demographic factors, 51, 52, 54–55;
  and etiology determination, 192;
  and IQ changes, 44, 45;
  longitudinal studies of, 44–45, 54;
  and motivational factors affecting performance, 10, 11, 14, 15 18, 19, 20, 21, 156, 268;
  possible outcomes of studying, 41–42, 55;
  pre-institutionalized social deprivation and, 44–45, 53–54;
  quality of life in, 45, 48, 50, 55;
  and social policy *re* the retarded, 42, 51, 55;
  and studies of rigidity, 74, 75, 77, 78;
  transferring from, and behavior, 55;
  as variable in mental retardation studies, 64, 174;
  variables considered in studies of, 42–43
IQ, 130, 132, 134, 137, 176, 215
  changes in and institutionalization, 44;
  definition, 203–204;
  in difference theories, 178, 207–209, 279–280;
  distribution of scores, 111–114, 156, 159, 184;
  factor analysis of tests, 170;
  as measure of cognitive processes, 196–199;
  relationship to cognitive functioning, 168–169, 208–209;
  relationship to stimulus trace, 136, 142, 144, 147, 148, 199–201;
  relationship to verbal ability, 114, 176;
  validity of MA obtained from, 208–209
Isomorphic stability, 277

J

Jastrow Illusion, 248
Judgment and Reasoning in the Child (Piaget), 251

L

Language, *see* verbal ability
Laughter, and Down's syndrome infants, 295–298
Learned helplessness, 27–38, 244,
  definition of, 28, 30, 36;
  etiology of, 33;

SUBJECT INDEX

failure and, 33–34, 37;
future research, 36, 38;
measures of, 29, 37;
negative feedback and, 31–32, 34–35, 37;
teacher estimation of, 30, 32;
and verbalization about task, 32–33
Linking, 102–104, 106, 109
Locus of control scale, 29
Logic, studies of development of, 238

M

MA,
  definition, 203–204, 244;
  and conservation, 258;
  mature levels and helplessness, 31, 36;
  as measure of cognitive skills, 130–133, 136, 148, 159, 160, 161, 169–177, 196–197, 198, 214, 242–243, and rate/level controversy, 207–208;
  as measure of noncognitive skills, 170;
  and moral judgment, 246;
  as predictor of behavior in institutions, 53;
  and role taking, 246;
  in stimulus trace theory, 200;
  in studies of similar structure, 248, 268;
  use of in rigidity studies, 62–63, 64, 67, 70, 73
Memory, 124, 125, 136, 139–147, 149, 255;
  and IQ level, 144;
  models of, 146–147;
  recency, 143, 144;
  storage loads, 145–146
Mental age, *see* MA
Mental retardation, *see also* etiology,
  definition of, 123, of behavior, 244;
  in developmental/difference controversy, 181–186;
  heterogenity of, 193–195;
  and organic impairment, 215;
  prevention, 27, 161;
  research:
    and ambiguity of determinants, 174, 176–177, 180;
    comparison studies, 123, 124;
    cross-sectional studies, 240–242;
    dependent variable in, 244–245;
    and developing sequencing hypotheses, 215;
    developmental theory, 277–313; adequate developmental model, 284–288, 290;
    developmental rates, 283; Down's syndrome infants, 293–308; heterogeneous/homogenous sub-group, 284, 290; individual differences, 277, 278; personality variables in, 249; process/achievement issue, 291; stages, 280–282, 286; suggestions for future research, 308–313;
  equal CA/MA in, 196–199;
  history of, 99–100, 121–122, 134, 189–190, 213–214;
  improvement of similar sequence studies, 241–261;
  longitudinal studies, 234–239, 240;
  and scaling procedures, 220, 228, 229, 231, 239, 240, 241;
  social deprivation, 75–77;
  social policy, 42, 51, 55;
  two-group approach to study, 111, 125–127, 183–184
Moral judgment, 230–231, 237–238, 245–246, 257
Motivation, 63, 70, 122, 180, 191, 196–197, 244, 260f, 268, 289, 310;
  and performance, 9, 12–13, 16–22, 27, 155–156, 159, 160–161, 164, 173–177, and effectance motivation, 18;
  in studies of cognitive rigidity, 74–79
Motor ability, 72, 95, 103, 105, 107–110
Mueller-Lyer illusion, 255–256

N

Number concepts, 256

O

Orthogenetic principle of development, 285
Outerdirectedness, 19, 116–117, 156, 176

P

Perception,
  depth, in infants, 298–300, 301;
  language as modifier of, 101–102

SUBJECT INDEX

Performance,
  cognitive determinants, *see also* cognition, 9–10, 173–174;
  and deficit theories, 124;
  motivational determinants, 9, 27, 155–156, 174, 183, 244, 289, 309;
  noncognitive factors, 281, 285;
  scaling methods to assess, 220, 228, 229, 231;
Perserverance, *see also* persistance, 30
  and institutionalization, 43;
  in rigidity studies, 71, 73, 77
Persistance, 62
Personality, 85,
  as determinant of behavior, 9–11, 27, 306;
  organizational approach to study, 277–280;
  and social deprivation, 11–13;
  static traits in, 277, 279
Perspective-taking/perceptual-spatial concepts, 247–249
Picture Integration Test, 247
Polygenic model of inheritance, 125–126, 164, 289, 308
Pre-Institutional experience, 42–44;
  and institutionalization, 53–54;
  relationship to social reinforcement, 44;
  and studies of cognitive rigidity, 76–77
Prelogical beliefs, 249–251
Prevention, 27, 161
Psychiatry, child, 83–85
Psychosis, 283–284

Q

Quality of life, 45, 48, 50, 55
Quantity, comparison of, 253

R

Reaction tendencies, 54,
  performance, and negative, 14, 15, 298–301;
  positive, 15
Rehearsal, 139, 140, 141, 145, 146, 149
Reinforcement, *see also* social reinforcement, 155–156, 175, 244;
  intrinsic, 18;
  and learned helplessness, 31–32, 34–35;
  tangible/intangible, 17–18

Relative thinking, 230
Resident Management Practices Inventory, 47, 48, 49, 50, 52, 54
Response initiation, studies of, 29, 30
Reversal learning tasks, and rigidity formulation, 72
Rigidity, 16, 108–109, 122,
  Lewin/Kounin theory of, 61–63, 64, 69, 78, 170–172, 175, 213,
    and criticism of, 66–70, 71–72, 74, 77;
    studies of, 70–74;
  motivational factors and, 70, 75–78, 79;
  persistance and, 62,
  perseveration and, 73;
  as predictor of rigid behaviors, 65–68, 76, and MA correlation, 70;
  secondary, 67–69;
  transfer, in studies of, 65, 73
Role-taking, 246–247

S

Self-image,
  developmental concept of, 20–21, 307;
  and learned helplessness, 29
Sensorimotor stage of cognitive development, 218–220, 234–236, 280, 308;
Seriation, 254,
Sex relationship to task performance, 246;
Scaling procedures, 220, 228, 229, 231, 239, 240, 241, 295, 298, 299, 308;
Short-term memory, 78, 125, 200, 201;
Signaling systems in concept attainment, 117–118;
Similar structure hypothesis, 242–269,
  analysis of research findings, 263–267, 268–269;
  etiology in research designs of, 243, 260, 267–269;
  as null hypothesis, 245, 262
Social deprivation, 11–13, 155,
  institutionalization and, 46;
  pre-institutionalized, 11, 13, 18, 44–45, 191, 194
Social learning theory, 134
Social reinforcement, 12–13, 244,
  in institutions, 43–46, 52–54;
  and performance, 27;
  and rigidity formulation, 75–77

Socialization, *see also* social deprivation, 85, 87, 100
Socioeconomic status, and motivation, 17–19, 176
Spatial concepts, 228–229
Speech, *see* verbal ability
Stanford-Binet test, 170, 243,
  and cognitive rididity, 70
Stimulus response, 101–104, 107–110,
  and effort, 297–298
Stimulus trace theory, *see also* trace conditioning, 122, 125, 135–138, 148, 156, 193;
  as behavioral theory, 128–129, 134, 135, 136;
  criticism of, 132–133, 199–202;
  model of, 136;
  and origin of deficits, 133;
  studies of, 138–147, 148–149
"Strange situation", 304–305, 306
Success,
  expectancy of, 27;
  formulation, 16, 19, 21
Surprise reactions, 259–260

T

Tension, 300–301, 306
Trace conditioning, 138–139, 148
Training, 79, 91, 97–98, 107, 124, 128–129, 161, 184, 217
Transfer, 65, 73, 78
Transitivity, 225, 254,
  Mueller-Lyer illusion to measure, 255–256

V

Verbal ability, 72, 89–93, 100, 134,
  acquiring, 101–106;
  relation to cognitive ability, 114–119, 156, 159, 176–177;
  and retardation, 106–111, 268, in Down's syndrome children, 310

W

Wariness, 14, 15, 27, 244,
  and institutionalization, 52–53
Wechsler Intelligence test, 170

THE LIBRARY
ST. MARY'S COLLEGE OF MARYLAND
ST. MARY'S CITY, MARYLAND 20686